1992

THE COMPLETE HANDBOOK OF
PRO
BASKETBALL

1992
THE COMPLETE HANDBOOK OF PRO
BASKETBALL

EDITED BY
ZANDER HOLLANDER

AN ASSOCIATED FEATURES BOOK

A SIGNET BOOK

ACKNOWLEDGMENTS

Short of the original peach basket, a bushel of 100 peaches atop a 7-foot birthday cake would be appropriate this December when basketball officially celebrates its 100th anniversary. With this 18th edition of *The Complete Handbook of Pro Basketball*, we offer a slam-dunk to the American-born sport (oddly, invented by a Canadian) that grew from the pits.

A special acknowledgment here to 93-year-old Original Celtic Nat Holman, and to contributing editor Eric Compton, the writers on the facing page and Lee Stowbridge, Linda Spain, Kevin Mulroy, Reid Grosky, Alex Sachare, Brian McIntyre, Terry Lyons, Marty Blake, the NBA team publicity directors, Elias Sports Bureau, Dot Gordineer of Libra Graphics, and Westchester/Rainsford Book Composition.

Zander Hollander

PHOTO CREDITS: Cover—NBA Photos/Andrew Bernstein. Inside photos—Ira Golden, Michael Hirsch, Malcolm Emmons, Vic Milton, Mitch Reibel, UPI, Wide World and the NBA and college team photographers, including Dave Cross, Einstein Photos, Bruce Kluckhorn, Mitchel Layton and Mike Maicher.

SIGNET
Published by the Penguin Group
Penguin Books USA Inc., 375 Hudson Street,
New York, New York 10014, U.S.A.
Penguin Books Ltd, 27 Wrights Lane,
London W8 5TZ, England
Penguin Books Australia Ltd, Ringwood,
Victoria, Australia
Penguin Books Canada Ltd, 10 Alcorn Ave.,
Toronto, Ontario, Canada M4V 3B2
Penguin Books (N.Z.) Ltd, 182-190 Wairau Road,
Auckland 10, New Zealand

Penguin Books Ltd, Registered Offices:
Harmondsworth, Middlesex, England

First Signet Printing, November, 1991
10 9 8 7 6 5 4 3

CONTENTS

Editor's Note: The material herein includes trades and rosters up to the final printing deadline.

UP, UP AND AWAY! CELEBRATING A CENTURY OF HOOPS

By JOE GERGEN

Dr. James Naismith started it all with a peach basket.

Magic and Michael in classic vis-a-vis in '91 NBA Finals.

Other sports look back on a long and glorious history. Basketball looks down. A century after Dr. James Naismith set a goal of upward mobility for his creation, Michael Jordan reigns over the NBA from a throne suspended in mid-air.

Appropriately, the most spectacular and celebrated flyer ever to lace up basketball sneakers led his team, the Chicago Bulls, to the championship of the world's greatest league in a milestone season. Naismith, a Canadian-born physical education instructor, introduced the concept to his students in December 1891. One hundred years later, Jordan carried the game to unprecedented

As a sports columnist for Newsday *and* The Sporting News, *Joe Gergen doesn't claim to be Methuselah. But he has seen more basketball than most and has interviewed many of the greats of the game.*

heights while achieving his first title at the expense of the Los Angeles Lakers.

No sooner had a custodian nailed two peach baskets to a gymnasium balcony in Springfield, Mass., at Naismith's request than the direction of the sport was established. But in the latter half of the 20th century, basketball stretched the limits of its original confines and soared with the imagination.

Players routinely play above the iron rim, which has replaced the bushel basket as the main objective of the game, and occasionally someone plays beyond the constraints of the mind. Jordan's takeoffs and landings are studied for their application to the laws of physics, his flights of fancy are captured on video tapes for the entertainment of a worldwide audience and his choice of shoes is copied by millions wanting to wear the right thing.

He is a contemporary Peter Pan, sporting a shaved head and baggy shorts, and he stands at the apex of the evolutionary process that began with William Davis, Eugene Libby, John Thompson (not the Georgetown coach), George Weller, Wilbert Carey, Ernest Hildner, Lyman Archibald, T. Duncan Patton, Finley MacDonald, Raymond Kaighn, Genzabaro Ishikawa, Franklin Barnes, Edwin Ruggles, Frank Mahan, William Chase, Benjamin French, George Day and Henri Gelan. The latter are the 18 students from Naismith's class who participated in the very first game. They were aligned nine to a side and used a soccer ball which they pursued with more zest than skill.

The sport spread quickly via the extensive network of YMCA facilities throughout the country. Leagues sprang up, district and regional tournaments were staged and basketball flourished. But the rough nature of the phenomenon and the fact that its emergence pushed all other physical activities at the "Y" into the background caused the officers of the organization to ban the game from their gymnasiums. Suddenly, the popular upstart was without a home court.

Unlike baseball, which gained a foothold in cow pastures, and football, which was conceived as a rite of autumn for collegians, basketball hurriedly was transformed into a professional enterprise out of necessity. There is documentation that within five years of Naismith's little exercise in Springfield, teams along the Eastern seaboard were charging admission. The explanation is that the athletes had to rent the halls in which they played and an audience was needed to defray the costs.

Although a team in Herkimer, N.Y., claimed to have been enriched by less than a buck a man for its performance against a Utica club as far back as 1893, there is substantial evidence that

At 5-4, 118 pounds, Barney Sedran was a giant performer in the early pro era with Carbondale, Pa., and Utica, N.Y.

a team in Trenton, N.J., set up shot at the Masonic Hall in 1896 and drew such a crowd that each player received $15 for his efforts, after expenses. Fred Cooper, the captain, earned an extra dollar for his leadership.

That Trenton team, which had learned its lessons in the local ''Y'', may have been the first exponent of Showtime. The players were outfitted in velvet trunks, long tights and frilled stockings designed by Cooper, a former soccer player. They also demonstrated a sophisticated passing attack, featuring Cooper and Al Bratton. Perhaps the most indispensible member of the club, however, was manager Fred Paderatz, a carpenter by trade. It was Paderatz who built the first cage out of chicken wire.

Cages, whether of wire or rope, were erected in the early years of the sport to protect the fans from the athletes or, more often than not, the athletes from the fans. They also kept the game moving since a ball deflecting off the cage remained in play. More

Joe Lapchick (left) and Nat Holman were Original Celtics.

than 60 years later, basketball players still were referred to as cagers by some newspaper headline writers.

These cagers were tough men. They had to be. They were subjected to a physical pounding inside their enclosure and frequently prodded with hatpins and lighted cigarettes by the more obstreperous customers. Yet the sport inched forward with the inception of the first professional league in 1898. The National Basketball League disbanded five years later but many of its players found employment in the Philadelphia League, which expanded into New York, New Jersey and other areas of Pennsylvania in 1909, forming the basis for the Eastern League.

The Hudson River League and the New York State League, founded shortly thereafter, produced the standout professional team of the era, Lew and Ed Wachter's Troy Trojans. Originally formed to challenge the celebrated Buffalo Germans, who had claimed the national amateur championship by overwhelming the opposition at the 1901 Pan American Exposition, the Trojans won two Hudson River League crowns and three titles in the four years that the New York State League was in operation.

Ed Wachter was a 6-6 center who not only was a superior athlete but an innovator. Whereas other teams of the day used short tosses on the fly to advance the ball, he had his team utilize

PRE-HISTORIC
ALL-STAR TEAM

The standout professional players before the advent of the NBA and the team with which they were most closely associated:

G—Barney Sedran, Carbondale (Pa.)
G—Nat Holman, Original Celtics
G—Bobby McDermott, Fort Wayne Pistons
C—Joe Lapchick, Original Celtics
C—Ed Wachter, Troy, (N.Y.) Trojans
C—Tarzan Cooper, New York Rens
F—John Beckman, Original Celtics
F—Dutch Dehnert, Original Celtics
F—Pop Gates, New York Rens
F—Reece (Goose) Tatum, Harlem Globetrotters

the bounce pass. The Trojans, known in the region as Wachter's Wonders, also freed players to run downcourt in anticipation of a long pass, creating a fast-break offense.

As various leagues ebbed and flowed, the better players tended to float from team to team. With no contracts to bind them, they sold their services to the highest bidder or played for more than one team at a time. One of the most exciting of the basketball gypsies was Barney Sedran, who led a Carbondale, Pa., team to 35 consecutive victories and the 1914-15 Tri-State League title while playing a complete schedule with Utica in the New York State League.

Sedran used his speed and accurate shot to offset a particular disadvantage. At 5-4, he was considered too short to play for his high-school team in New York, yet competed on 10 championship teams in 15 years as a pro. He also was credited with 17 baskets in one game, played without benefit of a backboard.

It wasn't until the Roaring '20s that one team became recognized as truly dominant in the sport. That team was the Original Celtics. Its roots could be traced to the formation of the New York Celtics, representing a settlement house on the city's tough West Side, in 1914. That club, which starred John Witte and Pete Barry, played together for three seasons before the U.S. entrance into the World War.

A New York promoter, Jim Furey, attempted to reorganize the team after the armistice but Frank McCormack, who had founded the New York Celtics, declined to authorize use of the name. So Furey settled on the Original Celtics, enlisted Witte and Barry and added the likes of Ernie Reich, Joe Trippe, Eddie White and Mike Smolick.

One year later, with the addition of Swede Grimstead, Henry (Dutch) Dehnert and Johnny Beckman, the Celtics became a powerhouse. Still, they had their challengers, among them the New York Whirlwinds, organized by Tex Rickard of Madison Square Garden. The Whirlwinds were led by Sedran, Chris Leonard and a deft ball-handler named Nat Holman.

By public demand, the two teams finally agreed to a three-game series at New York's 71st Regiment Armory in 1921. Before an overflow crowd reported at 11,000, the Whirlwinds won the first game, 40-27. The Celtics then responded with a 26-24 victory the following night. The third game never was played for fear of violence among the frenzied spectators.

Furey made the argument academic at the end of the season when he persuaded Leonard and Holman to jump to the Celtics. He made another shrewd move before the start of the 1922-23 season, signing all the Celtics to exclusive contracts with guaranteed salaries. Then he pursued additional talent, including Davey Banks, Nat Hickey, Horace (Horse) Haggerty and 6-5 Joe Lapchick, a smooth and accomplished big man.

The Celtics barnstormed, taking on different opponents night after night before big crowds in strange towns. Their familiarity evolved into teamwork of a kind unprecedented in that era. With little time for practice, they perfected basketball innovations under actual game conditions, including the pivot play (originated by Dehnert), the give-and-go and switching defenses.

Not even the advent of the American Basketball League, founded by Washington laundry tycoon George Preston Marshall in an attempt to provide the sport with a big-time environment, slowed their triumphant march. At first, the Celtics refused to join the ABL because it was more lucrative for them to barnstorm. They did, however, condescend to rout the league's teams in exhibition games.

When the ABL reacted by forbidding members to play the Celtics, sharply curtailing the independent team's revenue, the Celtics consented to join the league midway through the 1926-27 season. They promptly won 19 of 20 games and romped to the second-half title. A year later, they won both halves with relative

The Rens (left to right): Clarence (Fat) Jenkins, Bill Yancey, John Holt, James (Pappy) Ricks, Eyre Saith, Charles (Tarzan) Cooper and Wee Willie Smith. Inset: owner Bob Douglas.

ease and rolled over Fort Wayne in a championship playoff series.

In the end, they may have been too good for their own good. Attendance around the league began to drop and, in a desperate attempt to restore competitive balance, the league broke up the Celtics and parceled their players to other teams. Furey was in no position to prevent this, having been convicted of embezzlement and having moved into new quarters at Sing Sing.

But the Celtics' influence was unmistakeable in the success of the Cleveland Rosenblums after they acquired Lapchick, Dehnert and Barry. After winning the first-half title and finishing second behind Fort Wayne in the second half, the Rosenblums swept a four-game playoff series in convincing fashion.

From relative prosperity, the ABL was plunged into a depression with the stock market crash of 1929. Within two years, it suspended operations. The expiration of the league wasn't so traumatic for the Celtics, who reunited for another few years of barnstorming, although at reduced rates. But their time as kings of the road was passing. It was the Rens who reigned over basketball in the 1930s.

This was the New York Renaissance, a team of all-black players who once shared the Renaissance Casino ballroom in Harlem with the big bands of Count Basie and Jimmy Lunsford. The depression cost them their home court, so founder Bob Douglas took them on the road in a custom-fitted bus which all too often served as their hotel since they were denied accommodations in many cities. They endured an exhausting schedule and overt discrimination to compile a remarkable record of 473-49 in the period from 1932-36, including an 88-game winning streak.

Their battles against the older Celtics were classics and drew huge crowds in Cleveland and Louisville and Kansas City. The Rens won seven of eight such meetings in 1933 and, bolstered by two superb big men in Charles (Tarzan) Cooper and Wee Willie Smith, they dominated the rest of the decade. In 1939, they won 112 games, lost only seven and captured the world title in a Chicago tournament featuring the best pro teams of the era.

Ironically, the team that succeeded them as champions of that Chicago tournament was another all-black squad that would gain greater fame for its showmanship. The Harlem Globetrotters were organized in Chicago by Abe Saperstein in 1927, five years after the formation of the Rens. But it was not until 1940, when they edged the Rens and George Halas' Chicago Bruins in the world championship tournament, that they were taken seriously.

The recognition gave them entree to better facilities in bigger cities. Later that year they played the first of many games against a collection of college all-stars. Championship status also lured the two most illustrious performers in the team's history, Reece (Goose) Tatum and Marques Haynes. In the course of the decade, the Trotters became strong enough to defeat the Minneapolis Lakers, with George Mikan, and were so entertaining that Saperstein was able to launch a series of overseas tours as he had envisioned when he named them. More than 60 years after their founding, they continue as the clown princes (and chief ambassadors) of basketball.

One team that gained regional fame at the same time as the Rens and Globetrotters were dueling for national attention was the Philadelphia SPHAs. They had evolved from an amateur team created in 1918 by Eddie Gottlieb, Harry Passon and Hughie Black to represent the South Philadelphia Hebrew Association. They remained a strong independent club until John O'Brien reorganized the ABL into a Northeast circuit in 1933.

Gottlieb, who had assumed direction of the SPHAs, led them

Marques Haynes wowed followers of the Harlem Globetrotters.

to championships in three of the league's first four seasons. Overall, they claimed seven titles in the 13 years they competed before Gottlieb turned his attention to the Basketball Association of America in 1946.

By then, the National Basketball League was struggling with its identity and its vision of the future. Organized in 1937 by Lon Darling, the NBL sought to capitalize on the soaring popularity of the college game by signing former college stars and adapting college rules, including one that abolished the center jump after each basket. Its weakness was in its mostly midwestern markets. They included several large cities but many more small towns.

Of all the teams that shuffled in and out of the league before, during and after World War II, it was the Fort Wayne Zollner Pistons who had the strongest influence on the sport. Named for Fred Zollner's piston plant, the team began as a replacement franchise during the war and, in time, became a charter member of the National Basketball Association. The Pistons not only won consecutive championships in 1944 and 1945 and overwhelmed

The Minneapolis Lakers, with George Mikan (99), won the title in their first year in the BAA in 1949.

all opposition in the world championships in each of those years but they boasted one of basketball's most flamboyant players in Bobby McDermott.

The man had been a high-scoring attraction with the last of the Celtics' barnstorming teams and the top scorer in the downsized ABL. But it was in the NBL where the pugnacious guard flourished. Following the 1945 season, in which McDermott averaged an unprecedented 20.1 points per game, he was hailed as the greatest player in pro basketball history by a vote of league coaches.

His prominence would be eclipsed in short order. In the spring of 1946, the Chicago Gears signed hometown star George Mikan, who had grown into an overwhelming force at DePaul University. The 6-10 Mikan made his debut in the world championship tournament, where he scored 100 points in five games and was selected MVP even though the Gears were eliminated by Oshkosh in the semifinals.

The Chicago franchise received another jolt of energy midway through the 1946-47 season when McDermott was suspended for his part in a brawl and then dealt to the Gears, where he held the dual role of player-coach. The team eliminated Indianapolis and Oshkosh in the playoffs and then steamrollered the defending champion Rochester Royals in the championship finals.

What appeared to be a dynasty in the making came to a grinding halt when Gears' owner Maurice White pulled his team out of the NBL and announced the formation of his own 24-team league. He called his new venture the Professional Basketball League of America. It lasted less than a month and its players were redistributed among NBL members. McDermott was assigned to Sheboygan and Mikan, suddenly the biggest attraction in the sport, was sent to a first-year franchise in Minneapolis, where he teamed with former Stanford star Jim Pollard.

Together, they led the Lakers to the 1948 NBL title and the championship of the last world professional tournament. Surely, they would have dominated the league for more years but in the fall of 1948, the Lakers and three other prominent NBL franchises—Rochester, Fort Wayne and Indianapolis—jumped to the rival Basketball Association of America. The BAA controlled the major arenas in the populous Northeast. Now, with the addition of Mikan and Rochester's Bob Davies, they had the crowd-pleasers so essential to a new league.

In its first two seasons, the BAA had not gained a hold on the public despite the emergence of a star in Jumpin' Joe Fulks, a former Marine who relied on this newfangled jump shot. But the arrival of the four NBL franchises provided a vital shot in the arm. While the Lakers won a second championship in a second league in two years, the NBL played out the string with Anderson defeating Oshkosh in the finals.

The six surviving NBL franchises were incorporated into the BAA in time for the 1949-50 season and the new alignment was renamed the National Basketball Association. Of the six new members, only two would last more than a season: the Syracuse Nationals, who reached the finals where they lost to Minneapolis, and the Tri-Cities Hawks, who would bounce to Milwaukee, then to St. Louis and, finally, Atlanta.

While the Lakers continued to lead the championship parade (they would account for five titles in six years), two significant developments took place in the early years. One was the integration of the league and the other was the rise of an attraction equal in stature, if not size, to Mikan. The Celtics, as Walter Brown called his franchise in Boston, were doubly rewarded.

On April 25, 1950, Brown startled participants in the college draft at a Chicago hotel by selecting Chuck Cooper of Duquesne

The Rochester Royals' Bob Davies (vs. Knicks' Harry Gallatin) was an artful dribbler, playmaker and scorer.

at the start of the second round. Cooper was black and no black had participated in the NBA's first season. Emboldened, the Washington Capitals then picked forward Earl Lloyd of West Virginia State on the ninth round and the New York Knickerbockers later purchased Nat (Sweetwater) Clifton from the Globetrotters.

The schedule afforded Lloyd the honor of the being the first of his race to appear in an NBA game, on Oct. 31, in Rochester.

Philadelphia's Jumpin' Joe Fulks was known for his jump shot.

But Cooper, a sturdy 6-5 forward who specialized in rebounding, was the first black drafted and signed to an NBA contract. Clifton was a major contributor to the Knicks, who pushed Rochester to the limit in a seven-game final series.

Meanwhile, the Celtics were blessed by fate when the Chicago Stags went out of business three weeks before the start of the 1950-51 season. The team's two stars, Max Zaslofsky and Andy Phillip, were the objects of fierce competition among New York, Philadelphia and Boston. A third player on the Chicago roster was largely ignored. He was a rookie from Holy Cross, a ball-handling wizard named Bob Cousy.

The Celtics, who had been a financial as well as artistic failure, already had rejected the chance to acquire the popular Cousy as a territorial draft choice at the discretion of Red Auerbach, the brash coach who had spent the previous season at Tri-Cities. Resolution of the Stags' fallout fell into the ample lap of Maurice Podoloff, the NBA's first commissioner. When even his gift for compromise was insufficient to sway the three teams, he dropped three slips of paper into his hat.

Ned Irish, drawing on behalf of the Knicks, plucked Zaslof-

Bob Cousy (vs. Sweetwater Clifton) quarterbacked Celtics.

sky's name and gladly paid $15,000 for the rights to the high scorer he coveted. Eddie Gottlieb was not disappointed when he drew the name of Phillip, an accomplished playmaker. It cost the Philadelphia franchise $10,000. But that left Brown with no choice but to pay $8,500 for the privilege of obtaining a player his coach didn't want. In short order, of course, the 6-1½ Cousy became the most flamboyant star in the league.

Although the level of talent increased dramatically with each year, the game was constricted by stalling tactics and tactical fouling which slowed the pace to a crawl. The Pistons, playing with all deliberate speed, edged the defending champion Lakers, 19-18, on Nov. 22, 1950. And the 1953 and 1954 playoffs occasionally degenerated into wrestling matches. A solution was offered by Danny Biasone, the owner of the Syracuse Nats, at a meeting in 1954. He proposed a 24-second clock and the Board of Governors, faced with declining interest and shrinking attendance, voted to accept it. At the same time, team fouls were limited to six per quarter, after which the opposing team would shoot free

Great confrontations: Wilt Chamberlain vs. Bill Russell.

Wilt Chamberlain's 100-point night vs. Knicks in 1962.

throws for each violation.

The effect of the two changes was instantaneous and therapeutic. Fouling diminished and the average score per team jumped 13.6 points to 93.1 in the 1954-55 season. Before the decade was over, the Lakers lost another game worthy of a place in the record book. On Feb. 27, 1959, eight seasons after their 19-18 defeat, they were trounced by the Celtics, 173-139. Basketball was off and running.

In the interim, the Celtics had grown into the most powerful franchise in the NBA, thanks to the presence of Bill Russell at center. As he had done in the college ranks where he led San Francisco to 55 consecutive victories and successive NCAA championships, Russell revolutionized the pro game with his shot-blocking ability and defensive skills. Boston, due to pick sixth in the 1956 draft, was able to sign Russell only because Auerbach took the calculated risk of trading two stars, Easy Ed Macauley and Cliff Hagan, to St. Louis for the right to choose second.

Before retiring in 1969, Russell led the team to 11 NBA titles, the last two in the dual role of player-coach. Eight of those cham-

Oscar (The Big O) Robertson evades K.C. Jones in 1961.

pionships were achieved consecutively, from 1959 through 1966, establishing a dynasty that dwarfed those of the New York Yankees in baseball and the Montreal Canadiens in hockey.

While Russell helped the Celtics monopolize team prizes, the individual spotlight in the 1960s became the domain of Wilt Chamberlain. As a rookie, the 7-2 center, nicknamed Wilt the Stilt and the Big Dipper, led the league in both scoring and rebounding on behalf of the Philadelphia Warriors. He became a tremendous draw throughout the league and his duels with Russell were the stuff of legend.

In just his third pro season, Chamberlain surpassed Elgin Baylor's single-game scoring mark of 71 three times. On the third occasion, he wrapped up the honor, perhaps for all time, with a 100-point effort against the Knicks in Hershey, Pa. He completed the 1961-62 season with an average of 50.4 points per game.

During his career, he was credited with 49 of the top 57 scoring performances in league history. Yet, he didn't win his initial NBA title until 1967, the first season in which he failed to lead the league in scoring. He won his second and final championship ring

1947-63

PIONEER ALL-STAR TEAM

The NBA's greatest players whose professional careers began before 1963, and the teams with which they were most closely associated:

G—Oscar Robertson, Cincinnati Royals
G—Jerry West, Los Angeles Lakers
G—Bob Cousy, Boston Celtics
C—George Mikan, Minneapolis Lakers
C—Bill Russell, Boston Celtics
C—Wilt Chamberlain, Philadelphia Warriors
F—Bob Pettit, St. Louis Hawks
F—Dolph Schayes, Syracuse Nationals
F—Elgin Baylor, Los Angeles Lakers
F—John Havlicek, Boston Celtics

in 1972 when, asked to concentrate on rebounding and defense by Lakers' coach Bill Sharman, he averaged but 14.8 points per game.

The torch Cousy carried in the backcourt was passed to a pair of guards who were teammates on the 1960 U.S. Olympic team. Oscar Robertson and Jerry West entered the NBA in the same year, were rivals for 14 seasons, earned one well-deserved championship apiece and shared the designation as greatest guards in history. Robertson signed with the Royals, who had shifted their base of operations from Rochester to Cincinnati in 1957, and West began a lifelong affiliation with the Lakers, who were opening the West Coast to pro basketball.

In addition to the Royals, another small-town franchise that had been the backbone of the league in its formative years also went big time when the Fort Wayne Pistons resettled in Detroit. The NBA's major-league image was further enhanced in 1963 when the Syracuse Nationals, with their aging star Dolph Schayes now a player-coach, were sold and transferred to Philadelphia, a city which had been left vacant when the Warriors moved to San Francisco a year earlier. The new alignment strengthened the league's position on the sports market, which proved significant

Jerry West was the greatest backcourt scorer of his era.

with the creation of the American Basketball Association in the latter part of the decade.

The ABA came equipped with a red, white and blue ball, a three-point field goal it called a "home run," some tacky arenas, a few stars and an odd cast of supporting characters. Its first major attraction, former NBA scoring champ Rick Barry, had to sit out the first season to fulfill the option year on his contract with the Warriors. And franchises came and went with numbing regularity.

Perhaps the major miscalculation of the new league was in failing to outbid the NBA for the services of Lew Alcindor, the 7-2 center who had led UCLA to three consecutive NCAA cham-

High-scoring Rick Barry was ABA showcase with Oakland Oaks.

pionships. A native New Yorker, he favored the New York Nets—
based on suburban Long Island—over the Milwaukee Bucks, who
held his rights in the established league. But when the Nets' first
offer fell short, he opted for the NBA and combined with Robertson to lead the Bucks to a title in only his second professional
season.

Alcindor would change his name to Kareem Abdul-Jabbar in
1971 and orchestrate a trade to the Lakers in 1975. In his 20 years
of NBA service, he earned six Most Valuable Player awards, was
selected to 19 All-Star teams and scored more points than any
figure in league history.

Despite administrative shortcomings, undersized crowds and
an inability to attract a national television contract, the ABA lasted
nine seasons and showcased some exciting young talent. Four
teams—representing New York, Denver, Indiana and San Antonio—were absorbed into the NBA in time for the start of the 1976-
77 season. The established league was enriched by the arrival of
several outstanding players, most notably the transcendent Julius
Erving.

Already a basketball cult figure known as Dr. J, Erving had

Kareem Abdul-Jabbar won MVP award in 1985 NBA Finals.

led the Nets to two titles in the ABA's last three seasons. Following his sale to the 76ers, he not only carried Philadelphia to one championship but became the NBA's model citizen. And his flights of fancy set the stage for Jordan's spectacular air shows in the next decade.

The growth of the league in the 1980s, however, owed much to two charismatic players who met for the first time in the 1979 NCAA championship game. Although Magic Johnson and Larry Bird were 6-9, their games were so complete that they could fill

The celebrated Dr. J debuted with ABA's Virginia Squires.

any position on the court. Neither man was fast but both were superb passers who elevated the play of their teammates.

More than any of their contemporaries, they were treasured for their ability to win. Johnson's Lakers and Bird's Celtics combined for eight championships in the decade. The consecutive titles annexed by Los Angeles in 1987-88 were particularly notable because they were the first since those achieved by the Celtics of the Russell era two decades earlier.

Ironically, the Lakers were succeeded by Detroit, which also

Walt (Clyde) Frazier drove Knicks to titles in 1970 and '73.

won back-to-back titles. The Pistons were a physical, defensively-oriented club run with precision by a superb point guard. Isiah Thomas had rocketed to prominence in 1981 when, as a sophomore, he had led Indiana to an NCAA championship, then elected to turn pro.

The NBA's next great star would emerge from the 1982 NCAA title game, in which North Carolina edged Georgetown on Michael Jordan's last-minute jump shot. He was only a freshman at the time but his grace under pressure was evident even then. He entered the pro ranks two years later and almost single-handedly transformed Chicago into a basketball town.

After seven years in a Bulls' uniform, he has become basketball's greatest salesman and a major reason why the sport, starting its second century, continues to point skyward.

Larry Bird smokes Red Auerbach's cigar after '81 title win.

1964-91

CONTEMPORARY ALL-STAR TEAM

The NBA's greatest players whose careers began after 1963 and the teams with which they were most closely associated:

G—Magic Johnson, Los Angeles Lakers
G—Isiah Thomas, Detroit Pistons
G—Michael Jordan, Chicago Bulls
G—Walt Frazier, New York Knicks
C—Kareem Abdul-Jabbar, Los Angeles Lakers
C—Moses Malone, Philadelphia 76ers
F—Rick Barry, San Francisco Warriors
F—Larry Bird, Boston Celtics
F—Julius Erving, Philadelphia 76ers
F—Charles Barkley, Philadelphia 76ers

Isiah Thomas soared with champion Pistons in 1990.

BEHIND THE SCENES WITH AMAZING MICHAEL JORDAN

By MARK VANCIL

When Michael Jordan reached his destination in mid-June, tears rolling down his cheeks and Chicago's first NBA championship trophy held tight to his chest, the climb suddenly seemed so very distant.

For weeks, practice sessions leading to the deciding game against Los Angeles had been mob scenes. Mini-cams pinned Jordan into a corner, tape recorders and microphones pressed within an inch of his lips, pens and pencils scribbled every utterance as if it were his last. When he left his hotel room, either to play golf or step into another Bulls' bus, security guards shadowed every movement.

Yet through it all a calm accompanied Jordan, a learned tolerance perhaps, but clearly an acceptance of what has become ritual.

It started seven years earlier in a worn-out gymnasium on Chicago's North Side. Angel Guardian Gym, with its old wood bleachers pressed against the walls and cement-floored locker rooms, is where the chase began. Jordan was smaller then, his upper body not yet introduced to the private weight-training sessions that would eventually carry him through his first championship season.

Two, maybe three reporters occupied the sidelines as Jordan

As an NBA reporter, first for the Chicago Sun-Times *and most recently for the* National Sports Daily, *Mark Vancil has covered Michael Jordan and the Bulls since Air Jordan's debut in 1984.*

Michael Jordan climbed the mountain in 1990-91.

went through the paces for the first time. At the start at least, Kevin Loughery, the first of four coaches for whom Jordan would work, treated Jordan like he treated everyone else. And Jordan responded to Loughery like he no doubt responded to Dean Smith, his coach at North Carolina.

"I always show respect for the coach," Jordan said then. "That's just the way I was brought up."

Although there were prearranged press conferences in each NBA city, the hysteria that would become part of his daily life was limited. For the most part, he came and went like the others. When practice ended, Jordan walked through the old steel doors like everyone else. He didn't have to sneak through back exits, as would become habit years later.

"He understands it all," said Loughery. "Everything. He's unbelievable. He's in total control of everything that's going on around him. He's amazing."

For most of his first five months, Jordan enjoyed an almost idyllic existence. The first Air Jordan shoe elevated an entire corporation. Endorsements, commercials and remarkable success on the court rolled through Jordan in waves.

Until Indianapolis.

Jordan had feared problems as fans voted him a starting spot in the 1985 All-Star Game. In three short days, those fears were realized and a measure of innocence forever disappeared.

According to Dr. Charles Tucker, who fancied himself as a trusted confidant and advisor to Isiah Thomas, Magic Johnson and others, a few veteran stars had conspired to make Jordan look bad. Players were said to have been miffed at Jordan's decision to cover himself in Nike garb for the Slam-Dunk competition.

Jordan, who didn't play well in his first All-Star appearance, didn't hear the news until the following Monday morning when a film crew greeted him inside Angel Guardian.

The practice session became a war. The smile that Jordan usually carried through these routine rigors never showed. He was different. He was hurt. And he was angry.

Jordan vented his rage in a frenzied, if not brilliant end of the practice scrimmage. He dunked. He pushed. He shoved. He glared. And he never stopped running.

Twenty-four hours later, after Thomas and virtually everyone else involved in the alleged snub had issued denials, the rivalry began. Chicago's first game after the All-Star break was inside the Stadium against Thomas's Detroit Pistons.

The fury that had swept through Monday's practice found a new level. Jordan bombed the Pistons for 49 points, hitting

19-of-31 shots in a rousing 139-126 Bulls' victory.

Though his relationship with Thomas would thaw over the years, Jordan never doubted the conspiracy and he never forgot.

"That was the worst," Jordan would recall. "That was the lowest point."

But once inside the damp, crowded quarters of the ancient locker room, the pain remained. He spoke softly and looked down at the floor. There was only one reporter at the scene. No cameras. If his teammates knew about the alleged snub, they certainly didn't understand how much it affected him.

He said he was surprised. He didn't understand being a target. It was as close to tears as he would come publicly until Los Angeles. He said he planned to call his parents.

"Whenever I need to think, or need to be alone, I play the game of basketball," he said in slightly more than a whisper. "It relaxes me. I've always done it."

Although the hype would hit the first of many crescendos with the introduction of the first Air Jordan shoe, Jordan seemed virtually unaffected. He lived much like he had been raised.

His townhouse in suburban Chicago looked no different than all the others in the crowded subdivision. He cooked for himself, cleaned his own house and lived a remarkably normal life.

Jordan even did his own shopping, timing each trip so that he would arrive minutes before the grocery store would close. That way, he explained, there weren't many people around and he could get "everything I need and get home."

"I can cook and I can sew," said Jordan at the time. "I took home-economics classes in high school because I thought I'd be a bachelor. If I need a button put on or something like that, I can do it. I could make my own clothes if I had to."

He was also supremely confident. He would play anybody in any game anytime, convinced he would not lose. He played teammates in pool on a table in his basement and shot darts a few feet away. Even on the golf course in a game he was still learning, Jordan played as if he were invincible.

By the beginning of Jordan's second NBA season, his endorsement package had already become the standard. If O.J. Simpson and Arthur Ashe crossed the color line for commercial endorsements, Jordan obliterated it.

His Nike deal, which included stock options and an entire personal clothing line, instantly became the most lucrative shoe contract in the history of team sports. Coca-Cola, McDonald's and Chevrolet, the cream of corporate America, had also lined

An emotional Michael clutches the championship trophy.

up. And there were other smaller deals and appearances that brought in additional thousands.

But the next blow to Jordan's youth was straight ahead. It came at Golden State just three games into the the 1985-86 season and it forever changed Jordan's relationship with Bulls' management.

He came down hard on his left foot in a first-half play. Doctors eventually found a broken bone and Jordan's season, like that of the Bulls, was virtually over. Chicago was 3-0 at the time under new coach Stan Albeck. They would be 24-44 when Jordan returned and Albeck would be caught in a firestorm fanned by his desire to play.

For operations chief Jerry Krause, who would battle Jordan for years to come, the sparks started flying in a ludicrous late-night meeting at the suburban offices of owner Jerry Reinsdorf.

Jordan arrived with a pad of paper and a tape recorder. He wore glasses and once again the familiar smile had disappeared. Inside, Krause, Reinsdorf, Jordan, Albeck and team Dr. John Hefferon, the team physician, sat around a conference table and listened to a telephone conference call with other leading foot surgeons.

Jordan insisted the foot was fine. The doctors weren't sure. Reinsdorf mediated the meeting and finally decided Jordan could play. But he would play less than 10 minutes a half with his minutes increased by one each game. Jordan was furious at what seemed to be an arbitrary figure.

He accused the team of purposely devising the plan to insure more losses and a better draft position. At almost midnight, a hurried press conference was called, with Reinsdorf announcing the decision to allow Jordan's return.

Jordan had been playing pickup games back in North Carolina against the advice of doctors and management's demands. Jordan had approached the meeting like he had approached every game, every situation. Clearly he expected to win. His defiance, driven home when he told Reinsdorf that he would also tape the proceedings, was palpable.

In the weeks that followed, Jordan's minutes became an almost nightly issue. Albeck, under the threat of being fired, had to time each substitution to the minute so that Jordan would not go over the allotted time. As with the All-Star Game at Indianapolis, Jordan never forgot.

Considering the daily demands and the pace at which Jordan faces them, his basketball exploits seem even more extraordinary.

Early in his career, it wasn't uncommon for Jordan to start the day with some work on commercials, head to practice, go back to the commercial and then get home at 8 or 9 P.M. If his life seemed to be moving by in a blur, Jordan never noticed.

Indeed, he often appeared to feed off the action. He might get up with the sun to play nine holes of golf before heading off to practice. And after practice, if there were no other commitments, a rarity, Jordan might head back to the course. But nothing suffered, not even his practice performance.

"I never thought a man could play like he does every night and practice like he does every day," said Pete Myers, a lanky 6-5 guard who spent most of the 1986-87 season guarding Jordan in practice. "He'll do anything. He plays just like he does in games. He won't let you rest. He's tough. Nobody practices like that."

During a scrimmage, when Doug Collins was coach, Jordan got furious over a foul that wasn't called. He left the floor and the building. He felt that Collins was trying to purposely help the opposing team in the scrimmage in order to make things more interesting. He has screamed at teammates and coaches, and once even fired a punch at Will Perdue.

"I thought Jerry Sloan was the toughest practice player I ever saw," said Krause. "He would compete in practice. He would run rookies right out of the league. He wouldn't tolerate any bums. Sloan would beat the hell out of you.

"Michael won't beat a guy up, but he'll dunk over you and do anything to embarrass you. Michael plays as hard as Sloan. And that's the ultimate tribute."

Jordan has not only led the league in scoring for five straight seasons, but he's also made the All-Defensive team four consecutive years. Even more impressive considering the demands, the two-time regular-season MVP and 1991 Finals MVP has played in 424 of a possible 425 games since his foot injury. And he has never missed a playoff game.

"I play every game like it's my last," said Jordan.

He seems to approach life much the same way.

It's Friday night at the Spectrum in Philadelphia. The Bulls are favored but struggling against the Sixers in Game 3 of their 1990 Eastern Conference semifinal match.

A saddened Scottie Pippen is on the bench, contemplating his next two days, which include the funeral of his father. The Bulls had been forced to come back twice at home to take a 2-0 lead in the best-of-seven series. As the series moved to Philadelphia, however, the momentum flowed through the Sixers.

They blew open Game 3, leading 87-67 entering the fourth

Michael, Jeffrey and Juanita at Chicago's victory rally.

quarter. An obviously distracted Pippen had played poorly. Three other starters spent much of the remaining 12 minutes on the bench. Jordan and four reserves then took over.

In a stunning comeback, the Bulls come back to within a Jordan jumper of taking the lead. He scored 24 points in the fourth quarter and his three-pointer, which would have put Chicago ahead, banged off the front edge of the rim in the final seconds. Philadelphia, exhausted and surprised, escaped. But only briefly.

As Jordan walks off, he quietly announces, "We'll win Sunday."

He is reminded that Pippen probably won't even be in the building for Game 4.

"It doesn't matter," said Jordan. "We'll win. You wait. We'll beat 'em."

As the Spectrum's visiting locker room clears, the adrenalin is still pumping. Jordan whispers his hotel room number to a reporter and suggests a trip to Atlantic City. His inner circle, a group of friends from North Carolina, is waiting and it's after midnight when the trek begins.

It's prom night and there are no limousines. Two taxi drivers say it will cost $100 per car for the trip. Jordan rejects the proposed tab and instead he and his entourage pile into three private cars.

The Taj Majal is relatively quiet at 1:30 A.M. Jordan and his gang walk down an aisle walled by slot machines and gaming tables. A few people notice him, but most just stand and stare.

Jordan finds a blackjack table and starts to play as a crowd quickly forms around him. There are cheers when he wins. Security men eventually arrive to protect Jordan and lend some semblance of order to the area.

For much of the next four-and-a-half hours, Jordan moves between tables. He goes to the cash machine for more ammunition and returns to keep playing. He wins some, but loses more.

Jordan, like the rest of his group, is still playing when the last hand is dealt and the doors are closed at 6 A.M. Two hours later, after a stop for breakfast, Jordan walks through the doors of the team hotel. Coach Phil Jackson, just out of bed and preparing for a morning walk, walks past him.

"Hi, coach," says Jordan.

"Hello, Michael," responds Jackson. "See you at practice."

And so he does. Jordan catches a couple hours of sleep, goes to practice and contemplates an afternoon of golf. All this with Game 4, a game in which he virtually guaranteed victory, less than 24 hours away.

As expected, Pippen has returned home to be with family and will not play.

The Bulls fall behind again and trail in the third quarter. But Jordan leads another fourth-quarter sprint, scoring 18 of his game-high 45 points in the final period. Chicago, which trailed by nine with 12 minutes left, rolls to a 111-101 triumph.

"I told you," Jordan says.

Deep into his seventh NBA season, Jordan sat back after a private weight-training session in his basement. He had finished another typical practice and headed home for another hour of lifting.

The house, situated in a upper middle-class suburb, is remarkably modest, given Jordan's cash flow. There is a three-car garage, but no swimming pool, no tennis court or basketball facility. The backyard is average. Although decorated and appointed tastefully and at obvious expense, it is not what one might expect.

The basement is filled with state-of-the-art Cybex machines. There is a small putting green and Jordan's most valued awards fill cabinets along one wall. He keeps all his away uniforms, a few of those framed.

His endorsement deals, which now top $12 million annually, are still anchored by Nike, Chevy, Gatorade, Wilson and McDonald's. His charity foundation passes out millions of dollars to a variety of causes. And he has added a clothing deal, a personalized tuxedo line, videos and a toy line to his portfolio.

He is in such demand, in fact, that Jordan stunned even the Bulls' front office prior to the 1990-91 season by turning down a three-day, $250,000 appearance offer from a Canadian company.

And it all keeps on growing. Just weeks after the Bulls won the title, Gatorade entered negotiations to lure Jordan from his endorsement of Coca-Cola. In August, Gatorade announced it had achieved the switch when Jordan signed an estimated $18-million contract over the next 10 years. With his playing salary topping $3 million in 1991-92, Jordan, with stock options and all the other perks tied to his Nike deal, will top $15 million a year.

But there won't be many left.

"As soon as I quit, I'll be out of there so fast it will be unbelievable," said Jordan. "After basketball, I want to be a professional golfer. After what I will have gone through, then to own a team? And have people asking me about evaluating players, the team's expectations?

"Ask me how many birdies I'm going to make, how many putts it will take or what I'm going to shoot today. That's all I'll want to be asked about. If I'm near basketball, it's only because my sons want to play. But come to a Bulls' game? I didn't go before I came here. I had never been to an NBA game before I played in one.

"Five more years. After 12 years, I think I'll still be doing what I'm doing now. But then I'd start to go down and I can't play when I start to go down. I learned from what they did to Dr. J. They started saying he was too old and that he couldn't play anymore. He could still play. He had just made the expectations of him too high because of all that he had done. I don't want to be put in that position. No way."

As Jordan heads to his video room, it's clear that however fast it all moves around him, he remains in control. It's a trait that runs through him like a long, narrow stream. It's the difference between Michael, Magic, Larry and all the rest.

Sir Charles Barkley & The All-Interview Gang

By JAN HUBBARD

On any given night, Charles Barkley is capable of outscoring, outrebounding, outworking and outplaying anyone in the NBA. Almost always, he is more outrageous and outlandish. Sometimes, his emotions are so out of control that he is constantly disciplined by the league office, which leads to his image as an outlaw. In the locker room, however, he is outgoing and outspoken. And, to make up a word, no player in the NBA can outcooperate Charles Barkley, who may not have won a Most Valuable Player award yet, but is consistently the Most Popular Interview in the NBA.

And so, not surprisingly, when reporters were asked to vote on the All-Interview team, the free-wheeling 76er was the overwhelming choice for the first team, an accolade that he attributes to his blunt, sometimes brutal, but always humorous approach to life in general and interviews in particular.

"People sometimes get mad at me because I tell the truth," Barkley said. "But anybody who knows me, I think, likes me. I'm a very spontaneous person. Situations happen and I react to them in a funny way. I don't try to be a comedian. But life's got to be funny. If you're not enjoying it, you might as well be dead. You work hard and you play hard. That's my motto in life."

Barkley's approach makes a lot of jobs easier, and it's not just because of his often hilarious analysis of NBA games, his teammates or himself. Barkley adds the element of humor to pre- and

Tuned to the pearly quotes that surface in and out of the locker room, Jan Hubbard is NBA columnist for Newsday *and* The Sporting News.

Is notorious Donald Trump interviewing Charles Barkley?

postgame discussions with reporters, but, for professional writers, his most endearing trait is his accessibility.

It's nothing for Barkley to spend 20 minutes with a writer before the game, no matter how big or small the publication that the writer represents. Underneath it all, he's a thoughtful, intelligent observer of sports—and cooperative. The combination makes for good stories and, of course, this leads to his overwhelming popularity among reporters.

Barkley is aware of that popularity, but he acknowledges it by making fun of reporters. In 1990, Barkley was involved in a controversy when he announced that he probably would not play in the Miami All-Star Game because of a groin injury. The league office told Barkley that if he was healthy enough to playing in regular-season games, he had no choice but to play in the All-Star Game. If he chose not to, Barkley would be suspended for three games.

ALL-INTERVIEW TEAMS

Selected by writers and broadcasters

FIRST		SECOND	
Player	**Votes**	**Player**	**Votes**
Charles Barkley	58	Kevin Johnson	22
Magic Johnson	46	Kevin McHale	22
Michael Jordan	26	David Robinson	19
Karl Malone	23	Mychal Thompson	11
Doc Rivers	23	Clyde Drexler	7
Coach Cotton Fitzsimmons	20	Coach Chuck Daly	16

Barkley was irritated by the strong-arm tactics, but, as usual, he found a way to joke about it.

"It would have been nice to sit in Philadelphia freezing and relaxing," Barkley said, noting the difference between February weather in Miami and Philadelphia. "But I guess I have to suffer here in Florida and play with Michael Jordan, Isiah Thomas and Patrick Ewing. I'll make the best of it."

Barkley then looked at the surrounding media and said, "I wasn't going to do interviews all weekend and make everybody's life miserable. But then I said that wouldn't be the right thing to do. But I'll say one thing. I never realized you could get so many ugly guys together at one time."

Barkley received 58 of 76 media votes for the All-Interview first team. He was joined by the Lakers' Magic Johnson (46), Chicago's Michael Jordan (26), Utah's Karl Malone (23) and Doc Rivers (23), who was traded after the season from Atlanta to the Clippers. The coach was Phoenix's Cotton Fitzsimmons.

It says a lot about the quality of superstars in the NBA that the four leading vote-getters on the All-Interview team also have been on the NBA's All-NBA first team the last three years. The obvious conclusion that should be fascinating to fans is that the greatest players in the game are as cooperative off the court as they are proficient on it.

No player is more cooperative than Magic, who arrives at the arena for home games three hours before tipoff. Generally speaking, most players arrive about an hour and a half before tipoff, which means Johnson beats the crowd by a full 90 minutes. En-

Magic Johnson addresses reporters at 1991 NBA Finals.

terprising reporters have discovered that if they beat their competitors and get to the arena by an extra 30 or 45 minutes, Johnson will sit the entire time and discuss almost anything. His specialty, of course, is the NBA. Johnson is a keen observer of the game, and he keeps up with what is going on. If he has time, you could ask him questions about every other team in the NBA, and he would analyze their present state.

Jordan's accessibility is surprising because he is so overwhelmingly popular among fans that he seldom ventures into public. At airports, restaurants, or on the street, Jordan is mobbed. He simply has little freedom.

Catch him 90 minutes before gametime, however, and Jordan will talk and talk and talk. He will sit around in his street clothes and philosophize on the state of the Bulls, on endorsements, on golf, on just about anything. And considering how many people Jordan knows or has met, he has a remarkable ability to remember names. Jordan probably addresses about 50 regular NBA reporters by their first name.

In fact, he and Johnson are similar in one respect. They are so cooperative that they have an army of reporters believing that they

TNT's Hubie Brown (left) and Bob Neal listen to Karl Malone.

are the reporters' best friend. Neither player has to be that way, because each is bigger than the game. That's why profiles on each sometimes are so gushing. Jordan and Johnson not only are two of the best players in the history of the game, but they also are down-to-earth good guys who believe they have an obligation to help the press do a good job. They are good for everybody.

Six years ago, it seemed unlikely that Karl Malone would have been on the All-Interview team. He seemed destined for anonymity. It had been that way all his life. Malone played for a small high school in Summerfield, La. He received a scholarship offer to Arkansas, but instead went to Louisiana Tech, where he did well enough to be drafted by the Utah Jazz, who play in Salt Lake City, one of the smallest markets in the NBA.

Malone worked hard on his game and became a superstar. And when the press began talking to him, they found a refreshing sort of cooperativeness and humor that, perhaps because of his modest background, they did not expect. He turned out to be a great talker.

For instance, during one of Malone's many contract re-negotiations, he made the point that when a player exceeds the production expected of him and the market increases with lesser players making more money, the truly great player deserves a raise.

"It's like my dog," Malone said. "Every morning, I let him outside and he picks up the paper for me. When he comes in the house, he goes right by the cabinet and waits there, because he knows he's going to get a treat. He sits there until he gets his treat. Then when he gets it, he goes about his business. Same way here."

Was he saying that he intended to camp out in front of Jazz executive offices until he got a new contract?

"I'm going to sit by the door," Malone said, "and start howling."

The last member of the All-Interview first team is Rivers, whose forte is his courtesy. He is known as one of the NBA's good guys.

Rivers does not attempt to be a comic, but he is capable of flashy quotes and actions. When he got married, he wore pink sneakers to match the dress of his future wife. The marriage cer-emony, however, made him nervous.

"It's like playing one-on-one," he said. "I'm not nervous about the crowd. It's the ceremony that's on my mind. This is going to be too quiet. If they'd cheer, it'd be a lot easier."

Fitzsimmons, the first-team coach, is a gruff, blunt veteran of 18 seasons. His style always has been direct, but reporters began appreciating him more after his teams began winning. And there is little doubt that the recent success of the Suns has invigorated Fitzsimmons, who had a career record of 46 games under .500 before the Suns put together consecutive records of 55-27, 54-28 and 55-27. Fitzsimmons now has a 752-716 record. He is in the place of his choice, Phoenix, where he loves the climate. He has a popular TV show. And he's having a lot of fun, which is a far different experience than his last job in San Antonio. At times, fans were so negative there that Fitzsimmons was booed in grocery stores.

"The guys didn't realize it when they were in the Alamo," Fitzsimmons said. "But they got a break when they were killed. They just didn't realize it at the time."

After the Suns improved by 27 games in 1988-89, which led to Fitzsimmons' selection as Coach of the Year, he told the press before the next season, "I hope no one expects us to improve 27 games like we did last year. That would make us 82-0.''

The All-Interview second team also is impressive, and two players missed making the first team by only one vote. One was Boston's Kevin McHale, who delivers quotes in machine-gun style after games. McHale is forever amused by the complicated analysis offered by the so-called experts. After patiently answering questions for awhile, McHale inevitably will say, "Hey, guys, it's only a game. We're talking about basketball. Don't make like it's rocket science.''

And although he is acknowledged as one of the NBA's better talkers, McHale admits that he's not in Barkley's class.

"There are so many processed, sterilized drones in this league,'' said McHale, in a quote that indicates the type of stories he is able to generate. "We all trust the party line. Charles ruffles some feathers, and that's good. He says a lot of things we'd all like to say but don't dare. We are 290 drones in the league, and Charles.''

Phoenix's Kevin Johnson also missed the first team by only one vote, and he probably will make it in future years—just as he probably will begin making the All-NBA first team. Johnson, like the others, is cooperative, thoughtful and insightful. He's not particularly funny, but he is exuberant, which is refreshing and enjoyable.

"Off the court,'' Johnson said, "I'm happy-go-lucky, excited, energetic. That's just me, and I would never do anything to hurt someone. Once I get on the court, though, that's the battlefield. I used to talk a lot of mess on the court, and my game would really go to another level. But one guy I saw play in the parks helped change that. This guy would take all kinds of mess from other guys, but he wouldn't say anything. He would intimidate someone by playing hard and not saying anything. I mean, I didn't like to pop off, but I thought it helped my game. But as I got religious, I realized that boasting was not something you always wanted to be doing. You should be humble.''

That ability to weave a story while making a point makes Johnson's locker a popular one after games.

The Spurs' David Robinson also is heavily sought-after after games. Robinson not only is well-spoken and willing, he has a unique way of articulating his responses.

Once, Robinson was asked about his ability to block shots, and he responded by saying, "I can't let them drive the lane with impunity.''

Another time, Robinson was comparing himself to the other great centers in the league and said of himself and Hakeem Ola-

Cotton Fitzsimmons is head coach of All-Interview team.

juwon, "How can you compare me to Hakeem? His stats are much more audacious than mine."

In terms of an All-Interview team, the Lakers' Mychal Thompson is a Hall-of-Famer. Last season, he played only 1,077 minutes, but still was selected to the All-Interview second team, primarily because he remained a quote machine. Thompson not only is funny, but he is spontaneously witty. He can pop one-liners faster than a speeding bullet.

The examples are numerous, but indicative of his approach was a quote he once manufactured when in Portland. Thompson was talking about a change from a setup offense to a running game. "You can't make thoroughbreds pull a buggy," Thompson said. "You have to let them run free and wild."

Thompson claims that when he retires from basketball, he will return to his native Bahamas, where he eventually hopes to be the prime minister. Thompson said his popularity in the Bahamas helped make basketball "the No. 1 sport, partly because of myself, and partly, all of a sudden, because this other Michael came along. And Magic vacations in the Bahamas every summer and they treat him better than they treat me. To save my ego, I just catch the next banana boat out and spend some time in Miami."

During the last championship series, when Magic led the Lakers to a Game 1 victory over Chicago, Thompson said, "We've got the No. 1 general in the U.S." Then he thought about the recent Gulf War and amended his statement, saying, "Magic and Schwarzkopf—they are the two. You can't count Bush. What has he done? It's Magic and Norman."

The last member of the second team is a puzzling one, at least in terms of jocularity. Portland's Clyde Drexler is one of the truly nice and cooperative players in the league, but he's not that funny. Even Drexler admits that he sometimes is boring.

"Hey, what can I say?" he said. "Everybody wants me to be like Charles Barkley and I can't."

Drexler is a diplomat, usually careful to avoid anything controversial. But he does have his moments. One came when he talked about how the absence of an injured Olajuwon might hurt Houston.

"If you take away the foundation," Drexler said, "what do you have left? All you have left are sideboards."

The coach of the second team is the noted Prince of Pessimism, Detroit's Chuck Daly. Daly admits worrying about every situation. In 1989, when the Pistons had a 3-0 lead in the NBA Finals against a Lakers team that was playing without the injured Magic Johnson and Byron Scott, Daly was still worried.

"I never feel good about anything," Daly said. "That's what being the Prince of Pessimism is all about."

Daly is one of the more cooperative NBA coaches, freely giving out his home phone number to regular NBA beat reporters.

The only way to appropriately conclude an article about the best talkers in the NBA is to return to some of the Best of Barkley:

• On his desire to learn karate: "I want to be registered as a lethal weapon."

• On New York City: "I like New York City. I own a gun."

• On responding to obnoxious fans: "If people come to the zoo and feed the animals, they'd better be willing to get bit."

• On an agreement between him and former teammate Rick Mahorn to donate $1,000 to charity each time one got a technical foul. "We wanted to donate the money to the homeless, but they would have better houses than we would by the end of the season."

• Describing his wife delivering their first child: "(She) was calling me every name in the book during labor. But I just told her, 'Come on. It can't hurt that bad. I've played with sprained ankles before. It can't hurt worse than that."

• On teammate Hersey Hawkins: "He's the black Jack Benny. The cheapest guy in the NBA."

• To a referee who missed a call during the game: "You've got to make that call. You know Moe and Larry won't."

• On the Sixers' ability to play without him after he missed seven consecutive regular-season games: "We're 2-5. But who's counting?"

INSIDE THE NBA

By FRED KERBER
and
SCOTT HOWARD-COOPER

PREDICTED ORDER OF FINISH

ATLANTIC	CENTRAL	MIDWEST	PACIFIC
Boston	Chicago	Utah	Portland
Philadelphia	Detroit	San Antonio	L.A. Lakers
New York	Indiana	Dallas	Phoenix
Washington	Cleveland	Houston	Golden State
New Jersey	Milwaukee	Denver	Seattle
Orlando	Atlanta	Minnesota	L.A. Clippers
Miami	Charlotte		Sacramento

EASTERN CONFERENCE: Chicago
WESTERN CONFERENCE: Portland
CHAMPION: Portland

There doesn't appear to be anyone in the East to challenge the Bulls. But the West is another matter. The overall weakness of the East is not to suggest that the defending champion Bulls couldn't win in a more competitive setting. Of course they could, especially as long as Michael Jordan can draw a rarified breath.

It's just that from top to bottom, particularly in the Atlantic Division, the East is far less than overpowering. And this may be crazy logic but it is one reason why we're picking the Bulls' reign

---

Fred Kerber roams the NBA for the New York Post *and Scott Howard-Cooper has the Clipper beat for the* Los Angeles Times. *Howard-Cooper wrote the Western Conference, Kerber the Eastern Conference and the introduction after going one-on-one with his counterpart.*

UNLV's Larry Johnson enters Hornets' nest as No. 1 pick.

to end at one year and why the Portland Trail Blazers will ascend to the throne.

Chicago had it too easy last season. With Finals MVP Jordan finally receiving help, they flattened everybody in their path and figure to do so again, right up to the NBA Finals. Quite simply, there's nobody in the East capable of beating the Bulls four times in seven games. Or four times in 17 games, for that matter.

So the Bulls will waltz through but then they'll meet the Blazers, who are still young, are still deep, are still loaded with weaponry and are still the team to beat in the West. Figure the Bulls will be cocky. Figure the Bulls won't be as hungry. Figure the Blazers in seven.

In the Atlantic Division, the NBA's tribute to mediocrity, Boston will rise to the top whether or not Larry Bird is 100 percent. The most intriguing in-division story will be what Pat Riley can do with the Knicks—with or without Patrick Ewing. Hey, it's

Nets opted for Georgia Tech's Kenny Anderson as No. 2.

worth a shot; no one else could do anything. New Yorkers want a miracle. They'll probably get a third-place finish behind the Sixers, who will be carried into second place by Charles Barkley.

The Bullets are the pick for fourth, unless Bernard King averages triple-figure points. The Nets picked the most-talked-about point guard in eons in Kenny Anderson and figure to win—about five more games. Then comes the breathless battle of Florida as Miami and Orlando swap insults in an effort to avoid the cellar.

The Bulls will reign in the Central, followed by Detroit, which will slip farther away from the Bulls' level. Indiana could be intriguing with youth, shooters, an up-tempo style and a center (Rik Smits) whose game is developing slower than his mastery of the language. But if he blossoms, the Pacers could surprise.

Cleveland will make noise if Mark Price can walk. Age and injuries may take their toll in Milwaukee. Figure the Hawks will need until January just to figure out who's on the team and Charlotte will make strides with youth (especially No. 1 overall pick Larry Johnson), but still is at least two years from challenging for the playoffs.

In the Midwest, Utah should replace San Antonio at the top. Rod Strickland's offcourt antics have some Spurs grumbling. And the Jazz can't possibly choke two straight years, can they? We'll pick Dallas for third—or until Roy Tarpley goes on some kind of list.

Houston finishes fourth because at some point Hakeem Olajuwon will want to start scoring lots again. Denver still has no veterans, but will be improved through the drafting of defensive studs Mark Macon and Dikembe Mutombo. Minnesota? Go North Stars. The T-Wolves needed help at three positions so they drafted for one of the other two.

In the Pacific, Portland repeats as divisional champ, but this time continues through the playoffs. The Lakers will be a year better under Mike Dunleavy's system and Magic still has his own teeth, so L.A. will be tough. Phoenix rolled the dice last year with Xavier McDaniel. It didn't work and the Suns are running out of time.

The Warriors, bolstered by three utterly useless first-round picks, still have their Big Three waiting for a center to surround. The Sonics are the sleeper team in all the NBA, but lose credit with the presence of Benoit Benjamin. The Clippers got their veteran point guard in Doc Rivers, but are teams supposed to have 11 forwards on the roster? And finally, there are the Kings, who had a great young small forward last year in Lionel Simmons and promptly drafted a great young small forward in Billy Owens.

ATLANTA HAWKS

TEAM DIRECTORY: Pres.: Stan Kasten; GM: Pete Babcock; Dir. Pub. Rel.: Arthur Triche; Coach: Bob Weiss; Asst. Coaches: Johnny Davis, Bob Weinhauer. Arena: The Omni (16,371). Colors: Red, white and gold.

SCOUTING REPORT

SHOOTING: The Hawks were fine inside, led by Kevin Willis and Dominique Wilkins. From the perimeter, well, that was another story.

The lack of any outside consistency sent the Hawks searching the draft for a shooter and they were ecstatic to find Rodney Monroe around at No. 30 on the second round. But he is, after all, a rookie and can't be expected to cause a turnaround. What the Hawks need are a few more guys who can hit a turnaround. And hit off the dribble.

In the backcourt, only Sidney Moncrief (.488) shot with consistency. After him, the best was John Battle (.461), and now he's a Buck. Newly acquired Travis Mays (.406 with the Kings) doesn't figure to solve the ills. The Hawks abandoned their passing game in season but figure to try it again to improve the .464 team mark, which tied them for 20th in the league.

PLAYMAKING: Despite the presence of the passing game much of the season, the Hawks were down—way down—in the league among assists, ranking 22nd. And now Spud Webb and Doc Rivers, their two best playmakers (although Rivers played off-guard all season) are gone. So that means a lot of burden will fall upon second-year man Rumeal Robinson and rookie Monroe, a shooter with point-guard size (6-2).

DEFENSE: You don't really want to talk defense, do you? The Hawks didn't talk it—or play much of it, either. Opponents shot .494, the second straight season Atlanta gave up more than .490. Inside, the shot-blocking didn't overwhelm as Jon Koncak's 76 were a team high. Blair Rasmussen (30 with Denver) hardly can be expected to fill that void.

REBOUNDING: With Wilkins enjoying his finest rebounding season ever, the Hawks held their own on the boards, finishing eighth overall in the league.

Dominique Wilkins had best all-around campaign.

But they'll need improvement on the offensive glass, especially with the departure of warhorse Moses Malone. Although confined to the bench and getting reservist minutes, Moses still contributed

HAWK ROSTER

No.	Veterans	Pos.	Ht.	Wt.	Age	Yrs. Pro	College
33	Duane Ferrell	F	6-7	210	26	3	Georgia Tech
32	Jon Koncak	C	7-0	250	28	6	SMU
34	Gary Leonard	C	7-1	240	24	2	Missouri
1	Travis Mays	G	6-2	190	23	1	Texas
40	Tim McCormick	C	7-0	240	29	7	Michigan
15	Sidney Moncrief	G	6-3	181	34	11	Arkansas
41	Blair Rasmussen	C	7-0	260	28	6	Oregon
22	Rumeal Robinson	G	6-2	195	24	1	Michigan
8	Alexander Volkov	F	6-10	218	27	1	Kiev Institute
21	Dominique Wilkins	F	6-8	200	31	9	Georgia
42	Kevin Willis	F-C	7-0	235	29	6	Michigan State

Rd.	Rookies	Sel. No.	Pos.	Ht.	Wt.	College
1	Stacey Augmon	9	F	6-6	205	Nevada-Las Vegas
2	Rodney Monroe	30	G	6-2	185	North Carolina State

at the offensive end. Koncak is thus the man on the spot to make up the difference. 'Nique averaged nine boards once; asking for twice will be a bit much. On the defensive boards, the Hawks were third-best in the East.

OUTLOOK: Another new-look season beckons. And so do new questions. Last season, the story surrounded Bob Weiss, new coach. This season, it centers around what will be a new backcourt with the departure of Rivers and Webb, and the loss of John Battle. The Hawks traditionally have been an athletic team and the drafting of Stacey Augmon will enhance that rep. They'll renew their motion offense—but must improve on a stagnant defense that allowed opponents to shoot .494, the worst in the East last season.

The Hawks streaked in midseason but finished lamely, checking into the East playoffs as the sixth seed. They'll need considerable improvement just to maintain that status with expected improvement arriving in Cleveland and Indiana and, perhaps, New York.

HAWK PROFILES

DOMINIQUE WILKINS 31 6-8 200   Forward

The fans' clamoring of "trade 'Nique" quieted down . . . A career-best season tends to do that . . . Scoring (25.9), was his lowest in seven years, but he was still massively potent . . . More impressive were contributions elsewhere . . . Career high in rebounds (9.0, second only to Dennis Rodman among NBA small forwards). His 471 defensive boards bettered by 114 his previous high . . . One-game career best of 19 . . . Career-high assists (3.3) . . . Team-high 65 blocks were his most since his second season in the league after leaving Georgia in '82 . . . Seventh straight season of 2,000-plus points . . . Stopped leaping out on offense. Stayed in and soared for rebounds . . . Fewest shots in seven years . . . Wore down at end and had rough-shooting (.372) playoffs. But that was against Detroit and Rodman . . . All-Best-Dressed with Knicks' brother, Gerald . . . Underrated, hardworking defender . . . Born Jan. 12, 1960, in Sorbonne, France . . . Real name Jacques . . . No. 3 pick by Utah in '82. Hawks got him for John Drew, Freeman Williams and cash, Sept. 3, 1982 . . . Made $2.065 million.

Year	Team	G	FG	FG Pct.	FT	FT Pct.	Reb.	Ast.	TP	Avg.
1982-83	Atlanta	82	601	.493	230	.682	478	129	1434	17.5
1983-84	Atlanta	81	684	.479	382	.770	582	126	1750	21.6
1984-85	Atlanta	81	853	.451	486	.806	557	200	2217	27.4
1985-86	Atlanta	78	888	.468	577	.818	618	206	2366	30.3
1986-87	Atlanta	79	828	.463	607	.818	494	261	2294	29.0
1987-88	Atlanta	78	909	.464	541	.826	502	224	2397	30.7
1988-89	Atlanta	80	814	.464	442	.844	553	211	2099	26.2
1989-90	Atlanta	80	810	.484	459	.807	521	200	2138	26.7
1990-91	Atlanta	81	770	.470	476	.829	732	265	2101	25.9
	Totals	720	7157	.469	4200	.807	5037	1822	18796	26.1

KEVIN WILLIS 29 7-0 235   Forward-Center

Kevin, this man is your opponent. Try not to let him score . . . Has trouble defending. A lot of trouble . . . Bad guy in defensive rotations . . . Only slightly better in passing-game offense, which Hawks played—or tried to. Can be effective in very structured game . . . Suffice to say he doesn't have the best hands in the league, either . . . Sound athletic skills for the most part, runs the floor well but inconsistent . . . Has terrific drop-step baseline shot which went under-utilized . . . Led team in shooting at .504 . . . Was second to Wilkins in rebounding at 8.8 per . . . Led team in boards (9.0) and scored well in playoffs (15.4, nearly three points above career average). But he shot a dismal .403 . . . Born Sept. 6, 1962, in Los Angeles . . . Hawks' No. 11 pick out of Michigan State in '84 . . . Made $685,000.

Year	Team	G	FG	FG Pct.	FT	FT Pct.	Reb.	Ast.	TP	Avg.
1984-85	Atlanta	82	322	.467	119	.657	522	36	765	9.3
1985-86	Atlanta	82	419	.517	172	.654	704	45	1010	12.3
1986-87	Atlanta	81	538	.536	227	.709	849	62	1304	16.1
1987-88	Atlanta	75	356	.518	159	.649	547	28	871	11.6
1988-89	Atlanta				Injured					
1989-90	Atlanta	81	418	.519	168	.683	645	57	1006	12.4
1990-91	Atlanta	80	444	.504	159	.668	704	99	1051	13.1
	Totals	481	2497	.512	1004	.672	3971	327	6007	12.5

JON KONCAK 28 7-0 250   Center

If only outscoring the other team weren't so darn important . . . Smart defender, solid in the post. And not a bad rebounder . . . Offensively as sound as an S&L . . . Some face-up skills but bad post-up offense . . . Confidence in his scoring at low tide. With reason. Shot career-low .436, averaged 4.1 points . . . Awful from foul line: .593 last season, .603 career . . . Made $1.55 million, thanks to huge offer sheet tended by Pistons three years back . . . Should get better with scoring as Hawks get more involved and comfortable with their passing game . . . Began season on bench. Became a starter. Back to bench. Back to front five . . . Rebound average should be better (4.9) . . . Decent shot-blocker: 76 in 77 games . . . Born May 17, 1963, in Cedar Rapids, Iowa . . . No. 5 lottery pick in '85 out of SMU, where he became all-time rebounder in Southwest Conference . . . 1984 Olympic gold medalist.

Year	Team	G	FG	FG Pct.	FT	FT Pct.	Reb.	Ast.	TP	Avg.
1985-86	Atlanta	82	263	.507	156	.607	467	55	682	8.3
1986-87	Atlanta	82	169	.480	125	.654	493	31	463	5.6
1987-88	Atlanta	49	98	.483	83	.610	333	19	279	5.7
1988-89	Atlanta	74	141	.524	63	.553	453	56	345	4.7
1989-90	Atlanta	54	78	.614	42	.532	226	23	198	3.7
1990-91	Atlanta	77	140	.436	32	.593	375	124	313	4.1
	Totals	418	889	.496	501	.603	2347	308	2280	5.5

ALEXANDER VOLKOV 27 6-10 218   Forward

Two definitely not better than one here . . . Doctors found fractures in both wrists . . . Didn't play a minute. Placed on injured list Nov. 1 and underwent subsequent surgery . . . At least he didn't have to wait on line a month for bread . . . Lifted weights to get strength back . . . Tremendous moves to the basket. First step catches many by surprise . . . Needs upper-body strength and to limit silly clutch-and-grab fouls . . . MVP in Soviet Union in 1989 . . . Born March 29, 1964, in Kiev, USSR, where he later attended the Institute of Physical Culture (probably Russia's answer to Nevada-Las Vegas) . . . Sixth-round pick of Hawks in '86, he signed Aug. 1, '89 . . . Made $650,000.

Year	Team	G	FG	FG Pct.	FT	FT Pct.	Reb.	Ast.	TP	Avg.
1989-90	Atlanta	72	137	.482	70	.583	119	83	357	5.0
1990-91	Atlanta					Injured				
	Totals	72	137	.482	70	.583	119	83	357	5.0

TIM McCORMICK 29 7-0 240   Center

Never been confused with Jesse Owens . . . With Moses Malone and then Jon Koncak struggling as starters, he was given seven-game hiatus from bench and used as starter in March . . . Averaged 8.0 points and 3.7 rebounds. Not great, but better than season figures of 4.5 and 2.9 . . . Smart player with a decent shot and better-than-average low-post moves . . . Takes forever to get shot off, though . . . Obtained before 1990 training camp from Houston with John Lucas for Kenny Smith and Roy Marble . . . Accustomed to being traded. Drafted No. 12 by Cavs out of Michigan in '84 and traded twice on Draft Day, going to Washington, then Seattle . . . Born March 10, 1962, in Detroit . . . Made $775,000.

Year	Team	G	FG	FG Pct.	FT	FT Pct.	Reb.	Ast.	TP	Avg.
1984-85	Seattle	78	269	.557	188	.715	398	78	726	9.3
1985-86	Seattle	77	253	.570	174	.713	403	83	681	8.8
1986-87	Philadelphia	81	391	.545	251	.719	611	114	1033	12.8
1987-88	Phil-N.J.	70	348	.537	145	.647	467	118	841	12.0
1988-89	Houston	81	169	.481	87	.674	261	54	425	5.2
1989-90	Houston	18	10	.345	10	.526	27	3	30	1.7
1990-91	Atlanta	56	93	.497	66	.733	165	32	252	4.5
	Totals	461	1533	.536	921	.704	2332	482	3988	8.7

RUMEAL ROBINSON 24 6-2 195   Guard

If he knew how to run a team the way he knows how to score . . . Typical rookie point-guard transition . . . Doesn't see the floor as well as he should . . . Must lose score-first mentality . . . Extremely confident . . . Toward season's end, he improved decision-making. Realized he could pass on penetrations . . . Started 16 games, Hawks were 9-7 . . . Also sat 28 games, seven more with injury . . . Playoff non-entity . . . Notoriously bad foul shooter who makes them when they count . . . Won a state high-school title and the NCAAs for Michigan in '90 at line in closing seconds . . . Hawks took him at No. 11 and paid him $800,000 . . . Born Nov. 13, 1966, in Mandeville, Jamaica . . . Attended Rindge and Latin High in Cambridge, Mass., like another Jamaican-born player, Patrick Ewing.

Year	Team	G	FG	FG Pct.	FT	FT Pct.	Reb.	Ast.	TP	Avg.
1990-91	Atlanta	47	108	.446	47	.588	71	132	265	5.6

BLAIR RASMUSSEN 28 7-0 260   Center

Traded to Hawks from Nuggets just after draft . . . Coming off rotator-cuff surgery that caused him to miss final seven games . . . Should be ready for training camp but don't expect him to throw any sliders . . . Started team-high 69 games with Denver . . . Good outside shooter for a center . . . Consistent . . . Slow-footed . . . Tied career high with 16 rebounds and eight blocked shots March 2 against Orlando . . . Finished 11th in NBA in rebounding and 16th in blocks . . . Had 31 double-doubles . . . Born Nov. 13, 1962, in Auburn, Wash. . . . Attended Oregon and Denver made him 15th pick in 1985 draft . . . Made $2,185,000.

Year	Team	G	FG	FG Pct.	FT	FT Pct.	Reb.	Ast.	TP	Avg.
1985-86	Denver	48	61	.407	31	.795	97	16	153	3.2
1986-87	Denver	74	268	.470	169	.732	465	60	705	9.5
1987-88	Denver	79	435	.492	132	.776	437	78	1002	12.7
1988-89	Denver	77	257	.445	69	.852	287	49	583	7.6
1989-90	Denver	81	445	.497	111	.828	594	82	1001	12.4
1990-91	Denver	70	405	.458	63	.677	678	70	875	12.5
	Totals	429	1871	.472	575	.769	2558	355	4319	10.1

TRAVIS MAYS 23 6-2 190   Guard

Came to Hawks from Kings in Draft Day trade for Spud Webb and 1994 second-round draft pick ... Great first step, but not good yet at shooting quickly coming around a pick ... That tends to be a necessity for someone at that position ... His best game is to go to the hole, but he did finish 13th in league in three-point shooting ... Finished behind only Derrick Coleman, Lionel Simmons and Dennis Scott among rookie scorers ... Other problem is defending larger off-guards ... Left Texas as leading scorer in Southwest Conference history and the Kings picked him at No. 14 ... Born June 19, 1968, in Ocala, Fla. ... Made $800,000.

Year	Team	G	FG	FG Pct.	FT	FT Pct.	Reb.	Ast.	TP	Avg.
1990-91	Sacramento......	64	294	.406	255	.770	178	253	915	14.3

DUANE FERRELL 26 6-7 210   Forward

Before re-signing Nov. 2, seemed to get cut every other month ... Cut four times by Hawks since they originally signed him as an undrafted free agent in '88 out of Georgia Tech ... Figures to stick this time ... Tough player, good defender on small forwards and shooting guards ... Gets his points (6.1 ppg) on garbage baskets and drives ... Shot .489 ... Inconsistent on outside ... Born Feb. 28, 1965, in Baltimore ... Not bad for $125,000.

Year	Team	G	FG	FG Pct.	FT	FT Pct.	Reb.	Ast.	TP	Avg.
1988-89	Atlanta.........	41	35	.422	30	.682	41	10	100	2.4
1989-90	Atlanta.........	14	5	.357	2	.333	7	2	12	0.9
1990-91	Atlanta.........	78	174	.489	125	.801	179	55	475	6.1
	Totals	133	214	.472	157	.762	227	67	587	4.4

SIDNEY MONCRIEF 34 6-3 181   Guard

Doesn't approach what he once was, but still contributes ... Played 72 games, most since 1985-86 ... Came out of retirement after one year when knee injuries apparently ended career ... Can still dominate offensively and defensively for limited stretches ... Held Reggie Miller to one shot in 12 minutes in game where Pacer guard was toasting Hawks ... Understands his role completely. Only tries to score when it's there or necessary . . . Had decent playoff showing. His 11-of-22 made him only Hawk at .500 . . . Milwaukee picked him No. 5 out of Arkansas in '79 . . . Twice named Defensive Player of the Year . . . Born Sept. 21, 1957, in Little Rock, Ark. . . . Made $510,000 as free agent.

Year	Team	G	FG	FG Pct.	FT	FT Pct.	Reb.	Ast.	TP	Avg.
1979-80	Milwaukee	77	211	.468	232	.795	338	133	654	8.5
1980-81	Milwaukee	80	400	.541	320	.804	406	264	1122	14.0
1981-82	Milwaukee	80	556	.523	468	.817	534	382	1581	19.8
1982-83	Milwaukee	76	606	.524	499	.826	437	300	1712	22.5
1983-84	Milwaukee	79	560	.498	529	.848	528	358	1654	20.9
1984-85	Milwaukee	73	561	.483	454	.828	391	382	1585	21.7
1985-86	Milwaukee	73	470	.489	498	.859	334	357	1471	20.2
1986-87	Milwaukee	39	158	.488	136	.840	127	121	460	11.8
1987-88	Milwaukee	56	217	.489	164	.837	180	204	603	10.8
1988-89	Milwaukee	62	261	.491	205	.865	172	188	752	12.1
1990-91	Atlanta	72	117	.488	82	.781	128	104	337	4.7
	Totals	767	4117	.502	3587	.831	3575	2793	11931	15.6

GARY LEONARD 24 7-1 240   Center

Can't teach size, right? . . . Never given chance under what he called "demonic" leadership of Bill Musselman in Minnesota . . . Hawks like his natural skills . . . Didn't like them that much in regular season, however, as he got nine minutes in four cameos . . . No discernible defensive skills yet . . . Decent shooter . . . Minnesota made him a second-round pick out of Missouri in '89 . . . Signed as free agent for pro-rated minimum wage ($120,000).

Year	Team	G	FG	FG Pct.	FT	FT Pct.	Reb.	Ast.	TP	Avg.
1989-90	Minnesota	22	13	.419	6	.429	27	1	32	1.5
1990-91	Atlanta	4	0	.000	2	.500	2	0	2	0.5
	Totals	26	13	.419	8	.444	29	1	34	1.3

THE ROOKIES

STACEY AUGMON 23 6-6 205   Forward

Defensive Player of the Year as senior for 34-1 UNLV . . . Hawks traded Doc Rivers to get No. 9 pick from Clippers and draft him . . . Compared to Dennis Rodman . . . Only he is considered to have

better offensive skills . . . One of three Rebels drafted on first round
. . . Should fit in nicely with coach Bob Weiss' passing game . . .
Averaged 16.5 points, shot .587 . . . Tied for school steals record
with 275 . . . Born Aug. 1, 1968, in Pasadena, Cal.

RODNEY MONROE 23 6-2 185   **Guard**
Considered one of surprises in draft—the 30th pick after Hawks
had considered taking him at 15 . . . Excellent shooting touch
Hawks sought . . . Considered extremely streaky, though . . . Will
need help to create his shots . . . All-ACC as senior for North
Carolina State . . . School record 104-of-239 on three-pointers
(.435) . . . Born April 16, 1968, in Baltimore.

COACH BOBBY WEISS: Players' coach . . . Breaks it down
to simple terms and communicates well with
players . . . Very positive approach . . . "Everything we expected, Bob has done to the Nth
degree," said Hawks' GM Pete Babcock . . .
Mike Fratello's replacement posted 43-39 record, best by first-year Hawks' coach since
1972-73 . . . Coach of the Month for December
when Hawks went 11-3 . . . Amateur magician
. . . Head coach in San Antonio, 1986-88. Two-year stint produced
59-105 record . . . Instituted passing game with Hawks and found
early success after 4-10 start . . . Came out of Penn State and was
25th pick by Philadelphia in 1965 . . . Played for six teams in NBA
career that covered 12 seasons . . . Member of 1967 champ Sixers
. . . Averaged 7.6 points, 3.7 assists as a pro . . . Born May 7,
1942 in Easton, Pa.

GREATEST TEAM

In 1986-87, the Hawks forged a franchise-record 57 regular-
season victories, capping off a Central Division reign of terror
with a 13-2 April. But the Hawks, the November-to-April defensive kings behind a Dominique Wilkins-led roster renowned for
athleticism, died in the Eastern semis to Detroit. For all they
accomplished in the regular season, the Hawks didn't get it done.

But the 1957-58 Hawks of St. Louis did, despite only 41 pre-playoff victories, the 19th-best total in team history. One season after losing a double-OT seventh game to the Celtics, the Hawks exacted revenge in the finals.

With Celtic legend Bill Russell hobbled by a Game 3 ankle injury, St. Louis avoided a Game 7 in Boston as Bob Pettit, still the Hawks' all-time scoring leader, poured in 50 points to end the series in six. But the title run by the Hawks—the fifth different winner in five years—ended an age of parity. The following season, the Celts embarked on their staggering streak of eight straight titles.

ALL-TIME HAWK LEADERS

SEASON

Points: Bob Pettit, 2,429, 1961-62
Assists: Glenn Rivers, 823, 1986-87
Rebounds: Bob Pettit, 1,540, 1960-61

GAME

Points: Dominique Wilkins, 57 vs. Chicago, 11/10/86
Dominique Wilkins, 57 vs. New Jersey 4/10/86
Lou Hudson, 57 vs. Chicago, 11/10/69
Bob Pettit, 57 vs. Detroit, 2/18/61
Assists: Glenn Rivers, 21 vs. Philadelphia, 3/4/86
Rebounds: Bob Pettit, 35 vs. Cincinnati, 3/2/58
Bob Pettit, 35 vs. New York, 1/6/56

CAREER

Points: Bob Pettit, 20,880, 1954-65
Assists: Glenn Rivers, 3,866, 1983-91
Rebounds: Bob Pettit, 12,851, 1954-65

BOSTON CELTICS

TEAM DIRECTORY: Chairman: Don Gaston; Vice-Chairman/ Sec.: Paul Dupee; Vice-Chairman/Treas.: Alan Cohen; Pres.: Red Auerbach; Sr. Exec. VP: David Gavitt; Exec. VP/GM: Jan Volk; VP-Marketing/Communications: Tod Rosensweig; Dir. Pub. Rel.: Jeff Twiss; Dir. Publications and Inf.: David Zuccaro; Coach: Chris Ford; Asst. Coaches: Don Casey, John Jennings. Arena: Boston Garden (14,890) and Hartford Civic Center (15,134), Colors: Green and white.

SCOUTING REPORT

SHOOTING: The Celts were the league's best last season at .512. But with an asterisk. At the All-Star break, the Celts were shooting .522. From there, they were .499. That is by no means shabby, but the trend was toward a steady, consistent decrease

So much still depends on the flight of the Bird.

that could be traced to Larry Bird's back. Not that Bird's shooting meant that much. His setups and defensive rebounding did. As the rebounding faded, so did the fastbreaks and thus the shooting percentage.

Much of the Celts' fortunes this season will again hinge on Bird's back. Boston has the uncanny inside accuracy of Robert Parish (.598) and Kevin McHale (.553)—yeah, yeah, so they're a year older. When was the last time you didn't say that? On the perimeter, Reggie Lewis is an inch away from stud status, hitting virtually everything if left open. The Celts can't expect another .587 year from Kevin Gamble—but then they didn't expect anything like it last year, either.

PLAYMAKING: Perhaps the most interesting development in Chris Ford's second season at the helm will be the duel at point guard between Brian Shaw, who was lured back from Italy before last season, and Dee Brown, who usurped virtually all the point-guard duties except being on court for the opening tap in the playoffs. Either way, the Celts will have a young and skilled playmaker at the point.

But the real point for Boston could remain at forward. Before Bird's health became a legitimate concern again last season, much of the Celtics' offensive schemes passed through him. With it all, the Celtics still ranked eighth in the league in assists. Unselfish play is mandatory on all Celtic resumes.

DEFENSE: Foes shot .452, the best mark in the East, second-best in the NBA. The C's, always formidable defenders in the halfcourt with Parish and McHale, gave opponents fits in transition, too, with their backcourt speed, although they didn't force nearly enough turnovers (13.7). For all the offensive talk, it was the defense that enabled Boston to bolt at the start last season.

REBOUNDING: Here comes the age-old argument about the Celtics: old age. But as long as Bird, Parish and McHale tug on green and white uniforms and can remember their names, the Celtics will be a rebounding force. They were sixth overall in the league, despite the defensive-glass tailspin the team suffered when Bird's condition worsened and McHale's ankle gave him major headaches. Always, though, there was Parish, who was fourth among all centers in offensive rebounds.

OUTLOOK: Last season, when the young legs were spinning, the Celtics were winning. But the legs spun on fastbreaks and the

CELTIC ROSTER

No.	Veterans	Pos.	Ht.	Wt.	Age	Yrs. Pro	College
5	John Bagley	G	6-0	205	31	8	Boston College
33	Larry Bird	F	6-9	220	34	12	Indiana State
7	Dee Brown	G	6-1	161	22	1	Jacksonville
34	Kevin Gamble	G-F	6-5	210	25	4	Iowa
53	Joe Kleine	C	7-0	271	29	6	Arkansas
35	Reggie Lewis	G-F	6-7	195	25	4	Northeastern
32	Kevin McHale	F-C	6-10	225	33	11	Minnesota
00	Robert Parish	C	7-0	230	38	15	Centenary
54	Ed Pinckney	F	6-9	215	28	6	Villanova
20	Brian Shaw	G	6-6	190	25	2	Cal-Santa Barbara
43	Derek Smith	G-F	6-6	218	30	9	Louisville
11	Michael Smith	F	6-10	225	26	2	BYU
52	Stojko Vrankovic	C	7-2	260	27	1	Yugoslavia

Rd.	Rookies	Sel. No.	Pos.	Ht.	Wt.	College
1	Rick Fox	24	F-G	6-6	231	North Carolina
	Anderson Hunt		G	6-2	175	Nevada-Las Vegas

transitions began with the big three of Bird, McHale and Parish. After the two forwards were stricken, the major question for the Celtics was health. And it still is.

The guard position is well-stocked with youth and talent. Backup help for the frontline is questionable, though. Joe Kleine's minutes fell off the planet. Ed Pinckney is still considered inconsistent. Michael Smith, ugh. With McHale serving as sixth man, Gamble started. A playoff bust, Gamble must prove his regular season was not a one-year fluke. Rookies Rick Fox from North Carolina and Anderson Hunt, undrafted from Nevada-Las Vegas, will get a shot. But, as always, the major question will concern Bird.

CELTIC PROFILES

LARRY BIRD 34 6-9 220   Forward

Biggest question in Atlantic: how much legend is left in Larry? . . . Underwent offseason back surgery after missing 22 regular-season games . . . Averaged under 20 points (19.4) for second time. Was 19.3 in six-game injury-riddled 1988-89 . . . Don't bury him yet. He is Bird . . . In first-round Game 5 vs. Pacers, he made dramatic third-quarter return from nasty face-first fall. Scored 32 points to oust Indy . . . Decidedly human vs. Pistons in Eastern semis (13.4 ppg) . . . Back affected shooting most: .454 regular season, .408 playoffs (62-of-152) . . . Celtic running game faded without their best defensive rebounder (7.6 average, 8.5 overall) . . . Passing was Larry-like in point-forward role: 7.2 assists . . . All-NBA his first nine years . . . Three-time MVP (1984-85-86) . . . Passed 20,000 points, 5,000 assists . . . 13th all-time scorer (20,883) . . . 68 triple-doubles, including first playoff game vs. Indy . . . Celts' greatest playoff scorer . . . Born Dec. 7, 1956, in West Baden, Ind . . . Selected sixth as junior-eligible out of Indiana State in '78 . . . Made $1.5 million. Gets balloon payment of $7.1 million this season.

Year	Team	G	FG	FG Pct.	FT	FT Pct.	Reb.	Ast.	TP	Avg.
1979-80	Boston	82	693	.474	301	.836	852	370	1745	21.3
1980-81	Boston	82	719	.478	283	.863	895	451	1741	21.2
1981-82	Boston	77	711	.503	328	.863	837	447	1761	22.9
1982-83	Boston	79	747	.504	351	.840	870	458	1867	23.6
1983-84	Boston	79	758	.492	374	.888	796	520	1908	24.2
1984-85	Boston	80	918	.522	403	.882	842	531	2295	28.7
1985-86	Boston	82	796	.496	441	.896	805	557	2115	25.8
1986-87	Boston	74	786	.525	414	.910	682	566	2076	28.1
1987-88	Boston	76	881	.527	415	.916	703	467	2275	29.9
1988-89	Boston	6	49	.471	18	.947	37	29	116	19.3
1989-90	Boston	75	718	.473	319	.930	712	562	1820	24.3
1990-91	Boston	60	462	.454	163	.891	509	431	1164	19.4
	Totals	852	8238	.497	3810	.884	8540	5389	20883	24.5

ROBERT PARISH 38 7-0 230   Center

Still has his own teeth . . . Oldest active player in NBA . . . Ultimate team player . . . Career highs in shooting: from floor (.598, second in NBA) and line (.767) . . . Seventh in rebounding (10.6), third among Eastern centers . . . Nine-time All-Star . . . 21-point first quarter vs. Lakers on Feb. 15. Passed 19,000 points in process . . . Injured (ankles) in playoffs; missed game against Pistons, averaged 26.2 minutes. Shot .479 and .613 from line . . . Picks spots to run, does so with devastating effectiveness . . . Superior offensive rebounder . . . His 271 offensive boards led Eastern centers . . . Deadly baseline jumper and virtually unpreventable 12-foot turnaround . . . After career-low 69 blocks in 1989-90, responded with 103. Clogs lane, barks instructions and frustrates younger centers by knocking them out of position...Earned $2.5 million, with another year left...Born Aug. 30, 1953, in Shreveport, La....No. 8 pick of Warriors in '76 out of Centenary...Came to Celts June 9, 1980, with first-rounder (Kevin McHale) for two No. 1s.

Year	Team	G	FG	FG Pct.	FT	FT Pct.	Reb.	Ast.	TP	Avg.
1976-77	Golden State	77	288	.503	121	.708	543	74	697	9.1
1977-78	Golden State	82	430	.472	165	.625	680	95	1025	12.5
1978-79	Golden State	76	554	.499	196	.698	916	115	1304	17.2
1979-80	Golden State	72	510	.507	203	.715	783	122	1223	17.0
1980-81	Boston	82	635	.545	282	.710	777	144	1552	18.9
1981-82	Boston	80	669	.542	252	.710	866	140	1590	19.9
1982-83	Boston	78	619	.550	271	.698	827	141	1509	19.3
1983-84	Boston	80	623	.546	274	.745	857	139	1520	19.0
1984-85	Boston	79	551	.542	292	.743	840	125	1394	17.6
1985-86	Boston	81	530	.549	245	.731	770	145	1305	16.1
1986-87	Boston	80	588	.566	227	.735	851	173	1403	17.5
1987-88	Boston	74	442	.589	177	.734	628	115	1061	14.3
1988-89	Boston	80	596	.570	294	.719	996	175	1486	18.6
1989-90	Boston	79	505	.580	233	.747	796	103	1243	15.7
1990-91	Boston	81	485	.598	237	.767	856	66	1207	14.9
	Totals	1181	8025	.543	3469	.720	11986	1872	19519	16.5

KEVIN McHALE 33 6-10 225   Forward-Center

Another reason Celts' medical insurance premiums hit roof...Enjoyed typical "Big Three" season until Feb. 2 in Seattle when left ankle turned toward Miami...Re-aggravated injury, gummed up ligaments, faced surgery. Missed 14 games...Still had 146 blocks (2.15 per), eighth-best in league. And he had just one block after 15 games...Smarts and experience make up for bad lateral movement...Became fourth-best scorer in team history (15,793 points), passing Sam Jones...Scored 20.7 in playoffs, 20th-best...Primarily sixth-man role. Made 10 starts...Magnificent offensive rebounder whose long arms bring short follow-up jumpers that have crushed opponents for years... Has 39 career three-pointers, 38 in last two seasons...Born Dec. 19, 1957, in Hibbing, Minn....Got to Celts out of Minnesota as part of perhaps greatest swindle in sports history. Celts gave up slot to draft Joe Barry Carroll to Warriors. Got No. 3 pick in '80,

which brought McHale. They also got Robert Parish...Made
$1.4 million.

Year	Team	G	FG	FG Pct.	FT	FT Pct.	Reb.	Ast.	TP	Avg.
1980-81	Boston..........	82	355	.533	108	.679	359	55	818	10.0
1981-82	Boston..........	82	465	.531	187	.754	556	91	1117	13.6
1982-83	Boston..........	82	483	.541	193	.717	553	104	1159	14.1
1983-84	Boston..........	82	587	.556	336	.765	610	104	1511	18.4
1984-85	Boston..........	79	605	.570	355	.760	712	141	1565	19.8
1985-86	Boston..........	68	561	.574	326	.776	551	181	1448	21.3
1986-87	Boston..........	77	790	.604	428	.836	763	198	2008	26.1
1987-88	Boston..........	64	550	.604	346	.797	536	171	1446	22.6
1988-89	Boston..........	78	661	.546	436	.818	637	172	1758	22.5
1989-90	Boston..........	82	648	.549	393	.893	677	172	1712	20.9
1990-91	Boston..........	68	504	.553	228	.829	480	126	1251	18.4
	Totals	844	6209	.562	3336	.795	6434	1515	15793	18.7

DEE BROWN 22 6-1 161   Guard

Okay, at least 10 GMs, repeat after us: ''I
shoulda took Dee Brown, I shoulda
...''...Jacksonville star lasted until 19 and
promptly made All-Rookie team with lightning
quickness...Outraced Trump Shuttle from
LaGuardia to Logan...Supplanted Brian
Shaw in minutes (not starts) in Eastern semis.
Averaged 15.8 vs. Pistons, third-best on team
...Gained instant fame for winning Slam Dunk championship,
although gave blatant sneaker commercial before each jam. He
was first Celt ever entered in event...Nice rebounder for his size.
Uses explosive leap...One steal every 23 minutes...Jump shot
improved over season...Better than anyone thought...Born
Nov. 29, 1968, in Jacksonville, Fla....Paid $547,000.

Year	Team	G	FG	FG Pct.	FT	FT Pct.	Reb.	Ast.	TP	Avg.
1990-91	Boston..........	82	284	.464	137	.873	182	344	712	8.7

REGGIE LEWIS 25 6-7 195   Guard/Forward

Heir to Larry Bird's ''go-to'' crown...Career
highs in minutes, scoring (18.7), blocks, rebounds and free-throw shooting...Magnifi-
cent baseline move that has defenders cussing
...Shot .491 despite awful midseason stretch
...In keeping with club policy, nursed nagging
injury, sore back, for much of the season...
Part of Celts' young-legs brigade that terrorized
East for three-fourths of season...Explosive in open court, fills

the lanes well but not the greatest (though improved) ball-handler
... Quick hands made him solid defender (98 steals, 85
blocks) ... Career-high 42 points vs. Miami April 12 ... Led Celts
in playoff scoring (22.4) ... Boston took him at 22 in '87 out of
Northeastern ... Born Nov. 21, 1965, in Baltimore ... Swing
player earned $400,000, one of NBA's best bargains.

Year	Team	G	FG	FG Pct.	FT	FT Pct.	Reb.	Ast.	TP	Avg.
1987-88	Boston	49	90	.466	40	.702	63	26	220	4.5
1988-89	Boston	81	604	.486	284	.787	377	218	1495	18.5
1989-90	Boston	79	540	.496	256	.808	347	225	1340	17.0
1990-91	Boston	79	598	.491	281	.826	410	201	1478	18.7
	Totals	288	1832	.489	861	.801	1197	670	4533	15.7

BRIAN SHAW 25 6-6 190   Guard

Was having decent season, then came the playoffs ... Kept starting against Pistons in East
semis, but Dee Brown kept finishing ... After
soap-opera affair complete with court orders
brought him back from Italy, he became prime
trade-rumor target after playoffs ... Had a bum
right ankle in playoffs. Had a bum playoffs,
period ... Average dropped by over five points
... Missed Larry Bird in regular season. Celts played more halfcourt game so his outside inconsistency showed ... No real range
(3-of-27 on three-pointers) ... Good in transition, makes sound
decisions ... Has quickness and agility to handle smaller point
guards defensively ... Team-high 7.6 assists ... Turnover-prone
... Picked at 24 by Celts in '88 ... Played one year in Boston,
did a year in Italy, returned ... Born March 22, 1966, in Oakland
... UC-Santa Barbara product made $1.212 million.

Year	Team	G	FG	FG Pct.	FT	FT Pct.	Reb.	Ast.	TP	Avg.
1988-89	Boston	82	297	.433	109	.826	376	472	703	8.6
1990-91	Boston	79	442	.469	204	.819	370	602	1091	13.8
	Totals	161	739	.454	313	.822	746	1074	1794	11.1

KEVIN GAMBLE 25 6-5 210   Guard/Forward

Came back to earth, somewhat ... Was shooting about six-zillion percent early in the season.
At .625 at All-Star break, finished at .587 ...
Disappeared in playoffs. Average of 15.6
points in regular season plunged to 4.5 ... Regular-season play, which made him legit candidate for Most Improved, eased the Larry Bird
injury factor ... When Celts stopped running

as rebounding fell off, his effectiveness dropped . . . Pistons forced him wide . . . Regular season included career highs across the board . . . Originally a third-rounder to Blazers in '87, out of Iowa . . . Waived and did the CBA route before signing as a free agent with Celts on Dec. 15, 1988 . . . Born Nov. 13, 1965, in Springfield, Ill . . . Made $375,000.

Year	Team	G	FG	FG Pct.	FT	FT Pct.	Reb.	Ast.	TP	Avg.
1987-88	Portland	9	0	.000	0	.000	3	1	0	0.0
1988-89	Boston	44	75	.551	35	.636	42	34	187	4.3
1989-90	Boston	71	137	.455	85	.794	112	119	362	5.1
1990-91	Boston	82	548	.587	185	.815	267	256	1281	15.6
	Totals	206	760	.554	305	.784	424	410	1830	8.9

MICHAEL SMITH 26 6-10 225   Forward

Michael Stiff . . . See? Even the Celtics blow some draft picks . . . Another guy who couldn't win a starting job that was given to him . . . Nice shooting touch, which he'll use as often as he touches the ball . . . Liability in most departments . . . His shot gets blocked with uncanny frequency . . . Has short arms and doesn't extend . . . Started two of first six games . . . Then came Nov. 13, when he missed four shots (two blocked) in seven minutes and was re-introduced to the bench . . . First-round pick out of Brigham Young in '89 . . . Born May 19, 1965, in Rochester, N.Y . . . Paid $525,000.

Year	Team	G	FG	FG Pct.	FT	FT Pct.	Reb.	Ast.	TP	Avg.
1989-90	Boston	65	136	.476	53	.828	100	79	327	5.0
1990-91	Boston	47	95	.475	22	.815	56	43	218	4.6
	Totals	112	231	.475	75	.824	156	122	545	4.9

JOE KLEINE 29 7-0 271   Center

Only so many minutes to go around . . . Playing time (11.8 minutes) plunged to ocean floor with emergence of Kevin Gamble and use of Kevin McHale off bench . . . Celts ran most of the time and six-season vet from Arkansas isn't exactly a sprinter . . . Definite couch-potato potential if not an athlete . . . Played some spurts of five-to-seven minutes . . . Pure backup material. Banger, wide-body type . . . Sets picks that stop traffic on the expressway . . . Decent shooter, though rarely called . . . Rebound every 3.5 minutes . . . Born Jan. 4, 1962, in Colorado Springs,

Col. . . . Came to Celts with Ed Pinckney Feb. 23, 1989, from Kings for Brad Lohaus and Danny Ainge . . . No. 6 pick by Kings in '85 . . . Made $850,000.

Year	Team	G	FG	FG Pct.	FT	FT Pct.	Reb.	Ast.	TP	Avg.
1985-86	Sacramento	80	160	.465	94	.723	373	46	414	5.2
1986-87	Sacramento	79	256	.471	110	.786	483	71	622	7.9
1987-88	Sacramento	82	324	.472	153	.814	579	93	801	9.8
1988-89	Sac.-Boston	75	175	.405	134	.882	378	67	484	6.5
1989-90	Boston	81	176	.480	83	.830	355	46	435	5.4
1990-91	Boston	72	102	.468	54	.783	244	21	258	3.6
	Totals	469	1193	.461	628	.806	2412	344	3014	6.4

ED PINCKNEY 28 6-9 215   Forward

Okay, sometimes the transition from college takes a little longer than expected. But six years? . . . And it still isn't complete . . . Had a solid playoffs. Made 16-of-21 shots, took in 40 rebounds in 170 minutes . . . Progressed as season went on . . . Incredibly inconsistent . . . Couldn't win a starting job being handed to him . . . Has skills: long arms, quickness, a nice shooting touch. But displayed the concentration and attention span of a chili dog . . . Soft rep on defense . . . MVP of NCAA tourney when he led Villanova to stunning '85 upset of Georgetown . . . Selected No. 10 by Suns in '85 . . . Came to Celts via Kings with Joe Kleine for Danny Ainge and Brad Lohaus . . . Born March 27, 1963, in Bronx, N.Y. . . . Made $750,000.

Year	Team	G	FG	FG Pct.	FT	FT Pct.	Reb.	Ast.	TP	Avg.
1985-86	Phoenix	80	255	.558	171	.673	308	90	681	8.5
1986-87	Phoenix	80	290	.584	257	.739	580	116	837	10.5
1987-88	Sacramento	79	179	.522	133	.747	230	66	491	6.2
1988-89	Sac.-Bos.	80	319	.513	280	.800	449	118	918	11.5
1989-90	Boston	77	135	.542	92	.773	225	68	362	4.7
1990-91	Boston	70	131	.539	104	.897	341	45	366	5.2
	Totals	466	1309	.543	1037	.760	2133	503	3655	7.8

JOHN BAGLEY 31 6-0 205   Guard

Heads he stays, tails he goes . . . Probably will need 2-out-of-3 . . . Sat the entire season with cartilage damage in right knee . . . Underwent surgery in March . . . Will need to prove himself to win a job . . . Reported to camp overweight (as usual) and injured . . . Not a set-up point guard. Has trouble seeing over larger defenders . . . But is good penetrator and runs break.

There lies Boston's interest . . . Very effective against pressure defenses . . . Cavs picked him No. 12 out of Boston College as an undergrad in '82 . . . Celts got him from Nets in '89 for two second-rounders . . . Free agent, he won't get the $550,000 of last year.

Year	Team	G	FG	FG Pct.	FT	FT Pct.	Reb.	Ast.	TP	Avg.
1982-83	Cleveland	68	161	.432	64	.762	96	167	386	5.7
1983-84	Cleveland	76	257	.423	157	.793	156	333	673	8.9
1984-85	Cleveland	81	338	488	125	.749	291	697	804	9.9
1985-86	Cleveland	78	366	.423	170	.791	275	735	911	11.7
1986-87	Cleveland	72	312	.426	113	.831	252	379	768	10.7
1987-88	New Jersey	82	393	.439	148	.822	257	479	981	12.0
1988-89	New Jersey	68	200	.416	89	.724	144	391	500	7.4
1989-90	Boston	54	100	.459	29	.744	89	296	230	4.3
1990-91	Boston					Injured				
	Totals	579	2127	.437	895	.784	1560	3477	5253	9.1

STOJKO VRANKOVIC 27 7-2 260   Center

A Yugo . . . Celts brought in Dave Cowens to work with him . . . They're kind of curious to find out if he does anything other than sit up-right . . . Supposedly can defend, intimidate, rebound and leap . . . Running is another matter. Slow as mud in winter . . . Signed as rookie free agent . . . Actually, did display quality shot-blocking skills: one every five minutes (29 rejects in 166 minutes) . . . Bill Cartwright of Bulls had 15 rejects in 2,273 minutes . . . Born Jan. 22, 1964, in Ornis, Yugoslavia . . . Paid $222,000 . . . His Greek team advanced to European Final Four in 1990.

Year	Team	G	FG	FG Pct.	FT	FT Pct.	Reb.	Ast.	TP	Avg.
1990-91	Boston	31	24	.462	10	.556	51	4	58	1.9

DEREK SMITH 30 6-6 218   Guard-Forward

Career appeared to be over . . . But Celts gambled on this locker-room presence and were rewarded . . . Earned his $315,000 with superlative defensive effort against Chuck Person in first round . . . Came close to calling it quits but played 16 regular-season minutes, rehabbed some more and was activated on April 21 for playoffs . . . Was on the verge of true superstardom with Clippers in '85 when he tore knee cartilage . . . Four knee operations and three teams later, he's trying to decide if spot-specialist duty is worth it . . . Born Nov. 1, 1961, in Hogansville,

Ga. . . . Second-round pick by Golden State coming out of Louisville in 1982 . . . Celts got him as free agent in December.

Year	Team	G	FG	FG Pct.	FT	FT Pct.	Reb.	Ast.	TP	Avg.
1982-83	Golden State	27	21	.412	17	.680	38	2	59	2.2
1983-84	San Diego	61	238	.546	123	.755	170	82	600	9.8
1984-85	L.A. Clippers	80	682	.537	400	.794	427	216	1767	22.1
1985-86	L.A. Clippers	11	100	.552	58	.690	41	31	259	23.5
1986-87	Sacramento	52	338	.447	178	.781	182	204	863	16.6
1987-88	Sacramento	35	174	.478	87	.770	103	89	443	12.7
1988-89	Sac.-Phil.	65	216	.435	129	.686	167	128	568	8.7
1989-90	Philadelphia	75	261	.508	130	.699	172	109	668	8.9
1990-91	Boston	2	1	.250	3	.750	0	5	5	2.5
	Totals	408	2031	.499	1125	.753	1300	866	5232	12.8

THE ROOKIES

RICK FOX 22 6-6 231   Forward-Guard
Celts raised some eyebrows by picking him 24th . . . Must increase
strength . . . Small forward in college (North Carolina), no doubt
headed for off-guard in pros . . . Shooting dropped each season
from freshman year: .628, .583, .522, .453 . . . All-ACC and MVP
of ACC tournament as senior . . . Led Tar Heels in scoring and
steals . . . Born July 24, 1969, in Warshaw, Ind.

ANDERSON HUNT 22 6-2 175   Guard
Early-entry candidate as a junior, he was the only Nevada-Las
Vegas starter not selected in 1991 draft . . . Celtics liked his play
in Los Angeles Summer League . . . Averaged 17.2 ppg last season
and was MVP of 1990 NCAA Final Four when UNLV won crown
. . . Born May 5, 1969, in Detroit.

COACH CHRIS FORD: Won respect immediately when he
challenged Larry Bird about public comments
over planned running game . . . By season's
end, challenged everybody . . . Led Celts to 56
victories and a division title in first year as
replacement for Jimmy Rodgers . . . Became
fourth rookie coach to end up leading an All-
Star team. And he led East to victory . . .
Started season at 29-7, best ever by Celtic
rookie coach . . . Second-round pick by Detroit in 1972 after a
career at Villanova . . . Ten-year NBA career, averaged 9.2 points
. . . Traded to Celts in 1978 . . . Started for Celtics' 1981 cham-

pionship team in backcourt with Tiny Archibald . . . Made the first three-point shot in NBA history . . . Shot .375 on trifectas in his career . . . Born Jan. 11, 1949, in Atlantic City, N.J . . . A Celtic assistant from 1983-90.

GREATEST TEAM

Take your pick. Selecting the greatest Celtic team is sort of like choosing the prettiest Miss Universe. It's hard to go wrong. Close your eyes, pick a year and most likely, you'll find a stunner.

For percentage, the 1972-73 Celtics lost just 14 of 82 regular-season games enroute to an .829 all-time team mark. But they lost in the playoffs to the Knicks. And with the Celtics, a championship green and white banner up in the Boston Garden rafters is a must for a "greatest" team. The 1985-86 bunch with the Bird-Parish-McHale front line, an NBA title and a 67-15 regular-season mark deserves consideration.

But the pick here goes to the 1959-60 Celtic team of the Bill Russell-Bob Cousy era. That version of Gang Green won 59 of 75 games and then disposed of Philadelphia and St. Louis for the title. The Celtics had no less than eight Hall of Famers: Russell, Cousy, Frank Ramsey, K.C. Jones, Sam Jones, Tommy Heinsohn, Bill Sharman and coach Red Auerbach.

ALL-TIME CELTIC LEADERS

SEASON

Points: John Havlicek, 2,338, 1970-71
Assists: Bob Cousy, 715, 1959-60
Rebounds: Bill Russell, 1,930, 1963-64

GAME

Points: Larry Bird, 60 vs. Atlanta, 3/12/85
Assists: Bob Cousy, 28 vs. Minneapolis, 2/27/59
Rebounds: Bill Russell, 51 vs. Syracuse, 2/5/60

CAREER

Points: John Havlicek, 26,395, 1962-78
Assists: Bob Cousy, 6,945, 1950-63
Rebounds: Bill Russell, 21,620, 1956-69

CHARLOTTE HORNETS

TEAM DIRECTORY: Owner George Shinn; Pres.: Spencer Stolpen; Exec. VP: Tony Renaud; VP-Asst. to Pres.: Gene Littles; Player Personnel Dir.: Dave Twardzik; Dir. Pub. Rel.: Harold Kaufman; Coach: Allan Bristow; Asst. Coaches: Mike Pratt, Bill Hanzlik. Arena: Charlotte Coliseum (23,901). Colors: Teal, purple and white.

SCOUTING REPORT

SHOOTING: Maybe the less-than-average .467 wouldn't have looked so bad had the opposition not shot .493. Then again, maybe it would have. At season's end, the only regular at .500 or better

Kendall Gill hinted at future by making All-Rookie team.

was reserve forward Kenny Gattison (.532). Rex Chapman, a certified bricklayer his first two seasons, settled down and took more human shots. His percentage (.445) still wasn't worthy of handstands, but it was noticeably better.

Free-agent acquisition Johnny Newman (.470) provided some finishing skills on the break. Entering his second year in teal and white, he figures to be even more effective. With No. 1 draftee Larry Johnson, there should be lots more scoring inside that should open up the perimeter for Dell Curry (.471). Kendall Gill (.450) and Chapman, enhancing an already sound outside game.

New coach Allan Bristow will concentrate on improving last season's third-worst defense in the NBA and will utilize the motion offense that marked his years as Doug Moe's assistant at Denver.

PLAYMAKING: He is not the true point guard the Hornets covet but until something better comes along, Charlotte apparently will have Muggsy Bogues running the show. Bogues, 11th in the league in assists at 8.3, was the runaway leader in assists-to-turnovers ratio with 5.58. But all the numbers can't deny the defensive limitations he places upon the Hornets.

After Bogues, the Hornets overall are not a very good passing team, despite a middle-of-the-pack rating in assists (15th) and despite Gill, who earned boffo reviews for his first season—in all areas except his ability at point guard.

DEFENSE: They blocked fewer shots (304) than any team on earth. Only Denver and Atlanta surrendered a higher opponent-shooting yield than the Hornets' .493. Other than that, they were as solid as pudding. And that was one of the incentives for drafting Johnson.

REBOUNDING: The pits. The Hornets were the worst in the East, 26th out of 27 overall.

And that's why they loved Johnson above all others in the draft. With the Nevada-Las Vegas dynamo, Charlotte management hopes it obtained the interior toughness the team so desperately lacks. Newman never was and never will be anything of a re-bounder. J.R. Reid has been fairly clueless in his two-year tenure. Mike Gminski operates much of the time from the perimeter and, with the guards hoisting outside, there simply was no concerted effort on the backboards. With Johnson, the Hornets hope they have a Charles Barkley-type, good for nine or 10 boards a game.

HORNET ROSTER

No.	Veterans	Pos.	Ht.	Wt.	Age	Yrs. Pro	College
1	Tyrone Bogues	G	5-3	140	26	4	Wake Forest
3	Rex Chapman	G	6-4	195	26	3	Kentucky
30	Dell Curry	G	6-5	200	27	5	Virginia Tech
44	Kenny Gattison	F	6-8	252	27	5	Old Dominion
13	Kendall Gill	G	6-5	195	23	1	Illinois
42	Mike Gminski	C	6-11	260	32	11	Duke
4	Scott Haffner	G	6-3	180	25	2	Evansville
45	Eric Leckner	C	6-11	265	25	3	Wyoming
22	Johnny Newman	F	6-7	190	28	5	Richmond
34	J.R. Reid	F-C	6-9	263	23	2	North Carolina

Rd.	Rookies	Sel. No.	Pos.	Ht.	Wt.	College
1	Larry Johnson	1	F	6-5	245	Nevada-Las Vegas
2	Kevin Lynch	28	G	6-5	197	Minnesota

OUTLOOK: There will be improvement under the highly regarded Bristow. But realistically, all the Hornets can hope for is to avoid the Central Division cellar. And even that isn't very realistic.

The Hornets still are young and learning, still lacking a classic point guard. Two years were virtually thrown away trying to build a team around Reid, a no-win proposition. Now, the focus will be around Johnson. A major factor will be Gminski, whose elbow problems seriously curtailed his effectiveness. If Gminski, the first legitimate starting center in Hornets' history, is healthy, Charlotte could and should make considerable improvement on its 26-56 record, but not enough to make the playoffs.

HORNET PROFILES

KENDALL GILL 23 6-5 195   Guard

Stud on the horizon . . . Hornets knew they got a player at No. 5 in last year's draft. Never realized he'd be this good . . . First Hornet ever named to All-Rookie team . . . Averaged 11.0 points and set Hornet rookie highs for assists and steals . . . No obvious deficiency . . . "A steal for Charlotte," said Sonic coach K.C. Jones . . . Became starter at All-Star break. Averaged 12.9 after that . . . Quality rebounder (3.2 avg.) for size

and position...Real hard worker...Shot will only improve (.450)...Born May 25, 1968, in Matteson, Ill....Won NCAA Slam Dunk contest as Illini senior...Made $1.5 million—after GM Allan Bristow and his agent got into fight.

Year	Team	G	FG	FG Pct.	FT	FT Pct.	Reb.	Ast.	TP	Avg.
1990-91	Charlotte	82	376	.450	152	.835	263	303	906	11.0

JOHNNY NEWMAN 28 6-7 190   Forward

Surprise. Wasn't happy when season ended and his minutes were down...Wasn't happy in past when Knicks' seasons ended and his minutes were down...Only change was locale... Has his strengths—terrific open-court player, good finisher, great range on jumper (though often inconsistent), pesky defender, untiring worker...But has weaknesses. Doesn't rebound, although his 3.1 represented career high. Has often inflated opinion of skills. Entirely too thin-skinned, despite years in New York...Team-high and career-best 16.9 ppg...Didn't bring leadership Hornets hoped for when they gave him offer sheet worth $1.2 million a year...Born Nov. 28, 1963, in Danville, Va....Picked by Cavs out of Richmond on second round in '86 ...Waiver-wire steal by Knicks, who let him go to Hornets without compensation July 13, 1990.

Year	Team	G	FG	FG Pct.	FT	FT Pct.	Reb.	Ast.	TP	Avg.
1986-87	Cleveland	59	113	.411	66	.868	70	27	293	5.0
1987-88	New York	77	270	.435	207	.841	159	62	773	10.0
1988-89	New York	81	455	.475	286	.815	206	162	1293	16.0
1989-90	New York	80	374	.476	239	.799	191	180	1032	12.9
1990-91	Charlotte	81	478	.470	385	.809	254	188	1371	16.9
	Totals	378	1690	.462	1183	.817	880	619	4762	12.6

TYRONE (MUGGSY) BOGUES 26 5-3 140   Guard

A great complementary player, terrific when you want to throw a change-up to opposition ...Unfortunately, Hornets have him starting ...Finished strong. Averaged 10.8 points and shot .550 in April...Assists, though, were 7.0—down a full 4.0 from November...Unstoppable force in open court...Team highs in assists (8.3) and steals (1.69) for third straight year...Made $805,000 and has three more years at $1 million per . . . Obvious halfcourt liability—especially when not hitting his 15-footers . . . Born Jan. 9, 1965, in Baltimore . . . Washington's first-round pick in '87 . . . Came to Hornets in 1988 expansion draft.

Year	Team	G	FG	FG Pct.	FT	FT Pct.	Reb.	Ast.	TP	Avg.
1987-88	Washington	79	166	.390	58	.784	136	404	393	5.0
1988-89	Charlotte	79	178	.426	66	.750	165	620	423	5.4
1989-90	Charlotte	81	326	.491	106	.791	207	867	763	9.4
1990-91	Charlotte	81	241	.460	86	.796	216	669	568	7.0
	Totals	320	911	.448	316	.782	724	2560	2147	6.7

REX CHAPMAN 24 6-4 195   Guard

Rockets' coach Don Chaney once said of Chapman, "The easiest player to guard is the one who only shoots." . . . Well, Rex became a little tougher to guard last season . . . Shot selection infinitely better. Shot .445—compared to .414 and .408 of first two seasons . . . Voted MVP by teammates . . . Career best in assists (3.2 per). His 250 assists were over 100 more than he posted in 1989-90 . . . Still learning. Left Kentucky in '88 after sophomore season . . . Phenomenal vertical leap . . . Finished third in Slam Dunk contest . . . Born Oct. 5, 1967, in Bowling Green, Ky . . . Made $675,000 . . . Picked No. 8 in '88, first Hornet draft pick.

Year	Team	G	FG	FG Pct.	FT	FT Pct.	Reb.	Ast.	TP	Avg.
1988-89	Charlotte	75	526	.414	155	.795	187	176	1267	16.9
1989-90	Charlotte	54	377	.408	144	.750	179	132	945	17.5
1990-91	Charlotte	70	410	.445	234	.830	191	250	1102	15.7
	Totals	199	1313	.421	533	.797	557	558	3314	16.7

J.R. REID 23 6-9 256   Forward/Center

The moral of the story is don't draft just for the sake of hometown fans . . . Was No. 5 pick in '89 from North Carolina . . . Almost obligatory pick, playing in Hornets' backyard . . . Megaton bomb the first two seasons . . . Rebounds dropped from 8.4 to 6.3 in his second season . . . Played center for 30 games, then moved to power forward after arrival of Mike Gminski . . . Averaged 9.9 points, 6.6 boards at forward . . . Hornets ruefully discovered he has extremely limited skills . . . Doesn't quite drop from exhaustion practicing his game, either . . . Okay, he's a stiff... A $1.25-million stiff... Born March 31, 1968, in Virginia Beach, Va.

Year	Team	G	FG	FG Pct.	FT	FT Pct.	Reb.	Ast.	TP	Avg.
1989-90	Charlotte	82	358	.440	192	.664	691	101	908	11.1
1990-91	Charlotte	80	360	.466	182	.703	502	89	902	11.3
	Totals	162	718	.452	374	.682	1193	190	1810	11.2

DELL CURRY 27 6-5 200   Guard

Exceptional jump shooter... Um, good jump shot... Er, shoots a jumper well... Just not a heckuva lot about his game that thrills people, although he possesses the skills... Is basically the same player who arrived in Charlotte from Cleveland in the expansion draft June 23, 1988 ... Traumatic season. Father passed away in January... One of the league's premier stand-still jump-shooters. Possesses terrific range... Not at all a bad defender or passer amd has a good head... Born June 25, 1964, in Harrisonburg, Va.... Utah made him the No. 15 pick in 1986 after his career at Virginia Tech, where he finished as second-best all-time Metro Conference scorer behind Keith Lee... Paid $900,000.

Year	Team	G	FG	FG Pct.	FT	FT Pct.	Reb.	Ast.	TP	Avg.
1986-87	Utah	67	139	.426	30	.789	78	58	325	4.9
1987-88	Cleveland	79	340	.458	79	.782	166	149	787	10.0
1988-89	Charlotte	48	256	.491	40	.870	104	50	571	11.9
1989-90	Charlotte	67	461	.466	96	.923	168	159	1070	16.0
1990-91	Charlotte	76	337	.471	96	.842	199	166	802	10.6
	Totals	337	1533	.465	341	.846	715	582	3555	10.5

MIKE GMINSKI 32 6-11 260   Center

Finally, a legit center... Sixers gave him up for Armon Gilliam on Jan. 4... Philly felt his awful shooting (.384) meant he was washed up ... But G-Man maintained elbow problem was cause... After some rest and therapy, he shot .473 for Hornets... Posted a pair of 16-rebound games, one with Philly, one with Hornets... Holds his own against the center elite... Always a good perimeter shooter and has nice inside jump hook... Troubled in team-defense concept... Passed the 10,000-point mark... But his 844 points ended run of six straight 1,000-point seasons... Great free-throw center. His .810 was actually low. He's at .844 for career . . . Born Aug. 3, 1959, in Monroe, Conn. . . . Highest-paid Hornet at $1.65 million . . . No. 7 pick out of Duke by Nets in 1980.

Year	Team	G	FG	FG Pct.	FT	FT Pct.	Reb.	Ast.	TP	Avg.
1980-81	New Jersey	56	291	.423	155	.767	419	72	737	13.2
1981-82	New Jersey	64	119	.441	97	.822	186	41	335	5.2
1982-83	New Jersey	80	213	.500	175	.778	382	61	601	7.5
1983-84	New Jersey	82	237	.513	147	.799	433	92	621	7.6
1984-85	New Jersey	81	380	.465	276	.841	633	158	1036	12.8
1985-86	New Jersey	81	491	.517	351	.893	668	133	1333	16.5
1986-87	New Jersey	72	433	.457	313	.846	630	99	1179	16.4
1987-88	N.J.-Phil.	81	505	.448	355	.906	814	139	1365	16.9
1988-89	Philadelphia	82	556	.477	297	.871	769	138	1409	17.2
1989-90	Philadelphia	81	458	.457	193	.821	687	128	1112	13.7
1990-91	Phil.-Char.	80	357	.442	128	.810	582	93	844	10.6
	Totals	840	4040	.466	2487	.844	6203	1154	10572	12.6

SCOTT HAFFNER 25 6-3 180   Guard

Can compare expansion notes . . . Second-round pick in '89 by Heat, which waived him. Hornets signed him as a free agent on Jan. 21 . . . Appeared in seven games for Hornets, stretched right knee ligaments and spent last 31 games in a cast . . . Bankrupt in the offensive-skills department . . . Pretty average defender. Lacks size and strength . . . Pro-rated minimum wage ($120,000) . . . Born in Peoria, Ill. on Feb. 2, 1966 . . . Played at Illinois and Evansville.

Year	Team	G	FG	FG Pct.	FT	FT Pct.	Reb.	Ast.	TP	Avg.
1989-90	Miami	43	88	.406	17	.680	51	80	196	4.6
1990-91	Charlotte	7	8	.381	1	.500	4	9	17	2.4
	Totals	50	96	.403	18	.667	55	89	213	4.3

KENNY GATTISON 27 6-8 252   Forward

Eight career highs on two bum knees . . . Figured to be a CBA staple by now . . . Has stayed in league through hard work, delightful team attitude and some tough play . . . Career high in minutes and third on the team in rebounding . . . Does whatever is asked—including being a sacrificial lamb to the Ewings, Robinsons and Olajuwons . . . His 67 blocks were most ever by a Hornet . . . Good finisher . . . Rotten foul-shooter (.655 for career)... Free-agent pickup on Dec. 2, 1989... Drafted by Phoenix in '86 as third-rounder out of Old Dominion... Born May 23, 1964, in Wilmington, N.C.... Earned $355,000 the hard way.

Year	Team	G	FG	FG Pct.	FT	FT Pct.	Reb.	Ast.	TP	Avg.
1986-87	Phoenix	77	148	.476	108	.632	270	36	404	5.2
1988-89	Phoenix	2	0	.000	1	.500	1	0	1	0.5
1989-90	Charlotte	63	148	.550	75	.682	197	39	372	5.9
1990-91	Charlotte	72	243	.532	164	.661	379	44	650	9.0
	Totals	214	539	.519	348	.655	847	119	1427	6.7

ERIC LECKNER 25 6-11 265   Center

For a guy run out of town by Sacramento coach Dick Motta, he was a very pleasant surprise... Big body with bigger hands... Finishes well and can hit the 15-footer... Runs floor well, too. At least as long as he doesn't have to move laterally... Not a high-post center, so Kings yielded him for two second-rounders, Jan. 29, 1991... Must be considered one of three or four top backup centers in the league... Time increased from 11.8 to 18.6 minutes per after trade... Numbers also rose. Scored 5.8 points for Hornets, 2.8 for Kings... High-strung, hyper type ... Utah picked the Wyoming product 17th in 1988... Born May 27, 1966, in Manhattan Beach, Cal.... Made $485,000.

Year	Team	G	FG	FG Pct.	FT	FT Pct.	Reb.	Ast.	TP	Avg.
1988-89	Utah	75	120	.545	79	.699	199	16	319	4.3
1989-90	Utah	77	125	.563	81	.743	192	19	331	4.3
1990-91	Sac.-Char.	72	131	.446	62	.559	295	39	324	4.5
	Totals	224	376	.511	222	.667	686	74	974	4.3

THE ROOKIES

LARRY JOHNSON 22 6-5 245   Forward

Sir Lawrence?... Favorably compared to Charles Barkley because of superior inside strength and height... Consensus Player of the Year paced UNLV to 34-1 record as senior after leading charge to national title as a junior... Can shoot the jumper with range, but most of offense should come on tip-ins and spectacular offensive rebound skills... Good defender, smart player... No. 1 overall pick... Born March 14, 1969, in Dallas.

KEVIN LYNCH 22 6-5 197   **Guard**

Many feel Hornets came away with a downright steal getting him
at No. 28, first pick on second round . . . Compared to Craig Ehlo
and Jeff Hornacek . . . Displayed uncanny ability to come through
in clutch . . . Simply solid in all areas, but excels with perimeter
jumper . . . Minnesota's career leader in three-pointers (117)
. . . Born Dec. 24, 1968, in Bloomington, Minn.

COACH ALLAN BRISTOW: From NBA player to assistant
coach to front office to head coach . . . That's
bare resume of former 6-7 forward who replaced Gene Littles in July . . . He'd spent past
year as Hornets' VP-Basketball Operations and
now, as coach, though never the head honcho
before, he brings solid credentials to the bench
. . . Spent six years in Denver as top assistant
to Doug Moe . . . Regarded as intense, com-
petitive and a sharp analyst . . . Born Aug. 23, 1951, in Richmond,
Va. . . . Began college playing career at Toledo and moved to
Virginia Tech, where he averaged 23 ppg . . . Was first-round pick
(21st) of 76ers in 1973 and had 10-year career with Philadelphia,
San Antonio (under Moe), Utah and Dallas . . . He averaged
7.9 ppg, 4.0 rebounds and 3.2 assists . . . Came close to being
named Hornets' first head coach in 1988 (Dick Harter got the job)
. . . Front-office experience was invaluable, but he says he's now
"fulfilling my dream of being an NBA coach."

GREATEST TEAM

Let us not be too confused by the phrase "greatest team" here.
After only three seasons, the word "great" has not yet found its
way into the Hornet vocabulary.

So suffice to say that last season, 1990-91, was the least painful
for the embryonic Hornets. Pangs, however, were felt throughout
the community when the original Hugo mascot left before the start
of the season (some claimed in a contract dispute, others inferred
a tawdry affair with the Phoenix Gorilla).

The Hornets landed free-agent pickup Johnny Newman, late
of the Knicks, and acquired two centers in-season, Mike Gminski
from the Sixers and Eric Leckner from the Kings (they allowed

J.R. Reid to move from center to power forward where, however, he proved equally inept). Third-year wunderkind Rex Chapman finally started behaving like a pro on the court and Kendall Gill emerged as a marvelous No. 5 pick. The result was 26 victories— not great, but not bad by Hornet standards.

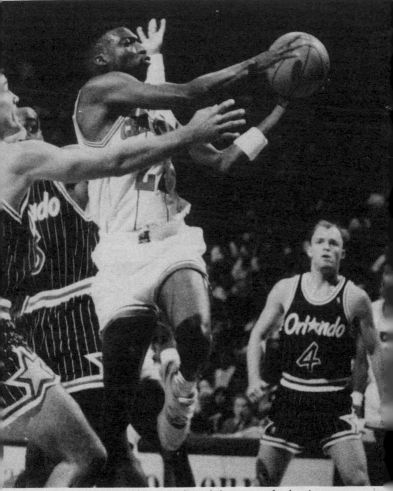

Ex-Knick Johnny Newman found the range for best pro year.

ALL-TIME HORNET LEADERS

SEASON

Points: Kelly Tripucka, 1,606, 1988-89
Assists: Tyrone Bogues, 867, 1989-90
Rebounds: Kurt Rambis, 703, 1988-89

GAME

Points: Kelly Tripucka, 40 vs. Philadelphia, 1/16/89
         Kelly Tripucka, 40 vs. Indiana, 12/14/89
         Kelly Tripucka, 40 vs. San Antonio, 2/25/89
         Johnny Newman, 40 vs. Dallas, 1/19/91
Assists: Tyrone Bogues, 19 vs. Boston, 4/23/89
Rebounds: Kurt Rambis, 22 vs. San Antonio, 2/25/89

CAREER

Points: Kelly Tripucka, 3,379, 1988-91
Assists: Tyrone Bogues, 2,156, 1988-91
Rebounds: J.R. Reid, 1,193, 1989-91

CHICAGO BULLS

TEAM DIRECTORY: Chairman: Jerry Reinsdorf; VP-Operations: Jerry Krause; Dir. Media Services: Tim Hallam; Coach: Phil Jackson; Asst. Coaches: John Bach, Tex Winter, Jim Cleamons. Arena: Chicago Stadium (17,339). Colors: Red, white and black.

SCOUTING REPORT

SHOOTING: Staggering. The Bulls were second in the league to Boston at .510 and there's no let-up in sight. Not as long as Michael Jordan breathes a superhuman breath. Four of the five starters were well over 50 percent. Only center Bill Cartwright (.490) was below break-even. With Jordan penetrating—or more like with Jordan just existing—double- and triple-teams are mandatory. So someone is left open. And as GM Jerry Krause noted, "When we built this team around Michael, we wanted shooters above all else." And they've got shooters. From everywhere. Their .366 on three-pointers was the best in the East.

John Paxson and Scottie Pippen are quality perimeter threats and Horace Grant makes his living with put-backs and dunks. The only sore spot is backup shooting guard, where Craig Hodges (.424) showed his age and Dennis Hopson (.426) showed he's Dennis Hopson.

PLAYMAKING: When coach Phil Jackson installed a "share the wealth" policy, Jordan was skeptical. But it worked and one of the greatest offensive forces the game has known became the central piece in a team-wide passing frenzy. Jordan still gets his points. But now, so does everyone else.

As a result, the Bulls racked up 2,212 assists, fourth-best in the league, second in the East. They came through Jordan's and Pippen's penetrations and kicks-outs. Paxson, the point guard, is around for his shooting, not passing. What other starting point guard ranked fourth on his team in assists?

DEFENSE: The NBA's premier pressing, trapping team. Just ask L.A. Of course, it helps when you have Jordan and Pippen, two guys who excel playing passing lanes, finishing in the top five in steals. Grant, the mobile key in the trap, compensates for the lack of a center shot-blocker.

Scottie Pippen blazed all the way to fat, new contract.

BULL ROSTER

No.	Veterans	Pos.	Ht.	Wt.	Age	Yrs. Pro	College
10	B.J. Armstrong	G	6-2	175	24	2	Iowa
24	Bill Cartwright	C	7-1	245	34	12	San Francisco
54	Horace Grant	F	6-10	220	26	4	Clemson
14	Craig Hodges	G	6-2	190	31	9	Long Beach State
2	Dennis Hopson	G	6-5	195	26	3	Ohio State
23	Michael Jordan	G	6-6	198	28	7	North Carolina
34	Stacey King	F-C	6-11	230	24	2	Oklahoma
53	Cliff Levingston	F	6-8	210	30	9	Wichita State
5	John Paxson	G	6-2	185	31	8	Notre Dame
32	Will Perdue	C	7-0	240	26	3	Vanderbilt
33	Scottie Pippen	G-F	6-7	210	26	4	Central Arkansas
42	Scott Williams	C	6-10	230	23	1	North Carolina

Rd.	Rookies	Sel. No.	Pos.	Ht.	Wt.	College
1	Mark Randall	26	F	6-7	230	Kansas

REBOUNDING: It was just that kind of year for Chicago. Everything worked. And rebounding was no exception.

Up front, the young, gifted and jumping-jack legs of Pippen and Grant, plus Jordan's spring from the backcourt, made the Bulls the league's fourth-best rebounding team overall. There was no standout stud on the boards; Grant was 20th in the league at 8.4. But four starters grabbed at least 485 rebounds and on the bench Will Perdue developed into a fine offensive rebounder at backup center. If the Bulls were ancient, there might be signs of letup. But they're not and there aren't.

OUTLOOK: The Bulls made one big mistake in their march to their first NBA championship last season: they made it look too easy. They won 61 in the regular season, then steamrollered the playoffs, sweeping the Knicks, taking Philly in five, sweeping the Pistons and knocking off the Lakers in five.

The Bulls will be among the elite again but the path will be a lot harder. One factor that could clear obstacles is the Bulls' own belief in their ability as a TEAM. They thought they could. Now they know they can. No longer are they Michael and the Jordan-aires. They are legitimate contenders for a second straight title.

BULL PROFILES

MICHAEL JORDAN 28 6-6 198   God, er, Guard

Only thing left is to run for President . . . Silenced any criticism when he led Bulls to championship and earned unanimous playoff MVP honors . . . Yes, he can make those around him better. Even makes those in the cheap seats better . . . Averaged 31.2 points in playoffs after 31.5 regular-season mark that brought his fifth straight scoring title. Only Wilt Chamberlain, with seven, won more consecutively . . . Scored his 15,000th point at Philly, Jan. 9. It came in his 460th game. Only Wilt made it quicker (358 games) . . . Won second MVP award . . . Was 12th in scoring (.539), third in steals (2.72) . . . Openly wept after Bulls completed five-game rout of Lakers in Finals . . . Born Feb. 17, 1963, in Brooklyn, N.Y. . . . Olympic gold medalist out of North Carolina . . . Picked third in 1984 draft by Bulls behind Hakeem (then Akeem) Olajuwon and Sam Bowie (don't remind Portland) . . . Has almost as many points as he does endorsements . . . Paid $2.5 million last season . . . May be in Muhammad Ali's class for transcending his sport . . . His Finals Game 2 switch-hands move is already legend.

Year	Team	G	FG	FG Pct.	FT	FT Pct.	Reb.	Ast.	TP	Avg.
1984-85	Chicago	82	837	.515	630	.845	534	481	2313	28.2
1985-86	Chicago	18	150	.457	105	.840	64	53	408	22.7
1986-87	Chicago	82	1098	.482	833	.857	430	377	3041	37.1
1987-88	Chicago	82	1069	.535	723	.841	449	485	2868	35.0
1988-89	Chicago	81	966	.538	674	.850	652	650	2633	32.5
1989-90	Chicago	82	1034	.526	593	.848	565	519	2753	33.6
1990-91	Chicago	82	990	.539	571	.851	492	453	2580	31.5
	Totals	509	6144	.520	4129	.849	3186	3018	16596	32.6

JOHN PAXSON 31 6-2 185   Guard

For 3:54, had world asking, "Yeah, so who is the Bulls' other guard with Paxson?" . . . Completed staggering shooting Finals when he scored 10 points in last 3:54—including six points in :51—of title-clinching Game 5 win over L.A. . . . The perfect complement to Jordan . . . He takes the kickouts and is deadly shooter: witness career-best .548 in regular season. Realizes and accepts role . . . Shot .653 in Finals, making

32-of-49 shots. Tied Finals record with 8-of-8 in Game 2 . . .
Middle name is MacBeth . . . Father, Jim, played two NBA seasons. Brother, Jim, was standout for Portland before finishing up
with Celtics . . . Signed as free agent by Bulls in '85 . . . Has started
every game past two seasons . . . First-round, No. 19, pick by
Spurs in 1983 after his career at Notre Dame . . . Born Sept. 29,
1960, in Dayton, Ohio . . . A bargain at $385,000 last season, his
final contract year.

Year	Team	G	FG	FG Pct.	FT	FT Pct.	Reb.	Ast.	TP	Avg.
1983-84	San Antonio	49	61	.445	16	.615	33	149	142	2.9
1984-85	San Antonio	78	196	.509	84	.840	68	215	486	6.2
1985-86	Chicago	75	153	.466	74	.804	94	274	395	5.3
1986-87	Chicago	82	386	.487	106	.809	139	467	930	11.3
1987-88	Chicago	81	287	.493	33	.733	104	303	640	7.9
1988-89	Chicago	78	246	.480	31	.861	94	308	567	7.3
1989-90	Chicago	82	365	.516	56	.824	119	335	819	10.0
1990-91	Chicago	82	317	.548	34	.829	91	297	710	8.7
	Totals	607	2011	.500	434	.805	742	2348	4689	7.7

SCOTTIE PIPPEN 26 6-7 210   Guard-Forward

And no migraines . . . Overcame the horrible
memory of his wimping out against Pistons with
headache in '90 with marvelous regular season
and playoffs . . . Many felt that Bulls would
float face down, Jordan or no Jordan, if Pippen
was off his game in playoffs . . . Only Bull to
outscore Jordan in any of the 17 playoff games
when he netted 32 in title-clincher . . . Averaged 20.4 in playoffs . . . Staggeringly good transition player . . .
Toasted bad defense rap when he hounded Magic Johnson throughout Finals . . . Fifth in league in regular season with 2.35 steals
. . . Competent rebounder, very sound off offensive glass . . . Handles ball with proficiency of guard . . . Bulls got him on Draft Day
of '87 by sending rights to Olden Polynice and a second-rounder
to Sonics, who picked him fifth out of Central Arkansas . . . Born
Sept. 26, 1965, at Hamburg, Ark. . . . Bitched about $765,000
salary all season and was rewarded with five-year, a $16-million
deal.

Year	Team	G	FG	FG Pct.	FT	FT Pct.	Reb.	Ast.	TP	Avg.
1987-88	Chicago	79	261	.463	99	.576	298	169	625	7.9
1988-89	Chicago	73	413	.476	201	.668	445	256	1048	14.4
1989-90	Chicago	82	562	.489	199	.675	547	444	1351	16.5
1990-91	Chicago	82	600	.520	240	.706	595	511	1461	17.8
	Totals	316	1836	.492	739	.667	1885	1380	4485	14.2

BILL CARTWRIGHT 34 7-1 245   Center

And how many championship rings does Patrick Ewing have?... Medical-Bill, Invisi-Bill, Horri-Bill got last laugh on New York as member of Bulls' title team... Averaged 9.6 points in regular season, making Chicago first champs since '78 Bullets to have center score under 10 ... Another complementary piece to Jordan. Did his job effectively. Clogged lane, took up space, scored when needed... Shot .490 in regular season, .519 in playoffs... Subject of controversy for all the opponents he floored with elbows, including Hakeem Olajuwon, who needed surgery... After career at U. of San Francisco, Knicks made him third pick in '79 draft... Years in New York plagued by twice-broken foot... Traded to Bulls for Charles Oakley and swap of first-round draft picks, June 27, 1988... Born July 30, 1957, in Lodi, Cal.... Earned $1.1 million in last year of contract.

Year	Team	G	FG	FG Pct.	FT	FT Pct.	Reb.	Ast.	TP	Avg.
1979-80	New York	82	665	.547	451	.797	726	165	1781	21.7
1980-81	New York	82	619	.554	408	.788	613	111	1646	20.1
1981-82	New York	72	390	.562	257	.763	421	87	1037	14.4
1982-83	New York	82	455	.566	380	.744	590	136	1290	15.7
1983-84	New York	77	453	.561	404	.805	649	107	1310	17.0
1984-85	New York				Injured					
1985-86	New York	2	3	.429	6	.600	10	5	12	6.0
1986-87	New York	58	335	.531	346	.790	445	96	1016	17.5
1987-88	New York	82	287	.544	340	.798	384	85	914	11.1
1988-89	Chicago	78	365	.475	236	.766	521	90	966	12.4
1989-90	Chicago	71	292	.488	227	.811	465	145	811	11.4
1990-91	Chicago	79	318	.490	124	.697	486	126	760	9.6
	Totals	765	4182	.535	3179	.780	5310	1153	11543	15.1

HORACE GRANT 26 6-10 220   Forward

Now do you know why Bulls traded Charles Oakley three years ago?... After Game 1 nerves-induced garbage game, he wrecked Lakers inside in Finals... Superb offensive rebounder... Has worked and worked since Bulls made him 10th pick in '87 draft out of Clemson... Superlative defender, he's the key to Chicago traps. Quick enough to trap up and then get back and rebound... Decent shot-blocker, seems to have flair for dramatic rejects... Shot career-best .547, using putbacks and tip-ins as his staple... Older twin of Bullets' Harvey...

Adapted goggles in regular season, abandoned them in playoffs. Brought them back for Game 2 of Finals. Bulls won four straight ... Playoffs helped shed underrated status ... Born July 4, 1965, in Augusta, Ga.... Earned $1 million.

Year	Team	G	FG	FG Pct.	FT	FT Pct.	Reb.	Ast.	TP	Avg.
1987-88	Chicago	81	254	.501	114	.626	447	89	622	7.7
1988-89	Chicago	79	405	.519	140	.704	681	168	950	12.0
1989-90	Chicago	80	446	.523	179	.699	629	227	1071	13.4
1990-91	Chicago	78	401	.547	197	.711	659	178	1000	12.8
	Totals	318	1506	.524	630	.689	2416	662	3643	11.5

B.J. ARMSTRONG 24 6-2 175   Guard

Even with a championship ring on his hand, he'd get proofed going to a PG-13 movie ... Matured in second year but still learning point-guard role. Has two-guard mentality at times ... Was consistent bench contributor in regular season ... Sort of lost in playoff shuffle as Michael Jordan and John Paxson tended to stay on floor a lot ... Averaged just 2.0 points in Finals ... Good penetrator, decent defender and passer ... Excellent free-throw shooter with .878 accuracy for two years ... Struggled late in season ... Made $425,000 ... Was 18th overall pick in '89 out of Iowa ... Born Sept. 9, 1967, in Detroit.

Year	Team	G	FG	FG Pct.	FT	FT Pct.	Reb.	Ast.	TP	Avg.
1989-90	Chicago	81	190	.485	69	.885	102	199	452	5.6
1990-91	Chicago	82	304	.481	97	.874	149	301	720	8.8
	Totals	163	494	.482	166	.878	251	500	1172	7.2

CRAIG HODGES 31 6-2 190   Guard

First, wait'll ya hear what he did in the three-point shootout ... Minutes drastically down in his ninth season: 843 minutes, more than 200 less than previous season, which was nearly 200 less than previous season, which was over 200 less ... You get the idea ... Had a great three-point shootout, y'know ... Missed 14-of-23 shots in Finals, but did make a couple of clutch baskets early in Game 5 ... Okay, the three-point thing. At All-Star bash, he banged home record 19 in a row en route to his second straight championship ... During regular season, wasn't quite that good, making 44-of-115 (.383) ... A specialist role player at this point . . . Arrived in December 1988 from Phoenix for Ed Nealy and second-rounder . . . Born June 27, 1960, in Park Forest, Ill. . . . Third-round '82 pick by Clips out of Long Beach State . . . Made $600,000.

Year	Team	G	FG	FG Pct.	FT	FT Pct.	Reb.	Ast.	TP	Avg.
1982-83	San Diego	76	318	.452	94	.723	122	275	750	9.9
1983-84	San Diego	76	258	.450	66	.750	86	116	592	7.8
1984-85	Milwaukee	82	359	.490	106	.815	186	349	871	10.6
1985-86	Milwaukee	66	284	.500	75	.872	117	229	716	10.8
1986-87	Milwaukee	78	315	.462	131	.891	140	240	846	10.8
1987-88	Mil.-Phoe.	66	242	.463	59	.831	78	153	629	9.5
1988-89	Phoe.-Chi.	59	203	.472	48	.842	89	146	529	9.0
1989-90	Chicago	63	145	.438	30	.909	53	110	407	6.5
1990-91	Chicago	73	146	.424	26	.963	42	97	362	5.0
	Totals	639	2270	.464	635	.826	913	1715	5702	8.9

STACEY KING 24 6-11 230   Forward-Center

Forget the regal name. Played like a queen . . . Can you say, "major bust," boys and girls? . . . Biggest debate on King was who was worse, him or Dennis Hopson . . . And he complained about his playing time. Walked out of a practice, was suspended by team in April . . . Ticked off teammates . . . Problem was lofty lottery-slot selection—No. 6 pick out of Oklahoma in '89 . . . Folks tend to want lottery picks to score their ring size . . . Ripped league for 5.5 points, .467 shooting . . . Had shown promise as a rookie, but seems easily distracted . . . Promise included a decent post defense and leaping ability . . . Paid $1 million . . . Born Jan. 29, 1967, in Lawton, Okla.

Year	Team	G	FG	FG Pct.	FT	FT Pct.	Reb.	Ast.	TP	Avg.
1989-90	Chicago	82	267	.504	194	.727	384	87	728	8.9
1990-91	Chicago	76	156	.467	107	.704	208	65	419	5.5
	Totals	158	423	.490	301	.718	592	152	1147	7.3

DENNIS HOPSON 26 6-5 195   Guard

Well, can't blame New Jersey any more . . . Acquired to steady bench . . . All he did was weigh it down so it didn't tip over . . . Major disappointment . . . One guy even Jordan didn't make better . . . Regarded as a "can't miss" out of Ohio State whom Nets made the No. 3 pick in '87 . . . Did miss. A lot . . . Bothered by nagging injuries which reduced already non-existent playing time . . . A shame because you'll rarely meet a nicer guy . . . Shot .426—which was actually the second-best mark in his four seasons . . . Minutes down over 1,800 from final year with Nets, who swapped him for a first and two second-rounders . . . Earned $915,000 . . . Born April 22, 1965, in Toledo, Ohio.

Year	Team	G	FG	FG Pct.	FT	FT Pct.	Reb.	Ast.	TP	Avg.
1987-88	New Jersey	61	222	.404	131	.740	143	118	587	9.6
1988-89	New Jersey	62	299	.419	186	.849	202	103	788	12.7
1989-90	New Jersey	79	474	.434	271	.792	279	151	1251	15.8
1990-91	Chicago	61	104	.426	55	.663	109	65	264	4.3
	Totals	263	1099	.423	643	.783	733	437	2890	11.0

WILL PERDUE 26 7-0 240   Center

Okay, a lot of folks were wrong. He can play . . . Not flashy, not spectacular, not enough to make you green with envy, but enough to make you admit he is a totally legit backup center, one of best in league . . . Always gave Patrick Ewing fits, now he has expanded it to rest of NBA . . . Bull-in-china-shop approach . . . Never quits on a ball . . . Good, solid defensive rebounder . . . No offense, but no one's complaining . . . Feet the size of Manhattan Island . . . Won't yield position underneath . . . Born Aug. 29, 1965, in Melbourne, Fla . . . Was 11th pick in '88 draft, a slot obtained from Knicks in Oakley-Cartwright trade . . . Vanderbilt product made $450,000.

Year	Team	G	FG	FG Pct.	FT	FT Pct.	Reb.	Ast.	TP	Avg.
1988-89	Chicago	30	29	.403	8	.571	45	11	66	2.2
1989-90	Chicago	77	111	.414	72	.692	214	46	294	3.8
1990-91	Chicago	74	116	.494	75	.670	336	47	307	4.1
	Totals	181	256	.445	155	.674	595	104	667	3.7

CLIFF LEVINGSTON 30 6-8 210   Forward

Lynch mob put noose away when he arose in the playoffs . . . Helped make Bulls' bench a major factor in the Finals . . . Best moment was Game 3, when he shot 5-for-5 with four rebounds, a steal and three blocks . . . Always considered an athletic type who'd go to boards tirelessly . . . Didn't fit in during regular season. Had trouble picking up the plays . . . Across-the-board lowest numbers of career . . . Bulls signed him as unrestricted free agent for $750,000 in October... Had spent six years in Atlanta... Born Jan. 4, 1961, in St. Louis... Wichita State product went to Pistons as ninth-pick undergrad in '82.

Year	Team	G	FG	FG Pct.	FT	FT Pct.	Reb.	Ast.	TP	Avg.
1982-83	Detroit	62	131	.485	84	.571	232	52	346	5.6
1983-84	Detroit	80	229	.525	125	.672	545	109	583	7.3
1984-85	Atlanta	74	291	.527	145	.653	566	104	727	9.8
1985-86	Atlanta	81	294	.534	164	.678	534	72	752	9.3
1986-87	Atlanta	82	251	.506	155	.731	533	40	657	8.0
1987-88	Atlanta	82	314	.557	190	.772	504	71	819	10.0
1988-89	Atlanta	80	300	.528	133	.696	498	75	734	9.2
1989-90	Atlanta	75	216	.509	83	.680	319	80	516	6.9
1990-91	Chicago	78	127	.450	59	.648	225	56	314	4.0
	Totals	694	2153	.520	1138	.686	3956	659	5448	7.9

SCOTT WILLIAMS 23 6-10 230   Center

Became playoff cult hero... Shoulder kept popping out, creating fascinating anecdote stuff. Example: It popped out from high-fiving teammates after sweep of Pistons... Only rookie on Bulls' roster... Played a total of 337 minutes in 51 regular-season games. Didn't exactly earn his own cheer from the Luv-a-Bulls ... But surprised in the Finals with quality minutes... Undrafted, signed as free agent out of North Carolina... Doesn't do anything exceptionally well, but doesn't do anything exceptionally bad... Active type, takes up space... Born Aug. 21, 1968, in Hacienda Heights, Cal.

Year	Team	G	FG	FG Pct.	FT	FT Pct.	Reb.	Ast.	TP	Avg.
1990-91	Chicago	51	53	.510	20	.714	98	16	127	2.5

THE ROOKIE

MARK RANDALL 23 6-7 230   Forward

Bulls a little surprised he was still there at No. 26... All-Big 8 at Kansas, he's smart, tough, rebounds well and shoots from the outside... A good passer... Likened to the Bucks' Frank Brickowski... Born Sept. 30, 1967, in Englewood, Col.

COACH PHIL JACKSON: Took one of the greatest offensive forces the game has ever known in Michael Jordan, convinced him (with some skepticism) that a share-the-wealth policy was in order and revved up the defense . . . Result was a 61-victory season and an NBA title. Not bad for a second-year coach. With 25-8 record, now owns best all-time playoff record for percentage . . . Cerebral type with just enough streak of flake . . . Only ninth guy to win an NBA title as a player (with the Knicks in 1973) and as a coach (Bulls) . . . First ever to coach championships in both CBA and NBA . . . Developed Bulls into league's premier pressing, trapping team . . . Preached defense and team play ad nauseam. "On defense, you don't have to share a basketball . . . just a defensive philosophy," he said . . . Two-time All-American at North Dakota under Bill Fitch . . . Second-round pick for Knicks in '67 had career hampered by back injury . . . Born Sept. 17, 1945, in Deer Lodge, Mont.

GREATEST TEAM

Gee, this is a toughie. The greatest team ever for the Bulls (pronounced "Da Bulls") might still be feeling the effects of last June's celebration.

The 1990-91 Bulls captured the Central Division title by winning 61 games—becoming only the ninth franchise with a 60-victory season. In the playoffs, the Knicks caused them to almost break a sweat. The Sixers supplied a mild case of heartburn. Then came the Pistons, the two-time champs. Forever, it seemed, Michael Jordan begged his "supporting cast" to step forward. Here was the challenge, both physically and mentally. For three straight years, Chicago's seasons ended against Detroit.

Challenge met and mastered.

"I realize they had arrived when they overcame the Detroit thing," Jordan said.

And with an effort that had TEAM stamped all over it in red and black, the Bulls (oops, Da Bulls) crushed the Lakers in five for NBA gold in the franchise's silver anniversary season, completing a 17-2 playoff run.

ALL-TIME BULL LEADERS

SEASON

Points: Michael Jordan, 3,041, 1986-87
Assists: Guy Rodgers, 908, 1966-67
Rebounds: Tom Boerwinkle, 1,133, 1970-71

GAME

Points: Michael Jordan, 69 vs. Cleveland, 3/28/90
Assists: Ennis Whatley, 22 vs. New York, 1/14/84
        Ennis Whatley, 22 vs. Atlanta, 3/3/84
Rebounds: Tom Boerwinkle, 37 vs. Phoenix, 1/8/70

CAREER

Points: Michael Jordan, 16,596, 1984-91
Assists: Norm Van Lier, 3,676, 1971-78
Rebounds: Tom Boerwinkle, 5,745, 1968-78

CLEVELAND CAVALIERS

TEAM DIRECTORY: Chairman: Gordon Gund; GM: Wayne Embry; Dir. Pub. Rel.: Bob Price; Coach: Lenny Wilkens; Asst. Coaches: Brian Winters, Dick Helm. Arena: The Coliseum (20,273). Colors: Blue, white and orange.

SCOUTING REPORT

SHOOTING: Terrific up front. Center Brad Daugherty plus forwards Larry Nance and Chucky Brown all shot .524 last season. So why did the Cavs finish middle-of-the-road 13th at .475, just slightly above the .474 league average? Mark Price. No injury in the East decimated a team like Price's torn knee hurt the Cavs. The Cavs not only missed his career .486 accuracy, they were

Brad Daugherty's finest year included third All-Star Game.

devastated by the loss of his superb penetrating setups.

The injury had a domino effect. Craig Ehlo vacated his sixth-man role and shot .445, his worst in four years. The backcourt gave nothing resembling consistency. The best came from Darnell Valentine, rescued from Mexican ball and a brief TV job in Portland.

The Cavs have every finger crossed that Price resembles the player he was before the injury. They drafted Terrell Brandon, the Pac-10's most prolific one-season scorer ever, to provide outside help and to lift a bench that shot awfully last season. And they've signed John Battle, who comes off his best year at Atlanta.

PLAYMAKING: Here's where numbers lie. The Cavs were second in assists last season, behind only Portland, with 2,240. Yet they were not an exceptional playmaking team. Again, the reason was Price.

There are good passers here: Valentine, Daugherty, who's the best at the center position, and Danny Ferry, who had a tough first year. But none of them is Price. If opposing point guards are generals, Price has been a field marshal to the Cavs' floor game. He must be healthy for a sound, efficient offense. Brandon put up points at Oregon, but passing didn't lead his scouting report.

DEFENSE: Inside, there's shot-blocker deluxe Larry Nance. And John Williams will reject his share. Ehlo is one of the most underrated man-to-man defenders. So why were the Cavs the second-worst defensive team, giving up .482 shooting and 2.5 more points than they scored? Price's absence was a big part. The Cavs forced only 15.0 turnovers (sixth-worst in the NBA) and made 643 steals (fifth-worst).

REBOUNDING: Way down, and here is one area they can't blame on Price. The Cavs ranked 20th overall in the league. Daugherty and Nance held their own, combining for over 1,500. But after them, the dropoff was severe.

A foot injury to John Williams vastly affected the Cavs' boarding and Ferry, when playing the four, simply didn't have the muscle to bang with other power forwards. So the Cavs got him on a bulk-up program at season's end. Ehlo gave nice numbers (4.7 average) for a shooting guard, but that was hardly adequate for a team's third-best figure.

OUTLOOK: In the Atlantic, they'll watch Larry Bird's back and Johnny Dawkins' knee. In the Central, the injury comeback stories will be Isiah Thomas' wrist and Price's knee.

CAVALIER ROSTER

No.	Veterans	Pos.	Ht.	Wt.	Age	Yrs. Pro	College
10	John Battle	G	6-2	175	28	6	Rutgers
20	Winston Bennett	F	6-7	210	26	2	Kentucky
52	Chucky Brown	F	6-8	214	23	2	North Carolina State
43	Brad Daugherty	C	7-0	263	26	5	North Carolina
3	Craig Ehlo	G-F	6-7	205	30	8	Washington State
35	Danny Ferry	F	6-10	230	25	1	Duke
32	Henry James	F	6-9	220	26	1	St. Mary's (Tex.)
4	Steve Kerr	G	6-3	180	26	3	Arizona
23	John Morton	G	6-3	183	24	2	Seton Hall
22	Larry Nance	F-C	6-10	235	32	10	Clemson
25	Mark Price	G	6-0	178	27	5	Georgia Tech
1	Darnell Valentine	G	6-1	183	32	9	Kansas
18	John Williams	F-C	6-11	238	29	5	Tulane

Rd.	Rookies	Sel. No.	Pos.	Ht.	Wt.	College
1	Terrell Brandon	11	G	5-11	180	Oregon
2	Jimmy Oliver	39	G-F	6-5	208	Purdue
2	Keith Hughes	47	F	6-6	235	Rutgers

Injuries and a trade of Ron Harper that has yet to produce any dividends on Lake Erie have turned the Cavs from one of the NBA's premier rising powers into a team nearly back at square one. Age is becoming a factor with Nance, who was brought in as a final-piece type a few years back. Health is coach Jerry Wilkens' major Cav concern. If they stay out of the emergency room, improve their shooting and get some legitimate help off the bench, then they could again make some serious noise. If not, it's another trip to the lottery.

CAVALIER PROFILES

BRAD DAUGHERTY 26 7-0 263   Center

All the people who swear they didn't think he was soft coming out of North Carolina as the No. 1 pick in '86 are the same folks who swear they didn't cry when Bambi's mother got shot . . . Enjoyed best season as a pro . . . Became Cavs' first-ever three-time All-Star . . . Career highs in points (21.6) and rebounds (10.9). First Cav to average 20 and 10 . . . Sixth in league in rebounding, second among Eastern centers (to Patrick Ewing) . . . Had career-high 24-board game vs. Kings on March 8 . . . Always regarded as a "complete" center: scores, boards and is best passer at the position. His 253 assists ranked him first among all NBA centers . . . Not a shot-blocker, though. Was fourth from the bottom among starting centers with only 42 . . . Offseason marriage had big impact. Wife, Heidi, a fitness and diet nut, so his body fat took incredible drop without affecting weight and strength. Thus, endurance was up . . . Nice country-boy type . . . Born Oct. 19, 1965, in Ashville, N.C . . . Made $1.32 million.

Year	Team	G	FG	FG Pct.	FT	FT Pct.	Reb.	Ast.	TP	Avg.
1986-87	Cleveland	80	487	.538	279	.696	647	304	1253	15.7
1987-88	Cleveland	79	551	.510	378	.716	665	333	1480	18.7
1988-89	Cleveland	78	544	.538	386	.737	718	285	1475	18.9
1989-90	Cleveland	41	244	.479	202	.704	373	130	690	16.8
1990-91	Cleveland	76	605	.524	435	.751	830	253	1645	21.6
	Totals	354	2431	.521	1680	.724	3233	1305	6543	18.5

JOHN WILLIAMS 29 6-11 238   Forward

How to make $26.5 million the easy way . . . First, be 6-11. Then average a rebound every four minutes. Finally, locate an expansion team . . . "Hot Rod" received the incredible seven-year offer from the Heat, which the Cavs matched (they had no choice) . . . Lucrative deal—including $4-million signing bonus—led to constant trade rumors involving Heat . . . To make it worse for Cavs, he sprained foot Nov. 16 and missed 37 games . . . Career worsts in everything except scoring (11.7) . . . Exceptional, but not extraordinary, rebounder and shot-blocker (still averaged better than 1.5 per) . . . Great leaper with good instincts around glass . . . In addition to signing bonus, drew $3.785 million paycheck . . . Had been durable: played 250 straight games before foot injury . . . Born Aug. 9, 1962, in Sorrento, La. . . . Central figure in Tulane point-shave scandal, but exonerated . . . College woes caused many to back off but Cavs grabbed him with 45th pick in '85 draft and waited one year to sign him.

Year	Team	G	FG	FG Pct.	FT	FT Pct.	Reb.	Ast.	TP	Avg.
1986-87	Cleveland	80	435	.485	298	.745	629	154	1168	14.6
1987-88	Cleveland	77	316	.477	211	.756	506	103	843	10.9
1988-89	Cleveland	82	356	.509	235	.748	477	108	948	11.6
1989-90	Cleveland	82	528	.493	325	.739	663	168	1381	16.8
1990-91	Cleveland	43	199	.463	107	.652	290	100	505	11.7
	Totals	364	1834	.488	1176	.736	2565	633	4845	13.3

MARK PRICE 27 6-0 178   Guard

Cavs' season went up in flames when this magnificent point guard tore the anterior cruciate ligament in left knee . . . Reconstructive surgery . . . Had been one of NBA's fastest points. And very deceptively so . . . Obviously, speed and quickness now are major concern and question . . . Downright wonderful human being . . . Cavs 9-7 at time of injury. Finished 33-49. That's 24-42 (.363) sans Price . . . In his cameo appearance, was leading league in free-throw shooting (.952) and ranked among leaders in assists (10.4) . . . His 2,145 career assists place him second on Cavs' all-time list . . . Choir boy from Enid, Okla., where he was born Feb. 15, 1964 . . . Person he'd most like to meet: Billy Graham . . . Paid $1.4 million . . . Georgia Tech, Class of '86 . . . Drafted by Dallas on second round (No. 25). Mavs sent him to Cavs after draft for '89 second-rounder.

Year	Team	G	FG	FG Pct.	FT	FT Pct.	Reb.	Ast.	TP	Avg.
1986-87	Cleveland	67	173	.408	95	.833	117	202	464	6.9
1987-88	Cleveland	80	493	.506	221	.877	180	480	1279	16.0
1988-89	Cleveland	75	529	.526	263	.901	226	631	1414	18.9
1989-90	Cleveland	73	489	.459	300	.888	251	666	1430	19.6
1990-91	Cleveland	16	97	.497	59	.952	45	166	271	16.9
	Totals	311	1781	.486	938	.887	819	2145	4858	15.6

DANNY FERRY 25 6-10 230   Forward

A little different stateside, huh? . . . Lured from Italy for $34 million over 10 years . . . After initial look, Cav fans suggested merely burning big bundles of cash . . . Awful start. Fouled like crazy. Ended with foul every 7.2 minutes. Oddly, only fouled out once . . . Too slow for small forward. Too small for power . . . But he progressed . . . Rebounding improved. Good on offensive glass . . . Good passer. Passed up a lot of shots—but then, he shot .428 . . . European trademark clutch-and-grab fouls early on . . . Immediately began offseason bulk-up program to play power forward . . . One of most controversial trades in Cavs' history brought his rights from Clippers along with bust Reggie Williams for Ron Harper, two first-rounders and a second on Nov. 16, 1989 . . . Hit Italy after Duke rather than play for Clips, who drafted him No. 2 in '89 . . . Led Duke to three Final Fours (no titles) . . . College Player of Year as senior . . . Son of Bob Ferry, former pro and ex-GM of Bullets... Born Oct. 17, 1966, in Hyattsville, Md. ... Made $2.64 million.

Year	Team	G	FG	FG Pct.	FT	FT Pct.	Reb.	Ast.	TP	Avg.
1990-91	Cleveland	81	275	.428	124	.816	286	142	697	8.6

LARRY NANCE 32 6-10 235   Forward

Be honest. Doesn't he look like he's 49? ... Still can flash signs of a 22-year-old, though ... Sixth in league in blocked shots at 2.50—tops among all forwards... That was the second-best season for blocks in Cavs' history... First full season after ankle surgery... Altered game a bit. Took the outside shot more ... Played in 80 games, most since 1983-84, his third year in league out of Clemson... Averaged 19.2 points, fourth-best of career... Second to Brad Daugherty in scoring and rebounding... Was 19th in NBA rebounding, averaging 8.6, his second-best total... One of 17 forwards with 200-plus offensive rebounds... Drag-race nut... No. 20 pick in 1981 by Suns, who traded him to Cavs as part of the massive Kevin Johnson deal Feb. 25, 1988... Born Feb. 12, 1959, in Anderson, S.C.... Made $1.26 million.

Year	Team	G	FG	FG Pct.	FT	FT Pct.	Reb.	Ast.	TP	Avg.
1981-82	Phoenix	80	227	.521	75	.641	256	82	529	6.6
1982-83	Phoenix	82	588	.550	193	.672	710	197	1370	16.7
1983-84	Phoenix	82	601	.576	249	.707	678	214	1451	17.7
1984-85	Phoenix	61	515	.587	180	.709	536	159	1211	19.9
1985-86	Phoenix	73	582	.581	310	.698	618	240	1474	20.2
1986-87	Phoenix	69	585	.551	381	.773	599	233	1552	22.5
1987-88	Phoe.-Clev.......	67	487	.529	304	.779	607	207	1280	19.1
1988-89	Cleveland	73	496	.539	267	.799	581	159	1259	17.2
1989-90	Cleveland	62	412	.511	186	.778	516	161	1011	16.3
1990-91	Cleveland	80	635	.524	265	.803	686	237	1537	19.2
	Totals	729	5128	.549	2410	.744	5787	1889	12674	17.4

CRAIG EHLO 30 6-7 205   Guard-Forward

Born to sub... Effectiveness hampered when he was thrust in as starter... Cavs had no choice... As a result, they had lowest-scoring starting backcourt in NBA (Ehlo 10.1, Darnell Valentine 9.4)... Terrific role player: off bench, of course... One of most underrated defenders in public's eye... He's best when he brings his brand of havoc in for 20-25 minutes a game. Not the 34 he averaged last season... Quality defensive rebounder at off-guard . . . Can handle small forwards defensively . . . Loss of Mark Price's penetration hurt his three-point production. Was 104-of-248 in 1989-90. Dropped to 49-of-149 last year . . . Surprisingly weak foul shooter (.674 career) . . . Only Cav in all 82 games . . . Born Aug. 11, 1961, in Lubbock, Tex. . . . Washington State, Class of '83. Drafted by Houston on third round . . . Steal for Cavs, who grabbed him as free agent in 1987 . . . Made $925,000.

Year	Team	G	FG	FG Pct.	FT	FT Pct.	Reb.	Ast.	TP	Avg.
1983-84	Houston	7	11	.407	1	1.000	9	6	23	3.3
1984-85	Houston	45	34	.493	19	.633	25	26	87	1.9
1985-86	Houston	36	36	.429	23	.793	46	29	98	2.7
1986-87	Cleveland	44	99	.414	70	.707	161	92	273	6.2
1987-88	Cleveland	79	226	.466	89	.674	274	206	563	7.1
1988-89	Cleveland	82	249	.475	71	.607	295	266	608	7.4
1989-90	Cleveland	81	436	.464	126	.681	439	371	1102	13.6
1990-91	Cleveland	82	344	.445	95	.679	388	376	832	10.1
	Totals	456	1435	.457	494	.674	1637	1372	3586	7.9

DARNELL VALENTINE 32 6-1 183   Guard

Never, ever get the sneakers bronzed . . . Had played in Mexico and was doing TV in Portland when Cavs called after Mark Price injury . . . Scored 13 his first game back. Had 24 the next night . . . Another sound backup . . . Unfortunately for Cavs, another starter . . . Can penetrate, direct the team and has a decent outside shot . . . Before he wears down, anyway . . . Too many minutes (28.3 average) . . . His .464 shooting was second-best in a nine-season career; his .831 from line was best ever . . . Out of NBA in 1989-90 . . . All-American at Kansas . . . Blazers made him 16th pick in '81 . . . Cavs originally obtained him in '88 from Heat for a second-rounder . . . Brought him back as free agent Dec. 3 last season . . . Born Feb. 3, 1959, in Chicago . . . Made $100,000.

Year	Team	G	FG	FG Pct.	FT	FT Pct.	Reb.	Ast.	TP	Avg.
1981-82	Portland	82	187	.413	152	.760	149	270	526	6.4
1982-83	Portland	47	209	.454	169	.793	117	293	587	12.5
1983-84	Portland	68	251	.447	194	.789	127	395	696	10.2
1984-85	Portland	75	321	.473	230	.793	219	522	872	11.6
1985-86	Port.-LAC	62	161	.415	130	.743	125	246	456	7.4
1986-87	L.A. Clippers	65	275	.410	163	.815	150	447	726	11.2
1987-88	L.A. Clippers	79	223	.418	101	.743	156	382	562	7.1
1988-89	Cleveland	77	136	.426	91	.813	103	174	366	4.8
1990-91	Cleveland	65	230	.464	143	.831	172	351	609	9.4
	Totals	620	1993	.437	1373	.787	1318	3080	5400	8.7

JOHN BATTLE 28 6-2 175   Guard

Most productive season ever and then, as unrestricted free agent, responded to Cavs' need for another reasonably healthy guard . . . A poor man's Vinnie Johnson. Not quite The Microwave, more like The Toaster Oven . . . Can provide tremendous bursts of offense . . . Range solid from 15 to 20 feet . . . Arthroscopes on both knees have hurt defense. Not nearly the defender he once was because he doesn't use his body . . . His 13.6 scoring average was best by Hawk reserve in eight years . . . Scored 23 points in fourth quarter April 19 vs. Celts . . . Career bests across the board . . . Put up points in playoffs, but shot poorly (.364). Great from line though: 24-of-25 . . . Made $590,000 . . . Born Nov. 9, 1962, in Washington, D.C . . . Fourth-rounder for Hawks out of Rutgers in '85.

Year	Team	G	FG	FG Pct.	FT	FT Pct.	Reb.	Ast.	TP	Avg.
1985-86	Atlanta	64	101	.455	75	.728	62	74	277	4.3
1986-87	Atlanta	64	144	.457	93	.738	60	124	381	6.0
1987-88	Atlanta	67	278	.454	141	.750	113	158	713	10.6
1988-89	Atlanta	82	287	.457	194	.815	140	197	779	9.5
1989-90	Atlanta	60	275	.506	102	.756	99	154	654	10.9
1990-91	Atlanta	79	397	.461	270	.854	159	217	1078	13.6
	Totals	416	1482	.465	875	.791	633	924	3882	9.3

WINSTON BENNETT 26 6-7 210   Forward

Range up to about a foot . . . No outside shot at all; at least he realizes it and never has tried a three-pointer . . . Shot .374 . . . Second-season catastrophe because of bum back. Missed 45 games . . . Okay, the up side. He's a real good, active defender with a work ethic even the most jaded coaches enjoy . . . Season highlights: career-high 23 points in 29 minutes vs. Nets March 23. And he went to foul line to shoot free throws for the injured John Williams with :17.2 left against Bucks Nov. 16. Made 'em both . . . Born Feb. 9, 1965, in Louisville, Ky. . . . Third-rounder in '88 draft, out of Kentucky . . . Earned $525,000.

Year	Team	G	FG	FG Pct.	FT	FT Pct.	Reb.	Ast.	TP	Avg.
1989-90	Cleveland	55	137	.479	64	.667	188	54	338	6.1
1990-91	Cleveland	27	40	.374	35	.745	64	28	115	4.3
	Totals	82	177	.450	99	.692	252	82	453	5.5

CHUCKY BROWN 23 6-8 214   Forward

See Cavs run. See Chucky excel . . . See Cavs play halfcourt. Where's Chucky? . . . Superb finisher, a knack for the basket on the break . . . Another guy who needs to be spotted just so many minutes . . . One rap is a lack of concentration . . . Needs help getting his shots . . . Plays both forward spots. Ball-handling a liability for small forward . . . Fairly aggressive defender . . . Athleticism around basket brought .524 shooting . . . A lot of teams like him . . . Cavs took him on second round in '89 . . . Born Feb. 29, 1968, in New York City . . . High school and college in ACC country: North Carolina State, Class of '89 . . . Made $630,000.

Year	Team	G	FG	FG Pct.	FT	FT Pct.	Reb.	Ast.	TP	Avg.
1989-90	Cleveland	75	210	.470	125	.762	231	50	545	7.3
1990-91	Cleveland	74	263	.524	101	.701	213	80	627	8.5
	Totals	149	473	.498	226	.734	444	130	1172	7.9

STEVE KERR 26 6-3 180   Guard

Probably wept as hard as Lenny Wilkens when Mark Price was injured . . . Fed off Price's penetrations in 1989-90. Went on veritable starvation diet last season . . . Pick a category, any category, and his numbers were down . . . Mediocre defender, average to atrocious ball-handler . . . A perimeter specialist . . . Terrific two-year Cleveland total of 101-of-206 on three-point shots. That's .490. A heckuva lot better than most guys shoot on twos . . . Guys like himself, who shot .441 on twos . . . Had fourth four-point play in Cav history—his third—at Indiana Dec. 8 . . . Born Sept. 27, 1965, in Beirut . . . Suns picked him on second round out of Arizona in '88, then sent him to Cavs Sept. 5, 1989, for a future second.

Year	Team	G	FG	FG Pct.	FT	FT Pct.	Reb.	Ast.	TP	Avg.
1988-89	Phoenix	26	20	.435	6	.667	17	24	54	2.1
1989-90	Cleveland	78	192	.444	63	.863	98	248	520	6.7
1990-91	Cleveland	57	99	.444	45	.849	37	131	271	4.8
	Totals	161	311	.444	114	.844	152	403	845	5.2

JOHN MORTON 24 6-3 183   Guard

Penetrates very well... But once inside, doesn't have a clue... Terrible decisions... One out of two isn't bad... Second season brought improvement on first, which was utter disaster... Shot 140 points higher than rookie season—and still he was just .438. Not a swell shooter... Scored career-high 21 at Seattle March 5. Ironically, he scored college-best 35 in Seattle in NCAA Final, which Morton's Seton Hall lost to Michigan in '89... Weak in a lot of areas... Born May 18, 1967, in Bronx, N.Y.... Paid $350,000... No. 25 to Cavs in '89.

Year	Team	G	FG	FG Pct.	FT	FT Pct.	Reb.	Ast.	TP	Avg.
1989-90	Cleveland	37	48	.298	43	.694	32	67	146	3.9
1990-91	Cleveland	66	120	.438	113	.813	103	243	357	5.4
	Totals	103	168	.386	156	.776	135	310	503	4.9

HENRY JAMES 26 6-9 220   Forward

Sounds like a writer, huh?... Well, his best works are authored behind three-point line... Tremendous outside shooter. Connected on 24-of-60 trifectas (.400) in his 37 games... Bounced around, did the CBA route after leaving St. Mary's (Tex.) in 1988... Undrafted, was signed by Cavs to a 10-day contract on New Year's Eve. One 10-day job led to another and he signed for rest of season... Bad ball-handler... Will never be mistaken for Charles Barkley off the boards, either (2.1 rebound average)... Not bad for a freebie pickup, though... Born July 29, 1965, in Centraville, Ala.... Happily took pro-rated $120,000 minimum.

Year	Team	G	FG	FG Pct.	FT	FT Pct.	Reb.	Ast.	TP	Avg.
1990-91	Cleveland	37	112	.441	52	.722	79	32	300	8.1

THE ROOKIES

TERRELL BRANDON 21 5-11 180   Guard

In case Mark Price can't make it back... Eleventh choice has point-guard's body with shooting-guard's scoring prowess... Averaged 26.6 for Oregon as a senior. Led Pac-10 in scoring (third-highest scoring average in conference history) and steals . . . Left after junior season . . . Size scared some . . . Born May 20, 1970, in Portland . . . No. 11 pick.

KEITH HUGHES 23 6-6 235   Forward
Drafted by Rockets but went to Cavaliers on Draft Day . . . Beat out Temple's Mark Macon to be named Player of the Year in Atlantic 10 Conference . . . Played first two years at Syracuse before transferring to Rutgers for junior and senior years . . . Career-high 40 points at Penn State in final season set record for most points by an opponent against Nittany Lions . . . Rockets made him 47th selection . . . Born June 29, 1968, in Carteret, N.J.

JIMMY OLIVER 22 6-5 208   Guard-Forward
Came on in postseason All-Star games . . . All-Big Ten first team for Purdue as a senior . . . Cavs desperate for help in backcourt. Must be; when was the last time a Purdue player did anything in pros? . . . Some like his versatility and strength . . . Born July 12, 1969, in Menifee, Ark . . . Was 19.2 senior scorer . . . No. 39 pick.

COACH LENNY WILKENS: Players' coach . . . He was a  player, wasn't he? . . . Has been playing last two years with short deck as injuries have wiped out key personnel . . . Cavs had 395 manpower games lost in last two seasons. At the expense of guys like Price, Daugherty, Williams, Nance . . . Keeps team playing hard, keeps them upbeat . . . Never publicly criticizes his players . . . Laid-back approach . . . Has 18-year coaching record of 758-696 (.521) . . . His five years with Cavs—second-longest continuous streak by an active coach—have brought break-even 205-205 . . . Hall of Fame player . . . Also in NIT Hall of Fame . . . A 15-year career left him among all-time leaders in assists (3,285) . . . 1971 All-Star Game MVP . . . Born Oct. 28, 1937, in Brooklyn, N.Y. . . . First-round pick by Hawks in 1960 after starring at Providence . . . Player-coach in both Seattle and Portland . . . Directed Seattle to NBA Finals twice, winning in 1978-79.

GREATEST TEAM

Three seconds. That was all the time the 1988-89 Cavaliers needed to hang on to a one-point lead to advance in the playoffs. But the other guys had this chap named Michael Jordan . . .

Jordan's 16-foot buzzer-beater in Game 5 of the first round ended the best season in Cav history. The Cavs exited disappointed but high about a future that has never blossomed. The following season, Cleveland traded Ron Harper, effectively derailing one of the NBA's premier on-the-rise teams.

The 1988-89 bunch won 57 games as the baby Cavs of Harper, Brad Daugherty, Mark Price and John "Hot Rod" Williams rose to maturity and prominence and blended with veteran Larry Nance, acquired the previous year. Before Jordan's heart-crushing shot, the Cavs set all kinds of team marks for accomplishment and pride. They beat Boston on the road twice. They won 11 straight games, 21 straight at home. They led the NBA in shooting (.504). There's no telling how far they could have gone if three seconds and one jumper didn't get in the way.

ALL-TIME CAVALIER LEADERS

SEASON

Points: Mike Mitchell, 2,012, 1980-81
Assists: John Bagley, 735, 1985-86
Rebounds: Jim Brewer, 891, 1975-76

GAME

Points: Walt Wesley, 50 vs. Cincinnati, 2/19/71
Assists: Geoff Huston, 27 vs. Golden State, 1/27/82
Rebounds: Rick Roberson, 25 vs. Houston, 3/4/72

CAREER

Points: Austin Carr, 10,265, 1971-80
Assists: John Bagley, 2,311, 1982-87
Rebounds: Jim Chones, 3,790, 1974-79

DETROIT PISTONS

TEAM DIRECTORY: Pres.: Bill Davidson; GM: Jack McCloskey; Dir. Pub. Rel.: Matt Dobek; Coach: Chuck Daly; Asst. Coaches: Brendan Malone, Brendan Suhr. Arena: The Palace, Auburn Hills (21,454). Colors: Red, white and blue.

SCOUTING REPORT

SHOOTING: Down, way down. At .465, Detroit was a paltry 19th in the league for accuracy. But again, there's an asterisk. The wrist surgery to Isiah Thomas threw the entire season out of whack. It forced Vinnie Johnson (now gone the waiver route) into a starter's role and dissected the Pistons' feared three-guard rotation.

Only one Piston made it to .500. And he was Scott Hastings (now a Nugget), whose .571 came amid just 113 minutes. Joe Dumars was forced to handle much of the point-guard duties and that wiped out his spot-up shots. Up front, Bill Laimbeer, James Edwards (traded to the Clippers), Dennis Rodman, Mark Aguirre and John Salley all were respectable, but overall the bench was a shooting nightmare. What also saved Detroit, as always, was defense, as opponents managed just .453. The Pistons need Thomas healthy and some far better consistency from Johnson (.434), who never quite got going.

Orlando Woolridge, in from Denver in the Hastings trade, should be a factor after a season in which he averaged 25.1 ppg on .498 shooting. Jeff Martin, who came from the Clippers in the Edwards deal, shot .424.

PLAYMAKING: Another plunge. Detroit ranked 23rd in assists. But with their style, with their penchant for games in the 90s, assists are always down anyway.

Still, the Pistons missed Isiah here, too. Dumars proved capable. But he also proved he's far more valuable and comfortable playing his normal off-guard role. The Pistons generate well more than half their offense on simple pick-and-rolls, but without Isiah, nothing ran as smoothly. They've added third-guard support with the acquisition of Darrell Walker from Washington.

DEFENSE: Synonymous with Pistons in recent years. Last year was—and this year should be—no exception. While the defense struggled without Thomas, the Rodman-led defense again topped the league, surrendering just 96.8 points.

Dennis Rodman: Two in row as Defensive Player of the Year.

REBOUNDING: With domination of the defensive boards (the Pistons rebounded with .710 efficiency against opponent misses), Detroit finished as the league's leading rebounding team.

The prime board force for Detroit is Rodman, whose 12.5 average was second in the league to David Robinson. Defense and rebounding are all Rodman wants to do. And he does them better than almost everybody. Laimbeer had a steady, if not spectacular, rebounding season. A plus should be Walker, who led all NBA guards in rebounding last season. With the likes of Salley and a bunch of give-a-foul guys on the bench, the Pistons should again hold their own on the boards.

OUTLOOK: "Three-peat" is officially history. But are the Pistons themselves? Detroit is one of the major question marks in the NBA. At one point last season, Thomas questioned the team's heart. Have two championship drives taken their toll? We'll soon find out.

PISTON ROSTER

No.	Veterans	Pos.	Ht.	Wt.	Age	Yrs. Pro	College
23	Mark Aguirre	F	6-6	232	31	10	DePaul
00	William Bedford	C	7-1	235	27	4	Memphis State
32	Lance Blanks	G	6-4	195	25	1	Texas
4	Joe Dumars	G	6-3	195	28	6	McNeese State
40	Bill Laimbeer	C-F	6-11	260	34	11	Notre Dame
—	Jeff Martin	G	6-5	195	24	2	Murray State
10	Dennis Rodman	F	6-8	210	30	5	SE Oklahoma State
22	John Salley	F-C	6-11	244	27	5	Georgia Tech
—	Brad Sellers	F	7-0	227	28	5	Ohio State
11	Isiah Thomas	G	6-1	182	30	10	Indiana
5	Darrell Walker	G	6-4	180	30	8	Arkansas
0	Orlando Woolridge	F	6-9	215	30	10	Notre Dame

Rd.	Rookies	Sel. No.	Pos.	Ht.	Wt.	College
2	Doug Overton	40	G	6-1	190	La Salle

Questions abound around several critical players. Thomas showed his value during his injury and how healthy he stays is beyond crucial. The Pistons were just another team when he was out. They'll still have some size up front, with 7-foot Brad Sellers, aboard from Greece, hoping to take up some of the slack resulting from the departure of Edwards and Hastings.

On paper, Chuck Daly's Pistons still look formidable. But they won't be exactly the same old Pistons. They will challenge but it appears their slip behind Chicago is an irreversible one, at least in the near future.

PISTON PROFILES

ISIAH THOMAS 30 6-1 182   Guard

Any question who's the heart and soul of this team?... Missed 34 games—more than the total missed in first nine years of career...Pistons went down without his leadership... Surgery fused three right-wrist bones...Out Jan. 29-April 5...Pistons went 18-14...In his 10 seasons, Detroit is 25-31 without him ...Should become all-time Piston scoring leader this season. Third at 15,130, trails Dave Bing (15,235) and Bob Lanier (15,488) . . . Third all-time in NBA assists (7,431) . . . Hobbled by hamstring in playoffs. Sat two more games . . . Shot .403 in 15 playoff games . . . One of greatest clutch players ever . . . Staggering roller-coaster career: 1990 Finals MVP; made THAT pass Bird stole in Game 5 of '87 Eastern Finals; two-time All-Star Game MVP; the sprained ankle in '88 Finals loss to Lakers; 16 points in 94 seconds of '84 Game 5 vs Knicks . . . Superb penetrations, uncanny ability for the big play, gets bored with regular season . . . Refused to congratulate Bulls for Eastern Finals sweep . . . Greatest little man ever . . . Drafted No. 2 by Pistons in '81 after leading Indiana to NCAA title . . . Born April 30, 1961, in Chicago . . . Made $2.72 million.

Year	Team	G	FG	FG Pct.	FT	FT Pct.	Reb.	Ast.	TP	Avg.
1981-82	Detroit	72	453	.424	302	.704	209	565	1225	17.0
1982-83	Detroit	81	725	.472	368	.710	328	634	1854	22.9
1983-84	Detroit	82	669	.462	388	.733	327	914	1748	21.3
1984-85	Detroit	81	646	.458	399	.809	361	1123	1720	21.2
1985-86	Detroit	77	609	.488	365	.790	277	830	1609	20.9
1986-87	Detroit	81	626	.463	400	.768	319	813	1671	20.6
1987-88	Detroit	81	621	.463	305	.774	278	678	1577	19.5
1988-89	Detroit	80	569	.464	287	.818	273	663	1458	18.2
1989-90	Detroit	81	579	.438	292	.775	308	765	1492	18.4
1990-91	Detroit	48	289	.435	179	.782	160	446	776	16.2
Totals		764	5786	.459	3285	.763	2840	7431	15130	19.8

JOE DUMARS 28 6-3 195 Guard

Was just Joe, not Superman, in Isiah Thomas' absence . . . Ran team at point guard and did commendable job. But he's Joe, not Isiah . . . Shouldered huge backcourt burden as three-guard rotation was nuked. Became first Piston in four years to play 3,000 minutes . . . Like Thomas, phenomenal in clutch . . . Has increased scoring every year in the league. Went for team-best 20.4 last season, first time he ever led Pistons . . . Twice equaled career-high 42 points . . . Established Piston free-throw record with 62 straight . . . MVP of '89 Finals, when Pistons won first title . . . Second-team All-Defense—takes charges, gets through picks. Not a big steals guy, but had career-high 89 . . . Great foul-shooter (.890, fourth straight year over .800) . . . Led Piston playoff scoring at 20.6. Had over one steal a game and just 17 turnovers in 15 games . . . Fundamentally-sound player . . . Quiet, decent gentleman . . . Born May 23, 1963, in Natchitoches,

La.... No. 18 in '85 draft from McNeese State... Made $1.035 million.

Year	Team	G	FG	FG Pct.	FT	FT Pct.	Reb.	Ast.	TP	Avg.
1985-86	Detroit	82	287	.481	190	.798	119	390	769	9.4
1986-87	Detroit	79	369	.493	184	.748	167	352	931	11.8
1987-88	Detroit	82	453	.472	251	.815	200	387	1161	14.2
1988-89	Detroit	69	456	.505	260	.850	172	390	1186	17.2
1989-90	Detroit	75	508	.480	297	.900	212	368	1335	17.8
1990-91	Detroit	80	622	.481	371	.890	187	443	1629	20.4
	Totals	467	2695	.485	1553	.842	1057	2330	7011	15.0

BILL LAIMBEER 34 6-11 260   Center-Forward

Became Pistons' all-time rebound leader (8,504), passing Bob Lanier... His 11.0 ppg was lowest since coming to Detroit Feb. 16, 1982, from Cavs with Kenny Carr for Phil Hubbard, Paul Mokeski and two draft choices... Has missed three games in career, none due to injury... Remarkable positional and intelligent rebounder. Athletic skills of Mt. Rainier, with a vertical jump the size of a snowflake. But gets rebounds in bunches. Twice in career had nine defensive boards in one quarter... Hates the media and pretty much is hated back outside Detroit... Superior foul-shooter. Six straight seasons of .800 plus... Legit perimeter threat with aggravatingly accurate tippy-toe shot... Shot below standards (.446) in playoffs... Responded to questions about Bulls' Eastern Finals sweep by saying, "They won" 34 times, by one Chicago writer's count... Born May 19, 1957, in Boston... Notre Dame product... Cavs drafted him on third round in '79... Made $1.51 million.

Year	Team	G	FG	FG Pct.	FT	FT Pct.	Reb.	Ast.	TP	Avg.
1980-81	Cleveland	81	337	.503	117	.765	693	216	791	9.8
1981-82	Clev.-Det.	80	265	.494	184	.793	617	100	718	9.0
1982-83	Detroit	82	436	.497	245	.790	993	263	1119	13.6
1983-84	Detroit	82	553	.530	316	.866	1003	149	1422	17.3
1984-85	Detroit	82	595	.506	244	.797	1013	154	1438	17.5
1985-86	Detroit	82	545	.492	266	.834	1075	146	1360	16.6
1986-87	Detroit	82	506	.501	245	.894	955	151	1263	15.4
1987-88	Detroit	82	455	.493	187	.874	832	199	1110	13.5
1988-89	Detroit	81	449	.499	178	.840	776	177	1106	13.7
1989-90	Detroit	81	380	.484	164	.854	780	171	981	12.1
1990-91	Detroit	82	372	.478	123	.837	737	157	904	11.0
	Totals	897	4893	.499	2269	.833	9474	1883	12212	13.6

Joe Dumars: Upped scoring, made All-Defense second team.

DENNIS RODMAN 30 6-8 210   Forward

The NBA was never warned... One of the most unique players in league history. Wants to defend and rebound. That's it... In five seasons, has averaged double-figure points once. But in his last four seasons, he has grabbed over 300 offensive rebounds each time... Second in the league in rebounding at 12.5... Had career-best 24 rebounds vs. Indy Feb. 13...
Defensive Player of the Year second straight season, first team All-Defense third straight... First Piston in five years with 1,000 rebounds (1,026)... Started slow with re-occurance of previous season's ankle injury... In pain in the playoffs, too, when he was

subpar. Got lit up by Scottie Pippen in Eastern finals and dealt Bulls' forward a staggeringly cheap shot from behind. Drew fine. Would have been arrested for assault on the streets . . . Second-round steal in '86 out of Southeastern Oklahoma State . . . Born May 13, 1961, in Trenton, N.J. . . . Made $880,000.

Year	Team	G	FG	FG Pct.	FT	FT Pct.	Reb.	Ast.	TP	Avg.
1986-87	Detroit	77	213	.545	74	.587	332	56	500	6.5
1987-88	Detroit	82	398	.561	152	.535	715	110	953	11.6
1988-89	Detroit	82	316	.595	97	.626	772	99	735	9.0
1989-90	Detroit	82	288	.581	142	.654	792	72	719	8.8
1990-91	Detroit	82	276	.493	111	.631	1026	85	669	8.2
	Totals	405	1491	.555	576	.601	3637	422	3576	8.8

WILLIAM BEDFORD 27 7-1 235   Center

At his height, he'll always have a job . . . That was Suns' thinking when they drafted him No. 6 out as an undergraduate of Memphis State in '86 . . . But they passed up Karl Malone, and Bedford began checkered career plagued by drugs . . . Clean for two seasons now and occasionally showing flashes of the offensive skills Suns—and others—coveted . . . A bit player again: 562 minutes . . . Got four starts at season's end . . . Attention span always a worry, doctors traced it to a chemical imbalance that eased with medication . . . A favorite of management . . . Pistons got him in '87 for a No. 1 . . . Born Dec. 3, 1963, in Memphis, Tenn. . . . Made $850,000.

Year	Team	G	FG	FG Pct.	FT	FT Pct.	Reb.	Ast.	TP	Avg.
1986-87	Phoenix	50	142	.397	50	.581	246	57	334	6.7
1987-88	Detroit	38	44	.436	13	.565	65	4	101	2.7
1989-90	Detroit	42	54	.432	9	.409	58	4	118	2.8
1990-91	Detroit	60	106	.438	55	.705	131	32	272	4.5
	Totals	190	346	.419	127	.608	500	97	825	4.3

MARK AGUIRRE 31 6-6 232   Forward

Hard to believe everything didn't just go swimmingly, huh? . . . Had an in-game spat or two with coach, expected to be traded. Finding takers was hard . . . Pistons were 7-6 with him starting . . . Bothered by back and eye injuries . . . Has sacrificed scoring for team game with Detroit. Of course, he really had no choice . . . No-doubt-about-it skills. One of toughest post-up small forwards. Good strength . . . Has range. Quality three-point threat . . . For second straight season, scoring was just over 14 points. Is a 22.0 lifetime scorer . . . Heart and attitude also in question . . . Born Dec. 10, 1959, in Chicago . . . First player picked in '81 draft, by Dallas (buddy Isiah Thomas was No. 2) . . . Came to Pistons for Adrian Dantley and a No. 1 . . . Made $1.115 million.

Year	Team	G	FG	FG Pct.	FT	FT Pct.	Reb.	Ast.	TP	Avg.
1981-82	Dallas	51	381	.465	168	.680	249	164	955	18.7
1982-83	Dallas	81	767	.483	429	.728	508	332	1979	24.4
1983-84	Dallas	79	925	.524	465	.749	469	358	2330	29.5
1984-85	Dallas	80	794	.506	440	.759	477	249	2055	25.7
1985-86	Dallas	74	668	.503	318	.705	445	339	1670	22.6
1986-87	Dallas	80	787	.495	429	.770	427	254	2056	25.7
1987-88	Dallas	77	746	.475	388	.770	434	278	1932	25.1
1988-89	Dal.-Det.	80	586	.461	288	.733	386	278	1511	18.9
1989-90	Detroit	78	438	.488	192	.756	305	145	1099	14.1
1990-91	Detroit	78	420	.462	240	.757	374	139	1104	14.2
	Totals	758	6512	.489	3357	.744	4074	2536	16691	22.0

JOHN SALLEY 27 6-11 244 Forward-Center

Good evening, ladies and germs . . . One of NBA's most natural comedians . . . Subpar season, due in part to nagging lower-back strain . . . Shot career-low .475 . . . Dropped over 100 rebounds from 1989-90 . . . Still, a valued sixth man, decided asset at both ends . . . For fourth straight season, he registered over 100 blocks . . . Good transitional player and a jumping-jack offensive rebounder . . . Defensive boarding, never a strength, was decidedly down . . . Playing for $575,000 and eyeing restricted free agency . . . Subpar free-throw shooter. His .727 was career best . . . Had 20 blocks in playoffs—but only one in four games vs. Bulls . . . Born May 16, 1964, in Brooklyn, N.Y. . . . Was taken No. 11 out of Georgia Tech in '86.

Year	Team	G	FG	FG Pct.	FT	FT Pct.	Reb.	Ast.	TP	Avg.
1986-87	Detroit	82	163	.562	105	.614	296	54	431	5.3
1987-88	Detroit	82	258	.566	185	.709	402	113	701	8.5
1988-89	Detroit	67	166	.498	135	.692	335	75	467	7.0
1989-90	Detroit	82	209	.512	174	.713	439	67	593	7.2
1990-91	Detroit	74	179	.475	186	.727	327	70	544	7.4
	Totals	387	975	.523	785	.697	1799	379	2736	7.1

ORLANDO WOOLRIDGE 30 6-9 215   Forward

Traded in August from Nuggets for Scott Hastings and 1992 second-round draft pick . . . He and Michael Adams were the show in Denver, such as it was . . . A great offensive year, especially the first half . . . Did not have enough points to qualify, but his average of 25.1 per game would have ranked 10th in the league . . . Needed 1,400 points to qualify and finished with 1,330 . . . Missed 22 games with detached retina in right eye . . . Scored 30 points or more 17 times, 20 or more 37 times . . . Demanded a new contract during season, but didn't get it . . . Scored 10,000th career point Dec. 5 at Boston . . . Played at Notre Dame . . . Born Dec. 16, 1969, in Bernice, La. . . . Drafted sixth by Bulls in 1981 . . . Made $805,000 in 1990-91.

Year	Team	G	FG	FG Pct.	FT	FT Pct.	Reb.	Ast.	TP	Avg.
1981-82	Chicago	75	202	.513	144	.699	227	81	548	7.3
1982-83	Chicago	57	361	.580	217	.638	298	97	939	16.5
1983-84	Chicago	75	570	.525	303	.715	369	136	1444	19.3
1984-85	Chicago	77	679	.554	409	.785	435	135	1767	22.9
1985-86	Chicago	70	540	.495	364	.788	350	213	1448	20.7
1986-87	New Jersey	75	556	.521	438	.777	367	261	1551	20.7
1987-88	New Jersey	19	110	.445	92	.708	91	71	312	16.4
1988-89	L.A. Lakers	74	231	.468	253	.738	270	58	715	9.7
1989-90	L.A. Lakers	62	306	.556	176	.733	185	96	788	12.7
1990-91	Denver	53	490	.498	350	.797	361	119	1330	25.1
	Totals	637	4045	.521	2746	.748	2953	1267	10842	17.0

JEFF MARTIN 24 6-5 195   Guard

Pistons got him in August from Clippers for James Edwards and 1995 second-round draft pick . . . Tied Charles Smith for Clipper lead in games played with 74 . . . Started 26 times, most during stretch of late December, January and early February when he got hot and Bo Kimble slumped . . . Moved back to bench soon after Ron Harper returned . . . Improved from rookie year at coming around pick and getting off shot . . . Problem: he shot 42.2 percent . . . Older brother, Wayne, was 1989 first-round draft choice of New Orleans Saints . . . Attended Murray State and in 1988 became first Ohio Valley Conference player to receive an invitation to Olympic trials . . . Born Jan. 14, 1967.

in Cherry Valley, Ark. . . . Has street named after him in Cherry Valley . . . Made $210,000.

Year	Team	G	FG	FG Pct.	FT	FT Pct.	Reb.	Ast.	TP	Avg.
1989-90	L.A. Clippers.....	69	170	.411	91	.705	159	44	433	6.3
1990-91	L.A. Clippers.....	74	214	.422	68	.680	131	65	523	7.1
	Totals	143	384	.417	159	.694	290	109	956	6.7

BRAD SELLERS 28 7-0 227 Forward

Returns to NBA after a year in Greece . . . Has been considered one of softest physical big men in the game, but experience abroad reportedly has toughened him. Pistons must have thought so or else he wouldn't have received two-year contract . . . Has nice shooting touch, but never has averaged more than 9.5 ppg . . . That was with Chicago, which drafted him ninth overall out of Ohio State in 1986 . . . Bulls traded him to Sonics for first-round draft choice in 1989 and he was traded to Timberwolves for Steve Johnson and 1991 second-round pick on Feb. 22, 1990 . . . Born Dec. 17, 1962, in Cleveland.

Year	Team	G	FG	FG Pct.	FT	FT Pct.	Reb.	Ast.	TP	Avg.
1986-87	Chicago	80	276	.455	126	.720	373	102	680	8.5
1987-88	Chicago	82	326	.457	124	.790	250	141	777	9.5
1988-89	Chicago	80	231	485	86	.851	227	99	551	6.9
1989-90	Sea.-Minn.	59	103	.406	58	.795	89	33	264	4.5
	Totals	301	936	.457	394	.782	939	375	2272	7.5

DARRELL WALKER 30 6-4 180 Guard

Butt-buster and overachiever came to Pistons from Bullets in September for two future second-round draft choices . . . Strained right knee ligament just before All-Star break. Lost a month . . . Third on team in rebounding at 7.0, most by any guard in the league . . . Good, strong defender . . . Handles Michael Jordan as well as Jordan can be handled . . . Four more triple-doubles, two consecutively . . . Yeah, there are some bad points. His shot continues to be downside proposition (.430) which limits ability at big guard. And his ball-handling and decisions on break aren't up to snuff for true point . . . Ideally suited as a third guard for any roster . . . Nice guy, too . . . Born March 9, 1961, in Chicago . . . Knicks' first-round pick in '83 . . . Traded from

Nuggets to Bullets with Mark Alarie for Michael Adams and Jay Vincent . . . Paid $610,500.

Year	Team	G	FG	FG Pct.	FT	FT Pct.	Reb.	Ast.	TP	Avg.
1983-84	New York	82	216	.417	208	.791	167	284	644	7.9
1984-85	New York	82	430	.435	243	.700	278	408	1103	13.5
1985-86	New York	81	324	.430	190	.686	220	337	838	10.3
1986-87	Denver	81	358	.482	272	.745	327	282	988	12.2
1987-88	Washington	52	114	.392	82	.781	127	100	310	6.0
1988-89	Washington	79	286	.420	142	.772	507	496	714	9.0
1989-90	Washington	81	316	.454	138	.687	714	652	772	9.5
1990-91	Washington	71	230	.430	93	.604	498	459	553	7.8
	Totals	609	2274	.437	1368	.722	2838	3018	5922	9.7

LANCE BLANKS 25 6-4 195   Guard

Is he a one? Is he a two? Or is he history? . . . Pistons seemed set on finding out and planned big minutes for him Feb. 13. Then he had what one Detroit writer called "the worst six minutes ever played." . . . Lost ball while getting instructions from sidelines, for example . . . Rookie out of Texas came with won't-back-down rep . . . Real Piston mold: gutsy, quick, long arms . . . And of course he can play either position. Supposedly . . . Only got 38 minutes and was on injured list (translate: holding list) with some sort of imaginary injury during playoffs . . . Born Sept. 9, 1966, in Houston . . . Paid $365,000.

Year	Team	G	FG	FG Pct.	FT	FT Pct.	Reb.	Ast.	TP	Avg.
1990-91	Detroit	38	26	.426	10	.714	20	26	64	1.7

THE ROOKIE

DOUG OVERTON 22 6-1 190   Guard

LaSalle product is in Piston mold . . . Shooter with point-guard size . . . Has quickness, can pass and defend (all-time LaSalle leader in assists, 671, and steals, 277) . . . Combined with Randy Woods to score NCAA-record 91 points in one game . . . Injuries slowed senior progress . . . Born Aug. 3, 1969, in Philadelphia . . . Picked 40th.

Wrist healed, Isiah Thomas will pass Piston scoring mark.

COACH CHUCK DALY: If we get a bronze again in the Olympics, he'll be living in Iceland... Named coach of 1992 U.S. Olympic Men's Basketball Team for Barcelona... And yes, the pros will play... Decided to return for one more season (at least), ending loads of speculation he intended to quit... Nine-year NBA record: 428-269 (.614), including eight-year 419-237 (.639) mark with Detroit... Became 20th coach to hit 400 victories... The 428 rank him 18th on all-time list... Longest continuous service of any current coach... Pistons had never enjoyed back-to-back winning seasons until he arrived in 1983. Since then, they've had eight straight winners (including two championships)... Has done incredible job juggling personalities and soothing egos... Considered defensive master... Has coached at every level, starting at high school in Punxsutawney, Pa., home of the groundhog... College stops at Penn, Boston College and Duke (assistant)... Assistant in Cleveland and Philly... Born July 20, 1930, in St. Mary's, Pa., and graduated from Bloomsburg (Pa.) State.

GREATEST TEAM

The style was better suited for thugs and goons, rather than athletes, and was more apt to be found in the darkened environs of New York's Central Park instead of NBA courts. But the bruising, physical game that featured defensive ferocity was the trademark of Detroit's 1988-89 "Bad Boys."

The Pistons rumbled to a 63-19 record, winning 30 of their final 35. Offseason golf proved more grueling than the playoffs as Detroit swept Boston and Milwaukee, ousted Chicago in six and then swept the injury-riddled Lakers in the finals. In 17 playoff games, only twice did the opponent reach 100 points, both times L.A.

The Pistons' three-guard rotation of Isiah Thomas, Joe Dumars and Vinnie Johnson sent the league into fits of envy and imitation. Not even a midseason trade—acquiring Mark Aguirre for Adrian Dantley—could deter the Pistons from their destiny. Aguirre joined a frontcourt peopled by the bruising likes of Rick Mahorn and Bill Laimbeer and he strengthened a bench already fortified by versatile John Salley and the finest defender in the galaxy, Dennis Rodman.

ALL-TIME PISTON LEADERS

SEASON

Points: Dave Bing, 2,213, 1970-71
Assists: Isiah Thomas, 1,123, 1984-85
Rebounds: Bob Lanier, 1,205, 1972-73

GAME

Points: Kelly Tripucka, 56 vs. Chicago, 1/29/83
Assists: Kevin Porter, 25 vs. Phoenix, 4/1/79
      Kevin Porter, 25 vs. Boston, 3/9/79
      Isiah Thomas, 25 vs. Dallas, 2/13/85
Rebounds: Bob Lanier, 33 vs. Seattle, 12/22/72

CAREER

Points: Bob Lanier, 15,488, 1970-80
Assists: Isiah Thomas, 7,431, 1981-91
Rebounds: Bill Laimbeer, 8504, 1982-91

INDIANA PACERS

TEAM DIRECTORY: Owners: Herb Simon, Melvin Simon; Pres.: Donnie Walsh; VP-Basketball: George Irvine; Media Rel. Dir.: Dale Ratermann; Coach: Bob Hill; Asst. Coaches: Billy Knight, Bob Ociepka. Arena: Market Square Arena (16,530). Colors: Blue and yellow.

SCOUTING REPORT

SHOOTING: With a roster containing pure shooters in Chuck Person (.504) and Reggie Miller (.512), plus versatile sixth man

Micheal Williams got his chance and took over as playmaker.

Detlef Schrempf (.520), it's little surprise that the Pacers had a near team-record-breaking season. They shot .493 from the field, the second-highest mark in club history, fourth-best in the league and third in the East. And it wasn't just all in-close stuff. The Pacers were .332 from three-point range, their third-best mark ever.

The Pacers figure on more of the same, perhaps better if center Rik Smits can rediscover some confidence in his offensive game. The Pacers' problems weren't so much offensively as defensively.

PLAYMAKING: Finally, the Pacers feel they found a creative floor leader in Micheal Williams. He's the disruptor they've sought, a guy with speed who was born to play point guard in a passing game. He still needs to develop a point guard's instincts and shake off a shooter's mentality, but the Pacers are very happy with the early results.

Aside from Person, the rest of the starting five rate as decent passers. Person could, too, but he's a shooter and scorer, not a big assist guy.

DEFENSE: The Achilles heel. And headache and pain in the butt. If the Pacers ever come up with some defense to match their crisp, fast-moving offense, they'll be trouble. But it's a big if, considering the limitations of Miller in the backcourt and Person up front. In the middle, Smits fouls too much to take advantage of his shot-blocking prowess. It all added up to the Pacers giving up 112.1 points, most in the East.

REBOUNDING: An area that has ailed the Pacers for so long. They hope they've solved a portion of their problem with Clemson monster Dale Davis, who led the ACC in rebounding three years running. Smits was a major bust, averaging only 4.7. Between him and Greg Dreiling (3.5), the Pacers got fewer rebounds from the center position than any team in the East.

Forwards Schrempf and LaSalle Thompson have proven adequate, even quality boarders, but not enough to prevent Indiana from ranking 21st in the league. Davis, they hope, will earn his pay immediately.

OUTLOOK: The future is decidedly upbeat in Indiana. Coach Bob Hill has inspired some enthusiasm and a family atmosphere. Now if he could just do something about the rebounding and defense.

PACER ROSTER

No.	Veterans	Pos.	Ht.	Wt.	Age	Yrs. Pro	College
54	Greg Dreiling	C	7-1	250	27	5	Kansas
10	Vern Fleming	G	6-5	185	29	7	Georgia
20	George McCloud	G-F	6-8	215	24	2	Florida State
31	Reggie Miller	G	6-7	185	26	4	UCLA
45	Chuck Person	F	6-8	225	27	5	Auburn
33	Mike Sanders	F	6-6	215	31	9	UCLA
11	Detlef Schrempf	F	6-10	230	28	6	Washington
24	Rik Smits	C	7-4	265	25	3	Marist
41	LaSalle Thompson	F-C	6-10	260	30	9	Texas
44	Kenny Williams	F	6-9	205	22	1	Elizabeth City State
4	Micheal Williams	G	6-2	175	25	3	Baylor
14	Randy Wittman	G	6-6	210	32	8	Indiana

Rd.	Rookies	Sel. No.	Pos.	Ht.	Wt.	College
1	Dale Davis	13	F	6-9	230	Clemson
2	Sean Green	41	G-F	6-5	210	Iona

One major problem for the Pacers, of course, is their location: the Central Division. Put them over in the Atlantic and they're a second-place team. In the Central, they can hope for no better than third, with fourth more likely. They have talent, but depth is always a concern. If they can get anything consistent out of a few of last year's no-shows (Mike Sanders, George McCloud) they could be a formidable opponent, perhaps a second-round playoff team.

PACER PROFILES

CHUCK PERSON 27 6-8 225　　　　　　　　Forward

Caused Indiana to fall in love with him all over again with often spectacular playoffs . . . Averaged 26.0—or 7.6 more than regular-season 18.4 ppg. Had third-best playoff average in NBA. Granted, it was only five games but he does play for Pacers, y'know . . . Interesting quote type. Of his two years as trade bait: "I'll be here longer than the Simons." Of course, they only own the team. Of his game: "It's not what you'd teach your kids." . . . Wants to be Charles Barkley dominator-type, but just can't . . . Great shooter with near-supernatural range. Often, sub-human selection, though . . . Not quite the chair-Person of the boards and defensively vulnerable overall. Except in post, where he's good both ways... Decent passer. Doesn't always do it... Became fourth Pacer to score 7,000 points... Had 38 games of 20 points... First-team All-Trash Talking... Full name is Chuck Connors Person, nicknamed "Rifleman."... Born June 27, 1964, in Brantley, Ala... Auburn '86, was Pacers' first-round No. 4 pick, breaking hearts of fifth-picking Knicks... Paid $2.15 million last season.

Year	Team	G	FG	FG Pct.	FT	FT Pct.	Reb.	Ast.	TP	Avg.
1986-87	Indiana.........	82	635	.468	222	.747	677	295	1541	18.8
1987-88	Indiana.........	79	575	.459	132	.670	536	309	1341	17.0
1988-89	Indiana.........	80	711	.489	243	.792	516	289	1728	21.6
1989-90	Indiana.........	77	605	.487	211	.781	445	230	1515	19.7
1990-91	Indiana.........	80	620	.504	165	.721	417	238	1474	18.4
	Totals	398	3146	.481	973	.748	2591	1361	7599	19.1

REGGIE MILLER 26 6-7 185   Guard

See Reggie in isolation. See Reggie get mugged and beaten to a bloody pulp. Yep, defenders have devised a way to handle the guy Charles Barkley said owns the NBA's prettiest shot... Has withstood the beatings. Tougher than he looks... Led NBA in free-throw shooting (.918, 551-of-600) so pummelings were worth something... Should try that defensive approach himself. His defense is as threatening as a candy cane. Stops no one with a working pulse... Scoring fell two full points to 22.6 as his number was called less and his isolations were down ... Adapted to passing game like a third-grader studying Kirkegaard. Offensive confidence sank... His .348 shooting on three-pointers was worst of his career. But no one in league has more range. If four-point line existed, he'd lead... Only Pacer ever to average 20 points in two seasons, let alone consecutively ... Born Aug. 24, 1965, in Riverside, Cal... Re-upped for five years, $15 million after Dick Versace's ouster as coach... No. 11 pick out of UCLA in '87... All-in-the-family type: sister, Cheryl, was Olympic gold medalist; two other sibs also sports standouts.

Year	Team	G	FG	FG Pct.	FT	FT Pct.	Reb.	Ast.	TP	Avg.
1987-88	Indiana.........	82	306	.488	149	.801	190	132	822	10.0
1988-89	Indiana.........	74	398	.479	287	.844	292	227	1181	16.0
1989-90	Indiana.........	82	661	.514	544	.868	295	311	2016	24.6
1990-91	Indiana.........	82	596	.512	551	.918	281	331	1855	22.6
	Totals	320	1961	.502	1531	.873	1058	1001	5874	18.4

LaSALLE THOMPSON 30 6-10 260   Forward-Center

Nicknamed "Tank." Has same size and almost as much mobility... Players' favorite Pacer. Great guy in locker room... Trade-rumor fodder for two-plus seasons, but his $2.0-million salary makes deal tough... Second straight relatively unproductive season... Should average more than 6.9 rebounds... Offense limited to face-up jump shot he can take to 17 feet...
Post offense almost extinct. Once-feared hook shot now successful with the frequency of pterodactyl sightings... Still a quality banger underneath... Too slow for power forward, too small for center... First Pacer in six years to have two 20-rebound games in same season... Shot .533 after Bob Hill became coach... Born June 23, 1961, in Cincinnati... Fifth pick in draft, as undergraduate out of Texas, by Kansas City in '82... Became a Pacer with Randy Wittman in the Feb. 20, 1989 trade that sent Wayman Tisdale and a second-rounder to Sacramento.

Year	Team	G	FG	FG Pct.	FT	FT Pct.	Reb.	Ast.	TP	Avg.
1982-83	Kansas City	71	147	.512	89	.650	375	33	383	5.4
1983-84	Kansas City	80	333	.523	160	.717	709	86	826	10.3
1984-85	Kansas City	82	369	.531	227	.721	854	130	965	11.8
1985-86	Sacramento	80	411	.518	202	.732	770	168	1024	12.8
1986-87	Sacramento	82	362	.481	188	.737	687	122	912	11.1
1987-88	Sacramento	69	215	.471	118	.720	427	68	550	8.0
1988-89	Sac.-Indiana	76	416	.489	227	.808	718	81	1059	13.9
1989-90	Indiana	82	223	.473	107	.799	630	106	554	6.8
1990-91	Indiana	82	276	.488	72	.692	563	147	625	7.6
	Totals	704	2752	.500	1390	.736	5733	941	6898	9.8

RIK SMITS 25 7-4 265   Center

"The Dunking Dutchman"... Can score, but best element of his game left him early and he never recovered... Pacers considering yanking his green card to get him to work in offseason. Saying "pullleeezze" hasn't worked... Disgracefully soft for size... Legit shot-blocker. With 430 rejects in three years—111 last season—he's Pacers' second all-time shot-blocker.
Failed to place in top 20, though... Good hands, good passer for center... Completely clueless rebounder. But he had 25 more than 6-foot Tim Hardaway. That's less than two per extra inch ... Scores with either hand, rebounds with neither... In-season surgery removed right elbow bone chips... Dec. 12 fight with

Pervis Ellison brought a one-game suspension. Ellison took off as pro. Smits stayed even . . . Earned $1.35 million in third year out of Marist . . . Born Aug. 23, 1966, in Einhoven, Holland . . . No. 2 pick in '88 draft . . . Allegedly participated in playoffs. In five games vs. Celts, he had 49 points, 18 rebounds, 23 fouls.

Year	Team	G	FG	FG Pct.	FT	FT Pct.	Reb.	Ast.	TP	Avg.
1988-89	Indiana	82	386	.517	184	.722	500	70	956	11.7
1989-90	Indiana	82	515	.533	241	.811	512	142	1271	15.5
1990-91	Indiana	76	342	.485	144	.762	357	84	828	10.9
	Totals	240	1243	.514	569	.768	1369	296	3055	12.7

GREG DREILING 27 7-1 250   Center

How far did Rik Smits fall? Here's his replacement . . . Had career year—for him. First off, he played . . . Scored 259 points, just 11 less than he managed in four seasons. And he lapped his career rebound total: his 255 last season passed the 239 he had since leaving Kansas as second-round pick in '86 . . . Contributed in 1990-91 with no-backdown approach . . . Superb work ethic . . . Does have offensive skills, but is too mechanical and slow in reactions . . . Look, Ma, no hands . . . Had four double-figure rebound games, raising career total to four . . . Like Smits, prone to early foul trouble . . . Evaporated in playoffs, but still equaled Smits' rebound total (18) in fewer minutes . . . Has known Bob Hill, seemingly, since he was conceived . . . Paid $300,000 . . . Born Nov. 7, 1963, in Wichita, Kan.

Year	Team	G	FG	FG Pct.	FT	FT Pct.	Reb.	Ast.	TP	Avg.
1986-87	Indiana	24	16	.432	10	.833	43	7	42	1.8
1987-88	Indiana	20	8	.471	18	.692	17	5	34	1.7
1988-89	Indiana	53	43	.558	43	.672	92	18	129	2.4
1989-90	Indiana	49	20	.377	25	.735	87	8	65	1.3
1990-91	Indiana	73	98	.505	63	.600	255	51	259	3.5
	Totals	219	185	.489	159	.660	494	89	529	2.4

DETLEF SCHREMPF 28 6-10 230   Forward

Probably a Hells' Angel in a former life . . . Born Jan. 21, 1963, in Leverkusen, West Germany. About as European as the Pittsburgh Steelers . . . NBA's Sixth Man Award winner and deservedly so, despite starter's minutes (second-most on team) . . . Led Pacers in rebounds (8.0), was third in scoring (16.1). Similar playoff numbers: 15.8 ppg, 7.2 rpg . . .

Probably team's most skilled player . . . Good work ethic. Gym-rat type who spent two years bulking up to play power forward . . . Sees decent minutes at small forward, could get more as Pacers like Chuck Person in post and Schrempf out on floor . . . Despite rebound proficiency, numbers don't measure with monster fours in NBA . . . Superb shooter with range. Shot career-best .520, led team in three-point accuracy at .375 . . . Only Pacer to get a vote for All-Defensive team . . . Earned $1.16 million . . . No. 8 pick out of Washington by Mavs in '85 . . . Stolen by Pacers for Herb Williams and a second-rounder in '89.

Year	Team	G	FG	FG Pct.	FT	FT Pct.	Reb.	Ast.	TP	Avg.
1985-86	Dallas	64	142	.451	110	.724	198	88	397	6.2
1986-87	Dallas	81	265	.472	193	.742	303	161	756	9.3
1987-88	Dallas	82	246	.456	201	.756	279	159	698	8.5
1988-89	Dal.-Indiana	69	274	.474	273	.780	395	179	828	12.0
1989-90	Indiana.	78	424	.516	402	.820	620	247	1267	16.2
1990-91	Indiana.	82	432	.520	441	.818	660	301	1320	16.1
	Totals	456	1783	.489	1620	.788	2455	1135	5266	11.5

MICHEAL WILLIAMS 25 6-2 175   Guard

So much for scouting reports. This guy bounced around like a crook on the lam . . . Turned into the find of the year . . . Gave Pacers coveted elements: legit quickness and disruptive defense at point guard . . . Born to be a point guard in passing offense . . . Not instinctive passer yet and hasn't yielded all of shooting-guard mentality he got at Baylor . . . Penetrates well, needs to finish better . . . Throws body recklessly, so can he last? . . . Has good 20-foot range . . . Not a great man-to-man defender but terrific passing-lane player with solid anticipation . . . Needs strengthening work . . . Stepped in as starter when Vern Fleming was injured, and remained . . . Averaged 14.7 points, 6.5 assists and 2.6 steals in 37 starts (Indy was 22-15). His overall 2.05 steals average was 11th-best in NBA . . . Outstanding play-offs, averaged 20.6 points . . . Earned $325,000 . . . Born July 23, 1966, in Dallas . . . Second-round pick of Pistons in '88. Signed with Pacers as free agent in August 1990 after failing to impress four other teams.

Year	Team	G	FG	FG Pct.	FT	FT Pct.	Reb.	Ast.	TP	Avg.
1988-89	Detroit	49	47	.364	31	.660	27	70	127	2.6
1989-90	Phoe.-Char.	28	60	.504	36	.783	32	81	156	5.6
1990-91	Indiana.	73	261	.499	290	.879	176	348	813	11.1
	Totals	150	368	.477	357	.844	235	499	1096	7.3

VERN FLEMING 30 6-5 185 Guard

Death, taxes and the Pacers looking to trade Vern Fleming . . . Ironically, Fleming's value rose when Pacers found starting replacement in Micheal Williams. Fleming hit injured list Jan. 16 for pinched nerve in neck. Returned and was on bench . . . Brass always felt he'd be ideal third guard and he was . . . One rap claims he's a rotten shooter, but has been over .500 every year since rookie season, including career-best .531 last season, fifth-best ever by a Pacer. Shot 9-of-9 in one game . . . Does have a frighteningly weird rotation on shot . . . Great finisher, nice team defender, probably Indy's best in halfcourt game . . . All-time Pacer leader in assists, went over the 3,000 mark at Philly Nov. 28 . . . Steady, unspectacular playoffs . . . Coach's delight: never moans, works hard . . . Earned $667,000 . . . Born Feb. 4, 1961, in Long Island City, N.Y. . . . Attended Georgia . . . Pacers plucked him at No. 18 in 1984.

Year	Team	G	FG	FG Pct.	FT	FT Pct.	Reb.	Ast.	TP	Avg.
1984-85	Indiana	80	433	.470	260	.767	323	247	1126	14.1
1985-86	Indiana	80	436	.506	263	.745	386	505	1136	14.2
1986-87	Indiana	82	370	.509	238	.788	334	473	980	12.0
1987-88	Indiana	80	442	.523	227	.802	364	568	1111	13.9
1988-89	Indiana	76	419	.515	243	.799	310	494	1084	14.3
1989-90	Indiana	82	467	.508	230	.782	322	610	1176	14.3
1990-91	Indiana	69	356	.531	161	.729	214	369	877	12.7
	Totals	549	2923	.507	1622	.774	2253	3266	7490	13.6

KENNY WILLIAMS 22 6-9 205 Forward

Could be major, major steal if he ever learns the plays—at least the ones involving him . . . One year of junior college (Elizabeth City State) didn't exactly prepare him for NBA . . . Fabulous leaper, earned invitation to Slam Dunk contest . . . Needs weight. Lots of weight. Stands sideways and resembles side-view of a door . . . Strangely, refused to bulk up in season. Will need to learn European currency exchanges if he doesn't . . . Showed legit shot-blocking instincts (blocked three on four occasions) . . . Shooter to 15 feet . . . Useless off the ball, only seems confident if it's in his hands . . . Pacers hoping he'll blossom, a la Shawn Kemp . . . Got $175,000 rookie pay as second-round pick . . . Born June 9, 1969, in Elizabeth City, N.C.

Year	Team	G	FG	FG Pct.	FT	FT Pct.	Reb.	Ast.	TP	Avg.
1990-91	Indiana	75	93	.520	34	.680	131	31	220	2.9

MIKE SANDERS 31 6-6 215 Forward

What happened? The best small forward in Pacer training camp gave season-long tribute to the Invisible Man . . . Shot career-low .417, averaged 5.8 points, worst in seven years . . . His usually limited offense was even more limited than usual . . . Will be fighting for a job this season, could be saved by his plus-side attributes: works hard, doesn't complain and is a solid defender. And a small forward who plays defense is almost as rare as a Rik Smits rebound . . . Has two years left on a free-agent contract that brought him from Cleveland in September 1989 and paid him $760,000 last season . . . Nondescript playoffs . . . Fourth-round pick by Kansas City out of UCLA in '82 . . . Landed in Cleveland in February 1988 as part of the Kevin Johnson-Larry Nance megatrade.

Year	Team	G	FG	FG Pct.	FT	FT Pct.	Reb.	Ast.	TP	Avg.
1982-83	San Antonio	26	76	.484	31	.721	94	19	183	7.0
1983-84	Phoenix	50	97	.478	29	.690	103	44	223	4.5
1984-85	Phoenix	21	85	.486	45	.763	89	29	215	10.2
1985-86	Phoenix	82	347	.513	208	.809	273	150	905	11.0
1986-87	Phoenix	82	357	.494	143	.781	271	126	859	10.5
1987-88	Phoe.-Clev.	59	153	.505	59	.776	109	56	365	6.2
1988-89	Cleveland	82	332	.453	97	.719	307	133	764	9.3
1989-90	Indiana.	82	225	.470	55	.733	230	89	510	6.2
1990-91	Indiana.	80	206	.417	47	.825	185	106	463	5.8
	Totals	564	1878	.476	714	.770	1661	752	4487	8.0

RANDY WITTMAN 32 6-6 210 Guard

Honest, he was on the team . . . At the end of the bench . . . Does anyone remember that he was drafted by Bullets out of U. of Indiana as a small forward in '83? . . . Always was a good spot-up shooter. Never could create own shot . . . Was re-signed ($500,000) primarily for leadership role, hometown appeal and for witty messages he left on Indy writers' answering machines . . . Just 26 points away from breaking 100 for season . . . Under Dick Versace, his inactivity was a mystery. In Bob Hill's passing game, he's just too slow . . . Not a bad team defender, but hard to gauge from bench . . . May be only 6-6 player who can't dunk . . . Born Oct. 28, 1959, in Indianapolis . . . Best years in Atlanta, came from Kings in the Wayman Tisdale trade.

Year	Team	G	FG	FG Pct.	FT	FT Pct.	Reb.	Ast.	TP	Avg.
1983-84	Atlanta.........	78	160	.503	28	.609	71	71	350	4.5
1984-85	Atlanta.........	41	187	.531	30	.732	73	125	406	9.9
1985-86	Atlanta.........	81	467	.530	104	.770	170	306	1043	12.9
1986-87	Atlanta.........	71	398	.503	100	.787	124	211	900	12.7
1987-88	Atlanta.........	82	376	.478	71	.798	170	302	823	10.0
1988-89	Sac.-Indiana.....	64	130	.455	28	.683	80	111	291	4.5
1989-90	Indiana.........	61	62	.508	5	.833	30	39	130	2.1
1990-91	Indiana.........	41	35	.443	4	.667	33	25	74	1.8
	Totals	519	1815	.502	370	.754	751	1190	4017	7.7

GEORGE McCLOUD 24 6-8 215   Guard-Forward

Tragic, traumatic season for second-year player . . . His mother died suddenly in February, then his father was suicide victim in June . . . Florida State product came into league as a shooter, but has yet to demonstrate he can do that. Shot .373 last season . . . For whatever reason, Pacers projected him as a point guard, looking for 6-8, Magic type . . . That idea fizzled very quickly . . . McCloud allegedly can rebound, defend and pass . . . Pacers would be real appreciative if he'd do that in games . . . Survived stormy relationship with Dick Versace . . . Almost got into a playoff game . . . Born May 27, 1967, in Daytona Beach, Fla . . . Paid $940,000—guys picked No. 7 in draft, like he was in '89, make that.

Year	Team	G	FG	FG Pct.	FT	FT Pct.	Reb.	Ast.	TP	Avg.
1989-90	Indiana.........	44	45	.313	15	.789	42	45	118	2.7
1990-91	Indiana.........	74	131	.373	38	.776	118	150	343	4.6
	Totals	118	176	.356	53	.779	160	195	461	3.9

THE ROOKIES

DALE DAVIS 22 6-9 230   Forward
Pacers hope he's their rebounding-forward answer . . . Clemson product, picked No. 13, led ACC in boarding three straight years. Averaged 12.1 rpg as senior . . . In ACC history, only Davis, Mike Gminski and Ralph Sampson had 1,500 points, 1,200 rebounds and 200 blocks . . . Born March 25, 1969, in Toccoa, Ga.

SEAN GREEN 21 6-5 210   **Guard-Forward**

Nicknamed "Rise" for 40-inch vertical leap . . . Called by some "the best athlete in the draft" . . . Pacers grabbed Iona product 41st . . . Averaged 23.2 ppg as senior . . . Led high school to No. 4 national ranking as senior and he won Slam Dunk contest at Dapper Dan Classic . . . Swing guy for pros . . . Born Feb. 2, 1970, in Santa Monica, Cal.

COACH BOB HILL: Took over on Dec. 20 when axe finally fell on Dick Versace . . . Led Pacers to 32-25 record, including 22-14 after All-Star break . . . Second time in NBA career he was asked to pick up the pieces . . . In 1986-87, he replaced Hubie Brown with the Knicks 16 games into the season. Knick brass never gave him fair shot and he was canned at season's end . . . Joined Pacers as assistant in 1989-90 . . . Players' coach, stresses family atmosphere stuff . . . Up-tempo philosophy. Had Pacers in passing game most of regular season . . . With 2-3 first-round record, became all-time winningest Pacer playoff coach . . . Assistant coach at three colleges, including alma mater Bowling Green (Class of '72) . . . Born Nov. 24, 1948, in Columbus, Ohio . . . Played minor-league baseball in the Padres' organization . . . Wisely, Pacers gave him contract extension . . . Great dresser.

GREATEST TEAM

Like the Nets, the Pacers' most glorious season dates to their pre-NBA history. The most dominant team Indiana ever fielded—outside of Bloomington, that is—played with the red, white and blue balls of the ABA in 1969-70.

That was when the Pacers stormed to a 59-25 (.702) record, first place in the East and the first of their three ABA titles. Behind the 23-point scoring of Roger Brown and the 17.6-rebounding of Mel Daniels, the Pacers ran amok in the regular season, then swept Carolina in four, ousted Kentucky in five and battered the Bill Sharman-coached L.A. Stars in six games for the championship.

Any bragging halted once the Pacers joined the NBA. In 15

NBA seasons, the Pacers have charted 11 losers, two of .500 (including last season) and just two above break-even. Their winningest NBA season came in 1980-81, when they achieved 44 victories with Billy Knight, George McGinnis, James Edwards and Johnny Davis. But the playoffs produced a quick, if not painless, exit as Philly routed the Pacers in two straight by an average of 13.5 points.

ALL-TIME PACER LEADERS

SEASON

Points: George McGinnis, 2,353, 1974-75 (ABA)
        Billy Knight, 2,075, 1976-77
Assists: Don Buse, 689, 1975-76 (ABA)
        Don Buse, 685, 1976-77
Rebounds: Mel Daniels, 1,475, 1970-71 (ABA)
        Clark Kellogg, 860, 1982-83

GAME

Points: George McGinnis, 58 vs. Dallas, 11/28/72 (ABA)
        Billy Knight, 52 vs. San Antonio, 11/11/80
Assists: Don Buse, 20 vs. Denver, 3/26/76 (ABA)
        Vern Fleming, 18 vs. Houston, 11/23/90
Rebounds: George McGinnis, 37 vs. Carolina, 1/12/74 (ABA)
        Herb Williams, 29 vs. Denver, 1/23/89

CAREER

Points: Billy Knight, 10,780, 1974-83 (ABA)
        Herb Williams, 8,637, 1981-89
Assists: Vern Fleming, 3,266, 1984-91
        Don Buse, 2,747, 1972-77, 1980-82 (ABA)
Rebounds: Mel Daniels, 7,622, 1968-74 (ABA)
        Herb Williams, 4,494, 1981-89

MIAMI HEAT

TEAM DIRECTORY: Partners: Ted Arison, Zev Bufman, Billy Cunningham, Lewis Schaffel (Managing Partner); Dir. Player Personnel: Stu Inman; Dir. Pub. Rel.: Mark Pray; Coach: Kevin Loughery; Asst. Coach: Bob Staak. Arena: Miami Arena (15,008). Colors: Orange, red, yellow, black and white.

SCOUTING REPORT

SHOOTING: You look at the Heat and you see reputed shooters: Willie Burton, Glen Rice, Kevin Edwards, Sherman Douglas,

Sherman Douglas adds heat with shooting and playmaking.

Rony Seikaly. Then you look at their shooting numbers. Then you begin to see why Steve Smith made sense as the No. 5 pick.

The Heat finished a miserable 22nd in the league, shooting .459. Douglas cracked 50 percent (.504) and Seikaly came in at .481, but there wasn't much after that. From the perimeter, the Heat left much to be desired, although Rice showed decent improvement. The addition of Smith will provide Miami with a potent perimeter rotation in Burton, Rice and Smith. At least it looks that way.

PLAYMAKING: Douglas brings good penetration—but he also brings turnovers in bunches. Unlike most point guards, Douglas is more apt to penetrate and then shoot. His insistence on going all the way to the basket brings batterings—and it also brings out his flair for the dramatic, which is one reason why the Heat are runaway leaders in turnovers. Overall, the Heat are as good at passing as they've been at winning.

DEFENSE: They don't block shots. They don't force turnovers. They give up too many points. The Heat's major weakness is inside muscle. They could make strides in the pressure department if Kevin Loughery sticks with the up-tempo game, but they still lack the gorilla force to shut down the lane.

REBOUNDING: Take your pick. What's the Heat's biggest weakness, their endless supply of turnovers or their lack of rebounds? Either way, you've got a strong case to argue.

And this area was why so many felt the Heat would opt for Doug Smith, rebounding stud from Missouri, over Steve Smith, shooter from Michigan State. It figured that the Heat would try for a center, moving Seikaly to power forward, or a big inside forward to keep Seikaly at center. Instead, they took another shooting guard. That gives them five. True power forwards? They have none.

OUTLOOK: There's a new look of sorts with a familiar face in Loughery. But what he'll be able to bring out that Ron Rothstein couldn't is anybody's guess. The Heat will continue to slowly improve with their youth—and they'll continue to get slaughtered on the backboards. They have the built-in rivalry within the Atlantic Division with Orlando officially joining the pack. That could provide about all the excitement the Heat will manage this season. They figure to be the weakest team in the weakest division.

HEAT ROSTER

No.	Veterans	Pos.	Ht.	Wt.	Age	Yrs. Pro	College
2	Keith Askins	G-F	6-8	197	23	1	Alabama
34	Willie Burton	G-F	6-8	219	23	1	Minnesota
12	Bimbo Coles	G	6-2	182	23	1	Virginia Tech
11	Sherman Douglas	G	6-1	180	24	2	Syracuse
21	Kevin Edwards	G	6-3	197	26	3	DePaul
33	Alec Kessler	F-C	6-11	245	24	1	Georgia
43	Grant Long	F	6-9	230	25	3	Michigan
53	Alan Ogg	C	7-2	235	24	1	Ala.-Birmingham
41	Glen Rice	F-G	6-8	220	24	2	Michigan
4	Rony Seikaly	C	6-11	252	26	3	Syracuse
20	Jon Sundvold	G	6-2	180	30	8	Missouri

Rd.	Rookies	Sel. No.	Pos.	Ht.	Wt.	College
1	Steve Smith	5	G	6-6	200	Michigan State
2	George Ackles	29	F-C	6-9	215	Nevada-Las Vegas

HEAT PROFILES

RONY SEIKALY 26 6-11 252   Center

Okay, he's been in the NBA long enough to spell his first name right... Heat would love him at power forward, but until legit center is found, they'll stay with his slug-like inside game... Has developed quality power moves since being Heat's first-ever pick, No. 9, in '88 ...Again turnover-prone: 3.2 per game, second only to Patrick Ewing among Eastern centers. Was second in league in turnovers a year ago, also at 3.2 ... Great strides in rebounding, especially on defensive boards. Overall 11.1 average would have placed him sixth, but he missed too many games... Had 13 more offensive rebounds than Ewing—in 17 fewer games... Six games of 20 or more boards... Sprained right-knee ligament in December... Attempted league-high 26 free throws Nov. 14 when he had Heat's first-ever 30-20 game: 30 points, 21 rebounds... Stinks at the line (.619), but what'd you expect? He's from Syracuse . . . Born May 10, 1965, in Beirut . . . Earned $765,000.

Year	Team	G	FG	FG Pct.	FT	FT Pct.	Reb.	Ast.	TP	Avg.
1988-89	Miami	78	333	.448	181	.511	549	55	848	10.9
1989-90	Miami	74	486	.502	256	.594	766	78	1228	16.6
1990-91	Miami	64	395	.481	258	.619	709	95	1050	16.4
	Totals	216	1214	.479	695	.578	2024	228	3126	14.5

SHERMAN DOUGLAS 24 6-1 180   Guard

He does do things differently . . . Thinks shooting first. Always . . . Only NBA point guard who led team in scoring (18.5) . . . Penetrates and shoots regardless of who or what is in the way. Tends to offset defenses playing off penetration. Also brings unnecessary beatings . . . Shot .504, more than enough to keep defenses honest . . . Little range . . . Treats his moves like a panel of East European judges are grading . . . Goes for spectacular over easy. One reason why Heat lead league in turnovers . . . His 3.70 turnovers per were second among Eastern point guards to Isiah Thomas (3.86 in 48 games) . . . His 8.5 assists were ninth-best in NBA . . . Throws alley-oop well . . . In Syracuse tradition, shot .686 from line . . . Restricted free agent when his second-year, $325,000 deal expired . . . Heat stole him on second round in 1990 and he made All-Rookie team . . . Born Sept. 15, 1967, in Washington, D.C.

Year	Team	G	FG	FG Pct.	FT	FT Pct.	Reb.	Ast.	TP	Avg.
1989-90	Miami	81	463	.494	224	.687	206	619	1155	14.3
1990-91	Miami	73	532	.504	284	.686	209	624	1352	18.5
	Totals	154	995	.499	508	.686	415	1243	2507	16.3

GLEN RICE 24 6-8 220   Forward-Guard

Some of life's great mysteries: Why are we here? Is there life after death? Where the heck is Oconomowoc? Is Glen Rice being played out of position? . . . Started the season at small forward, wound up at big guard for final 63 games . . . Must improve ball-handling skills for backcourt . . . Not a demon on the boards up front, anyway . . . Appears to have adjusted to the NBA three-pointer . . . After rotten .246 rookie year, improved to .386 . . . Averaged 17.8 ppg at big guard . . . Had back-to-back 30-point games, a first for Heat . . . Good free-throw shooter (.818).

Didn't go to Syracuse... Led Michigan to 1989 NCAA title and became No. 4 pick by Heat... Nice second-year progression... Mystery answers: Don't know, don't know, Wisconsin, who knows?... Is paid $1.555 million... Born May 28, 1967, in Flint, Mich.

Year	Team	G	FG	FG Pct.	FT	FT Pct.	Reb.	Ast.	TP	Avg.
1989-90	Miami	77	470	.439	91	.734	352	138	1048	13.6
1990-91	Miami	77	550	.461	171	.818	381	189	1342	17.4
	Totals	154	1020	.451	262	.787	733	327	2390	15.5

WILLIE BURTON 23 6-8 219   Guard-Forward

Could use a relaxation tape or two... Fine rookie season, but must get game under control... Relax, breathe deep, think happy thoughts... Started last 24 games and had 13-game run averaging 14.4 points... Like Glen Rice, Heat still determining his best position... Good open-court player. Has strong post-up skills at big guard... At 12.0, was fifth-highest-scoring rookie (fourth officially)... Range a question. Shot .441... Heat traded down last year from No. 3 to grab him ninth... Second all-time leading scorer at Minnesota behind Mychal Thompson... Scored 25 points in first game... Was second-team All-Rookie selection... Great potential... Born May 26, 1968, in Detroit... Top-paid Heat at $2 million.

Year	Team	G	FG	FG Pct.	FT	FT Pct.	Reb.	Ast.	TP	Avg.
1990-91	Miami	76	341	.441	229	.782	262	107	915	12.0

ALAN OGG 24 7-2 235   Center

Quick question: what nationality is Ogg?... Is Cro-Magnon a nationality?... Graduate of Manute Bol School of Body Building... Doesn't rebound, doesn't score, can block shots... Hey, he is 7-2... Undrafted out of Alabama-Birmingham... Heat signed him as a free agent in August, waived him. When Rony Seikaly went down, they brought him back... Averaged 2.09 blocks in first 11 games... Must have worn him down: had four blocks in remaining 20... Born July 5, 1967, in Lancaster, Ohio... Salary: $130,000.

Year	Team	G	FG	FG Pct.	FT	FT Pct.	Reb.	Ast.	TP	Avg.
1990-91	Miami	31	24	.436	6	.600	49	2	54	1.7

KEVIN EDWARDS 26 6-3 197   Guard

Shot with Dennis Hopson consistency... Three-year low of .410... Not that he fell that far: previous seasons produced .425 and .412 ... Swing guard, plays point and big guard... Misses with equal ease from both spots... Became a restricted free agent after his $425,000 season last year... Lukewarm interest around league... Scorer (12.1) despite awful shot... Began showing quality three-point skills at very end, hitting 7-of-16... Played in same DePaul backcourt as Rod Strickland... Some question intensity and concentration... Born Oct. 30, 1965, in Cleveland Heights, Ohio... No. 20 pick on first round by Heat in '88.

Year	Team	G	FG	FG Pct.	FT	FT Pct.	Reb.	Ast.	TP	Avg.
1988-89	Miami	79	470	.425	144	.746	262	349	1094	13.8
1989-90	Miami	78	395	.412	139	.760	282	252	938	12.0
1990-91	Miami	79	380	.410	171	.803	205	240	955	12.1
	Totals	236	1245	.416	454	.771	749	841	2987	12.7

KEITH ASKINS 23 6-8 197   Guard-Forward

Roster fodder... Undrafted free agent signed for $150,000 in 1990-91 preseason... Only played 266 minutes, so NBA game hard to gauge... Reputation as defensive type without a shot. His .420 limited-action accuracy didn't do anything to dispel the rep... Ditto his .480 from the line... Missed first month with left-ankle stress fracture... Alabama product... Born Dec. 15, 1967, in Athens, Ala... Hard-worker type, knows it's his only shot to stick in league.

Year	Team	G	FG	FG Pct.	FT	FT Pct.	Reb.	Ast.	TP	Avg.
1990-91	Miami	39	34	.420	12	.480	68	19	86	2.2

BIMBO COLES 23 6-2 182   Guard

Do any of these bench-guards shoot?... Must develop an outside shot. His .412 rookie-season accuracy isn't going to make it... Supported case that his lousy .404 senior year at Virginia Tech wasn't a fluke... Figured as backup point guard, but didn't shake the shooter's mentality ... Good in pressure-defense situations... Only Heat player to get in all 82 games...

Member of 1988 Olympic team . . . Decent 2.37 assist-to-turnover ratio . . . Drafted on second round by Kings, immediately swapped to Heat for veteran Rory Sparrow . . . Born April 22, 1968, in Covington, Va . . . Paid $290,000.

Year	Team	G	FG	FG Pct.	FT	FT Pct.	Reb.	Ast.	TP	Avg.
1990-91	Miami	82	162	.412	71	.747	153	232	401	4.9

GRANT LONG 25 6-9 230   Forward

Nice complementary player . . . If only there were more to complement . . . Parlays hustle and smarts into staying power . . . Career highs in rebounds (7.1) and shooting (.492) . . . Lacks the bulk Heat so desire . . . Extremely consistent about fouling out: tied for league lead two years ago. Last season, his 10 disqualifications made him high in East . . . Very smart player, runs the floor and hits the offensive boards with abandon . . . Makes the most of very ordinary talent . . . Second-round pick by Heat in '88 . . . Born March 12, 1966, in Wayne, Mich. . . . Eastern Michigan product made $300,000.

Year	Team	G	FG	FG Pct.	FT	FT Pct.	Reb.	Ast.	TP	Avg.
1988-89	Miami	82	336	.486	304	.749	546	149	976	11.9
1989-90	Miami	81	257	.483	172	.714	402	96	686	8.5
1990-91	Miami	80	276	.492	181	.787	568	176	734	9.2
	Totals	243	869	.487	657	.749	1516	421	2396	9.9

ALEC KESSLER 24 6-11 245   Forward-Center

Small forward in power forward's body . . . Good, quality perimeter game features Bill Laimbeer-type shot . . . Got to line a lot in college. Not so his rookie season: 131 FTs in 1,259 minutes . . . Averaged 4.3 rebounds and celebrates every board . . . Hunches over rebound, protects it for about a week. Sort of detrimental to running game . . . Georgia's all-time leading scorer was picked No. 12 by Rockets in '90. Went to Miami for rights to Carl Herrera and Dave Jamerson . . . Strength dulls the pain of his lack of quickness . . . Brainiac type: 3.9 grade-point average, Academic All-American . . . Missed 1990-91 preseason

with left-leg stress fracture . . . Born Jan. 13, 1967, in Minneapolis
. . . Drew $1.6 million.

Year	Team	G	FG	FG Pct.	FT	FT Pct.	Reb.	Ast.	TP	Avg.
1990-91	Miami	78	199	.425	88	.672	336	31	486	6.2

JON SUNDVOLD 30 6-2 180   Guard

Don't give up the day job . . . Strictly a specialist with his three-point shooting (225-of-575), .391 for career) . . . Non-existent season: 24 games. Came down with pneumonia at All-Star break and was out the rest of the way . . . Didn't mesh in before illness, anyway . . . Bad defender. That's what made him bit player with expansion team . . . Had NBA's best three-point season ever in 1988-89 when he went 48-of-92, an astounding .522 mark . . . Unfortunately, he was .444 on two-pointers . . . An original Heat, grabbed in '88 expansion draft from San Antonio . . . Was 19th overall pick, by Seattle, in '83 . . . Born July 2, 1961, in Sioux Falls, S.D . . . Missouri product earned $335,000.

Year	Team	G	FG	FG Pct.	FT	FT Pct.	Reb.	Ast.	TP	Avg.
1983-84	Seattle	73	217	.445	64	.889	91	239	507	6.9
1984-85	Seattle	73	170	.425	48	.814	70	206	400	5.5
1985-86	San Antonio	70	220	.462	39	.813	80	261	500	7.1
1986-87	San Antonio	76	365	.486	70	.833	98	315	850	11.2
1987-88	San Antonio	52	176	.464	43	.896	48	183	421	8.1
1988-89	Miami	68	307	.455	47	.825	87	137	709	10.4
1989-90	Miami	63	148	.408	44	.846	71	102	384	6.1
1990-91	Miami	24	43	.402	11	1.000	9	24	112	4.7
	Totals	499	1646	.452	366	.849	554	1467	3883	7.8

THE ROOKIES

STEVE SMITH 22 6-6 200   Guard

Consensus best shooter in draft . . . Heat wanted rebounding but couldn't pass on Michigan State's second-team All-American at No. 5 . . . Shot .487 over four years . . . Set Big Ten record with 45 straight free throws . . . Can dominate a game with outside threat and drives . . . Born March 31, 1969, in Detroit.

GEORGE ACKLES 24 6-8 215   Forward-Center

Heat hope he can bulk up and provide power-forward solution . . . Defensive force for UNLV who wasn't needed to score with great surrounding cast . . . A 17.0 scorer in junior college, 7.2 at UNLV . . . Set Rebel record for blocks in a season with 77 . . . Born July 4, 1967, in Manteo, N.C. . . . At No. 29, he was fourth UNLV starter chosen.

COACH KEVIN LOUGHERY: Walking proof of yard-sale mentality that nothing ever goes out of date . . . Won out over 20 candidates to claim his sixth pro head-coaching job . . . An assistant in Atlanta last season . . . Named Miami's second coach, succeeding Ron Rothstein, who left at season's end, on June 17. Hawks wouldn't give permission for him to join until after June 26 draft, which ticked off Heat. Hawks wanted him working on draft plans . . . Lifetime coaching record of 341-503. His .404 percentage is the worst of any coach with 200 victories . . . But if he goes .404 in Miami, he'll be mayor . . . Three winners in nine full NBA seasons . . . First head-coaching post in Philly in 1972-73. Lost 26 of 31 as interim . . . Did eight years with the Nets, including three in ABA. Led them to ABA titles in 1973-74 and 1975-76. Had two years with Hawks, two with Bulls, one full season and part of two others with Bullets . . . Born March 28, 1940, in the Bronx, N.Y. . . . St. John's grad played 11 pro seasons, averaging 15.3 points, with his best years with Bullets . . . Originally drafted on second round in '63 by Detroit.

GREATEST TEAM

Once again, greatness is relative here. Twenty-four victories ain't knee-slapping, hand-clapping stuff. Unless you happened to win 18 and 15 games in the two previous seasons.

Despite the Heat's best record in their three campaigns, coach Ron Rothstein said "enough" after last season. Whether a gun was at his head or not, Rothstein proclaimed there was only so much expansionist losing a guy could swallow. So he left a team pockmarked with talent holes but undoubtedly headed for better days.

The Heat, winners of seven of their last 12 to finish at 24-58, have quality youth in point guard Sherman Douglas, small forward Glen Rice, center Rony Seikaly (six 20-rebound games, tying him for second in the NBA in that category) and swingman Willie Burton, an All-NBA second-team rookie. But with youth comes mistakes and the Heat were the NBA's runaway leaders in turnovers in 1990-91, averaging 18.9 a game. So what if it was the most modest of improvements from the 19.0 a game of 1989-90? Everything's relative, don't forget.

ALL-TIME HEAT LEADERS

SEASON

Points: Sherman Douglas, 1,352, 1990-91
Assists: Sherman Douglas, 624, 1990-91
Rebounds: Rony Seikaly, 766, 1989-90

GAME

Points: Sherman Douglas, 42 vs. Denver, 12/27/91
Assists: Sherman Douglas, 17 vs. Atlanta, 2/26/90
Rebounds: Rony Seikaly, 22 vs. Orlando, 11/28/89

CAREER

Points: Rony Seikaly, 3,126, 1988-91
Assists: Sherman Douglas, 1,243, 1988-91
Rebounds: Rony Seikaly, 2,024, 1988-91

MILWAUKEE BUCKS

TEAM DIRECTORY: Pres.: Herb Kohl; VP-Bus. Oper.: John Steinmiller; Dir. Player Personnel: Lee Rose; Dir. Pub. Rel.: Bill King II; Coach: Del Harris; Asst. Coaches: Frank Hamblen, Mack Calvin, Larry Riley. Arena: Bradley Center (18,633). Colors: Kelly and forest green, lime and white.

Jay Humphries continues mastery at point guard.

SCOUTING REPORT

SHOOTING: Er, could you change the subject, please? The Bucks would rather not talk about this until they have a verdict on Dale Ellis. The herniated disc threatening Ellis' career casts a pall over the Bucks' offensive fortunes. With their inverted offense, the Bucks shot .480 last season, placing them 12th overall.

There will be some huge holes to fill. Jack Sikma was let go and although he was awful with .427 inaccuracy, he drew enough respect to lure opposing centers outside. Ellis, of course, is a prime concern. With Ricky Pierce gone, there isn't much from the perimeter. Jay Humphries is a mid-range type and Alvin Robertson lives off drives. The Bucks need someone who can drill from beyond 15 if Ellis isn't up to snuff. A long-shot is Bobby Phills, the 45th pick from Southern. Anthony Avent, the Bucks' first-rounder from Seton Hall, is Italy-bound.

PLAYMAKING: Again, the Bucks were middle-of-the-pack with a 13th-place showing for assists. But in Humphries and Robertson, they have two guys who form one of the league's most creative—and underrated—backcourt pairs. Humphries is a do-it-all type. A great passer, great penetrator. Robertson feeds off his defense, which again helped him lead the NBA in steals—and the Bucks are big on opportunity, scoring off turnovers.

DEFENSE: The Bucks hope that what starts in the backcourt with Robertson and Humphries will carry over into the middle with new resident Moses Malone. He is not the Moses of the Houston years, but he may be able to provide the plug that offense-oriented Sikma didn't.

REBOUNDING: Wasn't up to usual Buck standards. Sikma was hurt. Larry Krystkowiak was on the shelf. Danny Schayes and Frank Brickowski arrived in time to bang and bump, but overall the Bucks were a disappointing 19th in the league. And that's with a guard like Robertson, a better-than-average rebounding off-guard who racked up three triple-doubles.

What the Bucks need is a moose underneath. Maybe Malone, aboard from Atlanta, is that moose. While lots of guys put up "nice" numbers, no one overwhelmed. Schayes had 535, a team high. That was the lowest team-leading total in the East and the second-worst in the NBA. Only the rebound-bankrupt Warriors fared worse, with a team-best figure of 483.

BUCK ROSTER

No.	Veterans	Pos.	Ht.	Wt.	Age	Yrs. Pro	College
40	Frank Brickowski	F-C	6-10	240	32	7	Penn State
15	Lester Conner	G	6-4	185	32	8	Oregon State
7	Adrian Dantley	F	6-5	210	35	15	Notre Dame
3	Dale Ellis	G-F	6-7	215	31	8	Tennessee
20	Jeff Grayer	G-F	6-4	213	26	3	Iowa State
12	Steve Henson	G	5-11	177	23	1	Kansas State
24	Jay Humphries	G	6-3	185	29	7	Colorado
42	Larry Krystkowiak	F	6-10	240	27	5	Montana
54	Brad Lohaus	C-F	6-11	235	27	4	Iowa
8	Moses Malone	C	6-10	255	36	15	None
44	Fred Roberts	F	6-10	220	31	8	BYU
21	Alvin Robertson	G	6-4	202	29	7	Arkansas
10	Danny Schayes	C	6-11	260	32	10	Syracuse

Rd.	Rookies	Sel. No.	Pos.	Ht.	Wt.	College
2	Bobby Phills	45	G	6-4	210	Southern

OUTLOOK: Last year, Del Harris' Bucks were picked by many to be Central doormats and they rose up for 48 victories and a third-place division finish. This year, it catches up to them.

Sikma didn't supply much over the long haul last season, but when he was going good early the Bucks were tough, almost invincible at home. Now he's gone and although Schayes and Brickowski are both fully capable, the Bucks are one less strong on the depth chart up front. And if Ellis can't make it back, then the Bucks could be in deep trouble. They always find a way to the playoffs and probably will do so again. But the search figures to be a lot tougher this time.

BUCK PROFILES

JAY HUMPHRIES 29 6-3 185   Guard

Quick, name the best point guards around . . . Didn't even think of this guy, huh? . . . Vastly underrated player . . . Holds team together, great penetrator, outstanding in clutch, terrific defender, makes few turnovers (151, 1.89 avg., lowest in league for starting point guards), good mid-range jumper . . . Yet not considered in league's elite and was trade-rumored . . . Improved three-point shooting (.373). Never above .300 in a season before . . . Has started last 208 regular-season games for Bucks . . . Can't be blamed for team's playoff flameout: 15.0 points, 8.3 assists, 2.0 turnovers, shot .531 . . . Born Oct. 17, 1962, in Los Angeles . . . Drafted 13th by Phoenix, out of Colorado . . . Went to Milwaukee Feb. 25, 1988, for Craig Hodges and an 1988 second-rounder . . . A $650,000 wage-earner.

Year	Team	G	FG	FG Pct.	FT	FT Pct.	Reb.	Ast.	TP	Avg.
1984-85	Phoenix	80	279	.446	141	.829	164	350	703	8.8
1985-86	Phoenix	82	352	.479	197	.767	260	526	905	11.0
1986-87	Phoenix	82	359	.477	200	.769	260	632	923	11.3
1987-88	Phoe.-Mil	68	284	.528	112	.732	174	395	683	10.0
1988-89	Milwaukee	73	345	.483	129	.816	189	405	844	11.6
1989-90	Milwaukee	81	496	.494	224	.786	269	472	1237	15.3
1990-91	Milwaukee	80	482	.502	191	.799	220	538	1215	15.2
	Totals	546	2597	.487	1194	.784	1536	3318	6510	11.9

DANNY SCHAYES 32 6-11 260   Center

The son also rises . . . Son of Hall of Famer Dolph Schayes proved to be a pleasant surprise for Bucks, who gave Denver the draft rights to porker Terry Mills Aug. 1, 1990 . . . Faster than a traffic jam at the beach. Almost . . . Smart, intelligent player, makes the most of minimal athletic skills . . . Adapted well into organized sets better than days of helter-skelter teams in Denver . . . Sets great picks that take defenders a week and a half to get around . . . Took over starting center spot in January when Jack Sikma got hurt . . . Wide-body banger type . . . Averaged 13.3 points as a starter . . . Led team in rebounding, but had only 6.5 per . . . Quality at the line, shot .835, fourth-best among centers . . . Born May 10, 1959, in Syracuse, N.Y. . . . Academic All-American at Syracuse, was No. 13 pick by Utah in '81 . . . Made $1.5 million.

Year	Team	G	FG	FG Pct.	FT	FT Pct.	Reb.	Ast.	TP	Avg.
1981-82	Utah	82	252	.481	140	.757	427	146	644	7.9
1982-83	Utah-Den	82	342	.457	228	.773	635	205	912	11.1
1983-84	Denver	82	183	.493	215	.790	433	91	581	7.1
1984-85	Denver	56	60	.465	79	.814	144	38	199	3.6
1985-86	Denver	80	221	.502	216	.777	439	79	658	8.2
1986-87	Denver	76	210	.519	229	.779	380	85	649	8.5
1987-88	Denver	81	361	.540	407	.836	662	106	1129	13.9
1988-89	Denver	76	317	.522	332	.826	500	105	969	12.8
1989-90	Denver	53	163	.494	225	.852	342	61	551	10.4
1990-91	Milwaukee	82	298	.499	274	.835	535	98	870	10.6
	Totals	750	2407	.499	2345	.808	4497	1014	7162	9.5

DALE ELLIS 31 6-7 215   Guard-Forward

Model citizen for Bucks after biggest in-season trade . . . Yeah, but leave the car keys home anyway . . . Playing career jeopardized by herniated disc and ensuing surgery . . . No assurances, but Bucks insist he'll return . . . Missed last 10 games and playoffs . . . Traded by Seattle for Ricky Pierce, Feb. 15, 1991 . . . One of NBA's best pure shooters. Career 625-of-1,562 (.400) on three-pointers . . . Led Bucks in scoring in his 21 games, averaging 19.3 points . . . Doesn't sustain defense, typical of scorer . . . Missed first 17 games with Sonics due to right-foot injury . . . Complex offcourt problems in Seattle, most stemming from driving cars in wrong place (like highway medians) at wrong time (like after a party) . . . Played NBA-record 69 minutes, Nov. 9, 1989 for Sonics in 5-OT game vs. Bucks . . . Most Improved Player in 1986-87 . . . No. 9 pick by Mavs in '83 out of Tennessee . . . Born Aug. 6, 1960, in Marietta, Ga. . . . Paid $1.25 million.

Year	Team	G	FG	FG Pct.	FT	FT Pct.	Reb.	Ast.	TP	Avg.
1983-84	Dallas	67	225	.456	87	.719	250	56	549	8.2
1984-85	Dallas	72	274	.454	77	.740	238	56	667	9.3
1985-86	Dallas	72	193	.411	59	.720	168	37	508	7.1
1986-87	Seattle	82	785	.516	385	.787	447	238	2041	24.9
1987-88	Seattle	75	764	.503	303	.767	340	197	1938	25.8
1988-89	Seattle	82	857	.501	377	.816	342	164	2253	27.5
1989-90	Seattle	55	502	.497	193	.818	238	110	1293	23.5
1990-91	Sea.-Mil.	51	340	.474	120	.723	173	95	857	16.8
	Totals	556	3940	.490	1601	.779	2196	953	10106	18.2

ALVIN ROBERTSON 29 6-4 202   Guard

"The Real Steal" . . . Led NBA in thefts with 3.04. Third time in seven-year career he led league . . . Set Milwaukee record with 246 steals . . . Also led in complaints about contract . . . Got deal redone: $13 million for six years . . . Curious season . . . An absolute demon in first half, stats off the charts. Had 10 steals Nov. 19 vs. Utah . . . Then rocked boat over money . . . Play dipped, even after contract was settled . . . Made All-Star team, which surprised even him . . . Game was frustrated by arrival of Dale Ellis as he moved to perimeter. Has no outside shot to speak of . . . Three triple-doubles . . . One of NBA's best rebounding guards . . . Tied for second on team in boards at 5.7

... His 5.5 assists was third-best in league for off-guards, behind Michael Jordan and Clyde Drexler... Arkansas product chosen No. 7 by Spurs in 1984... Came to Bucks May 28, 1989, with Cadillac Anderson and second-rounder for Terry Cummings... Born July 22, 1962, in Barberton, Ohio.

Year	Team	G	FG	FG Pct.	FT	FT Pct.	Reb.	Ast.	TP	Avg.
1984-85	San Antonio	79	299	.498	124	.734	265	275	726	9.2
1985-86	San Antonio	82	562	.514	260	.795	516	448	1392	17.0
1986-87	San Antonio	81	589	.466	244	.753	424	421	1435	17.7
1987-88	San Antonio	82	655	.465	273	.748	498	557	1610	19.6
1988-89	San Antonio	65	465	.483	183	.723	384	393	1122	17.3
1989-90	Milwaukee	81	476	.503	197	.741	559	445	1153	14.2
1990-91	Milwaukee	81	438	.485	199	.757	459	444	1098	13.6
	Totals	551	3484	.485	1480	.752	3105	2983	8536	15.5

FRANK BRICKOWSKI 32 6-10 240　　　Forward-Center

As in Brick House... Supplied the limited muscle and trash talk on team... An enforcer and locker-room joker who irritates some... Was a good pickup, especially considering the down year Paul Pressey had in San Antonio. Straight trade went down Aug. 1, 1990... Started 73 games at power forward... Averaged 12.7 points and 5.7 rebounds, both the third-best marks of a career that began when the Knicks drafted him on the third round out of Penn State in '81. Knicks always regretted letting him go... Nothing fancy, just effective... His .527 shooting was second-best on team... Real good playoff series, averaged 18.3... Just a tough New York-type with playground inside game... Born Aug. 15, 1959, in Bayville, N.Y.... Earned $905,000.

Year	Team	G	FG	FG Pct.	FT	FT Pct.	Reb.	Ast.	TP	Avg.
1984-85	Seattle	78	150	.492	85	.669	260	100	385	4.9
1985-86	Seattle	40	30	.517	18	.667	54	21	78	2.0
1986-87	LAL-S.A.	44	63	.508	50	.714	116	17	176	4.0
1987-88	San Antonio	70	425	.528	268	.768	483	266	1119	16.0
1988-89	San Antonio	64	337	.515	201	.715	406	131	875	13.7
1989-90	San Antonio	78	211	.545	95	.674	327	105	517	6.6
1990-91	Milwaukee	75	372	.527	198	.798	426	131	942	12.6
	Totals	449	1588	.523	915	.736	2072	771	4092	9.1

BRAD LOHAUS 27 6-11 235   Center-Forward

The Man Without a Position . . . Is he a center? Nah, too weak in rebounding . . . Is he a small forward? At 6-11? . . . Is he a power forward? Not the way he hangs out on the perimeter . . . Without a defined position to concentrate on, Lohaus pulled more than his share of disappearing acts . . . Showed nothing before the All-Star break as his scoring (4.1) and rebounding (2.0) averages combined didn't equal his hat size . . . Improved a bit after the break . . . Made 33 three-pointers. Missed 86 . . . Runs the floor well . . . Reportedly participated in the playoffs . . . Paid $1.275 million (is this a great country or what?) . . . Born Sept. 29, 1964, in New Ulm, Minn. . . . Celtics made his second-round pick out of Iowa in '87 . . . Came from T-Wolves in January 1990 for Randy Breuer and a swap of future No. 2s.

Year	Team	G	FG	FG Pct.	FT	FT Pct.	Reb.	Ast.	TP	Avg.
1987-88	Boston	70	122	.496	50	.806	138	49	297	4.2
1988-89	Bos.-Sac.	77	210	.432	81	.786	256	66	502	6.5
1989-90	Minn.-Mil.	80	305	.460	75	.728	398	168	732	9.2
1990-91	Milwaukee	81	179	.431	37	.685	217	75	428	5.3
	Totals	308	816	.451	243	.755	1009	358	1959	6.4

MOSES MALONE 36 6-10 255   Center

Question all season was where Moses' next exodus will take him. The answer is Milwaukee . . . Legs not those of a starter any more . . . So he went to bench Nov. 30 . . . Played well in reserve during last year of contract . . . Can still score in the paint (but 10.6 ppg was career low) and be a competent position rebounder (averaged 8.1 boards) . . . But those stats couldn't justify $2.406-million salary with Hawks . . . Three-time MVP . . . MVP of '83 playoffs when he led Sixers to title . . . No. 1 active scorer with 27,908 points . . . Left Petersburg (Va.) High and was third-round pick by ABA's Utah Stars in '74. Sold to Spirits of St. Louis in '75, selected in ABA dispersal draft by Portland and sold to Buffalo . . . Houston, Philly and Washington made the re-

sume before Hawks signed him Aug. 16, 1988, as free agent. . .
Born March 23, 1955, in Petersburg, Va.

Year	Team	G	FG	FG Pct.	FT	FT Pct.	Reb.	Ast.	TP	Avg.
1974-75	Utah (ABA)	83	591	.571	375	.635	1209	82	1557	18.8
1975-76	St. Louis (ABA) . .	43	251	.512	112	.612	413	58	614	14.3
1976-77	Buf.-Hou.	82	389	.480	305	.693	1072	89	1083	13.2
1977-78	Houston	59	413	.499	318	.718	886	31	1144	19.4
1978-79	Houston	82	716	.540	599	.739	1444	147	2031	24.8
1979-80	Houston	82	778	.502	563	.719	1190	147	2119	25.8
1980-81	Houston	80	806	.522	609	.757	1180	141	2222	27.8
1981-82	Houston	81	945	.519	630	.762	1188	142	2520	31.1
1982-83	Philadelphia	78	654	.501	600	.761	1194	101	1908	24.5
1983-84	Philadelphia	71	532	.483	545	.750	950	96	1609	22.7
1984-85	Philadelphia	79	602	.469	737	.815	1031	130	1941	24.6
1985-86	Philadelphia	74	571	.458	617	.787	872	90	1759	23.8
1986-87	Washington.	73	595	.454	570	.824	824	120	1760	24.1
1987-88	Washington.	79	531	.487	543	.788	884	112	1607	20.3
1988-89	Atlanta	81	538	.491	561	.789	956	112	1637	20.2
1989-90	Atlanta	81	517	.480	493	.781	812	130	1528	18.9
1990-91	Atlanta	82	280	.468	309	.831	667	68	869	10.6
	Totals	1290	9709	.498	8486	.759	16772	1796	27908	21.6

LESTER CONNER 32 6-4 185   Guard

Hands-down worst nickname in league: "Lester the Molester." For his defense . . . Doubtful that will ever get him speaking gigs at elementary schools . . . Bucks wanted two things: a steady backup point guard and to dump Cadillac Anderson . . . Well, they dumped Anderson in three-team trade that brought the Molester on Jan. 16 . . . Filled his need adequately for a while . . . Gave little offense (2.9 points in 39 games) but continued his rep as a strong defender (2.7 steals per) . . . Decent distributor . . . Limited range on shot . . . Sometimes, no range at all . . . Not a good penetrator, either . . . Originally selected by Warriors as No. 14, in 1982 out of Oregon State . . . Born Sept. 17, 1959, in Memphis, Tenn. . . . Made $900,000.

Year	Team	G	FG	FG Pct.	FT	FT Pct.	Reb.	Ast.	TP	Avg.
1982-83	Golden State	75	145	.479	79	.699	221	253	369	4.9
1983-84	Golden State	82	360	.493	186	.718	305	401	907	11.1
1984-85	Golden State	79	246	.451	144	.750	246	369	640	8.1
1985-86	Golden State	36	51	.375	40	.741	62	43	144	4.0
1987-88	Houston	52	50	.463	32	.780	38	59	132	2.5
1988-89	New Jersey	82	309	.457	212	.788	355	604	843	10.3
1989-90	New Jersey	82	237	.414	172	.804	265	385	648	7.9
1990-91	N.J.-Mil.	74	96	.464	68	.723	112	165	260	3.5
	Totals	562	1494	.456	933	.755	1604	2279	3943	7.0

FRED ROBERTS 31 6-10 220   Forward

The ultimate role player, a tribute to hard work, smarts and using capabilities to the max... Only Buck to start all 82 games... Averaged career-best 10.8 points... Once was traded for a scheduled exhibition game. Traded another time for a coach (draft rights traded by Nets to Spurs, who relinquished rights to Stan Albeck)... Doesn't have quickness. Doesn't have a consistent shot. Doesn't have imagination with the ball. Doesn't have bulk... But he does have a place in the league... Uncanny movement without the ball... Just seems to find the right place to be... Shot team-best .533, 14th in NBA... Average playoffs... Born Aug. 14, 1960, in Provo, Utah... Originally drafted by Bucks out of Brigham Young in '82 on second round... Came back from Miami in '88 for a second-rounder... Made $690,000.

Year	Team	G	FG	FG Pct.	FT	FT Pct.	Reb.	Ast.	TP	Avg.
1983-84	San Antonio	79	214	.536	144	.837	304	98	573	7.3
1984-85	S.A.-Utah	74	208	.498	150	.824	186	87	567	7.7
1985-86	Utah	58	74	.443	67	.770	80	27	216	3.7
1986-87	Boston	73	139	.515	124	.810	190	62	402	5.5
1987-88	Boston	74	161	.488	128	.776	162	81	450	6.1
1988-89	Milwaukee	71	155	.486	104	.806	209	66	417	5.9
1989-90	Milwaukee	82	330	.495	195	.783	311	147	857	10.5
1990-91	Milwaukee	82	357	.533	170	.813	281	135	888	10.8
	Totals	593	1638	.506	1082	.804	1723	703	4370	7.4

LARRY KRYSTKOWIAK 27 6-10 240   Forward

You're not being a homer to root for this guy... Sat the entire season rehabbing his surgically-reconstructed left knee... Activated just before playoffs... Played 25 nondescript minutes... Key word is "played"... Blew out the knee, tearing medial capsule and collateral ligaments 25 seconds into Game 3 of 1989 Eastern semis... Returned in March, 1990, and played in 16 of final 20 games... A type every team wants. Works his butt off in practice. Tough inside player and banger... Mobility, of course, will be suspect... Born Sept. 23, 1964, in Missoula, Mont.... Drafted out of Montana on second round by Bulls in 1986 . . . Came to Bucks from Spurs for Charles Davis in 1987 . . . Made $605,000.

Year	Team	G	FG	FG Pct.	FT	FT Pct.	Reb.	Ast.	TP	Avg.
1986-87	San Antonio	68	170	.456	110	.743	239	85	451	6.6
1987-88	Milwaukee	50	128	.481	103	.811	231	50	359	7.2
1988-89	Milwaukee	80	362	.473	289	.823	610	107	1017	12.7
1989-90	Milwaukee	16	43	.364	26	.788	76	25	112	7.0
1990-91	Milwaukee.					Injured				
	Totals	214	703	.462	528	.801	1156	267	1939	9.1

STEVE HENSON 23 5-11 177   Guard

Looks like he's on his way to the high-school prom with Betty Lou . . . Plays and practices like he's coming from a parole-board review . . . Leads team in floor burns. Makes the absolute most of limited skills and treats every opportunity like the secret of life . . . A good outside shooter . . . Fan favorite . . . Only the fourth non-first rounder (picked 44th out of Kansas State) to make Bucks' opening-day roster since 1980 . . . Cameo appearances, averaged 3.1 points and 1.9 assists . . . Extremely smart. Not real quick. No glaring deficiency . . . Born Feb. 2, 1968, in Junction City, Kan. . . . Got $120,000 minimum wage.

Year	Team	G	FG	FG Pct.	FT	FT Pct.	Reb.	Ast.	TP	Avg.
1990-91	Milwaukee	68	79	.418	38	.905	51	131	214	3.1

ADRIAN DANTLEY 35 6-5 210   Forward

A good try . . . Had very little left from his once feared post-up game . . . Sat virtually the entire season after getting himself out of contract in Dallas . . . Nobody came knocking. Until the Bucks, who signed him April 2 after Dale Ellis went down . . . A.D. played in 10 games and scored 57 points. But they enabled him to move past Elgin Baylor into ninth place on the all-time scoring list . . . Originally the No. 6 pick in '76 by the Buffalo Braves after starring at Notre Dame . . . Earned $300,000 and about a $4,500 (guaranteed) playoff share . . . Former Rookie of the Year and two-time scoring champ was born Feb. 28, 1956, in Washington, D.C.

Year	Team	G	FG	FG Pct.	FT	FT Pct.	Reb.	Ast.	TP	Avg.
1976-77	Buffalo.........	77	544	.520	476	.818	587	144	1564	20.3
1977-78	Ind.-L.A.	79	578	.512	541	.796	620	253	1697	21.5
1978-79	Los Angeles	60	374	.510	292	.854	342	138	1040	17.3
1979-80	Utah	68	730	.576	443	.842	516	191	1903	28.0
1980-81	Utah	80	909	.559	632	.806	509	322	2452	30.7
1981-82	Utah	81	904	.570	648	.792	514	324	2457	30.3
1982-83	Utah	22	233	.580	210	.847	140	105	676	30.7
1983-84	Utah	79	802	.558	813	.859	448	310	2418	30.6
1984-85	Utah	55	512	.531	438	.804	323	186	1462	26.6
1985-86	Utah	76	818	.563	630	.791	395	264	2267	29.8
1986-87	Detroit.........	81	601	.534	539	.812	332	162	1742	21.5
1987-88	Detroit	69	444	.514	492	.860	227	171	1380	20.0
1988-89	Det.-Dal.	73	470	.493	460	.810	317	171	1400	19.2
1989-90	Dallas	45	231	.477	200	.787	172	80	662	14.7
1990-91	Milwaukee	10	19	.380	18	.692	13	9	57	5.7
	Totals	955	8169	.540	6832	.818	5455	2830	23177	24.3

JEFF GRAYER 26 6-4 213   Forward-Guard

Coach Harris, this is Jeff Grayer . . . For whatever reason, Grayer's playing time was as consistent as the weather . . . Seemed to do well when utilized. Then seemed to fall off the planet . . . Another knee-rehab case . . . Played 11 games as rookie (1988-89) after he blew out his left knee . . . Very versatile. Sort of . . . Can play three positions. Playing them well is another matter . . . Bucks envisioned him as heir to Paul Pressey's point-forward role . . . But he's only slightly above-average ballhandler . . . Decent passer and penetrator, though . . . Shooting very suspect (.433) . . . Limited playoff use . . . Good rebounder. Was fourth on team in offensive boards but eighth in minutes . . . No. 13 pick out of Iowa State in '88 . . . Born Dec. 17, 1965, in Flint, Mich. . . . Paid $605,000.

Year	Team	G	FG	FG Pct.	FT	FT Pct.	Reb.	Ast.	TP	Avg.
1988-89	Milwaukee	11	32	.438	17	.850	35	22	81	7.4
1989-90	Milwaukee	71	224	.460	99	.651	217	107	548	7.7
1990-91	Milwaukee	82	210	.433	101	.687	246	123	521	6.4
	Totals	164	466	.446	217	.680	498	252	1150	7.0

THE ROOKIE

BOBBY PHILLS 21 6-4 210   **Guard**
His 28.4 senior scoring at Southern (La.) made him the nation's fourth-best scorer . . . Has good range: hit 11 three-pointers in one game . . . His .407 shooting as senior, though, was shaky . . . All-SWAC selection . . . Born Dec. 20, 1969, in Baton Rouge, La.

COACH DEL HARRIS: Nothing, repeat, nothing escapes his preparation for a game . . . Regarded as a master technician . . . Players, however, grumbled that he had them over-prepared for the Sixers. And guess who took heat when Sixers swept? . . . Of course, mumblings died when it was formally announced that Harris, also VP of Basketball Operations, was coming back . . . Just a heckuva nice guy who's all basketball . . . His idea of a joke starts: "These two post-up men walk into a bar." . . . Led team that was picked for fifth in the Central and brought them third with 48 victories . . . Great regular season despite injuries and major in-season trade, lousy playoffs . . . Four-season record in Milwaukee: 183-145 (.558) . . . Overall, in eight NBA seasons (including Houston), he's 324-332 . . . Is 21-31 in playoffs, 6-15 with Milwaukee . . . Only Chuck Daly and Lenny Wilkens have been with same club longer . . . Born June 18, 1937, in Orleans, La. . . . Played at Milligan (Tenn.), coached at Earlham (Ind.).

GREATEST TEAM

On March 19, 1969, then-NBA Commissioner Walter Kennedy flipped a coin and Phoenix called heads. It landed tails and set in motion the structure for the greatest team in Bucks' history.

Milwaukee, of course, selected Kareem Abdul-Jabbar, who before becoming such a central figure in the Lakers' storied history, lifted the Bucks to their only NBA championship. Kareem achieved superstar status overnight, but it wasn't until the Bucks traded for legend Oscar Robertson before 1970-71 that they achieved the ultimate.

With Kareem and The Big O providing a devastating one-two

MILWAUKEE BUCKS • 161

combo, the Bucks blended the talents of Jon McGlocklin, Bobby Dandridge and Greg Smith in a first five that helped accumulate a staggering 66 victories. Milwaukee established six NBA records, including home wins (34), shooting (.509) and assists (2,249). Kareem swept to the MVP award almost as easily as the Bucks rode to the title. They ousted San Francisco, L.A. and Baltimore, losing two playoff games along the way.

ALL-TIME BUCK LEADERS

SEASON

Points: Kareem Abdul-Jabbar, 2,822, 1971-72
Assists: Oscar Robertson, 668, 1970-71
Rebounds: Kareem Abdul-Jabbar, 1,346, 1971-72

GAME

Points: Kareem Abdul-Jabbar, 55 vs. Boston, 12/10/71
Assists: Guy Rodgers, 22 vs. Detroit, 10/31/68
Rebounds: Swen Nater, 33 vs. Atlanta, 12/19/76

CAREER

Points: Kareem Abdul-Jabbar, 14,211, 1969-75
Assists: Paul Pressey, 3,272, 1982-90
Rebounds: Kareem Abdul-Jabbar, 7,161, 1969-75

NEW JERSEY NETS

TEAM DIRECTORY: Chairman: Alan Aufzien; Pres.: Jerry Cohen; Exec. VP-Chief Oper. Officer: Bob Casciola; Sr. VP-Basketball Oper.: Willis Reed; Dir. Pub. Rel.: John Mertz; Coach: Bill Fitch; Asst. Coaches: Tom Newell, Rick Carlisle. Arena: Brendan Byrne Meadowlands Arena (20,039). Colors: Red, white and blue.

SCOUTING REPORT

SHOOTING: Hey, you can't blame all of this on Chris Morris. He may have the worst shot selection on the planet, but he alone can't bring a team down to .444, the worst mark in the East. Morris had help. Lots of help. Of the regulars, only Drazen Petrovic was at .500 at season's end. No one else was even in the neighborhood.

The Nets have to replace Europe-gone Reggie Theus, their top scorer (.468 with 18.6 ppg). Rookie of the Year Derrick Coleman was .467 with 18.4 ppg.

And so one of the grand designs behind the selection of Georgia Tech's Kenny Anderson (besides filling the seats with fans who can't do a thing about that percentage) is to get a great setup guy who's going to deliver the ball to the right people at the right time. Sounds good. Let's see it happen.

PLAYMAKING: This was a major area of concern that the Nets feel they've solved with Anderson. Mookie Blaylock, the incumbent point guard, made more than a fair share of questionable decisions. And with the mentality of a shooting guard, the Nets' play from the point was questionable at best. So veteran shooter Theus was forced to assume a lot of the playmaking chores. All that will change if Anderson can be one-half as good as some believe.

DEFENSE: With centers Chris Dudley and Sam Bowie plus forwards Coleman and Morris, the Nets were runaway leaders in blocked shots. Unfortunately, with a sieve-like transition defense, too many teams ran away from them. With a sound halfcourt defense, if the Nets can match their offensive rebounding prowess on the defensive glass, they could make some real progress.

REBOUNDING: With centers Sam Bowie and Chris Dudley plus Coleman, the Nets were the East's best offensive rebounding

Derrick Coleman went from No. 1 pick to Rookie of Year.

NET ROSTER

No.	Veterans	Pos.	Ht.	Wt.	Age	Yrs. Pro	College
10	Mookie Blaylock	G	6-1	185	23	2	Oklahoma
31	Sam Bowie	C	7-1	240	30	7	Kentucky
35	Jud Buechler	F	6-6	220	23	1	Arizona
44	Derrick Coleman	F	6-10	230	24	1	Syracuse
22	Chris Dudley	C	6-11	240	26	4	Yale
12	Tate George	G	6-5	190	23	1	Connecticut
54	Jack Haley	F	6-10	240	27	3	UCLA
23	Roy Hinson	F	6-9	215	30	8	Rutgers
5	Terry Mills	F	6-10	240	23	1	Michigan
34	Chris Morris	F	6-8	210	25	3	Auburn
3	Drazen Petrovic	G	6-5	195	27	2	Yugoslavia

Rd.	Rookies	Sel. No.	Pos.	Ht.	Wt.	College
1	Kenny Anderson	2	G	6-0	168	Georgia Tech
2	Von McDade	53	G	6-2	185	Wis.-Milwaukee

team, second in the league only to Seattle. Of course, with their shooting, there were lots of offensive rebounds to be had. A better barometer came at the other end. The Nets were the East's worst defensive-rebounding team, second from the bottom, ahead of only Golden State.

But overall, rebounding still shapes up as a strength on a team riddled with weaknesses. They get boarding up front—Morris, too, can rebound—but receive very little from the backcourt. Anderson won't get any rebounds, but coach Bill Fitch is hoping he can break down defenses enough to provide better team positioning.

OUTLOOK: Hold your breath. In drafting Anderson over Billy Owens at No. 2, the Nets have taken one of the biggest gambles in their history. Bigger than trading Buck Williams. Bigger than re-signing Micheal Ray Richardson. Bigger than shutting off beer sales after the third quarter. They are a team with a solid future slowly emerging before them.

If Anderson proves to be a pick of Coleman's ilk, that future could start happening this season in the form of a playoff bid. If he's another Dennis Hopson, the owners might not be able to give the franchise away for a bag of donuts. If Anderson is ready and holds his own, and if Morris plays to this athletic capabilities, then Net fans may finally have cause to cheer.

NET PROFILES

DERRICK COLEMAN 24 6-10 230   Forward

The Nets didn't screw up, the Nets didn't screw up . . . They picked the plum of the '90 draft with the runaway Rookie of the Year at No. 1 . . . Far cry from such luminary picks as Dennis Hopson, Chris Morris, Pearl Washington . . . Remarkably consistent, Syracuse product led team in rebounding (10.3, tied for eighth-best in the league) and the most by Net rookie since Buck Williams . . . Was second to Reggie Theus in scoring (18.4) . . . The total package. Muscle inside, range on jumper, quality transition player . . . Needs field-goal improvement: .467 . . . And dose of modesty. Of David Robinson, he noted, "He reminds me a lot of myself." . . . In first season, established himself as a prime force at his position . . . Good defender, had 1.34 blocks, 0.96 steals . . . Quiet rap from some teammates: needs to think TEAM more, but not so much on court . . . Born June 21, 1967, in Mobile, Ala. . . . Lengthy contract talks brought five-year, $15-million deal that paid $2.1 million last year.

Year	Team	G	FG	FG Pct.	FT	FT Pct.	Reb.	Ast.	TP	Avg.
1990-91	New Jersey	74	514	.467	323	.731	759	163	1364	18.4

MOOKIE BLAYLOCK 23 6-1 185   Guard

Why former Net Reggie Theus was so valuable: Theus was off-guard who often had to play like point because this point too often played like off-guard . . . But now may be asked to play more off-guard with the arrival of wunderkind Kenny Anderson . . . Got it? . . . Showed steady, if not rapid, improvement over second season . . . Needs to penetrate more and shred his score-first mentality . . . Placed third on the team in scoring with 14.1 ppg . . . But shot a woeful .416 . . . Still makes awful decisions . . . Was sixth in the league in steals at 2.35, thanks to con-man quick hands and quality anticipation. That was fourth-best mark in East . . . Assists were 6.1, though, placing him fifth from bottom in East among starting point guards . . . Was his first full season. Missed big chunk of rookie campaign with broken finger... Born March 20, 1967, in Garland, Tex... Paid $525,000... Nets picked him No. 12 in '89 out of Oklahoma.

Year	Team	G	FG	FG Pct.	FT	FT Pct.	Reb.	Ast.	TP	Avg.
1989-90	New Jersey	50	212	.371	63	.778	140	210	505	10.1
1990-91	New Jersey	72	432	.416	139	.790	249	441	1017	14.1
	Totals	122	644	.400	202	.786	389	651	1522	12.5

CHRIS MORRIS 25 6-8 210   Forward

Incredibly gifted athlete... Incredibly dumb decisions... May have the hands-down worst shot-selection in league... Bad attitude, too... Terrible at finishing... Needs to reduce turnovers. At least the costly ones... But if Nets could ever harness those skills, they'd have a stud... How much longer can they wait?... Was the No. 4 pick in the '88 draft out of Auburn... Scored at 13.2, shot at .425... Heaves up three-pointers with abandon... Outstanding leaping ability. Nets call him "Doctor" for Dr. J-like legs. But also has Dennis Hopson-like shot... Gave glimpse of potential in final game when he registered a triple-double of 17 points, 14 rebounds, 10 assists... And he was second on the team in steals... Born Jan. 20, 1966, in Atlanta... Paid $750,000.

Year	Team	G	FG	FG Pct.	FT	FT Pct.	Reb.	Ast.	TP	Avg.
1988-89	New Jersey	76	414	.457	182	.717	397	119	1074	14.1
1989-90	New Jersey	80	449	.422	228	.722	422	143	1187	14.8
1990-91	New Jersey	79	409	.425	179	.734	521	220	1042	13.2
	Totals	235	1272	.434	589	.724	1340	482	3303	14.1

SAM BOWIE 30 7-1 240   Center

Quick word association: Sam Bowie. What do you think of, injuries or the guy drafted instead of Michael Jordan by Portland?... Those two reps will continue to haunt the Kentucky product. Was injured again (broken finger) and had tendinitis. And Jordan won a championship... When healthy, proved to be a serviceable center at both ends, although he griped about decreased role in the offense... Offensively inconsistent. Shot .434 and averaged 12.9 ppg... Decent rebound (7.7) and blocked-shot (1.45) numbers... Set single-game career highs in rebounds (21), points (38) and blocks (9)... Born March 17, 1961, in Lebanon,

Pa. . . . $2-million salary . . . Has missed 352 games through injury—including the entire 1987-88 season after suffering one of his three broken-leg injuries—since Blazers drafted him No. 2, one spot ahead of Jordan in '84 . . . Came to Nets in Buck Williams trade June 24, 1989.

Year	Team	G	FG	FG Pct.	FT	FT Pct.	Reb.	Ast.	TP	Avg.
1984-85	Portland	76	299	.537	160	.711	656	215	758	10.0
1985-86	Portland	38	167	.484	114	.708	327	99	448	11.8
1986-87	Portland	5	30	.455	20	.667	33	9	80	16.0
1987-88	Portland					Injured				
1988-89	Portland	20	69	.451	28	.571	106	36	171	8.6
1989-90	New Jersey	68	347	.416	294	.776	690	91	998	14.7
1990-91	New Jersey	62	314	.434	169	.732	480	147	801	12.9
	Totals	269	1226	.458	785	.730	2292	597	3256	12.1

DRAZEN PETROVIC 27 6-5 195   Guard

One of the best stand-still shooters in the league . . . Couldn't guard a closed door, however . . . Came to Nets Jan. 23 from Portland, for future first-rounder as part of three-team trade that saw Nets send Cadillac Anderson to Denver and also get Terry Mills . . . First time a Cadillac was traded for a Yugo . . . Only player to finish season with team who shot .500 (211-of-422) . . . A definite streak-shooter. Will go 8-of-10 or 0-of-8 . . . A rumor around the league says he can pass . . . Seven-assist game vs. Heat strengthened report . . . Born Oct. 22, 1964, in Sibenik, Yugoslavia . . . Third-round pick by Blazers in 1986 . . . Made $1.2 million.

Year	Team	G	FG	FG Pct.	FT	FT Pct.	Reb.	Ast.	TP	Avg.
1989-90	Portland	77	207	.485	135	.844	111	116	583	7.6
1990-91	Port.-N.J.	61	243	.493	114	.832	110	86	623	10.2
	Totals	138	450	.489	249	.838	221	202	1206	8.7

CHRIS DUDLEY 26 6-11 240   Center

Okay, no more cracks about his lousy free-throw shooting (.534, a vast improvement) . . . The guy should be known for other things. Like quietly becoming the best back-up center in NBA . . . Phenomenal offensive rebounder and shot-blocker. Consider: four-season pro from Yale had 229 offensive rebounds in 1,560 minutes. Patrick Ewing,

in twice as many minutes (3,104) had 194 offensive boards...
And this guy is a great shot-blocker. His 153 rejects—again,
considering minutes, superior to Ewing's 258—helped make Nets
the best reject team in NBA... A solid defensive position player
who'll bang... Turned in career-high 7.1 ppg... Drafted by Cavs
in fourth round in '87... Nets stole him for a pair of second-
rounders Feb. 21, 1990... Made $950,000... Born Feb. 22,
1965, in Stamford, Conn.... Grandfather was ambassador to
Denmark.

Year	Team	G	FG	FG Pct.	FT	FT Pct.	Reb.	Ast.	TP	Avg.
1987-88	Cleveland	55	65	.474	40	.563	144	23	170	3.1
1988-89	Cleveland	61	73	.435	39	.364	157	21	185	3.0
1989-90	Clev.-N.J.	64	146	.411	58	.319	423	39	350	5.5
1990-91	New Jersey	61	170	.408	94	.534	511	37	434	7.1
	Totals	241	454	.422	231	.431	1235	120	1139	4.7

TERRY MILLS 23 6-10 240

At least he met lots of people... Rookie
drafted by Milwaukee No. 16. Didn't sign...
Traded to Denver. Didn't resemble a human in
shape... Traded to Nets in Cadillac Anderson
deal Jan. 23. Didn't do much... Aside from
that, he had a fun time in his first year out of
Michigan... Showed flashes of rebounding
(11 boards vs. Lakers, Jan. 29) and passing
skills, but in 540 minutes he didn't exactly wow 'em in New
Jersey... Was never in shape, so he never did enough to be of
value... Made $600,000... Born Dec. 21, 1967, in Romulus,
Mich.

Year	Team	G	FG	FG Pct.	FT	FT Pct.	Reb.	Ast.	TP	Avg.
1990-91	Den.-N.J.	55	134	.465	47	.712	229	33	315	5.7

TATE GEORGE 23 6-5 190   Guard

No matter what he does, will always be known
for "The Shot" from college... Hit buzzer-
prayer in third NCAA round in '90 to lift his
UConn club to win over Clemson... Something to tell the grandkids. He won't want to
talk about his rookie shooting... Clanged for
.415... Nets took him No. 22 on first round
in '90 because of defensive rep... But lacks

quickness of a top-flight defender . . . Needs more time to develop skills . . . Born May 29, 1968, in Newark, N.J. . . . Paid $410,000.

Year	Team	G	FG	FG Pct.	FT	FT Pct.	Reb.	Ast.	TP	Avg.
1990-91	New Jersey	56	80	.415	32	.800	47	104	192	3.4

ROY HINSON 30 6-9 215   Forward

Return could require minor miracle . . . Has been counted out before, though . . . Played nine games, totaled 91 minutes . . . Began season on injured list for second straight year . . . Was recovering from February, 1990, right-knee arthroscope . . . Activated in January, made brief contribution and then needed another 'scope . . . Only 34 games in last two years for a guy once traded by Cavs to Sixers for a No. 1 pick (Brad Daugherty) . . . Came to Nets in trade involving Mike Gminski Jan. 16, 1988 . . . $1.25-million salary . . . Cavs drafted him from Rutgers No. 20 in '83 . . . Born May 2, 1961, in Trenton, N.J.

Year	Team	G	FG	FG Pct.	FT	FT Pct.	Reb.	Ast.	TP	Avg.
1983-84	Cleveland	80	184	.496	69	.590	499	69	437	5.5
1984-85	Cleveland	76	465	.503	271	.721	596	68	1201	15.8
1985-86	Cleveland	82	621	.532	364	.719	639	102	1606	19.6
1986-87	Philadelphia	76	393	.478	273	.758	488	60	1059	13.9
1987-88	Phil.-N.J.	77	453	.487	272	.775	517	99	1178	15.3
1988-89	New Jersey	82	495	.482	318	.757	522	71	1308	16.0
1989-90	New Jersey	25	145	.507	86	.869	172	22	376	15.0
1990-91	New Jersey	9	20	.513	1	.333	19	4	41	4.6
	Totals	507	2776	.499	1654	.741	3452	495	7206	14.2

JUD BUECHLER 23 6-6 220   Forward

Poor man's Dan Majerle . . . Real poor . . . Wrong-side-of-the-tracks poor . . . Okay, he's nowhere near Majerle but Nets hope he will be . . . No fear, won't back down, gives no hint of being intimidated . . . Shot .416 from the floor, .652 from the line . . . Real good team guy. Stands on head if asked . . . Can and will defend. Gets good position . . . Nice passer . . . Nets stole him in '90 from Sonics. Agreed not to draft Dennis Scott, who they didn't want to draft anyway. And they got Buechler's rights from Seattle, which grabbed him on second round from Arizona... Born June 19, 1968, in San Diego... Made $225,000.

Year	Team	G	FG	FG Pct.	FT	FT Pct.	Reb.	Ast.	TP	Avg.
1990-91	New Jersey......	74	94	.416	43	.652	141	51	232	3.1

JACK HALEY 27 6-10 240   Forward

All-Towel-Waving team... Cheerleader type with not many real athletic skills... Will hustle, bang, challenge anybody (gets into it with Charles Barkley once a season)... Strongest forte is rebounding... He averaged 4.6 in 154.1 minutes... Had a career-high 18 boards vs. Hornets on Dec. 10... Wife, Stacey, is a model/actress... Sister is press secretary for Barbara Bush... Has appeared in five national commercials and an Aerosmith music video... Made $360,000... Drafted by Bulls on fourth round out of UCLA in '87... Waived Dec. 18, 1989, and claimed by Nets two days later... Born Jan. 27, 1964, in Long Beach, Cal.

Year	Team	G	FG	FG Pct.	FT	FT Pct.	Reb.	Ast.	TP	Avg.
1988-89	Chicago	51	37	.474	36	.783	71	10	110	2.2
1989-90	Chi.-N.J.	67	138	.398	85	.680	300	26	361	5.4
1990-91	New Jersey......	78	161	.469	112	.619	356	31	434	5.6
	Totals	196	336	.438	233	.662	727	67	905	4.6

THE ROOKIES

KENNY ANDERSON 21 6-0 168   Guard

Many feel he'll be simply great... "An extraordinary talent," raved Hall of Famer Bob Cousy... Caused Nets major decision at No. 2: Anderson, who may need some time after leaving Georgia Tech after soph year, or Billy Owens, Syracuse stud who would have helped immediately... Nod went to 25.9 point-guard scorer with quickness and moves he hasn't used yet... Born Oct. 5, 1970, in Queens, N.Y.

VON McDADE 24 6-2 185   Guard

Next-to-last player drafted at No. 53... Magnificent shooter when he gets on a roll... Likened to Pistons' Vinnie Johnson... Averaged 28.8 at Wisconsin-Milwaukee as senior... Set or tied nine school records... Born June 7, 1967, in Milwaukee.

If Chris Morris gets court smarts to go with body, look out!

COACH BILL FITCH: Only looking for respectability, not the long haul here... Twenty-year veteran has compiled lifetime 805-835 (.491) record with four teams... Endured a typical Net season: lots of injuries (248 manpower games lost); lots of losses (56), lots of hope because of the lottery (Kenny Anderson)... Employed 17 lineups ... No-nonsense approach but nothing like hard-line rule adopted in former stops, like at Boston and Houston... Different team, different style... Two-time NBA Coach of the Year... Won NBA title in 1980-81 with Celts... Five division titles in all... Spent nine seasons with Cavs, four with Celts and five with Rockets... Two-year Nets' total is 43-121... Ranks fourth in all-time coaching wins with 805. Only Red Auerbach, Jack Ramsay and Dick Motta have more ... A good quote with a sense of humor... Born May 19, 1934, in Davenport, Ia.... Head coach at alma mater Coe (Iowa) College, North Dakota, Bowling Green and Minnesota... Earned master's degree in educational psychology at Creighton, where he was assistant basketball coach and head baseball coach.

GREATEST TEAM

This is a joke, right? A great season for the Nets? Well, boys and girls, once upon a time there was a zany place known as the ABA...

And in the ABA lived a man who forever changed the face of basketball, Julius Erving. Having led the Nets to the ABA title in 1973-74, Dr. J and the team said farewell to the league two years later, 1975-76, when they won 55 games, three off the franchise record, and went on to claim the final league championship. Erving was MVP of the regular season and the playoffs.

The Nets, minus Dr. J, who was sold to keep the franchise afloat, entered the NBA and things haven't been the same. There have been some high moments; unfortunately, there have been some high players, too, as drug problems plagued the organization in the late '80s. But the grandest, out-of-court, on-court moment came after a 45-victory season in 1983-84, when Buck Williams, Darryl Dawkins and Otis Birdsong led the Nets to a first-round upset of the defending champion 76ers, the only NBA playoff series victory in team history.

ALL-TIME NET LEADERS

SEASON

Points: Rick Barry, 2,518, 1971-72 (ABA)
Assists: Kevin Porter, 801, 1977-78
Rebounds: Billy Paultz, 1,035, 1971-72 (ABA)

GAME

Points: Julius Erving, 63 vs. San Diego (4 OT), 2/14/75 (ABA)
Assists: Kevin Porter, 29 vs. Houston, 2/24/78
Rebounds: Billy Paultz, 33 vs. Pittsburgh, 2/17/71 (ABA)

CAREER

Points: Buck Williams, 10,440, 1981-89
Assists: Billy Melchionni, 2,251, 1969-75 (ABA)
Rebounds: Buck Williams, 7,576, 1981-89

NEW YORK KNICKS

TEAM DIRECTORY: Pres.: David Checketts; VP-Player Personnel: Ernie Grunfeld; VP-Pub. Rel.: John Cirillo; Mgr. Media Rel.: Tim Donovan; Mgr. Publications and Inf.: Dennis D'Agostino; Dir. Scouting Services: Dick McGuire; Coach: Pat Riley; Asst. Coaches: Dick Harter, Paul Silas, Jeff Van Gundy. Arena: Madison Square Garden (19,081). Colors: Orange, white and blue.

(Editor's note: At press time, Patrick Ewing was still a Knick. Stay tuned.)

SCOUTING REPORT

SHOOTING: You look at the Knick shooting numbers: .485, tied for eighth in the league and fourth-best in the East. Seems like there's no problem. Wrong. See, you can come out to .485 by shooting .530 one night and .440 the next. Which is typical Knicks. A monument to inconsistency, the Knicks can look great one night, unworthy of a quick and painless execution the next.

The numbers among the regulars were fine: ranging from Charles Oakley's .516 and Patrick Ewing's .514 down to third guard Mark Jackson's .492. Then the dropoff was dramatic. Under Pat Riley, the pace should be decidedly upbeat and uptempo. The Knicks want athletes who can run. And freed from a halfcourt concept, Gerald Wilkins, the most athletically gifted Knick, should flourish, as he once did under Bob Hill and later Rick Pitino.

PLAYMAKING: A strange category for the Knicks. They ranked seventh in the league and fourth in the East for assists. And yet they're not an exceptionally gifted passing team.

The numbers rose through John MacLeod's use of the motion game. But that was a last-ditch effort because the Knicks were awful in everything else. Ewing's passing has come light years, but he must abandon his penchant to shoot first, second, third and fourth, then pass. Maurice Cheeks and Jackson are both superb passers at point guard—as is first-round draft pick Greg Anthony, who now creates a major logjam at the spot. Wilkins and Oakley can rack up impressive numbers—but both must improve their decisions. John Starks, slated for third guard, must stop telegraphing his passes.

DEFENSE: Riley has promised a return to the scrappy, pressing ways that made the Knicks a force three years ago. An inept

Will Patrick Ewing be a Knick when the season opens?

transition team, the Knicks at times played tough D—but too infrequently. Despite the middle presence of Ewing, the overall lack of quickness makes them highly vulnerable.

REBOUNDING: There were only two major board studs: Ewing and Oakley, the lone set of teammates in the top 10 boards last season. So what's the problem? After them, there's little.

Kiki Vandeweghe provides little inside work at small forward

KNICK ROSTER

No.	Veterans	Pos.	Ht.	Wt.	Age	Yrs. Pro	College
1	Maurice Cheeks	G	6-1	180	35	13	West Texas State
33	Patrick Ewing	C	7-0	240	29	6	Georgetown
13	Mark Jackson	G	6-3	205	26	4	St. John's
—	Anthony Mason	F	6-7	250	25	2	Tennessee State
32	Jerrod Mustaf	F	6-10	244	22	1	Maryland
34	Charles Oakley	F	6-9	245	27	6	Virginia Union
23	Brian Quinnett	F	6-8	236	25	2	Washington State
3	John Starks	G	6-5	180	26	2	Oklahoma State
6	Trent Tucker	G	6-5	190	31	9	Minnesota
55	Kiki Vandeweghe	F	6-8	220	33	11	UCLA
21	Gerald Wilkins	G	6-6	195	28	6	Tenn.-Chattanooga

Rd.	Rookies	Sel. No.	Pos.	Ht.	Wt.	College
1	Greg Anthony	12	G	6-0	190	Nevada-Las Vegas
2	Joe Wylie	38	F	6-9	210	Miami (Fla.)

and the backcourt doesn't always board with consistency. In short, the Knicks are basically a two-man rebound team. And their two best are flawed. Both Ewing and Oakley are apt to fire from 17 feet, leaving themselves out of offensive rebound position.

Thus, despite Ewing and Oakley's might, the Knicks were 19th on the offensive glass and 17th overall. They'll need help from the continually emerging Brian Quinnett and Jerrod Mustaf, both of whom gained some quality minutes under MacLeod last season.

OUTLOOK: Perhaps the most intriguing team in the league because of Riley and Ewing. They make the national story. But much depends on the rest of the team.

If they sacrifice, if they do the little necessary things, if they straighten up their locker-room act which reeks of bad chemistry, then the Knicks can be more than decent. But they didn't do it for Stu Jackson. Or MacLeod. So skepticism can be forgiven over claims they'll do it for Riley.

In Ewing, the Knicks have one of the game's three best centers, a guy capable of playing like No. 1 every night. Maybe he can get back into the team game he abandoned much of last year. The team needs remain: an inside scoring forward, backup center, perimeter shooting. Until those needs are met, Riley or no Riley, Ewing or no Ewing, the Knicks are no better than a second-round playoff team.

KNICK PROFILES

PATRICK EWING 29 7-0 240   Center

In cause celebre, he rejected six-year contract extension, went to arbitration and lost... So unless traded, he will make do with remaining four years of present contract totaling $14.2 million... Second-team All-NBA: 26.6 ppg, career-best 11.2 rpg. And his season was a downer... Far too much offensive burden... First option in crunch time. Failed more times than not... Teammates rapped him anonymously for taking too many shots. He rapped teammates for anonymously rapping him ... Great season by human standards... First Knick ever to post two 2,000-point seasons. Did it consecutively... After enduring so much losing in early years, then tasting success, he was bummed by team relapse... Enjoyed John MacLeod's motion offense as much as a root canal... Reverted to jump-shooting ways late in season... Bombed in playoffs... When he's pumped, no center can stop him one-on-one... Born Aug. 5, 1962, in Kingston, Jamaica... Fabled career at Georgetown. Object of first-ever draft lottery, grabbed No. 1 in '85.

Year	Team	G	FG	FG Pct.	FT	FT Pct.	Reb.	Ast.	TP	Avg.
1985-86	New York	50	386	.474	226	.739	451	102	998	20.0
1986-87	New York	63	530	.503	296	.713	555	104	1356	21.5
1987-88	New York	82	656	.555	341	.716	676	125	1653	20.2
1988-89	New York	80	727	.567	361	.746	740	188	1815	22.7
1989-90	New York	82	922	.551	502	.775	893	182	2347	28.6
1990-91	New York	81	845	.514	464	.745	905	244	2154	26.6
	Totals	438	4066	.532	2190	.742	4220	945	10323	23.6

MAURICE CHEEKS 35 6-1 180   Guard

Probably wonders how he ticked off the Almighty to land in Knick situation of past two years... Typical New York sports discussion: "Start Mo. Start Mark. Trade Mo. Trade Mark. Shoot 'em both." ... Thoroughly professional in often zoo-like atmosphere... Not the Mo of six years ago, but still a competent, smart point guard... Wore down from too many minutes ... Nagging injuries taking toll... All-time NBA steals leader... Asked to shoot more and take bigger offensive role. Uncomfortable spot for career set-up guy . . . As usual, raised game in playoffs . . . Took exception to Patrick Ewing's beef about not getting ball enough in Game 1 of first round . . . Total team guy . . . Endures media. Prefers they'd collectively fall off a cliff . . . Chatty as a peach pit . . . Member of '83 champ Sixers . . . Born Sept. 8, 1956, in Chicago . . . Second-round pick by Philly out of West Texas State . . . Traded for Rod Strickland from Spurs Feb. 21, 1990 . . . Paid $1 million, promised more.

Year	Team	G	FG	FG Pct.	FT	FT Pct.	Reb.	Ast.	TP	Avg.
1978-79	Philadelphia	82	292	.510	101	.721	254	431	685	8.4
1979-80	Philadelphia	79	357	.540	180	.779	274	556	898	11.4
1980-81	Philadelphia	81	310	.534	140	.787	245	560	763	9.4
1981-82	Philadelphia	79	352	.521	171	.777	248	667	881	11.2
1982-83	Philadelphia	79	404	.542	181	.754	209	543	990	12.5
1983-84	Philadelphia	75	386	.550	170	.733	205	478	950	12.7
1984-85	Philadelphia	78	422	.570	175	.879	217	497	1025	13.1
1985-86	Philadelphia	82	490	.537	282	.842	235	753	1266	15.4
1986-87	Philadelphia	68	415	.527	227	.777	215	538	1061	15.6
1987-88	Philadelphia	79	428	.495	227	.825	253	635	1086	13.7
1988-89	Philadelphia	71	336	.483	151	.774	183	554	824	11.6
1989-90	S.A.-N.Y.	81	307	.504	171	.847	240	453	789	9.7
1990-91	New York	76	241	.499	105	.814	173	435	592	7.8
	Totals	1010	4740	.525	2281	.795	2951	7100	11810	11.7

CHARLES OAKLEY 27 6-9 245　　　　Forward

Just rebound, Charles . . . Was third in NBA rebounding at 12.1 per . . . Wants bigger hand in the offense . . . Knicks want same but his only legit offensive skill is often erratic outside jumper . . . Lack of post offense for his size is baffling . . . Good, tough defender, especially in post . . . Dives and hustles for loose balls, a rarity on Knicks . . . Could be an even better boarder if he worked on positioning, instead of merely using strength . . . Tries quarterback outlet passes, but throws a lot of incompletions and interceptions . . . A big plus despite minuses . . . Hard worker . . . Disappeared offensively in playoffs (7.7 ppg) . . . Can follow up 18-point, 16-rebound night with two-point, four-rebound effort . . . Injuries hit last two seasons. Bothered by sore knee in 1990-91 . . . Underpaid at $1.05 million, sorest spot with him . . . Born Dec. 18, 1963, in Cleveland . . . Drafted by Cavs No. 9 in 1985, out of Virginia Union . . . Cavs then did incredibly dumb thing: traded him to Bulls for Keith Lee . . . Came to New York for Bill Cartwright in '88.

Year	Team	G	FG	FG Pct.	FT	FT Pct.	Reb.	Ast.	TP	Avg.
1985-86	Chicago	77	281	.519	178	.662	664	133	740	9.6
1986-87	Chicago	82	468	.445	245	.686	1074	296	1192	14.5
1987-88	Chicago	82	375	.483	261	.727	1066	248	1014	12.4
1988-89	New York	82	426	.510	197	.773	861	187	1061	12.9
1989-90	New York	61	336	.524	217	.761	727	146	889	14.6
1990-91	New York	76	307	.516	239	.784	920	204	853	11.2
	Totals	460	2193	.494	1337	.731	5312	1214	5749	12.5

KIKI VANDEWEGHE 33 6-8 220   Forward

Great comeback year few noticed . . . After 2½ years of basic inactivity, averaged 16.3 points and shot .494 . . . Team's leading scorer in playoff sweep by Bulls. With Knicks, that was as impressive as being Iraq's best general . . . Massive hands, still owns explosive first step for drive and dunk . . . Not what it once was, though . . . Effective range on jumper. Always was a pure shooter . . . Staggeringly efficient from line: .899 last season, .873 career . . . Age and chronic back woes have taken toll . . . Strange trait of dominating first halves, then disappearing. Example: scored 25 by halftime against T-Wolves, finished with 26 points . . . Dad a former Knick . . . Mom a former Miss America . . . Sister a former Olympic swimmer . . . He's a former All-Star . . . UCLA bred, No. 11 pick by Mavs in 1980. Didn't sign, traded to Denver . . . Laid-back Californian . . . Real name Ernest Maurice . . . Born Aug. 1, 1958, in Weisbaden, Germany . . . Obtained from Blazers for 1989 first-rounder . . . Made $1.025 million.

Year	Team	G	FG	FG Pct.	FT	FT Pct.	Reb.	Ast.	TP	Avg.
1980-81	Denver	51	229	.426	130	.818	270	94	588	11.5
1981-82	Denver	82	706	.560	347	.857	461	247	1760	21.5
1982-83	Denver	82	841	.547	489	.875	437	203	2186	26.7
1983-84	Denver	78	895	.558	494	.852	373	238	2295	29.4
1984-85	Portland	72	618	.534	369	.896	228	106	1616	22.4
1985-86	Portland	79	719	.540	523	.869	216	187	1962	24.8
1986-87	Portland	79	808	.523	467	.886	251	220	2122	26.9
1987-88	Portland	37	283	.508	159	.878	109	71	747	20.2
1988-89	Port.-N.Y.	45	200	.469	80	.899	71	69	499	11.1
1989-90	New York	22	102	.442	44	.917	53	41	258	11.7
1990-91	New York	75	458	.494	259	.899	180	110	1226	16.3
	Totals	702	5859	.527	3361	.873	2649	1586	15259	21.7

GERALD WILKINS 28 6-6 195   Guard

Biggest threat to Pat Riley's fashion statements . . . Downright likeable, quotable guy . . . Had the injury of the year: bruised thigh when he stomped foot laughing on charter flight . . . Suffered severe ankle sprain several games later. No laughing matter. Thus, played career-low 68 games . . . Yeah, he's Dominique's little brother, a label he has fought his whole life to lose . . . Incredible quickness, the one Knick who can break down a defense and blow past defender . . . Perimeter shot always an iffy proposition . . . Can get out of control and make decisions that warrant firing squad . . . Was the only Knick to win an NBA "Player of Week" honor in 1990-91 . . . Career-best .820 from foul line . . . Can bring points in bunches. Can bring turnovers in bunches . . . Underrated defender . . . Great curl-in move that has been underutilized . . . Earned $725,000 . . . Born Sept. 11, 1963, in Atlanta . . . Second-round steal in '85 out of Tennessee-Chattanooga.

Year	Team	G	FG	FG Pct.	FT	FT Pct.	Reb.	Ast.	TP	Avg.
1985-86	New York	81	437	.468	132	.557	208	161	1013	12.5
1986-87	New York	80	633	.486	235	.701	294	354	1527	19.1
1987-88	New York	81	591	.446	191	.786	270	326	1412	17.4
1988-89	New York	81	462	.451	186	.756	244	274	1161	14.3
1989-90	New York	82	472	.457	208	.803	371	330	1191	14.5
1990-91	New York	68	380	.473	169	.820	207	275	938	13.8
	Totals	473	2975	.463	1121	.735	1594	1720	7242	15.3

MARK JACKSON 26 6-3 205   Guard

Knicks tried to trade him, but made him as marketable as a virus . . . Starter, reserve, starter, reserve, suspended, benched . . . Ironically, his two-game suspension for "conduct detrimental to the best interest of the team" (he complained about playing time) and subsequent benching that included eight DNPs in 14 games, coincided with Knicks' best surge of season . . . Has lots of talent, but tends to say wrong thing at worst time . . . His $1.8-million salary halted several trades . . . Over 800 minutes less than previous year . . . Turned in 36-minute triple-double vs. Pacers March 28 . . . The guy has an NBA life; question is where . . . Tremendous leadership qualities . . . Feeds team with his own emotion. Thrives on crowd . . . Won back fickle Garden crowd . . .

Outside shot questionable, but is superb penetrator and easily team's best passer... Awful one-on-one defender. Decent in up-tempo team scheme... Born April 1, 1965, in Brooklyn, N.Y.... St. John's grad picked 18th in '87... Was 1987-88 Rookie of the Year.

Year	Team	G	FG	FG Pct.	FT	FT Pct.	Reb.	Ast.	TP	Avg.
1987-88	New York	82	438	.432	206	.774	396	868	1114	13.6
1988-89	New York	72	479	.467	180	.698	341	619	1219	16.9
1989-90	New York	82	327	.437	120	.727	318	604	809	9.9
1990-91	New York	72	250	.492	117	.731	197	452	630	8.8
	Totals	308	1494	.453	623	.734	1252	2543	3772	12.2

JERROD MUSTAF 22 6-10 244   Forward

Part of John MacLeod's Knick legacy. In his brief stint, he insisted on playing the rookie from Maryland... Nice face-up skills and strong post moves... He was the second-youngest player in NBA. Left Maryland after sophomore season... Knicks projected him as a high lottery pick in two years, so grabbed him at 17... Typical rookie learning experiences. In first start, he was paired against Dominique Wilkins... Six minutes, three fouls and 11 'Nique points later, he was learning from bench... Really came on after he complained on Western trip about playing time and MacLeod read riot act rapping his attitude and work habits. Rookie took off from there, slowed only by bad tendinitis problem in knee... Backs up center and power forward... Born Oct. 28, 1969, in Whiteville, N.C... Paid $565,000.

Year	Team	G	FG	FG Pct.	FT	FT Pct.	Reb.	Ast.	TP	Avg.
1990-91	New York	62	106	.465	56	.644	169	36	268	4.3

BRIAN QUINNETT 25 6-8 236   Forward

Dare you to find a more honest, decent guy... And guess what? He really can play... Began to blossom in some areas in second year, which for all intents was his rookie season... Played just 193 minutes as a rookie in 1989-90 after Knicks made him second-round pick from Washington State... Can shoot, run floor, rebound and defend... Did all those things in practice. In games, it was another story... Confidence level was below basement... Turning point came in his first pro start—

Jan. 19 in Philly. He hit first two shots . . . Good range on jumper . . . Kiki Vandeweghe raves about his shooting prowess . . . Born May 30, 1966, in Cheney, Wash . . . Re-upped for $360,000.

Year	Team	G	FG	FG Pct.	FT	FT Pct.	Reb.	Ast.	TP	Avg.
1989-90	New York	31	19	.328	2	.667	28	11	40	1.3
1990-91	New York	68	139	.459	26	.722	145	53	319	4.7
	Totals	99	158	.438	28	.718	173	64	359	3.6

JOHN STARKS 26 6-5 180   Guard

Just a nice find . . . Signed as a free agent in October, presumably as training-camp fodder . . . Emerged as, in John MacLeod's favorite words, "a tiger" . . . Instant energy infusion . . . Played both guard spots . . . Needs work on ball-handling to play point, needs work on perimeter shot to play off guard . . . Tenacious defender and a good finisher the other way . . . Not talking all-star here, just a pleasant find for the bench . . . Problem was Knicks often called upon him to start (10 games) or play starter's minutes . . . Sometimes, questionable selection on perimeter shots and sometimes tries to do too much . . . Four colleges in four years raised some eyebrows . . . Last was at Oklahoma State, 1988 . . . Undrafted, originally signed as free agent with Warriors in 1988 . . . Did the CBA bit . . . Born Aug. 10, 1965, in Tulsa, Okla . . . Got the $120,000 minimum wage.

Year	Team	G	FG	FG Pct.	FT	FT Pct.	Reb.	Ast.	TP	Avg.
1988-89	Golden State	36	51	.408	34	.654	41	27	146	4.1
1990-91	New York	61	180	.439	79	.752	131	204	466	7.6
	Totals	97	231	.432	113	.720	172	231	612	6.3

TRENT TUCKER 31 6-5 190   Guard

Dial 1-800-TRENT-4-3 . . . Incredible last-moment heroics with three-point shots continued for the seventh player to reach 500 trifectas, making him one of NBA's all-time leaders (504-of-1,231, .409) . . . Nailed trey with :00.2 on clock to beat Bullets Feb. 23 . . . Four games later, hit one off-balance at buzzer to beat Pistons on road . . . In two other games, three-pointers sealed win in last minute . . . With 634 steals, ranked third on all-time Knick list behind Micheal Ray Richardson (810) and

Ray Williams (750) . . . Good, intelligent player. May be Knicks' best one-on-one defender . . . Always a cautious, low-risk player. Thus, low turnover rates . . . Only shot 27 free throws in 1,194 minutes . . . Team's elder statesman. Knicks made him sixth pick in '82 draft out of Minnesota . . . Real name Kelvin . . . Born Dec. 20, 1959, in Tarboro, N.C., but reared in Flint, Michigan . . . Made $835,000.

Year	Team	G	FG	FG Pct.	FT	FT Pct.	Reb.	Ast.	TP	Avg.
1982-83	New York	78	299	.462	43	.672	216	195	655	8.4
1983-84	New York	63	225	.500	25	.758	130	138	481	7.6
1984-85	New York	77	293	.483	38	.792	188	199	653	8.5
1985-86	New York	77	349	.472	79	.790	169	192	818	10.6
1986-87	New York	70	325	.470	77	.762	135	166	795	11.4
1987-88	New York	71	193	.424	51	.718	119	117	506	7.1
1988-89	New York	81	263	.454	43	.782	176	132	687	8.5
1989-90	New York	81	253	.417	66	.767	174	173	667	8.2
1990-91	New York	65	191	.440	17	.630	105	111	463	7.1
	Totals	663	2391	.459	439	.750	1412	1423	5725	8.6

ANTHONY MASON 25 6-7 250   Forward

Signed after impressive summer-league showing . . . Built like a brickhouse . . . Strong rebounder with good post-up skills . . . Didn't play ball until junior year of high school . . . Was small forward throughout college years at Tennessee State . . . Bulked up to power-forward size . . . Was third-round draft pick by Portland in 1988 . . . Played in Turkey in 1988-89 . . . Had cameos with New Jersey and Denver . . . Bounced around CBA . . . Born Dec. 14, 1966, in Miami . . . Grew up in Queens, N.Y. . . . Signed to one-year minimum ($120,000) contract.

Year	Team	G	FG	FG Pct.	FT	FT Pct.	Reb.	Ast.	TP	Avg.
1989-90	New Jersey	21	14	.350	9	.600	34	7	37	1.8
1990-91	Denver	3	2	.500	6	.750	5	0	10	3.3
	Totals	24	16	.364	15	.652	39	7	47	2.0

THE ROOKIES

GREG ANTHONY 23 6-0 190   Guard
UNLV team leader is third point guard drafted by Knicks in five years . . . Extremely intelligent. Interned at World Economic Sum-

mit in Houston; started own T-shirt business, grossing $400,000 in one year; ambition is to be a U.S. Senator . . . Steady, no-flash team player . . . Compared to his idol, Maurice Cheeks . . . Born Nov. 15, 1967, in Las Vegas . . . Taken at No. 12.

JOE WYLIE 23 6-9 210   **Forward**
Miami product was 38th selection, by Clippers, then was traded to Knicks for 1993 second-round draft choice . . . Led Hurricanes in scoring and rebounding for second consecutive year . . . Averaged 18.4 ppg as junior and senior . . . Also blocked-shot specialist . . . Heat's Stu Inman said, "People see him in (Dennis) Rodman terms as a big-time jumper and runner, quick on offense, more of a scorer than shooter." . . . Voted to NCAA Independent All-America team . . . Born Feb. 10, 1968, in Washington, D.C.

COACH PAT RILEY: Knicks sought marquee name. Who's bigger? . . . Named sixth Knick coach in seven seasons on May 31 . . . Had all the leverage: team needed and wanted him. And he knew it . . . Thus, five-year contract worth $1.2-million per in salary, $1.5-million per with perks . . . Exactly what Knicks need, not only as a draw, but to straighten out the knuckleheads . . . Known for intense practices plus psychological approach. May need to enlist Freud with this bunch . . . All-time best winning percentage of .733 figures to take a dip for a while . . . His .685 playoff percentage, in 149 games, ranks second only to Phil Jackson, who took over first last June with just 33 games . . . Has created most excitement around New York basketball circles since the Ewing lottery victory . . . Coached Lakers to four NBA titles in nine seasons, including back-to-back jobs in 1987 and '88 after he "guaranteed" repeat . . . Opposing coaches praise his preparation . . . Question of why he'd risk legendary image to rebuild group of underachievers may provide his biggest motivation . . . First-round pick by San Diego in 1967, out of Kentucky . . . Nine-year playing career included 5½ seasons with Lakers . . . Had 7.4 career scoring average . . . Stock in Armani suits went off the NYSE board . . . Born March 20, 1945, in Rome, N.Y.

GREATEST TEAM

The greatest Knicks' season ended, for all intents, about two hours before the completion of the final game.

That was when captain Willis Reed, his leg heavily braced after a Game 5 fall, limped to the court at Madison Square Garden for the seventh game of the 1969-70 NBA Finals.

"I looked at the Lakers and their faces dropped. In my mind, they were defeated," said Dave DeBusschere.

If not, then they were when Reed, the regular-season and All-Star Game MVP, hit his first two shots for his only points. The Knicks scored a 113-99 victory, completing a near-mythical stretch during which the Jets and Mets also brought world titles to New York.

Reed was the top scorer and rebounder for a team that preached and practiced intelligent, unselfish basketball. Reed played up front between Bill Bradley, in his pre-U.S. Senator days, and DeBusschere.

At guard were the lord of cool, Walt "Clyde" Frazier, a master thief who was second in the NBA in assists, plus shooter Dick Barnett. The Knicks set team records with 60 victories, 18 consecutively. For all their offense, the trademark of Red Holzman's Knicks was defense—they allowed only 105.9 ppg, nearly six full points less than second-place L.A.

ALL-TIME KNICK LEADERS

SEASON

Points: Patrick Ewing, 2,347, 1989-90
Assists: Mark Jackson, 868, 1987-88
Rebounds: Willis Reed, 1,191, 1968-69

GAME

Points: Bernard King, 60 vs. New Jersey, 12/25/85
Assists: Richie Guerin, 21 vs. St. Louis, 12/12/58
Rebounds: Harry Gallatin, 33 vs. Ft. Wayne, 3/15/53
Willis Reed, 33 vs. Cincinnati, 2/2/71

CAREER

Points: Walt Frazier, 14,617, 1967-77
Assists: Walt Frazier, 4,791, 1967-77
Rebounds: Willis Reed, 8,414, 1964-74

ORLANDO MAGIC

TEAM DIRECTORY: General Partner: William duPont III; Pres./ GM: Pat Williams; Dir. Scouting: John Gabriel; Dir. Publicity/ Media Rel.: Alex Martins; Coach: Matt Guokas; Asst. Coaches: John Gabriel, Brian Hill, George Scholz. Arena: Orlando Arena (15,077). Colors: Electric blue, quick silver and magic black.

SCOUTING REPORT

SHOOTING: In the Magic's 64th game last season, Dennis Scott hoisted 33 shots and missed 25, seven from three-point range. "They all felt good," he claimed. Feeling good and being good tend to be different things. So as a second-year team, the Magic overall felt good about their .455 shooting. But it wasn't good. Not when it placed them 23rd.

One reason for offensive failure was the lack of a substantial inside game. The often-moody Terry Catledge and the offensively-poor Greg Kite are not keys to offensive happiness. So Orlando has bulked up with draftees Brian Williams and Stanley Roberts, he of the nearly 300-pound girth, in hopes of establishing something inside. Roberts is an intriguing rookie. An offensive force in his year at LSU before going to Spain, he was considered a lottery pick with his scoring skills. But his rapid weight gain dropped him to No. 23. He might help.

PLAYMAKING: Orlando has a good one in Scott Skiles, voted the NBA's Most Improved Player last season. A superb penetrator with an uncanny knack for finding the open man, Skiles set a league record with 30 assists in one game. But after him, well, Orlando would have trouble passing the ball in a fire-bucket brigade line. Their sub-standard shooting played a big part, but only the Nets accounted for fewer assists than the Magic's 1,809.

DEFENSE: For a second-year team, the Magic made big strides, knocking nearly eight points off their defense yield. But with an up-tempo attack and the "expansion" word still echoing, the Magic are still a very bottom-rung defensive combine. They're counting on rookie Williams for inside muscle and defensive rebounding.

Scott Skiles proved himself as Most Improved Player.

REBOUNDING: The Magic proved to be a surprisingly efficient rebounding team: they tied for 13th in offensive boarding, were eighth in defensive rebounding and thus placed ninth overall.

While Jeff Turner did a complementary job at power forward, he has neither the size nor strength to handle the position on a nightly basis. That's why the Magic were so enchanted with Williams, Arizona's 6-9 early-entry stud. The Magic are a rebound-by-committee team: 10 players managed 235 boards or more.

OUTLOOK: Could be worse. Matty Guokas' gang made major strides in just its second year and figures to improve on the record with a move into the weak Atlantic Division. There is some quality youth developing but the downside is youthful mistakes (like Scott's bombs-away approach—whether it's a good shot or not, it's still a shot). There'll be some overall harnessing and some third-year team growth. Last season, the Magic ended the second half with the ninth-best record in the West. They could conceivably

MAGIC ROSTER

No.	Veterans	Pos.	Ht.	Wt.	Age	Yrs. Pro	College
42	Mark Acres	F-C	6-11	225	28	4	Oral Roberts
25	Nick Anderson	F-G	6-6	205	22	2	Illinois
33	Terry Catledge	F	6-8	230	28	6	South Alabama
34	Greg Kite	C	6-11	260	30	8	Brigham Young
35	Jerry Reynolds	F-G	6-8	206	28	6	Louisiana State
3	Dennis Scott	G-F	6-8	229	23	1	Georgia Tech
4	Scott Skiles	G	6-1	180	27	5	Michigan State
32	Otis Smith	G-F	6-5	210	27	5	Jacksonville
31	Jeff Turner	F	6-9	240	29	5	Vanderbilt
11	Sam Vincent	G	6-2	185	28	6	Michigan State
20	Morlon Wiley	G	6-4	192	25	3	Long Beach State

Rd.	Rookies	Sel. No.	Pos.	Ht.	Wt.	College
1	Brian Williams	10	F	6-9	240	Arizona
1	Stanley Roberts	23	C	7-0	285	Louisiana State
2	Chris Corchiani	36	G	5-11	186	North Carolina State

finish ahead of one of the Atlantic also-rans, the Nets or Bullets, as well as the Heat, with a similar effort.

MAGIC PROFILES

SCOTT SKILES 27 6-1 180   Guard

Whopping improvement—on the court and in the wallet . . . In season that included an NBA all-time single-game high of 30 assists (vs. Denver, Dec. 30), former Michigan State star was voted by media as NBA's Most Improved Player, edging Boston's Kevin Gamble and Houston's Kenny Smith . . . And his bank account grew. Started season as $400,000 player. Signed four-year deal worth $7.2 million . . . The 30 assists broke 12-year-old record held by Kevin Porter . . . Played 48 minutes nine times . . . Fiery, competitive type. Would slit your throat to win a Scrabble game . . . Great ball-handler, unquestioned team leader . . . Defense leaves much to be desired against the jet-pack point guards . . . His 17.2 ppg more than doubled his previous high (7.7) . . . Tenth in NBA in assists (8.4) . . . Was selected No. 22 by Bucks in '86 . . . After injury-plagued stint in Indiana, he came to Orlando in '89 expansion draft... Born March 5, 1964, in LaPorte, Ind.

Year	Team	G	FG	FG Pct.	FT	FT Pct.	Reb.	Ast.	TP	Avg.
1986-87	Milwaukee	13	18	.290	10	.833	26	45	49	3.8
1987-88	Indiana.........	51	86	.411	45	.833	66	180	223	4.4
1988-89	Indiana.	80	198	.448	130	.903	149	390	546	6.8
1989-90	Orlando	70	190	.409	104	.874	159	334	536	7.7
1990-91	Orlando	79	462	.445	340	.902	270	660	1357	17.2
	Totals	293	954	.431	629	.891	670	1609	2711	9.3

DENNIS SCOTT 23 6-8 229   Guard-Forward

Tremendous range, although clanged his three-point attempts from the Canadian Pavillion at Epcot Center... The Lethal Weapon from Georgia Tech gave a foreshadowing in his first NBA game. He knocked down his first two three-point attempts—then missed next three—at Atlanta Nov. 2... Could use some discretion. Like in his 8-of-33 shooting horror (including 0-of-7 on treys) on March 18 vs. Sixers... Wound up taking 334 trifectas, hitting 125 (.375). No one in East attempted more... Made at least one trey in 62 games... Needs lots of work rebounding. Awful off the boards. Averaged 2.9 but had just 62 offensive boards in 82 games, including 73 starts... His 15.7 ppg was third-best among rookies... College Player of the Year as a senior... Magic tabbed him at No. 4 and paid him $1.56 million... Born Sept. 5, 1968, in Hagerstown, Md.

Year	Team	G	FG	FG Pct.	FT	FT Pct.	Reb.	Ast.	TP	Avg.
1990-91	Orlando	82	503	.425	153	.750	235	134	1284	15.7

GREG KITE 30 6-11 260   Center

Emergency-room regular... Staggering array of cuts, bumps and bruises: 23 stitches resulting from six facial cuts, bruised larynx, torn right-hand ligament, dislocated finger and broken nose... Yet he started every game... Best statistical season of eight-year career... Rugged, hard-working sort with a game that's as pretty as an oil slick... Physical defense, invisible offense... Knows he has six fouls to give every night... Scored in double figures just eight times in 82 games... Selected 21st by Celtics out of Brigham Young in '83 and proceeded to make four trips to NBA Finals, winning title rings in '84 and '86...

Stops with the Clippers, Hornets and Kings before Magic signed him as free agent Aug. 14, 1990.

Year	Team	G	FG	FG Pct.	FT	FT Pct.	Reb.	Ast.	TP	Avg.
1983-84	Boston	35	30	.455	5	.313	62	7	65	1.9
1984-85	Boston	55	33	.375	22	.688	89	17	88	1.6
1985-86	Boston	64	34	.374	15	.385	128	17	83	1.3
1986-87	Boston	74	47	.427	29	.382	169	27	123	1.7
1987-88	Bos.-LAC	53	92	.449	40	.506	264	47	224	4.2
1988-89	LAC-Char.	70	65	.430	20	.488	243	36	150	2.1
1989-90	Sacramento	71	101	.432	27	.500	377	76	230	3.2
1990-91	Orlando	82	166	.491	63	.512	588	59	395	4.8
	Totals	504	568	.443	221	.480	1920	286	1358	2.7

JERRY REYNOLDS 28 6-8 206   Forward-Guard

Six years and still some rookie mistakes... That's why a guy with lots of tools hasn't blossomed... That and a .425 lifetime shooting mark... Absolutely wonderful finisher, good open-floor player... But can look so bad with his decisions... Reluctant to pass... Gets caught in bad spots... And turnover-prone. Over 2.1 a night in 23 minutes per... Bad outside shooter, yet he insists on taking the shots... Deceptively good defender who impresses off the defensive boards... If he gets it all together, could be major asset and halt the bouncing around (three teams in last four seasons)... Bucks picked him at No. 22 in '85 out of LSU as hardship... Born Dec. 23, 1962, in Bronx, N.Y.... Paid $450,000.

Year	Team	G	FG	FG Pct.	FT	FT Pct.	Reb.	Ast.	TP	Avg.
1985-86	Milwaukee	55	72	.444	58	.558	80	86	203	3.7
1986-87	Milwaukee	58	140	.393	118	.641	173	106	404	7.0
1987-88	Milwaukee	62	188	.449	119	.773	160	104	498	8.0
1988-89	Seattle	56	149	.417	127	.760	100	62	428	7.6
1989-90	Orlando	67	309	.417	239	.742	323	180	858	12.8
1990-91	Orlando	80	344	.434	336	.802	299	203	1034	12.9
	Totals	378	1202	.425	997	.739	1135	741	3425	9.1

TERRY CATLEDGE 28 6-8 230   Forward

C'mon Terry, play hard tonight. Please! ... Needs to be motivated constantly... One of the reasons Bullets let him go in the '89 expansion draft... Very moody, often selfish. Maybe a Louisville Slugger to the skull would help... Irritating part is he can be so darn effective when playing hard and motivated. And what motivates him is scoring... He averaged

14.6 points (Magic's third-highest)—but was benched 19 games, injured 12 others . . . Can be almost comatose on defense . . . Good offensive rebounder, bad on defensive glass . . . Passing non-existent . . . Sixers took South Alabama product No. 21 in '85 . . . Born Aug. 22, 1963, in Houston, Miss. . . . Made $1.085 million.

Year	Team	G	FG	FG Pct.	FT	FT Pct.	Reb.	Ast.	TP	Avg.
1985-86	Philadelphia	64	202	.469	90	.647	272	21	494	7.7
1986-87	Washington.	78	413	.495	199	.594	560	56	1025	13.1
1987-88	Washington.	70	296	.506	154	.655	397	63	746	10.7
1988-89	Washington.	79	334	.490	153	.602	572	75	822	10.4
1989-90	Orlando	74	546	.474	341	.702	563	72	1435	19.4
1990-91	Orlando	51	292	.462	161	.624	355	58	745	14.6
	Totals	416	2083	.483	1098	.643	2719	345	5267	12.7

NICK ANDERSON 22 6-6 205   Forward-Guard

Young A.D. under construction? . . . Second-year swingman developing into fine post-up player, taking opposing off-guards one-on-one, much like Adrian Dantley . . . Has to because the outside shot isn't there . . . Magnificent upper-body strength . . . Needs help getting off his shot . . . Needs work on ball-handling and defense . . . Struggled to learn team concepts . . . But decent instincts (74 steals, 44 blocks) indicate a foundation to build upon . . . Was first collegiate pick in Magic history . . . Taken No. 11 in '89 as hardship out of Illinois . . . Born Jan. 20, 1968, in Chicago . . . Paid $725,000.

Year	Team	G	FG	FG Pct.	FT	FT Pct.	Reb.	Ast.	TP	Avg.
1989-90	Orlando	81	372	.494	186	.705	316	124	931	11.5
1990-91	Orlando	70	400	.467	173	.668	386	106	990	14.1
	Totals	151	772	.480	359	.686	702	230	1921	12.7

MARK ACRES 28 6-11 225   Forward-Center

Vanilla ice cream . . . Steady, rarely makes mistakes, but rarely lifts you out of your seat . . . Ability to leap over a turnip with an updraft . . . No discernible natural skills . . . Gives what he's got and is grateful for the playing time . . . Had seven games with double-figure points in 68 outings . . . Typical backup-center numbers: 4.2 points, better-than-average 5.3 rebounds . . . Only four other backup centers in NBA had more than his 359 rebounds . . . Double-figure rebounds eight times . . . Came out of

Oral Roberts in '85 and was drafted on second round by Mavs
... Played two years in Belgium and signed with Celtics as a free
agent... Came to Orlando in expansion draft... Born Nov. 15,
1962, in Inglewood, Cal.... Made $437,000.

Year	Team	G	FG	FG Pct.	FT	FT Pct.	Reb.	Ast.	TP	Avg.
1987-88	Boston	79	108	.532	71	.640	270	42	287	3.6
1988-89	Boston	62	55	.482	26	.542	146	19	137	2.2
1989-90	Orlando	80	138	.484	83	.692	431	67	362	4.5
1990-91	Orlando	68	109	.509	66	.653	359	25	285	4.2
	Totals	289	410	.502	246	.647	1206	153	1071	3.7

JEFF TURNER 29 6-9 240   Forward

Think he'd still make Bobby Knight's Olympic
team over Charles Barkley?... Rescued career
from garbage dump and has been pleasant surprise for Magic, who signed him as free agent
in July 1989, after a two-year tour in Europe
... Started final 40 games and averaged 11.2
points and 6.0 rebounds to finish with career
highs in each category... A perimeter player
who was surprisingly effective on the defensive glass... Too slow
to guard small forwards, not brutish enough to handle power forwards... But a decent, unselfish do-what-he's-told performer...
Was a first-round pick of Nets in '84 from Vanderbilt... Made
$410,000... Born in Bangor, Maine, April 9, 1962.

Year	Team	G	FG	FG Pct.	FT	FT Pct.	Reb.	Ast.	TP	Avg.
1984-85	New Jersey	72	171	.454	79	.859	218	108	421	5.8
1985-86	New Jersey	53	84	.491	58	.744	137	14	226	4.3
1986-87	New Jersey	76	151	.465	76	.731	197	60	378	5.0
1989-90	Orlando	60	132	.429	42	.778	227	53	308	5.1
1990-91	Orlando	71	259	.487	85	.759	363	97	609	8.6
	Totals	332	797	.465	340	.773	1142	332	1942	5.8

SAM VINCENT 28 6-2 185   Guard

Another identity-crisis case. Shooting guard in
point guard's body... Fourth NBA city in six
seasons... Rap of inconsistency has followed
him, especially on defense. Doesn't put body
on anyone... Put up decent numbers as a
starter: 12.6 points, 5.2 assists in 30.2 minutes
for 17 games... Brother of well-travelled Jay
Vincent... Developing as solid backup. But

another identity crisis: drawing a starter's salary. Made $980,000 last season as part of three-year, $2.5-million deal signed in 1989-90 . . . A good open-perimeter shooter and good penetrator who could be better . . . Had first triple-double in Magic history Jan. 30, 1990 . . . Born May 18, 1963, in Lansing, Mich. . . . Celtics picked him 20th out of Michigan State in '85 . . . Magic took him in expansion draft from Bulls.

Year	Team	G	FG	FG Pct.	FT	FT Pct.	Reb.	Ast.	TP	Avg.
1985-86	Boston	57	59	.364	65	.929	48	69	184	3.2
1986-87	Boston	46	60	.441	51	.927	27	59	171	3.7
1987-88	Sea.-Chi.	72	210	.456	145	.868	152	381	573	8.0
1988-89	Chicago	70	274	.484	106	.822	190	335	656	9.4
1989-90	Orlando	63	258	.457	188	.879	194	354	705	11.2
1990-91	Orlando	49	152	.431	99	.825	107	197	406	8.3
	Totals	357	1013	.452	654	.866	718	1395	2695	7.5

OTIS SMITH 27 6-5 210   Guard-Forward

Helium in his socks . . . A gifted athlete whose five-season career has been hampered by injury (three knee operations), lack of a defined position (is he a 2 or 3?) and lack of a defined role (started 39 of 75 games) . . . Came up with career-high numbers in scoring (13.9), rebounds (5.2), assists (2.3), minutes and all shooting categories . . . Enormous drive and determination . . . Shaky, at best, outside shot . . . Defensive liability at small forward due to size. Susceptible to post-ups . . . But he did have 85 steals . . . Good quickness to move around larger forwards . . . Spectacular dunks . . . Another original Magic, taken in expansion draft from Warriors . . . Second-round pick of Nuggets in '86 out of Jacksonville . . . Made $450,000 . . . Born Jan. 30, 1964, in Jacksonville, Fla.

Year	Team	G	FG	FG Pct.	FT	FT Pct.	Reb.	Ast.	TP	Avg.
1986-87	Denver	28	33	.418	12	.571	34	22	78	2.8
1987-88	Den.-G.S.	72	325	.491	178	.777	247	155	841	11.7
1988-89	Golden State	80	311	.435	174	.798	330	140	803	10.0
1989-90	Orlando	65	348	.492	169	.761	300	147	875	13.5
1990-91	Orlando	75	407	.451	221	.734	389	169	1044	13.9
	Totals	320	1424	.464	754	.761	1300	633	3641	11.4

MORLON WILEY 25 6-4 192   Guard

Beats digging ditches for a living . . . Weak shooter (.417) who has few discernible offensive skills . . . Can run the break or can break the running game with turnovers . . . Is considered a more than capable defender, however . . . Fire-hose arms, aggressive, get-up-on-opponent sort with admirable quickness . . . Works hard but has been unable to earn anything resembling consistent minutes in three seasons since leaving Long Beach State . . . Mavs took him on second round in '88, let him go in expansion draft to Magic . . . Born Sept. 24, 1966, in New Orleans . . . Made $347,000.

Year	Team	G	FG	FG Pct.	FT	FT Pct.	Reb.	Ast.	TP	Avg.
1988-89	Dallas	51	46	.404	13	.813	47	76	111	2.2
1989-90	Orlando	40	92	.442	28	.737	52	114	229	5.7
1990-91	Orlando	34	45	.417	17	.680	17	73	113	3.3
	Totals	125	183	.426	58	.734	116	263	453	3.6

THE ROOKIES

BRIAN WILLIAMS 22 6-9 240   Forward

Magic needs rebounding so they took Arizona's All-Pac-10 inside force at No. 10 . . . Left a year early . . . Averaged 14.0 points, 7.8 rebounds . . . Plays at both ends . . . Stock rose in NCAAs . . . Led conference with .619 shooting . . . Born April 6, 1969, in Santa Monica, Cal.

STANLEY ROBERTS 21 7-0 285   Center

Was a sure-fire lottery pick until he ate himself down to No. 23 . . . Marvelous offensive talent. Could be next Kevin Duckworth, could be next Mel Turpin . . . Played next to Shaquille O'Neal for one year at LSU. Grade problems sent him to Spain . . . Born Feb. 7, 1970, in Roberts, S.C . . . Draft's most intriguing player.

CHRIS CORCHIANI 23 5-11 186   Guard

Superb court vision . . . NCAA's all-time assist leader with 1,038, first ever to top 1,000 . . . Averaged 9.6 assists as senior at North Carolina State . . . That also was highest one-season average in

ACC history . . . Decent shooter, exceptional from foul line . . .
Born March 28, 1968, in Miami . . . Magic grabbed him at
No. 36.

COACH MATT GOUKAS: Outstanding second-season job
. . . Magic were 17-18 after the All-Star break
(leaving them just one game off a playoff
pace) . . . And they won 15 of last 20 . . . Considered an offensive-minded coach, his gang
improved defense by 9.9 points over previous
season . . . Of course, they still gave up 109.9
ppg . . . Very patient with young, aspiring team
. . . Players' coach. Former players usually are
. . . Ten-year playing career covered six cities and included championship with '67 Sixers . . . Passed a lot of future coaches in his
trades. Once was part of deal involving Dave Wohl. Later was
traded for Bobby Weiss . . . Good, sound Xs-and-Os guy . . .
Shields players from any controversy with in-family approach . . .
Assistant in Philly to Bill Cunningham for 3½ seasons, including
'83 title year . . . Head man in Philly for 2½ years. Produced
119-88 record . . . Career mark now 168-203 . . . Father, Matt Sr.,
a former pro . . . First-round pick by Philadelphia out of St. Joseph's (Pa.) . . . Born Feb. 25, 1944, in Philadelphia.

GREATEST TEAM

You really must search the memory banks for this one and go
all the way back to April 20, 1991. When the Magic beat the
Nets, 120-110, for its 31st victory, it was the fifth-best mark ever
by a second-year expansion team.

Fact is, after the All-Star break, Orlando bore little resemblance
to an expansionist. The Heat was 17-18 after the break, ninth-best in the West. With a league-high drop of 9.9 points in defense
from 1989-90, with home-court strength established (Orlando won
15 of the last 20 at home), Most Improved Player honoree Scott
Skiles wasn't far off when after the final game he proclaimed,
"We're a playoff team right now."

But even modest success has a price, as GM Pat Williams
ruefully noted on draft lottery day. The 31 victories allowed the
Magic to place two balls (out of 66) in the lottery drawing. Orlando

got the 10th pick in the draft. "You can't have 31 wins, have a great season on the court and get a lot of ping pong balls," Williams said.

ALL-TIME MAGIC LEADERS

SEASON

Points: Reggie Theus, 1,438, 1989-90
Assists: Scott Skiles, 660, 1990-91
Rebounds: Sidney Green, 588, 1989-90
            Greg Kite, 588, 1990-91

GAME

Points: Terry Catledge, 49 vs. Golden State, 1/13/90
Assists: Sam Vincent, 17 vs. Indiana, 1/30/90
          Scott Skiles, 17 vs. New York, 3/20/90
Rebounds: Sidney Green, 19 vs. Chicago, 2/14/90

CAREER

Points: Terry Catledge, 2,180, 1989-91
Assists: Scott Skiles, 994, 1989-91
Rebounds: Terry Catledge, 918, 1989-91

PHILADELPHIA 76ERS

TEAM DIRECTORY: Owner: Harold Katz; GM: Gene Shue; Asst. GM: Bob Weinhauer; Dir. Pub. Rel.: Zack Hill; Coach: Jim Lynam; Asst. Coaches: Fred Carter, Bob Weinhauer, Buzz Braman. Arena: The Spectrum (18,168). Colors: Red, white and blue.

SCOUTING REPORT

SHOOTING: In the regular season—a campaign that included 78 games without the starting point guard—the 76ers were slightly above average at .475. Charles Barkley was among the best at

Hersey Hawkins was acknowledged with All-Star selection.

.570, fourth in the league. Hersey Hawkins, the prime perimeter threat, continued his year-by-year improvement, finishing at .472.

Then came the playoffs. More specifically, then came the second round of the playoffs. Minus Barkley and his 64 percent accuracy, the Sixers shot .405. Yeah, there's room for improvement.

The Sixers were wounded at center after the trade of Mike Gminski. Rick Mahorn, who has been let go as a free agent, performed commendably, but was overmatched. So Philly lacked legitimate inside scoring from the five spot, thus increasing Barkley's already fearsome burden and adding emphasis on a perimeter game that lacked beyond Hawkins. And whenever Manute Bol enters, the offense immediately plays 4-on-5.

The Sixers hope to get some mileage out of Mitchell Wiggins, who shot 15.5 ppg in 1989-90 at Houston after being suspended for drug use.

PLAYMAKING: This is coach Jim Lynam's biggest question in 1991-92. Johnny Dawkins began rehabbing his surgically reconstructed knee immediately after the season and the Sixers expect him back for the start. But will he be ready?

The Sixers compiled a makeshift alignment at point guard with veteran castoff Rickey Green and perennial 10-day contract king Andre Turner. The results were far better than realistically could have been expected. Green and Turner played well, but not well enough to keep Philly from ranking 24th in assists.

Despite his dominant status in the Sixer offense, Barkley is a sound, knowledgeable passer who reacts to double teams exceptionally well. It is an area of his game for which he rarely gets credit.

DEFENSE: The Sixers were the only winning team that was outshot and outscored by oppponents. In fact, they were virtually out-everythinged. They played half the season minus a legitimate center and while Bol disrupts defensively, he's too big an offensive gamble. The 76ers hope 6-10 ex-Net Charles Shackleford, back from Europe, can provide some of the inside toughness and rebounding of Mahorn.

REBOUNDING: How can a team with Barkley, Mahorn and Armon Gilliam place 23rd in rebounding? Sounds unlikely, but the Sixers managed it.

For starters, Barkley missed 15 games with injuries/suspensions and wasn't among the top 10 in rebounding for the first time in

SIXER ROSTER

No.	Veterans	Pos.	Ht.	Wt.	Age	Yrs. Pro	College
20	Ron Anderson	F	6-7	215	33	7	Fresno State
34	Charles Barkley	F	6-6	250	28	7	Auburn
11	Manute Bol	C	7-7	225	29	6	Bridgeport
12	Johnny Dawkins	G	6-2	170	28	5	Duke
35	Armon Gilliam	F	6-9	245	27	4	Nevada-Las Vegas
14	Rickey Green	G	6-0	172	37	13	Michigan
33	Hersey Hawkins	G	6-3	190	26	3	Bradley
40	Dave Hoppen	C	6-11	240	27	4	Nebraska
31	Brian Oliver	G	6-4	210	23	1	Georgia Tech
21	Kenny Payne	F	6-8	220	24	2	Louisville
—	Charles Shackleford	F	6-10	225	25	2	North Carolina State
4	Andre Turner	G	6-4	199	32	5	Florida
—	Mitchell Wiggins	G	5-11	160	27	6	Memphis State
55	Jayson Williams	F	6-10	240	23	1	St. John's

Rd.	Rookies	Sel. No.	Pos.	Ht.	Wt.	College
	Tharon Mayes		G	6-3	175	Florida State

five seasons. Gilliam didn't come until Jan. 4. Mahorn played out of position at center. That's how the Sixers landed 23rd. That, and proving to be the East's worst offensive-rebounding team.

OUTLOOK: With Barkley, they're always a bit more than okay. They're in the NBA's weak-sister division, where a second-place finish can go to any team capable of a five-game winning streak. The Sixers must find a center, they must have a healthy Dawkins and they must form some plan on the Barkley-Gilliam alignment that sends two players with vastly similar styles on the court together.

SIXER PROFILES

CHARLES BARKLEY 28 6-6 250   Forward

There is only one . . . Part man, part tornado . . . Listed at 6-6, he's closer to 6-4 . . . Came back from offseason shoulder surgery . . . Fourth in MVP voting . . . Fourth in league in scoring (27.6) . . . Wasn't in the top 10 in rebounding for first time in five years. Averaged 10.1 . . . His 27.6 was second-best scoring average of career . . . Free throws at five-year low but he moved to wing when Armon Gilliam arrived... Third straight All-Star start. Won MVP with stunning 22-rebound performance, the most in 24 years... Only Sixer regular whose shooting didn't drop significantly in playoffs vs. Chicago. Instead, soared to .640... Missed 15 games: 14 through injury, one by suspension... Gives NBA security and operations offices lots of stuff to do. Fined for spitting at fan; got summons from city of Milwaukee for tossing water tray at fan, etc... What others call outspoken, he calls honest... All-Interview team... SEC Player of the Decade at Auburn... Born Feb. 20, 1963, in Leeds, Ala.... No. 5 pick as undergrad by Sixers in '84... Made $2.9 million.

Year	Team	G	FG	FG Pct.	FT	FT Pct.	Reb.	Ast.	TP	Avg.
1984-85	Philadelphia	82	427	.545	293	.733	703	155	1148	14.0
1985-86	Philadelphia	80	595	.572	396	.685	1026	312	1603	20.0
1986-87	Philadelphia	68	557	.594	429	.761	994	331	1564	23.0
1987-88	Philadelphia	80	753	.587	714	.751	951	254	2264	28.3
1988-89	Philadelphia	79	700	.579	602	.753	986	325	2037	25.8
1989-90	Philadelphia	79	706	.600	557	.749	909	307	1989	25.2
1990-91	Philadelphia	67	665	.570	475	.722	680	284	1849	27.6
	Totals	535	4403	.580	3466	.738	6249	1968	12454	23.3

HERSEY HAWKINS 26 6-3 190   Guard

If only the stock market kept his trend... Has gone up in scoring, shooting, rebounds, assists, steals and three-pointers each season since entering the league three years ago out of Bradley... Selected to All-Star team... Average defensively, but has made big strides. Real good anticipation. His 2.23 steals were eighth-best in NBA, third among Eastern off-guards...
Has trouble getting around picks... Durable. One of 17 players with over 3,000 minutes... Excellent range on jumper. Was 108-of-270 (.400) on three-pointers, seventh in league, second in East for percentage... Sixers' all-time three-point man in just three seasons... Deadly on baseline play Sixers used for years with Andrew Toney... College Player of Year as senior... Clippers drafted him No. 6 in '88. Traded to Philly in three-team Draft Day deal... Made $1 million... Born Sept. 29, 1965, in Chicago.

Year	Team	G	FG	FG Pct.	FT	FT Pct.	Reb.	Ast.	TP	Avg.
1988-89	Philadelphia	79	442	.455	241	.831	225	239	1196	15.1
1989-90	Philadelphia	82	522	.460	387	.888	304	261	1515	18.5
1990-91	Philadelphia	80	590	.472	479	.871	310	299	1767	22.1
	Totals	241	1554	.463	1107	.868	839	799	4478	18.6

ARMON GILLIAM 27 6-9 245   Forward

Seemed like a good idea at the time . . . Sixers acquired him Jan. 4, 1991, with Dave Hoppen from Charlotte for Mike Gminski . . . Idea was to create more offense . . . But he created more problems . . . Similar in style to Charles Barkley . . . Averaged 15.0 points and 7.3 rebounds with Sixers, both healthy drops from his Charlotte numbers (19.7 and 9.3) . . . Good left hand . . . Major increase from the line (.815 from .723) . . . Scoring (16.2) fine but shooting (.429) evaporated in second round vs. Bulls . . . Runs the floor well though not consistently . . . Heart and drive always have been questioned . . . Nicknamed "Hammer." Some in Philly media opted for "Chisel." . . . Can disappear in games with alarming quickness . . . Consensus All-American at Nevada-Las Vegas . . . Drafted No. 2 overall in '87 by Phoenix, which sent him to Charlotte in December 1989 . . . Made $1.2 million . . . Born May 28, 1964, in Pittsburgh.

Year	Team	G	FG	FG Pct.	FT	FT Pct.	Reb.	Ast.	TP	Avg.
1987-88	Phoenix	55	342	.475	131	.679	434	72	815	14.8
1988-89	Phoenix	74	468	.503	240	.743	541	52	1176	15.9
1989-90	Phoe.-Char.	76	484	.515	303	.723	599	99	1271	16.7
1990-91	Char.-Phil.	75	487	.487	268	.815	598	105	1242	16.6
	Totals	280	1781	.496	942	.745	2172	328	4504	16.1

RON ANDERSON 33 6-7 215   Forward

Wait a minute, don't be hasty. Could be showing up against Bulls any minute now . . . Shot horribly disappointing .320 in Eastern semis after .485 regular season and .500 first-round showings . . . Sixers' injury situation forced him into more minutes than designed . . . Only effective scorer off bench . . . When he starts, Sixer bench is as potent as a stifled sneeze . . . Devastating off-baseline screens . . . Drove far more than he did in past . . . Age is slowing him, however . . . Adequate defender who still positions well. Scorer's mentality . . . Second-best rebounding season (4.5) . . . Didn't play in high school . . . Was a second-round pick out of Fresno State by Cavs in '84 . . . After a stop in Indiana, was stolen by Sixers for draft rights to Everette

Stephens (or was it Stephen Everettes?) Oct. 3, 1988 . . . Born Oct. 15, 1958, in Chicago . . . Made $425,000.

Year	Team	G	FG	FG Pct.	FT	FT Pct.	Reb.	Ast.	TP	Avg.
1984-85	Cleveland	36	84	.431	41	.820	88	34	210	5.8
1985-86	Clev.-Ind.	77	310	.494	85	.669	274	144	707	9.2
1986-87	Indiana	63	139	.473	85	.787	151	54	363	5.8
1987-88	Indiana	74	217	.498	108	.766	216	78	542	7.3
1988-89	Philadelphia	82	566	.491	196	.856	406	139	1330	16.2
1989-90	Philadelphia	78	379	.451	165	.838	295	143	926	11.9
1990-91	Philadelphia	82	512	.485	165	.833	367	115	1198	14.6
	Totals	492	2207	.480	845	.805	1797	707	5276	10.7

JOHNNY DAWKINS 28 6-2 170   Guard

THE question for Sixers in 1991-92 . . . What will he have after reconstructive knee surgery? . . . Was playing above and beyond—though only four games—when he suffered complete tear of anterior cruciate ligament in right knee Nov. 8 . . . Helped Sixers stun Bulls in Chicago with 25 points opening night . . . His quickness has always been chief asset; now that's chief concern along with durability . . . Began workouts after season ended . . . Four-year career at Duke, was first ACC player with 2,000 points, 500 assists and 500 rebounds . . . Picked No. 10 by Spurs in '86. Traded to Sixers in deal for Maurice Cheeks Aug. 28, 1989 . . . Born Sept. 28, 1963, in Washington, D.C. . . . Paid $1.5 million.

Year	Team	G	FG	FG Pct.	FT	FT Pct.	Reb.	Ast.	TP	Avg.
1986-87	San Antonio	81	334	.437	153	.801	169	290	835	10.3
1987-88	San Antonio	65	405	.485	198	.896	204	480	1027	15.8
1988-89	San Antonio	32	177	.443	100	.893	101	224	454	14.2
1989-90	Philadelphia	81	465	.489	210	.861	247	601	1162	14.3
1990-91	Philadelphia	4	26	.634	10	.909	16	28	63	15.8
	Totals	263	1407	.471	671	.861	737	1623	3541	13.5

RICKEY GREEN 37 6-0 172   Guard

Sixers signed him as free agent before season . . . Lucky. Johnny Dawkins went down in fourth game . . . Elevated from backup to the oldest starting point guard in the history of the NBA . . . Shot okay (.463) but offered little penetration . . . Averaged 10.0 points, his most in five years . . . Far below average for position in steals—57 in 2,248 minutes. Rather soft defense for point guard . . . Below-par playoffs. But then every Sixer except Charles Barkley was atrocious against Bulls . . . Golden State picked him No. 16 out of Michigan in 1977, when he was consensus All-American . . . Bulk of career in Utah, but also did time in Detroit, Charlotte, Milwaukee and Indiana . . . Two-time Junior College All-American at Vincennes (Ind.), where he broke Bob McAdoo's scoring record . . . Considering need and result, an utter bargain at $120,000 . . . Born Aug. 18, 1954, in Chicago.

Year	Team	G	FG	FG Pct.	FT	FT Pct.	Reb.	Ast.	TP	Avg.
1977-78	Golden State	76	143	.381	54	.600	116	149	340	4.5
1978-79	Detroit	27	67	.379	45	.672	40	63	179	6.6
1980-81	Utah	47	176	.481	70	.722	116	235	422	9.0
1981-82	Utah	81	500	.493	202	.765	243	630	1202	14.8
1982-83	Utah	78	464	.493	185	.797	223	697	1115	14.3
1983-84	Utah	81	439	.486	192	.821	230	748	1072	13.2
1984-85	Utah	77	381	.477	232	.869	189	597	1000	13.0
1985-86	Utah	80	357	.471	213	.852	135	411	932	11.7
1986-87	Utah	81	301	.467	172	.827	163	541	781	9.6
1987-88	Utah	81	157	.424	75	.904	80	300	393	4.9
1988-89	Char.-Mil.	63	129	.489	30	.909	69	187	291	4.6
1989-90	Indiana	69	100	.433	43	.843	54	182	244	3.5
1990-91	Philadelphia	79	334	.463	117	.830	137	413	793	10.0
	Totals	920	3548	.469	1630	.808	1795	5153	8764	9.5

ANDRE TURNER 27 5-11 160   Guard

Might finally be able to unpack suitcase . . . Cut eight times all over NBA and saw CBA up close before Sixers signed him as free agent in wake of Johnny Dawkins' injury . . . Season-saver . . . Provided quick, solid penetrations . . . Excellent in trapping defense . . . Shooting (.439) shaky at best . . . Size will always be a hindrance . . . Career highs across the board . . . Well, he played a lot more: 1,407 minutes. Previous career total was 245 . . . Originally drafted by Lakers on third round in '86 . . . Lots of 10-day contracts, rookie-camp invites . . . Born March 13, 1964, in Memphis, Tenn. . . . Starred on Memphis State's Final Four team as junior . . . Made pro-rated $110,000.

Year	Team	G	FG	FG Pct.	FT	FT Pct.	Reb.	Ast.	TP	Avg.
1986-87	Boston	3	2	.400	0	.000	2	1	4	1.3
1987-88	Houston	12	12	.353	10	.714	8	23	35	2.9
1988-89	Milwaukee	4	3	.500	0	.000	3	0	6	1.5
1989-90	LAC-Char.	11	11	.289	4	1.000	8	23	26	2.4
1990-91	Philadelphia	70	168	.439	64	.736	152	311	412	5.9
	Totals	100	196	.421	78	.743	173	358	483	4.8

BRIAN OLIVER 23 6-4 210   Guard

Don't give up the day job... Especially if there's another .408 shooting season on horizon... Very spotty rookie year... Second-round pick from Georgia Tech showed he can defend and run floor... But also wasn't quick enough to drive lane in set offense... A rebound every 10 minutes; not bad considering position... Hustling type with heart who's willing to take a beating... Averaged 21.3 points as senior... Born June 1, 1968, in Chicago... Made $445,000.

Year	Team	G	FG	FG Pct.	FT	FT Pct.	Reb.	Ast.	TP	Avg.
1990-91	Philadelphia	73	111	.408	52	.732	80	88	279	3.8

CHARLES SHACKLEFORD 25 6-10 225   Forward

Rebounder deluxe... Played two seasons in New Jersey before fleeing to Europe in the wake of numerous offcourt problems... Averaged 21 points and 16.7 rebounds for Phonola Caserta in the Italian League last year... Averaged 8.2 points, 6.8 rebounds for Nets in 1989-90... Nets took him on second round in 1988 as an undergraduate out of North Carolina State... Pistons also scouted him in Europe... Born April 22, 1966, in Kinston, N.C.... With release of Rick Mahorn and his $1.33-million salary, Sixers were able to sign Shackleford.

Year	Team	G	FG	FG Pct.	FT	FT Pct.	Reb.	Ast.	TP	Avg.
1988-90	New Jersey	60	83	.494	21	.500	153	21	187	3.1

MANUTE BOL 29 7-7 225   Center

Two-way game disruptor. His defense disrupts opponents, his offense disrupts teammates... Set team record with 247 blocks, 3.01 average. Fourth-best in league behind center trio of Olajuwon, Robinson and Ewing... Added eight in three playoff games vs. Bucks, just four in five games vs. Bulls... Sixers funneled opponents his way on defense... Hoped, however, he'd get out of the way on offense, where he's a severe liability (1.9 points, .396 shooting) . . . Was read riot act about his three-point heaves. Cut down attempts to 14 (from 48 and 91 two previous years). Made one . . . Drafted by Bullets in second round in '85 . . . Attended U. of Bridgeport . . . Sixers got him from Warriors for a No. 1 pick . . . Born Oct. 16, 1962, in Gogrial, Sudan . . . Made $1.3 million.

Year	Team	G	FG	FG Pct.	FT	FT Pct.	Reb.	Ast.	TP	Avg.
1985-86	Washington	80	128	.460	42	.488	477	23	298	3.7
1986-87	Washington	82	103	.446	45	.672	362	11	251	3.1
1987-88	Washington	77	75	.455	26	.531	275	13	176	2.3
1988-89	Golden State	80	127	.369	40	.606	462	27	314	3.9
1989-90	Golden State	75	56	.331	25	.510	276	36	146	1.9
1990-91	Philadelphia	82	65	.396	24	.585	350	20	155	1.9
	Totals	476	554	.410	202	.564	2202	130	1340	2.8

DAVE HOPPEN 27 6-11 240   Center

Used sparingly despite size and Sixers' obvious wants in middle . . . That sort of says it all . . . Ripped up left knee as college senior at Nebraska and altered whatever was to be of career . . . No certain moves to speak of . . . Does have decent face-up shot. Hits to mid-range . . . Drafted on third round by Hawks in '87 . . . Has visited Golden State, Milwaukee and Charlotte . . . Averaged 2.1 ppg, 1.3 rpg for Sixers . . . Arrived Jan. 4 with Armon Gilliam in Mike Gminski trade . . . Born March 13, 1964, in Omaha . . . Made $400,000.

Year	Team	G	FG	FG Pct.	FT	FT Pct.	Reb.	Ast.	TP	Avg.
1987-88	Mil.-G.S.	39	84	.459	54	.871	174	32	222	5.7
1988-89	Charlotte	77	199	.564	101	.727	384	57	500	6.5
1989-90	Charlotte	10	16	.390	8	.800	36	6	40	4.0
1990-91	Char.-Phil.	30	24	.545	16	.727	39	3	64	2.1
	Totals	156	323	.520	179	.768	633	98	826	5.3

KENNY PAYNE 24 6-8 220   Forward

Second year a mirror of first. And he didn't prove much as a rookie in 1989-90 . . . Disappointment, considering he was regarded as second-best pure shooter to Glen Rice in '89 draft . . . Just not a pure shot-maker . . . Good free-throw shooter, has range, but shot .360 from the floor . . . Sixers have problem finding him time . . . Needs more minutes to bolster some sagging confidence . . . Has size to be a big small forward, but that spot is sort of occupied by Charles Barkley . . . Born Nov. 25, 1966, in Laurel, Miss. . . . No. 19 pick out of Louisville . . . Paid $400,000.

Year	Team	G	FG	FG Pct.	FT	FT Pct.	Reb.	Ast.	TP	Avg.
1989-90	Philadelphia	35	47	.435	16	.889	26	10	114	3.3
1990-91	Philadelphia	47	68	.360	26	.897	66	16	166	3.5
	Totals	82	115	.387	42	.894	92	26	280	3.4

MITCHELL WIGGINS 32 6-4 199   Guard

Ready to resume NBA career . . . Was double-figure scorer in two of first four seasons before drawing two-and-a-half-year suspension for drug abuse as a Rocket Jan. 13, 1987 . . . Reinstated July 27, 1989, and had best scoring season in 1989-90 with 15.5 ppg at Houston . . . Born Sept. 28, 1959, in Lenoir County, N.C. . . . Indiana drafted him 23rd out of Florida State in 1983 and he was immediately traded to Chicago, where he started 40 games as a rookie.

Year	Team	G	FG	FG Pct.	FT	FT Pct.	Reb.	Ast.	TP	Avg.
1983-84	Chicago	82	399	.448	213	.742	328	187	1018	12.4
1984-85	Houston	82	318	.484	96	.733	235	119	738	9.0
1985-86	Houston	78	222	.454	86	.729	159	101	531	6.8
1986-87	Houston	32	153	.437	49	.754	133	76	355	11.1
1989-90	Houston	66	416	.488	192	.810	286	104	1024	15.5
	Totals	340	1508	.466	636	.759	1141	587	3666	10.8

JAYSON WILLIAMS 23 6-10 240   Forward

Williams or Kenny Walker? Cast your vote for worst hairdo in NBA . . . Could be a tie . . . Typical rookie learning experience . . . Showed flashes of potential offensive domination but was soft defensively despite obvious NBA body . . . Blocked six shots, only one after December . . . Needs better practice habits and attention span. Brain wanders at bad times. Like in games . . . Suns picked him at 21 out of St. John's . . . Messy contract squabble. Became Sixer for '93 first-rounder ... Born Feb. 22, 1968, in Ritter, S.C.... Made $500,000.

Year	Team	G	FG	FG Pct.	FT	FT Pct.	Reb.	Ast.	TP	Avg.
1990-91	Philadelphia	52	72	.447	37	.661	111	16	182	3.5

COACH JIM LYNAM: Should be given monster raise just for handling Charles Barkley so masterfully, keeping him in tune with teammates ... That's one reason. The fact that he is a darn good coach is another ... Several GMs call him the best in the league ... Despite injuries and a strange array of talent, he led Sixers to 44-38 record in his third full season. And that was his worst Sixer mark ... In his three full seasons in Philly, has a 143-103 record (.579) ... Including interim stint with Sixers and one-plus season with Clippers, is 211-217 ... Succeeded Matt Guokas Feb. 8, 1988, on Sixer bench ... Offensive-minded guy whose favored transition game went up in smoke with Johnny Dawkins' knee injury in season's fourth game ... Led Sixers to Atlantic Division title two seasons ago, their first since '83 championship year ... Had 158-118 (.572) 10-season college coaching career at Fairfield, American U. and alma mater St. Joseph's in hometown Philadelphia, where he played three seasons under Jack Ramsay ... Born Sept. 15, 1941.

GREATEST TEAM

A high-water mark for any franchise is 60 victories, a feat accomplished by far less than half of the NBA franchises. The 1966-67 Celtics were one of Boston's many 60-win teams and yet they were a full eight games behind the 1966-67 76ers, the second-winningest single-season team in the history of the league.

Expansion helped. But the 68-13 record (.840) compiled by those Wilt Chamberlain-led Sixers ranks second only to the 69-13 record (.841) compiled by the Wilt Chamberlain-led Lakers of 1971-72. Before Wilt moved West, he led the 1967 playoff rampage that devastated Cincinnati, Boston and San Francisco en route to the NBA crown.

Those Sixers were more than Wilt. They had Billy Cun-

All-Everything Charles Barkley was fourth in MVP voting.

ningham, Matt Goukas, Luke Jackson, Hal Greer and Chet Walker. Averaging 125.2 points per game—four players averaged 18.5 or better, topped by Wilt's 24.1—the Sixers ran up a 28-2 home record. Wilt also ranked third in assists (this was the first year of his share-the-wealth program) and led the league in rebounding. The Sixers won 45 of their first 49 games and never once glanced in the rear-view mirror.

ALL-TIME 76ER LEADERS

SEASON

Points: Wilt Chamberlain, 2,649, 1965-66
Assists: Maurice Cheeks, 753, 1985-86
Rebounds: Wilt Chamberlain, 1,957, 1966-67

GAME

Points: Wilt Chamberlain, 68 vs. Chicago, 12/16/67
Assists: Wilt Chamberlain, 21 vs. Detroit, 2/2/68
Maurice Cheeks, 21 vs. New Jersey, 10/30/82
Rebounds: Wilt Chamberlain, 43 vs. Boston, 3/6/65

CAREER

Points: Hal Greer, 21,586, 1958-73
Assists: Maurice Cheeks, 6,212, 1978-89
Rebounds: Dolph Schayes, 11,256, 1948-64

WASHINGTON BULLETS

TEAM DIRECTORY: Chairman: Abe Pollin; Pres.: Susan O'Malley; VP: Jerry Sachs; GM: John Nash; Dir. Pub. Rel.: Matt Williams; Coach: Wes Unseld; Asst. Coaches: Bill Blair, Jeff Bzdelik. Arena: Capital Centre (18,756). Colors: Red, white and blue.

SCOUTING REPORT

SHOOTING: Get help for Bernard. Period. End of discussion.

Bernard King assumed a staggering offensive burden and for 64 games met the challenge. But one guy can only do so much and with little coming from Ledell Eackles, from whom so much was expected, and next to nothing arriving from John Williams, who began the season still rehabbing his knee, Bernard simply wore down. And now he's out for an indefinite period following knee surgery in September.

There were, however, two pleasant offensive surprises for the Bullets, who ranked 18th in field-goal percentage: Harvey Grant emerged and was vastly improved and Pervis Ellison flashed signs that maybe he wasn't a bust as the No. 1 pick two years ago. But the Bullets had a pitiful perimeter game devoid of any range. They tried the fewest (284) and made the fewest (55) three-pointers of any team in the NBA. In fact, they were the only team with a three-point percentage under .200 (.194). The next closest were the Clippers at .260. The trey shooting, of course, will change with the addition of flinging Michael Adams from Denver.

PLAYMAKING: This was why Louisville's LaBradford Smith was so appealing in the draft. The Bullets gave up Darrell Walker to Detroit in September, but with Adams aboard as well as Smith, they still figure to be potent in passing-game offense.

When it wasn't Walker running the show, the Bullets gave the point to Haywoode Workman, but he has opted to take his wares to Italy. And although the Bullets moved the ball well, they lacked the creative, good-decision type.

DEFENSE: Not great, but getting better. The development of Ellison in the middle certainly will help. Scorers King and Eackles don't defend, so the Bullets sought the big defensive plays elsewhere—and rarely found them. Adams should help create some pressure havoc for a team that forced just 15.3 turnovers per game.

Bernard King highlighted season with two 50-point sprees.

REBOUNDING: All things considered, it could have been worse under the boards for the Bullets. Power forward Williams made it to only 33 games. Center Ellison didn't start establishing himself until late in the season. And King, though competent, has never been an exceptionally gifted boarder.

But what the Bullets do is rebound in force. Everybody goes to the boards. That's why year in, year out, Walker was such a rebounding marvel. If Tom Hammonds, a two-year lottery-pick bust, can provide anything off the bench and if Williams returns to form, the Bullets could be far more formidable than their 18th-place finish.

OUTLOOK: The Bullets can never be counted out because of the work ethic they employ for coach Wes Unseld. With GM John

BULLET ROSTER

No.	Veterans	Pos.	Ht.	Wt.	Age	Yrs. Pro	College
—	Michael Adams	G	5-10	165	28	6	Boston College
31	Mark Alarie	F	6-8	225	27	5	Duke
21	Ledell Eackles	G	6-5	215	24	3	New Orleans
43	Pervis Ellison	F-C	6-10	225	24	2	Louisville
14	A.J. English	G	6-3	180	24	1	Virginia Union
42	Greg Foster	C	6-11	240	23	1	Texas-El Paso
44	Harvey Grant	F	6-9	215	26	3	Oklahoma
12	Tom Hammonds	F	6-9	225	24	2	Georgia Tech
32	Byron Irvin	G	6-5	190	24	2	Missouri
23	Charles Jones	F-C	6-9	225	34	8	Albany State
30	Bernard King	F	6-7	205	34	13	Tennessee
2	Larry Robinson	G	6-5	185	23	1	Centenary
34	John Williams	F	6-9	255	25	4	LSU

Rd.	Rookies	Sel. No.	Pos.	Ht.	Wt.	College
1	LaBradford Smith	19	G	6-3	205	Louisville

Nash entrenched now, the Bullets appear to have halted their skid and begun reversing their field.

Playoff team? Probably not, especially with King's newest problem. If offensive help arrives for King, if Grant makes an improvement resembling anything like the jump he had last year, if Eackles settles in and becomes the shooting guard some project he can be, then the Bullets could surprise. With a break or two from the Central Division, they might even challenge for the eighth playoff spot. But there are an awful lot of "ifs" involved.

BULLET PROFILES

BERNARD KING 34 6-7 205   Forward

Comeback complete . . . Coming back wasn't enough. He wanted All-Star status . . . He got it, starting for East . . . Shouldered incredible scoring burden, especially early due to holdout of Ledell Eackles and rehab of John Williams . . . Had two 50-point games, nine of 40 . . . His 52 points vs. Denver Dec. 29 set team and Cap Centre record . . . Wore down, sat last 13 games with sore back . . . Underwent arthroscopic knee surgery in September that will keep him out of action for a while at least . . . Third in NBA scoring at 28.4, only third Bullet ever in top three, first since Earl Monroe in 1968-69 . . . Is 17th on all-time scoring list, 568 points away from 20,000 . . . Most incredible game may have been 49-pointer against old team Knicks at MSG. Scored 23 in fourth quarter. Crowd went nuts . . . Still has some of best post-up moves around . . . As good as anyone finishing left . . . Jumper improved but not automatic . . . Never a good defender and if anterior cruciate surgery left any residue, it's decreased lateral movement . . . Born Dec. 4, 1956, in Brooklyn, N.Y. . . . All-American at Tennessee . . . No. 7 pick by New Jersey in '77 . . . Won 1984-85 scoring title with Knicks. Back-to-back 50-point games that season . . . Signed as free agent without compensation Oct. 17, 1987 . . . Made $1.6 million.

Year	Team	G	FG	FG Pct.	FT	FT Pct.	Reb.	Ast.	TP	Avg.
1977-78	New Jersey	79	798	.479	313	.677	751	193	1909	24.2
1978-79	New Jersey	82	710	.522	349	.564	669	295	1769	21.6
1979-80	Utah	19	71	.518	34	.540	88	52	176	9.3
1980-81	Golden State	81	731	.588	307	.703	551	287	1771	21.9
1981-82	Golden State	79	740	.566	352	.705	469	282	1833	23.2
1982-83	New York	68	603	.528	280	.722	326	195	1486	21.9
1983-84	New York	77	795	.572	437	.779	394	164	2027	26.3
1984-85	New York	55	691	.530	426	.772	317	204	1809	32.9
1985-86	New York				Injured					
1986-87	New York	6	52	.495	32	.744	32	19	136	22.7
1987-88	Washington	69	470	.501	247	.762	280	192	1188	17.2
1988-89	Washington	81	654	.477	361	.819	384	294	1674	20.7
1989-90	Washington	82	711	.487	412	.803	404	376	1837	22.4
1990-91	Washington	64	713	.472	383	.790	319	292	1817	28.4
	Totals	842	7739	.518	3933	.730	5984	2845	19432	23.1

PERVIS ELLISON 24 6-10 225   Forward-Center

Caution: legit center under construction . . . Finally began showing the promise that made him No. 1 overall pick by Kings in '89 draft after MVP Final Four showing for Louisville . . . Kings quit waiting for his health and dealt him to Bullets for Jeff Malone (then sent to Utah) and a second-rounder . . . Washington was going nowhere, so Ellison had more time to work in . . . Silent for first two months, then quality for 34 games before finger injury KO'd him in last three... Averaged 15.3 points, 9.4 boards and shot .555 as a starter... His 2.07 blocks were 10th in league... Great hands, good post scorer with nice turnaround jumper on baseline... Strong defensive instincts but needs more bulk to hold the bigger bodies in place. Weak lower body... Long arms make him Kevin McHale-like rebounder... Born April 3, 1967, in the Bronx, N.Y.... Made $2.3 million.

Year	Team	G	FG	FG Pct.	FT	FT Pct.	Reb.	Ast.	TP	Avg.
1989-90	Sacramento	34	111	.442	49	.628	196	65	271	8.0
1990-91	Washington	76	326	.513	139	.650	585	102	791	10.4
	Totals	110	437	.493	188	.644	781	167	1062	9.7

MICHAEL ADAMS 28 5-10 165   Guard

Bullets could have saved themselves lots of trouble by keeping him originally... Waived twice and traded once by Bullets, who got him back in June from Denver, along with swap of first-round picks... Drafted by Kings on No. 66 out of Boston College in '85... Sacramento to CBA... Washington signed him as free agent in May '86... Waived him in September. Re-signed him four days later. Waived him 30 days later. Then, of course, re-signed him in 24 days... Traded him to Denver with Jay Vincent for Darrell Walker and Mark Alarie Nov. 2, '87... Ran Denver's helter-skelter offense with license to shoot the three... Attempted league-high 564, made league all-time high 167 for not-league-high .296... Attempted 1,943 trifectas in last five years... Holds record, spanning two seasons, for making a trey in 79 straight games... Career-best 26.5 ppg. Don't forget, it was in Denver... Born Jan. 19, 1963, in Hartford, Conn. ... Made $825,000.

Year	Team	G	FG	FG Pct.	FT	FT Pct.	Reb.	Ast.	TP	Avg.
1985-86	Sacramento	18	16	.364	8	.667	6	22	40	2.2
1986-87	Washington	63	160	.407	105	.847	123	244	453	7.2
1987-88	Denver	82	416	.449	166	.834	223	503	1137	13.9
1988-89	Denver	77	468	.433	322	.819	283	490	1424	18.5
1989-90	Denver	79	398	.402	267	.850	225	495	1221	15.5
1990-91	Denver	66	560	.394	465	.879	256	693	1752	26.5
	Totals	385	2018	.416	1333	.849	1116	2447	6027	15.7

JOHN WILLIAMS 25 6-9 255   Forward

Okay, can the fat jokes right now. Don't listen to 'em, John. Now get on the ground and we'll roll you home . . . Sorry . . . Didn't get back until February from rehabilitating a torn anterior cruciate ligament in his right knee and then losing the incredible bulk he added while out . . . Ballooned to over 300 pounds and was placed on suspended list . . . Actually looked good by end of season . . . Marvelously versatile, gifted player . . . Projected as a four-position type who left LSU after soph season in '86 when Bullets picked him 12th . . . The team's best passer, he averaged 4.0 assists . . . Had little jumping ability before injury. Virtually less than none after, so any rebounds come through positioning . . . His baseline move suffered in his short comeback and he shot .417 . . . Improvement needed this season . . . Born Oct. 26, 1966, in Los Angeles . . . Made $1 million.

Year	Team	G	FG	FG Pct.	FT	FT Pct.	Reb.	Ast.	TP	Avg.
1986-87	Washington	78	283	.454	144	.646	366	191	718	9.2
1987-88	Washington	82	427	.469	188	.734	444	232	1047	12.8
1988-89	Washington	82	438	.466	225	.776	573	356	1120	13.7
1989-90	Washington	18	130	.474	65	.774	136	84	327	18.2
1990-91	Washington	33	164	.417	73	.753	177	133	411	12.5
	Totals	293	1442	.459	695	.732	1696	996	3623	12.4

HARVEY GRANT 26 6-9 215   Forward

He ain't Horace, but he's no rabbit, either . . . One of league's most improved players . . . Second on team in scoring and rebounding . . . Huge improvement in field-goal percentage (.498 from .473 and .464) . . . Could always shoot . . . Doesn't have twin brother's inside skills . . . Runs the court well, real good in transition and filling the lanes . . . Ball-handling a zilch. Doesn't come off screens because he doesn't put ball on floor well enough to get around anybody . . . Willing defender who doesn't have the necessary bulk to do damage . . . Had 32 games of 20 points or more . . . Born July 4, 1965, in Augusta, Ga., just after Horace . . . No. 12 pick out of Oklahoma in '88 . . . Made $475,000.

Year	Team	G	FG	FG Pct.	FT	FT Pct.	Reb.	Ast.	TP	Avg.
1988-89	Washington......	71	181	.464	34	.596	163	79	396	5.6
1989-90	Washington......	81	284	.473	96	.701	342	131	664	8.2
1990-91	Washington......	77	609	.498	185	.743	557	204	1405	18.2
	Totals	229	1074	.485	315	.711	1062	414	2465	10.8

LEDELL EACKLES 24 6-5 215   Guard

What a waste . . . Held out and basically threw away a season . . . Got his $605,000 and wasn't worth the $250,000 he earned prior . . . Made it into 67 games and quickly learned the difference between being in shape and being in NBA shape . . . Still shot career-best .453 and averaged 13.0 ppg, but so much more was expected of the '88 second-round pick from New Orleans . . . Was instant-offense type in first two seasons; last year he was expected to assume the void left by Jeff Malone . . . With the way he reported, he got stuck in void . . . Spent first 11 games on suspended list . . . A quality shooter, good driver with decent hang time . . . Defense? Hey, he's a scorer . . . Can get way out of control . . . Good at drawing fouls . . . Game hasn't expanded much in three seasons . . . Born Nov. 24, 1966, in Baton Rouge, La.

Year	Team	G	FG	FG Pct.	FT	FT Pct.	Reb.	Ast.	TP	Avg.
1988-89	Washington......	80	318	.434	272	.786	180	123	917	11.5
1989-90	Washington......	78	413	.439	210	.750	175	182	1055	13.5
1990-91	Washington......	67	345	.453	164	.739	128	136	868	13.0
	Totals	225	1076	.442	646	.762	483	441	2840	12.6

A. J. ENGLISH 24 6-3 180   Guard

A scorer in college, he maintained his rep quickly by becoming first rookie with a 30-point game last season . . . Gets off shot regardless of position, circumstance, time of day, position of the planets . . . Lots of one-on-one skills, still learning system approach . . . Another product of Virginia Union (Charles Oakley's alma mater) . . . Found decent time (1,443 minutes in 70 games) with the mess Bullet backcourt evolved into through injuries and departure of Jeff Malone . . . Shooter's mentality negates his chances at point . . . Started 12 games, averaged 15.1 points and 6.0 assists in those outings . . . Second-round pick, No. 37 overall . . . Paid $275,000.

Year	Team	G	FG	FG Pct.	FT	FT Pct.	Reb.	Ast.	TP	Avg.
1990-91	Washington......	70	251	.439	111	.707	147	177	616	8.8

MARK ALARIE 27 6-8 225　　　　　　　　Forward

Was spotted on the court several times last season by usually reliable witnesses . . . Missed last 27 games with tendinitis in knee . . . Some say he also missed first 55 games with apparent attention span of a fern . . . Got married in off-season, may have dampened his game fire . . . Never into it. Played 587 minutes . . . Before last season, he was developing nicely as a strong bench-role type who ran floor, crashed boards, shot more than adequately (.470 to .490 range) and defended well down low . . . Like a lot of Bullets, has a lot to prove this season . . . Born Dec. 11, 1963, in Phoenix . . . First-round (No. 18) pick by Denver in 1986 out of Duke . . . Came to Washington in the Michael Adams-Darrell Walker trade . . . Was paid $500,000.

Year	Team	G	FG	FG Pct.	FT	FT Pct.	Reb.	Ast.	TP	Avg.
1986-87	Denver.........	64	217	.490	67	.663	214	74	503	7.9
1987-88	Washington......	63	144	.480	35	.714	160	39	327	5.2
1988-89	Washington......	74	206	.478	73	.839	255	63	498	6.7
1989-90	Washington......	82	371	.473	108	.812	374	142	860	10.5
1990-91	Washington......	42	99	.440	41	.854	117	45	244	5.8
	Totals	325	1037	.475	324	.775	1120	363	2432	7.5

CHARLES JONES 34 6-9 225　　　　Forward-Center

Seems like he has been around since McKinley administration . . . Undersized center held down middle until Pervis Ellison arrived . . . Took benching in classy fashion . . . Cardboard cutouts have a better offensive game . . . Range to about seven inches . . . Always known for defense, it's what kept him in league since Phoenix selected him on eighth round in 1979 out of Albany State . . . Suffered the obligatory Bullet injury and missed last 19 games with groin pull... Rebounds, blocks shots, occasionally knocks a ball in with his nose and does the best he can against the Ewings and Parishes of the East... Three brothers all played in NBA... Signed by seven teams, played with three ... Signed on as free agent March 8, 1986... Made $675,000.

Year	Team	G	FG	FG Pct.	FT	FT Pct.	Reb.	Ast.	TP	Avg.
1983-84	Philadelphia	1	0	.000	1	.250	0	0	1	1.0
1984-85	Chi.-Wash.......	31	67	.528	40	.690	184	26	174	5.6
1985-86	Washington......	81	129	.508	54	.628	321	76	312	3.9
1986-87	Washington......	79	118	.474	48	.632	356	80	284	3.6
1987-88	Washington......	69	72	.407	53	.707	325	59	197	2.9
1988-89	Washington......	53	60	.480	16	.640	257	42	136	2.6
1989-90	Washington......	81	94	.508	68	.648	504	139	256	3.2
1990-91	Washington......	62	67	.540	29	.580	359	48	163	2.6
	Totals	457	607	.489	309	.645	2306	470	1523	3.3

GREG FOSTER 23 6-11 240   Center

Will somebody please tell this guy he's 6-11? Maybe he's too busy studying his tattoo to notice... Bullets happy with this second-round pick (No. 35) out of UTEP... Has a nice jump shot for a near 7-footer. Problem is, that's really all he wants to do... Good drop step and turnaround... Could develop into a nice backup. Showed first-season promise, averaging 4.4 points and 2.8 boards... Started last three games and doubled output... Typical rookie with big-man foul trouble... Blocks some shots and is a decent athlete but has to shake the soft tendencies... Born Sept. 3, 1968, in Oakland... Made $275,000.

Year	Team	G	FG	FG Pct.	FT	FT Pct.	Reb.	Ast.	TP	Avg.
1990-91	Washington......	54	97	.460	42	.689	151	37	236	4.4

LARRY ROBINSON 23 6-5 185   Guard

After just one go-round in NBA, seems headed for a life of 10-day contracts... Signed with Bullets as an undrafted free agent after playing at Centenary... Played 10 games, then was felled by tendinitis in ankle... Waived... Picked up by Warriors... Waived... Re-signed by Bullets for last two games... Good defender... Came out of college with rep as shooter, but in 36 games with Bullets and Warriors blistered for .413... Did have a 12-rebound game for Washington, however

. . . Born Jan. 11, 1968, in Bossier City, La. . . . Minimum wage all the way.

Year	Team	G	FG	FG Pct.	FT	FT Pct.	Reb.	Ast.	TP	Avg.
1990-91	Wash.-G.S.	36	62	.413	15	.556	51	35	139	3.9

TOM HAMMONDS 24 6-9 225   Forward

Everybody makes mistakes. Like the Bullets did in picking this guy at No. 9 in '89 . . . No wonder they traded their lottery pick last June . . . Bullets wanted him to rebound. And he tore opposition for 2.9 boards a game in his second season . . . In 218 more minutes than his rookie year, he managed to grab three less offensive rebounds . . . Just doesn't crash the boards . . . A pretty good shooter with decent offensive moves—unless he's finishing . . . Was allegedly spotted playing defense once a couple of years back . . . Born March 27, 1967, in Crestview, Fla . . . Played up-tempo at Georgia Tech and Bullets figured he'd fit in nicely. Wrong . . . Uses up an $800,000 salary cap slot.

Year	Team	G	FG	FG Pct.	FT	FT Pct.	Reb.	Ast.	TP	Avg.
1989-90	Washington.	61	129	.437	63	.643	168	51	321	5.3
1990-91	Washington.	70	155	.461	57	.722	206	43	367	5.2
	Totals	131	284	450	120	.678	374	94	688	5.3

BYRON IRVIN 24 6-5 190   Guard

Didn't this guy make disaster films or something? . . . If so, he could always film his NBA career . . . He's the guy Portland drafted in 1989 with the first-round pick (No. 22) they got from Knicks for Kiki Vandeweghe . . . He's the guy Sacramento got in trade for Danny Ainge . . . He's the guy Kings gave to Bullets for Steve Colter . . . Decent offensive rebounder for a guard . . . Can't shoot consistently, can't handle the ball . . . Very mechanical . . . A fair passer . . . Born Dec. 2, 1966, in LaGrange, Ill . . . Missouri product.

Year	Team	G	FG	FG Pct.	FT	FT Pct.	Reb.	Ast.	TP	Avg.
1989-90	Portland	50	96	.473	61	.670	74	47	258	5.2
1990-91	Washington.	33	60	.465	50	.820	45	24	171	5.2
	Totals	83	156	.470	111	.730	119	71	429	5.2

THE ROOKIE

LaBRADFORD SMITH 22 6-3 200   Guard

The guy Bullets wanted but they never thought they'd find at No. 19 . . . Big body for a point guard . . . Some felt he underachieved at Louisville . . . Led team in scoring, free-throw shooting, assists and steals . . . Good defender with average outside shot . . . Rep for disappearing in big games . . . Born April 3, 1969, in Bay City, Tex.

COACH WES UNSELD: Never heard of any player mutinies in Washington, huh? . . . If Unseld got ticked, he might break a spine or two. Then show his anger . . . One of the all-time great players . . . As an undersized center out of Louisville, he became only player other than Wilt Chamberlain to win MVP and Rookie of the Year the same season (1968-69) . . . Added another nifty dust-collector when he was playoff MVP for '78 championship Bullets . . . Played the game with heart, hustle and a no-quarter approach . . . Set picks that left opponents counting teeth and dislocated discs . . . Simply a superb rebounder who employed positioning and strength. Eighth-best of all time . . . Third-best playoff rebounder . . . No threat to Pat Riley as Atlantic's best-dressed coach . . . Players admire and respect his treat-'em-all-the-same approach . . . Team trademark is hard work . . . Hasn't had much to work with, in terms of a full team. Hence, a 131-170 record that isn't as bad as it looks . . . Born March 14, 1946, in Louisville, Ky . . . No. 2 pick in '68 draft behind Elvin Hayes, later a teammate with Bullets.

GREATEST TEAM

Washington's greatest regular-season team, the 1974-75 unit that won a franchise-best 60 games, ended its expedition in utter failure—a 4-0 sweep in the finals by the heavily underdog Golden State Warriors. The talent and expectations were there; it just didn't go by the script for the Bullets.

But the Bullets took another route in 1977-78. They landed a

Michael Adams brings his three-point shot to Washington.

ho-hum second place in the Central Division, eight games behind San Antonio at 44-38. Then they donned their Cinderella slippers in the playoffs. Washington bounced Atlanta in two straight, upset the Spurs in six and did the same to Atlantic champ Philadelphia.

With playoff MVP Wes Unseld, Elvin Hayes, free-agent pickup Bobby Dandridge and unlikely Charley Johnson, the Bullets met a would-be Cinderella in Seattle and won the last two games of a seven-game set to win the title and eradicate the frustrations of 1974-75.

ALL-TIME BULLET LEADERS

SEASON

Points: Walt Bellamy, 2,495, 1961-62
Assists: Kevin Porter, 734, 1980-81
Rebounds: Walt Bellamy, 1,500, 1961-62

GAME

Points: Earl Monroe, 56 vs. Los Angeles, 2/3/68
Assists: Kevin Porter, 24 vs. Detroit, 3/23/80
Rebounds: Walt Bellamy, 37 vs. St. Louis, 12/4/64

CAREER

Points: Elvin Hayes, 15,551, 1972-81
Assists: Wes Unseld, 3,822, 1968-81
Rebounds: Wes Unseld, 13,769, 1968-81

DALLAS MAVERICKS

TEAM DIRECTORY: Pres.: Donald Carter; Chief Oper. Off./GM: Norm Sonju; VP Basketball Oper.: Rick Sund; Dir. Communications: Allen Stone; Dir. Media Services: Kevin Sullivan; Coach: Richie Adubato; Asst. Coaches: Gar Heard, Bob Zuffelato. Arena: Reunion Arena (TBA). Colors: Blue and green.

Iron man Derek Harper and his Mavs must turn it around.

SCOUTING REPORT

SHOOTING: Surely, some of the problems can be blamed on the injuries. But 1990-91 was bad; try 99.9 points a game, 40 times under 100 and 14 times under 90, all franchise-record lows. Only Minnesota and Sacramento had a worse scoring average. Their .471 shooting was middle of the road, but their 6,890 attempts ranked 22nd in the league.

This is okay if the team is young and developing. In other words, the opposite of the Mavericks. And they were probably only that potent because of the late emergence of Herb Williams as a low-post scoring threat to take the entire load off the backcourt of Derek Harper and Rolando Blackman.

Steps have already been taken to rectify the problem, most notably drafting Missouri's Doug Smith for front-line scoring. Fat Lever's healthy comeback would obviously help, as would a full season from Roy (Don't Hold Your Breath) Tarpley.

PLAYMAKING: Harper finished only 16th in assists, but it's no question that he is held in higher regard than many in the top 15. His scoring continues to increase, and a career assist-to-turnover ratio of 3.1-1 after eight seasons of at least 77 games is admirable. The return of Lever, who averaged 6.5 assists in his final season with Denver before coming to the Mavericks, would provide relief.

DEFENSE: The 104.5 points allowed per game, 12th in the NBA, marked the first time the Mavericks did not improve since Richie Adubato joined the club as an assistant coach before the 1986-87 season. They had climbed from 21st to fourth before tripping. They could use some shot-blocking from 7-foot center Donald Hodge, the second-round draft choice. Take away Tarpley and no one averaged more than Williams' 1.47 blocks per game.

REBOUNDING: See above, in 1990-91 problems and possible solutions. Actually, it may even have been worse. They finished 24th in rebounding, and the 3,344 total was second-worst in franchise history.

OUTLOOK: No team in the conference has more uncertainty while awaiting the return of key players. Phoenix won't be as good if Tom Chambers and Dan Majerle are not at full strength, but Dallas, as was proven last season, will be downright bad if Lever and Tarpley don't return. The result could be the Mavericks'

MAVERICK ROSTER

No.	Veterans	Pos.	Ht.	Wt.	Age	Yrs. Pro	College
22	Rolando Blackman	G	6-6	206	32	10	Kansas State
15	Brad Davis	G	6-3	183	35	14	Maryland
40	James Donaldson	C	7-2	280	34	11	Washington State
12	Derek Harper	G	6-4	200	30	8	Southern Illinois
21	Lafayette Lever	G	6-3	175	31	9	Arizona State
1	Rodney McCray	F	6-8	235	30	8	Louisville
42	Roy Tarpley	F	7-0	250	26	5	Michigan
5	Kelvin Upshaw	G	6-2	180	28	3	Utah
33	Randy White	F	6-8	249	24	2	Louisiana Tech
32	Herb Williams	F-C	6-11	242	33	10	Ohio State

Rd.	Rookies	Sel. No.	Pos.	Ht.	Wt.	College
1	Doug Smith	6	F	6-10	220	Missouri
2	Donald Hodge	33	C	7-0	230	Temple
2	Mike Iuzzolino	35	G	5-10	180	St. Francis (Pa.)

first back-to-back losing seasons since 1981-82 and 1982-83.

One positive that emerged through the rubble of 1990-91 is that they went 9-6 in games decided by three points or less, one of only eight teams to have winning records in that category with at least 10 chances. The theory is that good teams win the close games, by composure or competence. That says a lot of how good the Mavericks could be if 100 percent.

MAVERICK PROFILES

ROLANDO BLACKMAN 32 6-6 206   Guard

Still the go-to guy in clutch situations, and it made no difference that everybody knew it . . . Mavs' leading scorer three straight seasons . . . His 19.9 last year was highest average since 1986-87 . . . Team's all-time leading scorer . . . One of five active NBA players with runs of at least 10 1,000-point seasons . . . Others are Robert Parish (14), Tom Chambers (10), Magic

Johnson (10) and Kevin McHale (10)... Only player in Western Conference from draft class of 1981 to be with team that originally picked him (No. 9)... Has streak of not fouling out at 790 games, second-best ever... Only Wilt Chamberlain, who never fouled out (1,045), went longer... Born Feb. 26, 1959, in Panama City, Panama... Attended Kansas State... Made $1.85 million.

Year	Team	G	FG	FG Pct.	FT	FT Pct.	Reb.	Ast.	TP	Avg.
1981-82	Dallas	82	439	.513	212	.768	254	105	1091	13.3
1982-83	Dallas	75	513	.492	297	.780	293	185	1326	17.7
1983-84	Dallas	81	721	.546	372	.812	373	288	1815	22.4
1984-85	Dallas	81	625	.508	342	.828	300	289	1598	19.7
1985-86	Dallas	82	677	.514	404	.836	291	271	1762	21.5
1986-87	Dallas	80	626	.495	419	.884	278	266	1676	21.0
1987-88	Dallas	71	497	.473	331	.873	246	262	1325	18.7
1988-89	Dallas	78	594	.476	316	.854	273	288	1534	19.7
1989-90	Dallas	80	626	.498	287	.844	280	289	1552	19.4
1990-91	Dallas	80	634	.482	282	.865	256	301	1590	19.9
	Totals	790	5952	.500	3262	.836	2844	2544	15269	19.3

HERB WILLIAMS 33 6-11 242   Forward-Center

Played in career-low 60 games because of chronic knee problems, but got better as season went on... Finished strongly as Mavericks' only low-post scoring threat... His 50.7 percent from field established career high... Was twice inadvertently kicked in right knee and developed bursitis... Sat out 19 consecutive games Dec. 14-Jan. 19... Returned Jan. 23 and didn't miss any more time rest of way... Averaged 13.8 points and 6.2 rebounds and shot 52 percent in those final 45 games... Went 17.7, 7.0 and 59 percent in March... Born Feb. 16, 1958, in Columbus, Ohio, and played at Ohio State in his hometown... Drafted 14th by Indiana in 1981... Made $1 million.

Year	Team	G	FG	FG Pct.	FT	FT Pct.	Reb.	Ast.	TP	Avg.
1981-82	Indiana	82	407	.477	126	.670	605	139	942	11.5
1982-83	Indiana	78	580	.499	155	.705	583	262	1315	16.9
1983-84	Indiana	69	411	.478	207	.702	554	215	1029	14.9
1984-85	Indiana	75	575	.475	224	.657	634	252	1375	18.3
1985-86	Indiana	78	627	.492	294	.730	710	174	1549	19.9
1986-87	Indiana	74	451	.480	199	.740	543	174	1101	14.9
1987-88	Indiana	75	311	.425	126	.737	469	98	748	10.0
1988-89	Ind.-Dal.	76	322	.436	133	.686	593	124	777	10.2
1989-90	Dallas	81	295	.444	108	.679	391	119	700	8.6
1990-91	Dallas	60	332	.507	83	.638	357	95	747	12.5
	Totals	748	4311	.474	1655	.698	5439	1652	10283	13.7

DEREK HARPER 30 6-4 200   Guard

The most marketable Maverick during the off-season . . . One of premier guards in the Western Conference because he's solid on offense and defense . . . More importantly, he's a good point guard . . . First player in NBA history to increase scoring average each of first eight seasons . . . Fourth-highest-scoring point guard in league . . . Has missed only 14 games in eight seasons . . . Born Oct. 13, 1961, in Elberton, Ga. . . . Left Illinois after junior year . . . Was 11th pick in 1983 by Mavs . . . Made $1.519 million.

Year	Team	G	FG	FG Pct.	FT	FT Pct.	Reb.	Ast.	TP	Avg.
1983-84	Dallas	82	200	.443	66	.673	172	239	469	5.7
1984-85	Dallas	82	329	.520	111	.721	199	360	790	9.6
1985-86	Dallas	79	390	.534	171	.747	226	416	963	12.2
1986-87	Dallas	77	497	.501	160	.684	199	609	1230	16.0
1987-88	Dallas	82	536	.459	261	.759	246	634	1393	17.0
1988-89	Dallas	81	538	.477	229	.806	228	570	1404	17.3
1989-90	Dallas	82	567	.488	250	.794	244	609	1473	18.0
1990-91	Dallas	77	572	.467	286	.731	233	548	1519	19.7
	Totals	642	3629	.485	1534	.749	1747	3985	9241	14.4

ROY TARPLEY 26 7-0 250   Forward

A franchise held hostage, year six . . . As James Donaldson said, "You have to wonder when the next slip-up will be. It could be next week, next month, next season. But it's almost to a point where you know there will be another one." . . . Had second arrest for DWI in 16 months when stopped in late March . . . It was especially disheartening because rehabilitation from knee surgery had been going so well . . . Tore anterior cruciate ligament in right knee in fifth game of season . . . Injury was sustained when he landed after making fast-break layup with 37.5 seconds left in first quarter of Nov. 9 home game against Orlando . . . In the four full games he played, he averaged 24 points and 12.3 rebounds and shot 54.3 percent . . . Played 75 games as a rookie, 81 in second season, 69 in three years since . . . Mavericks have held off notion of trade because they know return would be minimal because of other problems . . . And then there's his salary: $8.45 million next three seasons . . . Born Nov. 28, 1964, in Detroit, and played at Michigan . . . Seventh pick in 1986 . . . Made $765,000 in 1990-91.

Year	Team	G	FG	FG Pct.	FT	FT Pct.	Reb.	Ast.	TP	Avg.
1986-87	Dallas	75	233	.467	94	.676	533	52	561	7.5
1987-88	Dallas	81	444	.500	205	.740	959	86	1093	13.5
1988-89	Dallas	19	131	.541	66	.688	218	17	328	17.3
1989-90	Dallas	45	314	.451	130	.756	589	67	758	16.8
1990-91	Dallas	5	43	.544	16	.889	55	12	102	20.4
	Totals	225	1165	.485	511	.728	2354	234	2842	12.6

RODNEY McCRAY 30 6-8 235   Forward

Very good complementary player . . . But not the guy to pick up a team when Roy Tarpley is out . . . Not offensive-minded . . . Played 813 more minutes than Alex English, but took 55 fewer shots . . . Still Mavs' No. 1 small forward because of all-around game . . . Tied career high with 18 rebounds March 18 vs. Sacramento . . . Hit career-best 80.3 percent from the line . . . Born Aug. 29, 1961, in Mt. Vernon, N.Y. . . . Member of 1980 Olympic team . . . Played on 1980 NCAA champion Louisville and was third pick by Rockets in 1983 draft . . . Made $985,000.

Year	Team	G	FG	FG Pct.	FT	FT Pct.	Reb.	Ast.	TP	Avg.
1983-84	Houston	79	335	.499	182	.731	450	176	853	10.8
1984-85	Houston	82	476	.535	231	.738	539	355	1183	14.4
1985-86	Houston	82	338	.537	171	.770	520	292	847	10.3
1986-87	Houston	81	432	.552	306	.779	578	434	1170	14.4
1987-88	Houston	81	359	.481	288	.785	631	264	1006	12.4
1988-89	Sacramento	68	340	.466	169	.722	514	293	854	12.6
1989-90	Sacramento	82	537	.515	273	.784	669	377	1358	16.6
1990-91	Dallas	74	336	.495	159	.803	560	259	844	11.4
	Totals	629	3153	.511	1779	.765	4461	2450	8115	12.9

JAMES DONALDSON 34 7-2 280   Center

Only NBA center to start every game in 1990-91 . . . So much for that career-threatening knee injury in March 1989 . . . A guy worth rooting for . . . Can still outplay counterparts eight years younger . . . To think all it took to get him was sending Kurt Nimphius to the Clippers in 1985 . . . Not the first time he's been undersold: he had only two scholarship offers out of high school in Sacramento before going to Washington State . . . His 8.9-rebound average last season was 15th in league . . . Scoring and minutes also highest since 1986-87 . . . Future as spot player and backup . . . Has played longer than anyone in league without trying a three-pointer . . . Born Aug. 16, 1957, in Heacham, England, where father was stationed in Air Force . . . Was fourth-round pick by Seattle in 1979 . . . Made $880,000.

Year	Team	G	FG	FG Pct.	FT	FT Pct.	Reb.	Ast.	TP	Avg.
1980-81	Seattle	68	129	.542	101	.594	309	42	359	5.3
1981-82	Seattle	82	255	.609	151	.629	490	51	661	8.1
1982-83	Seattle	82	289	.583	150	.688	501	97	728	8.9
1983-84	San Diego	82	360	.596	249	.761	649	90	969	11.8
1984-85	L.A. Clippers	82	351	.637	227	.749	668	48	929	11.3
1985-86	LAC-Dal.	83	256	.558	204	.803	795	96	716	8.6
1986-87	Dallas	82	311	.586	267	.812	973	63	889	10.8
1987-88	Dallas	81	212	.558	147	.778	755	66	571	7.0
1988-89	Dallas	53	193	.573	95	.766	570	38	481	9.1
1989-90	Dallas	73	258	.539	149	.700	630	57	665	9.1
1990-91	Dallas	82	327	.532	165	.721	727	69	819	10.0
	Totals	850	2941	.576	1905	.734	7067	717	7787	9:2

LAFAYETTE (FAT) LEVER 31 6-3 175   Guard

Healthy return could still give Mavericks championship-caliber, three-guard rotation . . . Right knee inflamed during 1990 training camp and he was held out of final three preseason games to get him ready for opening night . . . Came off the bench first four games, his first action as a reserve since March 14, 1986 . . . Knee continued to bother him . . . Underwent arthroscopic surgery Nov. 13 and was gone the rest of the season . . . It was first time he didn't participate in playoffs . . . Needs 469 points to reach 10,000 . . . In 1989-90, with Denver, he became smallest NBA player to ever lead his team in scoring, assists and rebounding . . . Became known for versatility while at Arizona State . . . Born Aug. 18, 1960, in Pine Bluff, Ark. . . . Was 11th pick by Portland in 1982 draft . . . Made $1.519 million.

Year	Team	G	FG	FG Pct.	FT	FT Pct.	Reb.	Ast.	TP	Avg.
1982-83	Portland	81	256	.431	116	.730	225	426	633	7.8
1983-84	Portland	81	313	.447	159	.743	218	372	788	9.7
1984-85	Denver	82	424	.430	197	.770	411	613	1051	12.8
1985-86	Denver	78	468	.441	132	.725	420	584	1080	13.8
1986-87	Denver	82	643	.469	244	.782	729	654	1552	18.9
1987-88	Denver	82	643	.473	248	.785	665	639	1546	18.9
1988-89	Denver	71	558	.457	270	.785	662	559	1409	19.8
1989-90	Denver	79	568	.443	271	.804	734	517	1443	18.3
1990-91	Dallas	4	9	.391	11	.786	15	12	29	7.3
	Totals	640	3882	.452	1648	.772	4079	4376	9531	14.9

RANDY WHITE 23 6-8 249   Forward

Obviously unfair to compare him to fellow Louisiana Tech graduate Karl Malone . . . But shouldn't someone have warned Mavericks that he wouldn't compare to many starting forwards, period? . . . Still having trouble making transition from college back-to-the-basket center to NBA small forward . . . Shooting 40 percent would be a start . . . Did surpass rookie totals in every category in 1990-91, nearly tripling scoring and rebounding figures . . . The No. 8 pick overall two years ago . . . Born Nov. 4, 1967, in Shreveport, La. . . . Made $730,000.

Year	Team	G	FG	FG Pct.	FT	FT Pct.	Reb.	Ast.	TP	Avg.
1989-90	Dallas	55	93	.369	50	.562	173	21	237	4.3
1990-91	Dallas	79	265	.398	159	.707	504	63	695	8.8
	Totals	134	358	.390	209	.666	677	84	932	7.0

BRAD DAVIS 35 6-3 183   Guard

The last Maverick remaining from the first season re-signed after being unrestricted free agent . . . Can still play competent 10 or 12 minutes, but there may not be a roster spot available . . . Made most appearances since 1986-87, but 42.6 percent shooting was lowest since rookie season . . . Franchise all-time leader in games and assists . . . Among guards active at the end of 1990-91, only Rickey Green, Walter Davis and Robert Reid were older . . . Born Dec. 17, 1955, in Monaca, Pa. . . . Attended Maryland . . . Drafted 15th as an undergraduate by Lakers in 1977 . . . Made $600,000.

Year	Team	G	FG	FG Pct.	FT	FT Pct.	Reb.	Ast.	TP	Avg.
1977-78	Los Angeles	33	30	.417	22	.759	35	83	82	2.5
1978-79	L.A.-Ind.	27	31	.564	16	.696	17	52	78	2.9
1979-80	Ind.-Utah	18	35	.556	13	.813	17	50	83	4.6
1980-81	Dallas	56	230	.561	163	.799	151	385	626	11.2
1981-82	Dallas	82	397	.515	185	.804	226	509	993	12.1
1982-83	Dallas	79	359	.572	186	.845	198	565	915	11.6
1983-84	Dallas	81	345	.530	199	.836	187	561	896	11.1
1984-85	Dallas	82	310	.505	158	.888	193	581	825	10.1
1985-86	Dallas	82	267	.532	198	.868	146	467	764	9.3
1986-87	Dallas	82	199	.456	147	.860	114	373	577	7.0
1987-88	Dallas	75	208	.501	91	.843	102	303	537	7.2
1988-89	Dallas	78	183	.483	99	.805	108	242	497	6.4
1989-90	Dallas	73	179	.490	77	.770	93	242	470	6.4
1990-91	Dallas	80	159	.426	91	.771	118	230	431	5.4
	Totals	928	2932	.511	1645	.828	1705	4643	7774	8.4

KELVIN UPSHAW 28 6-2 180 — Guard

Backup point guard . . . Went into summer as unrestricted free agent . . . Used to being a yo-yo . . . Waived by Dallas in final reduction of 1990 training camp . . . Re-signed to one-year contract Nov. 12 to take Roy Tarpley's roster spot . . . Waived Dec. 24 prior to deadline for contracts becoming guaranteed for season . . . Probably just a coincidence . . . Re-re-signed to pair of 10-day deals . . . With Fat Lever still rehabilitating, re-re-re-signed to another pact for remainder of season . . . Also had two 10-day signings in 1989-90, so he's officially signed eight contracts with Mavericks . . . Appeared in 35 of 38 games after All-Star break . . . Set career highs in nine categories . . . Undrafted out of Utah in 1986 . . . Born Jan. 24, 1963, in Chicago . . . Made $30,000.

Year	Team	G	FG	FG Pct.	FT	FT Pct.	Reb.	Ast.	TP	Avg.
1988-89	Mia.-Bos.	32	99	.467	18	.692	49	117	219	6.8
1989-90	Bos.-Dal.-G.S.	40	64	.438	28	.757	41	54	160	4.0
1990-91	Dallas	48	104	.450	55	.859	55	86	270	5.6
	Totals	120	267	.453	101	.795	145	257	649	5.4

THE ROOKIES

DOUG SMITH 22 6-10 220 — Forward

Along with Danny Manning and Wayman Tisdale, the only player in Big 8 history with more than 2,000 points and 1,000 rebounds . . . Holds Missouri career records for rebounds, field-goals made and attempted, and ranks second in scoring, steals and blocked shots . . . Has great opportunity with Mavericks, who need his scoring on the frontline . . . No. 6 pick overall . . . Named two-time conference Player of the Year by UPI . . . Born Sept. 17, 1969, in Detroit.

DONALD HODGE 22 7-0 230 — Center

Mavericks would love to convert 33rd pick in the draft into James Donaldson's eventual replacement . . . But Hodge played only two years of college ball . . . Did not play as a freshman at Temple in order to become academically eligible and then left after junior year . . . Teammate of much publicized Mark Macon helped Owls to final eight of NCAA tournament in 1991 by shooting 63.3 percent and averaging 9.8 points in four games . . . Born Feb. 25, 1969, in Washington, D.C.

Rolando Blackman is Mavs' all-time scoring leader.

MIKE IUZZOLINO 23 5-10 180   **Guard**
Played first two years at Penn State, then moved to St. Francis
(Pa.) . . . Red Flash lost to Arizona in first round of NCAA tournament last season, but he had 20 points and six assists . . . Broke
Maurice Stokes' school record for points in a season . . . Two-time
academic All-American . . . No. 35 selection . . . Needs to improve
defense . . . Born Jan. 22, 1968, in Altoona, Pa.

COACH RICHIE ADUBATO: Opened first full season as head
coach last season with 4-1 record . . . Then had
rug pulled out from underneath him by injuries
. . . More people were sympathizing than crit-
icizing after 28-54 finish . . . Refs weren't
among the sympathizers . . . Hit with 22 tech-
nical fouls and one ejection . . . Also suspended
for going after official after Jan. 16 game at
San Antonio . . . Led all coaches with 20 tech-
nicals in 1989-90, the season he took over for fired John MacLeod
11 games in . . . Third coach in Mavs' history . . . Got first head-
coaching shot as interim replacement for Dick Vitale in Detroit
12 games into 1979-80 season . . . Later scouted for Hawks and
was assistant with the Knicks for four years before being hired as
MacLeod's No. 1 assistant at Dallas in 1986 . . . Son, Scott, was
seventh-round draft pick by Sacramento in 1987 . . . Born Nov.
23, 1936, in East Orange, N.J.

GREATEST TEAM

In the medieval days of 1987-88, which seems so long ago in
the light of recent events, the Mavericks were the franchise other
expansion teams wanted to copy. They had Rolando Blackman,
Derek Harper, Sam Perkins, Detlef Schrempf, Mark Aguirre,
James Donaldson and Roy Tarpley.

The Mavericks went 55-27 the season before and won the
division, but got bounced in the first round of the playoffs, so
there was pressure come the fall of '87. It turned out they were
never better: a 53-29 record, two victories fewer than the campaign
before, but made far better by an appearance in the conference
finals, where they pushed the Lakers to seven games before falling.

Aguirre and Donaldson were outstanding. Tarpley was the

NBA's best sixth man and became the first reserve ever to finish in the top 10 in rebounding. He also played in 81 games, more than he's played in the three seasons since combined.

ALL-TIME MAVERICK LEADERS

SEASON

Points: Mark Aguirre, 2,330, 1983-84
Assists: Derek Harper, 4,643, 1987-88
Rebounds: James Donaldson, 973, 1986-87

GAME

Points: Mark Aguirre, 49 vs. Philadelphia, 1/28/85
Assists: Derek Harper, 18 vs. Boston, 12/29/88
Rebounds: James Donaldson, 27 vs. Portland (3 OT), 12/29/89

CAREER

Points: Rolando Blackman, 15,269, 1981-91
Assists: Brad Davis, 4,458, 1980-91
Rebounds: James Donaldson, 4,319, 1985-91

DENVER NUGGETS

TEAM DIRECTORY: Owners: Peter C.B. Bynoe; Robert Wussler; GM: Bernie Bickerstaff; Dir. Pub. Rel.: Jay Clark: Coach: Paul Westhead. Asst. Coaches: Jim Boyle, Mike Evans, Judas Prada. Arena: McNichols Sports Arena (17,022). Colors: White, blue, green, yellow, red, purple and orange.

Will Dikembe Mutombo be mile-high in Denver?

SCOUTING REPORT

SHOOTING: The Nuggets check their consciences at the door. The only rule is: Don't stop firing. Michael Adams, who was traded to Washington in June, set disciplined shooters back to the Naismith generation when he stole a ball just beyond halfcourt, crossed the 10-second line, looked around to find no close pursuers and, instead of going for the easy layup, launched a three. That he made it wasn't the point.

The Nuggets led the NBA in scoring and still shot only 44 percent, worst in the league. (Orlando Woolridge did average 25.1 on .498 shooting, but he's a Piston now.) Only Minnesota (.449) and New Jersey (.444) were close. They had 1,409 more attempts than anyone, an average of 17.2 per game. Don't worry about a dropoff. Adams will be flinging for the Bullets, but more time for Chris Jackson and the arrival of rookie Mark Macon at shooting guard should compensate.

PLAYMAKING: Adams and Jackson couldn't play together in the same backcourt because it presented obvious matchup problems. So Adams was traded and Jackson will become the one and only point guard.

He, like the Nuggets, will continue to pay for youth and the style of play. Jackson's assist-to-turnover ratio was less than 2-1 last season, his rookie campaign, and the team as a whole wasn't even close (24.5-16.2).

DEFENSE: Yeah, right. They were the only team in the league last season not to hold an opponent below 100 points at least once. The Suns set NBA records Nov. 10 with 107 points in a half and 57 in a quarter, and Orlando's Scott Skiles broke another mark at their expense with 30 assists Dec. 30. Ex-Piston Scott Hastings promises to add a measure of defense.

The defense turned out to be as bad as most expected—and the locals feared. The Nuggets could create turnovers, but against teams that didn't panic the layups came with great frequency. That won't change until Denver's approach does.

REBOUNDING: The Nuggets set a league record for most offensive rebounds in a season (1,520) and finished No. 1 for 1990-91 in total rebounds at 4,050, good enough for a Denver NBA-era mark, but that is largely because of the number of shots taken. In the most telling statistic, percentage of rebound opportunities converted, they were only average.

NUGGET ROSTER

No.	Veterans	Pos.	Ht.	Wt.	Age	Yrs. Pro	College
33	Greg Anderson	F-C	6-10	230	27	4	Houston
45	Anthony Cook	F-C	6-9	215	24	1	Arizona
—	Winston Garland	G	6-2	175	26	4	SW Missouri State
—	Scott Hastings	C-F	6-11	245	31	9	Arkansas
3	Chris Jackson	G	6-1	170	22	1	Louisiana State
35	Jerome Lane	F	6-6	232	24	3	Pittsburgh
30	Marcus Liberty	F	6-8	205	23	1	Illinois
21	Todd Lichti	G	6-4	205	24	2	Stanford
34	Reggie Williams	F-G	6-7	195	27	4	Georgetown
42	Joe Wolf	C	6-11	230	26	4	North Carolina

Rd.	Rookies	Sel. No.	Pos.	Ht.	Wt.	College
1	Dikembe Mutombo	4	C	7-2	245	Georgetown
1	Mark Macon	8	G	6-3	185	Temple
1	Kevin Brooks	18	F	6-6	200	SW Louisiana

Even with Jerome Lane, there remains much to prove. Dikembe Mutombo arrives with a reputation for rebounding and shot-blocking, but at the expense of Blair Rasmussen being traded to Atlanta. Rasmussen averaged 9.7 boards last season and Mutombo is, after all, only a rookie.

OUTLOOK: More Rocky Mountain low. The growing pains will continue to hurt, but good showings by first-rounders Mutombo and Macon, continued development by Jackson and Lane and a healthy return by Todd Lichti would at least provide an anesthetic. But the only real hope for Paul Westhead's troupe is to avoid last place in the Midwest, maybe even the Western Conference.

NUGGET PROFILES

CHRIS JACKSON 22 6-1 170 Guard

Drafted from Louisiana State to be a point guard, but no one is sure where he really belongs . . . Scores like off guard, but a liability on defense there . . . May need to be paired with a big guard . . . Showed potential as a great shooter and scorer, as advertised . . . Went for at least 30 points four times and 20 points 16 times . . . His 14.1 average was the highest by a Denver rookie since the Nuggets joined the NBA . . . Born March 9, 1969, in Gulfport, Miss. . . . Was third pick in 1990 draft . . . Made $1,660,000 in 1990-91.

Year	Team	G	FG	FG Pct.	FT	FT Pct.	Reb.	Ast.	TP	Avg.
1990-91	Denver	67	417	.413	84	.857	121	206	942	14.1

TODD LICHTI 24 6-4 205   Guard

Most marketable Nugget . . . Teams almost always ask about him when they call to talk trade . . . A shooting guard who can drive and handle the ball well enough to play point in a pinch . . . Fair outside shooter, but doesn't get a lot of flexibility in offensive scheme that always puts him in the corner . . . Stanford product played just 29 games in injury-filled 1990-91 . . . Scored 20 points or more seven times in that time . . . Arthroscopic surgery on left knee Jan. 28 finished his season . . . Born Jan. 8, 1967, in Walnut Creek, Wash. . . . Was 15th pick by Denver in 1989 draft . . . Made $565,000 in 1990-91.

Year	Team	G	FG	FG Pct.	FT	FT Pct.	Reb.	Ast.	TP	Avg.
1989-90	Denver	79	250	.486	130	.747	151	116	630	8.0
1990-91	Denver	29	166	.439	59	.855	112	72	405	14.0
	Totals	108	416	.466	189	.778	263	188	1035	9.6

JEROME LANE 24 6-6 232   Forward

Left a good final impression heading into the offseason . . . Tied franchise record for rebounds in a game in next-to-last outing, then broke it in the season finale with 25 against Houston . . . Also set Nuggets NBA-era record with 280 offensive rebounds . . . Guess what his strong suit is? . . . It's not free-throw shooting. He hit 41.1 percent from the line . . . Has roundish, Barkleyesque look, but he's definitely not soft on boards . . . Former NCAA rebounding champion at Pitt despite small size . . . Has proven to be a good passer and ball-handler who was used by former coach Doug Moe at the point in emergency situations . . . Can be good . . . He'll also be the first to tell you that . . . Poor defense, erratic shooting . . . Born Dec. 4, 1966, in Akron, Ohio

. . . Drafted 23rd by San Antonio in 1987 . . . Made $500,000 in 1990-91.

Year	Team	G	FG	FG Pct.	FT	FT Pct.	Reb.	Ast.	TP	Avg.
1988-89	Denver	54	109	.426	43	.384	200	60	261	4.8
1989-90	Denver	67	145	.469	44	.367	361	105	334	5.0
1990-91	Denver	62	202	.438	58	.411	578	123	463	7.5
	Totals	183	456	.444	145	.389	1139	288	1058	5.8

MARCUS LIBERTY 23 6-8 205   Forward

Had off-and-on rookie year with flashes of big-time skills as an athlete and finisher . . . But has yet to prove he can consistently play at this level . . . Classic example of player who could have used another year in college . . . Ineligible as a freshman at Illinois and passed up senior year to enter draft . . . Had a tough transition to open-court style after playing predominantly with his back to the basket in college . . . Played in team-high 76 games, with 18 starts . . . Born Oct. 27, 1968, in Chicago . . . Selected 15th in 1990 draft . . . Made $210,000 in 1990-91.

Year	Team	G	FG	FG Pct.	FT	FT Pct.	Reb.	Ast.	TP	Avg.
1990-91	Denver	76	216	.421	58	.630	221	64	507	6.7

JOE WOLF 26 6-11 230   Center

Made a good move to leave the Clippers, where he wouldn't have played . . . Signed free-agent contract in summer of 1990 . . . Got in 74 games in 1990-91 and started 38 times, including 32 of his last 33 . . . Appears to be part of long-term puzzle, though may not ultimately as a starter . . . Nuggets see him as the perfect reserve—someone with the right attitude who hustles and can play more than one position . . . His 400 rebounds were only 103 less than he had previous two years combined . . . Went to Denver expecting to play center or power forward in the open-court style of play that didn't require him to be a post player, but flourished in second half of season as small forward . . . Born Dec. 17, 1964, in Kohler, Wis. . . . Attended North Carolina . . .

Clippers made him 13th pick in 1987 draft . . . Made $990,000 in 1990-91.

Year	Team	G	FG	FG Pct.	FT	FT Pct.	Reb.	Ast.	TP	Avg.
1987-88	L.A. Clippers.....	42	136	.407	45	.833	187	98	320	7.6
1988-89	L.A. Clippers.....	66	170	.423	44	.688	271	113	386	5.8
1989-90	L.A. Clippers.....	77	155	.395	55	.775	232	62	370	4.8
1990-91	Denver.........	74	234	.451	69	.831	400	107	539	7.3
	Totals	259	695	.422	213	.783	1090	380	1615	6.2

SCOTT HASTINGS 31 6-11 245   Center-Forward

Traded in August by Pistons with 1992 second-round draft pick for Orlando Woolridge . . . Tough defensive type who'll bang and grab some rebounds . . . No real offensive threat . . . Good passer and foul-shooter . . . Great practice player . . . A second-round pick by Knicks in '82 out of Arkansas . . . Public-relations degree. Has written columns during playoffs for Detroit papers . . . Good sense of humor, can laugh at himself . . . Made some defensive contributions in early playoff rounds . . . Born June 6, 1960, in Independence, Kan. . . . Made $450,000 . . . Detroit got him as free agent after 1988-89 season.

Year	Team	G	FG	FG Pct.	FT	FT Pct.	Reb.	Ast.	TP	Avg.
1982-83	N.Y.-Atl.	31	13	.342	11	.550	41	3	37	1.2
1983-84	Atlanta.........	68	111	.468	82	.788	270	46	305	4.5
1984-85	Atlanta.........	64	89	.473	63	.778	159	46	241	3.8
1985-86	Atlanta.........	62	65	.409	60	.857	124	26	193	3.1
1986-87	Atlanta.........	40	23	.338	23	.793	70	13	71	1.8
1987-88	Atlanta.........	55	40	.488	25	.926	97	16	110	2.0
1988-89	Miami	75	143	.436	91	.850	231	59	386	5.1
1989-90	Detroit.........	40	10	.303	19	.864	32	8	42	1.1
1990-91	Detroit.........	27	16	.571	13	1.000	28	7	48	1.8
	Totals	462	510	.439	387	.818	1052	224	1433	3.1

GREG (CADILLAC) ANDERSON 27 6-10 230   F-C

Still looking to duplicate early years in San Antonio . . . First Spur ever named to the All-Rookie team . . . Played in 41 games for Nuggets after January trade . . . They thought he would be a rebounder who could also run the court . . . Started twice . . . Only had double-figure rebounds six times . . . But 5.8 average in 16.1 minutes equated to around 10 for a normal game . . . Terrible passer . . . Backed up Hakeem Olajuwon as a freshman at Houston University and started final three seasons . . . Born June 22, 1964, in Houston . . . Made $1,365,000 in 1990-91.

Year	Team	G	FG	FG Pct.	FT	FT Pct.	Reb.	Ast.	TP	Avg.
1987-88	San Antonio	82	379	.501	198	.604	513	79	957	11.7
1988-89	San Antonio	82	460	.503	207	.514	676	61	1127	13.7
1989-90	Milwaukee	60	219	.507	91	.535	373	24	529	8.8
1990-91	Mil.-N.J.-Den.	68	116	.430	60	.522	318	16	292	4.3
	Totals	292	1174	.495	556	.547	1880	180	2905	9.9

REGGIE WILLIAMS 27 6-7 195   Forward-Guard

Potential realized? Not quite, but a nice start . . . Had the best year of his career while playing with fourth team in year and a half . . . Averaged 16.1 points as a Nugget after being cut by Spurs . . . Cavaliers couldn't waive him fast enough the season before . . . Scored 20 points or more 15 times . . . Confidence went way up with Nuggets . . . Insists he's mentally tough enough to play in NBA, but countless others, past employers included, claim former Georgetown star is way too frail . . . Nice guy, so a lot of people are rooting for him to shake label as big-time disappointment . . . Former No. 4 pick in draft by Clippers . . . Born March 5, 1964, in Baltimore.

Year	Team	G	FG	FG Pct.	FT	FT Pct.	Reb.	Ast.	TP	Avg.
1987-88	L.A. Clippers	35	152	.356	48	.727	118	58	365	10.4
1988-89	L.A. Clippers	63	260	.438	92	.754	179	103	642	10.2
1989-90	LAC-Clev.-S.A. . . .	47	131	.388	52	.765	83	53	320	6.8
1990-91	S.A.-Den.	73	384	.449	166	.843	306	133	991	13.6
	Totals	218	927	.419	358	.790	686	347	2318	10.6

WINSTON GARLAND 26 6-2 175   Guard

Nuggets got him from Clippers for future second-round pick on Draft Day . . . Had been acquired from Golden State in 1989-90 to be a role player, a third guard, but he was starting at the point by the end of last season . . . Won't win any games with flash, but doesn't throw any away, either . . . Was in backcourt opening lineup 26 times, including final 17 games of season . . . Clippers were 9-8 when he started at point guard . . .

Born Dec. 19, 1964, in Gary, Ind.... Recruited to Southwest Missouri State by current Clipper assistant coach John Hammond ... Drafted 40th by Bucks in 1987 ... Made $450,000.

Year	Team	G	FG	FG Pct.	FT	FT Pct.	Reb.	Ast.	TP	Avg.
1987-88	Golden State	67	340	.439	138	.879	227	429	831	12.4
1988-89	Golden State	79	466	.434	203	.809	328	505	1145	14.5
1989-90	G.S.-LAC	79	230	.401	102	.836	214	303	574	7.3
1990-91	L.A. Clippers	69	221	.426	118	.752	198	317	564	8.2
	Totals	294	1257	.427	561	.817	967	1554	3114	10.6

ANTHONY COOK 24 6-9 215 — Forward-Center

Plays bigger than his height ... Finished second on the team in blocked shots ... Averaged 10.3 rebounds in 14 games in January, 8.7 in 25 games as starter ... Missed 20 games after tearing a ligament in his lower right leg, returned for three games, then sat out final three because of continued problem ... Originally drafted by Phoenix (No. 24) and traded to Detroit ... Played in Greece in 1989-90 ... Born May 19, 1967, in Los Angeles ... Improved scoring each year at the University of Arizona ... Never shot worse than 54 percent in college ... Made $370,000 in 1990-91.

Year	Team	G	FG	FG Pct.	FT	FT Pct.	Reb.	Ast.	TP	Avg.
1990-91	Denver	58	118	.417	71	.550	326	26	307	5.3

THE ROOKIES

DIKEMBE MUTOMBO 25 7-2 245 — Center

Big East Defensive Player of the Year as a senior at Georgetown ... Fourth in the nation in blocked shots ... First center picked and No. 4 overall ... Needs to develop offensive skills ... At least he knows his range—he shot better than 70 percent twice in three years of college, with low of .586 ... Has competed for Zaire national team ... Speaks five languages ... Born June 25, 1966, in Kinshasa, Zaire.

MARK MACON 22 6-3 185 — Guard

Offensive exploits are well documented ... But Nuggets also got best defensive guard in the draft with the eighth pick ... Made two trips to the final eight with Temple . . . All-Atlantic 10 Conference each of his four years . . . Led nation's freshmen in scoring in 1988 . . . Became only third first-year player nominated for Wooden Award, joining Patrick Ewing and Ralph Sampson . . . Most attempts in a season at Temple was 622 . . . That's pregame warmups where he's going . . . Born April 14, 1969, in Saginaw, Mich.

KEVIN BROOKS 22 6-6 200   **Forward**
Was Bucks' 18th pick, but landed in Denver in trade that sent 15th choice Anthony Avent from Atlanta to Milwaukee . . . A scorer . . . Averaged 21.2 ppg as a a senior and shot .522 over four years at Southwestern Louisiana . . . Finished third on Ragin' Cajuns' all-time scoring list (2,294) behind Dwight Lamar and Andrew Toney . . . Born Oct. 29, 1969, in White Castle, La.

COACH PAUL WESTHEAD: What would Shakespeare say at a time like this? . . . Common man would say, "Let's hope he is renting." . . . Despite problems last season, players past and present say his system works with time . . . NBA career record is 159-164, the first time he's been below .500 . . . Last two years in the pros were the toughest—28-54 with 1982-83 Bulls and 20-62 last season . . . In between, had three 20-winning seasons at Loyola Marymount . . . Started as head coach at Division I level with nine seasons at LaSalle . . . Coached Lakers to 1980 title, going 50-18 after taking over for Jack McKinney and 12-4 in the playoffs . . . Born Feb. 21, 1939, in Malverne, Pa. . . . Played at St. Joseph's.

GREATEST TEAM

With other franchises, we've used as a guideline that only teams in their current sites will be considered; no ancestors like the Buffalo Braves or San Diego Rockets. With the Nuggets, Spurs, Pacers and Nets, it goes to another level: no ABA. While that may exclude the likes of some of Denver's greatest players, Mack Calvin or Ralph Simpson included, it also takes away the notion of comparing victories over the Minnesota Muskies or Anaheim

With Michael Adams gone, opportunity beckons Chris Jackson.

Amigos with wins over the Boston Celtics.

Even allowing the days of red, white and blue balls, the 1984-85 Nuggets may still deserve the title as the best. While going 52-30—granted, two wins fewer than the next season—they had a 20-game home winning streak and went 8-7 in the playoffs, the only plus-.500 postseason in the team's NBA life, before losing to the eventual champion Lakers in the Western Conference finals.

The 120 points-per-game was the Nuggets' lowest mark in four seasons, but the 117.6 against was also the best showing by the defense in the same stretch and represented the first time they had a point differential of more than plus–1 since their first year in the NBA. Alex English led the way with 27.9 points an outing.

ALL-TIME NUGGET LEADERS

SEASON

Points: Spencer Haywood, 2,519, 1969-70 (ABA)
  Alex English, 2,414, 1985-86
Assists: Michael Adams, 693, 1990-91
Rebounds: Spencer Haywood, 1,637, 1969-70 (ABA)
  George McGinnis, 864, 1978-79

GAME

Points: David Thompson, 73 vs. Detroit, 4/9/78
Assists: Larry Brown, 23 vs. Pittsburgh, 2/20/72 (ABA)
  Lafayette Lever, 23 vs. Golden State, 4/21/89
Rebounds: Spencer Haywood, 31 vs. Kentucky, 11/13/69 (ABA)
  Jerome Lane, 25 vs. Houston, 4/21/91

CAREER

Points: Alex English, 21,645, 1979-90
Assists: Alex English, 3,679, 1979-90
Rebounds: Dan Issel, 6,630, 1975-85

GOLDEN STATE WARRIORS

TEAM DIRECTORY: Owner: Jim Fitzgerald; Pres.: Daniel Finnane; GM/Coach: Don Nelson; Dir. Player Personnel: Sam Schuler; Dir. Scouting: Ed Gregory; Asst. Coaches: Donn Nelson, Garry St. Jean; Dir. Media Rel.: Julie Marvel. Arena: Oakland Coliseum (15,025). Colors: Gold and blue.

SCOUTING REPORT

SHOOTING: The Warriors are dangerous not just because they have three scorers, but because the three play off each other so well. Tim Hardaway provides quickness. Chris Mullin is the guy who wasn't supposed to be a star because he didn't have enough speed. Mitch Richmond dominates opposing guards with his strength.

That doesn't even get into the bench, where Sarunas Marciulionis shot 50.1 percent and Rod Higgins must be respected for three-point shooting. You quickly get the idea that offense isn't one of the problem areas for the Warriors, whose 116.6 points a game was second only to Denver. If they add anything at power forward or center, even the Nuggets may not be able to run fast enough to keep up.

PLAYMAKING: Hardaway embodies the Warriors' explosiveness. He was eleventh in NBA scoring and 10th in three-point shooting. This has much to do with his success as point guard because teams can't lay back and simply deny his penetration.

Get past Hardaway, though, and the dropoff of capable ballhandlers is significant. Last season's backup, Kevin Pritchard, was shipped to San Antonio. Or maybe the plan is that Hardaway just won't ever come out—he averaged 39.2 minutes a game last season.

DEFENSE: Hurt when opponents capitalized on the short lineup and lack of a low-post stopper, the Warriors allowed an alarming 115 points a game, second-worst in the NBA behind Denver and some three points more than No. 3 Indiana. In a league where defense wins championships, Golden State won't be a real contender until removing the red carpet leading to the basket.

Strange as this is, no team forced more turnovers, not even the Nuggets, who surely had more opportunities. The biggest impact was felt when they won nine games by three points or less, more

The cat who is a catalyst: Tim Hardaway.

than most. The 18.7 turnovers per game they forced turned into an average of 23 Warrior points.

REBOUNDING: What's one step up from lousy? Golden State was outrebounded 71 times in 1989-90, but improved to 60 last season, and the deficit went from 9.7 per game to 4.3. In the 22 outings when they outrebounded their opponents, the Warriors were 16-6.

WARRIOR ROSTER

No.	Veterans	Pos.	Ht.	Wt.	Age	Yrs. Pro	College
4	Vincent Askew	G	6-6	226	25	2	Memphis State
20	Mario Elie	G	6-5	210	27	1	American Int.
10	Tim Hardaway	G	6-0	175	25	2	Texas-El Paso
22	Rod Higgins	F	6-7	205	31	9	Fresno State
32	Tyrone Hill	F	6-9	243	23	1	Xavier
51	Les Jepsen	C	7-0	237	24	1	Iowa
53	Alton Lister	C-F	7-0	240	33	10	Arizona State
13	Sarunas Marciulionas	G	6-5	200	27	2	Lithuania
17	Chris Mullin	F	6-7	215	28	6	St. John's
43	Jim Petersen	F-C	6-10	235	29	7	Minnesota
23	Mitch Richmond	G	6-5	215	26	3	Kansas State
34	Tom Tolbert	F	6-7	240	26	3	Arizona

Rd.	Rookies	Sel. No.	Pos.	Ht.	Wt.	College
1	Chris Gatling	16	F	6-10	220	Old Dominion
1	Victor Alexander	17	F-C	6-9	265	Iowa State

Obviously, that's still not good enough. Searching for a center and a power forward just in case Tyrone Hill doesn't develop, Don Nelson went into the offseason looking for help up front. With three choices in the first round, the Warriors went with Chris Gatling, Victor Alexander and Italy-bound Shaun Vandiver, all power players. One working out would solve a major problem.

OUTLOOK: There's too much firepower and Nelson coaching hocus-pocus (Mario Elie torturing the Lakers in the playoffs?) not to like them. To an extent. Rebounding and defense will be their Achilles heel until proven otherwise.

WARRIOR PROFILES

CHRIS MULLIN 28 6-7 215   Forward

Basketball's answer to the change-up... He has as much quickness as long hair, but he has such great body control that he can twist and get the shot off... Reached new heights in 1990-91... Second-team All-NBA... Logged 3,315 minutes, the most since Moses Malone went 3,398 for Houston in 1981-82... Has reached double-figure points in 175 consecutive games in regular season, second only to Michael Jordan (419) and Patrick Ewing (208)... Became the first Warrior All-Star starter since Rick Barry in 1978... At 88 percent, he's currently fifth-best free-throw shooter of all time, behind Barry, Calvin Murphy, Larry Bird and Bill Sharman... More than the inspirational story of a recovering alcoholic... A great player under any circumstances... But feel free to rip his haircut... Born July 30, 1963, in Brooklyn, N.Y.... Local hero at St. John's... Seventh pick in 1985 draft... Made $2,650,000 in 1990-91.

Year	Team	G	FG	FG Pct.	FT	FT Pct.	Reb.	Ast.	TP	Avg.
1985-86	Golden State	55	287	.463	189	.896	115	105	768	14.0
1986-87	Golden State	82	477	.514	269	.825	181	261	1242	15.1
1987-88	Golden State	60	470	.508	239	.885	205	290	1213	20.2
1988-89	Golden State	82	830	.509	493	.892	483	415	2176	26.5
1989-90	Golden State	78	682	.536	505	.889	463	319	1956	25.1
1990-91	Golden State	82	777	.536	513	.884	443	329	2107	25.7
	Totals	439	3523	.516	2208	.880	1890	1719	9462	21.6

ROD HIGGINS 31 6-7 205   Forward

Bulls are still kicking themselves for cutting him... Twice... Jerry Krause isn't the only one... Higgins played with four teams in 1985-86 and has averaged double-figure scoring three of last four seasons, just missing in 1990-91... A good offensive rebounder for his size... Fresno State product has not missed a game since March 10, 1989, a run of 187 in a row... Warriors' all-time leader in three-point shots made (228) and attempted (637)... Has increased number of successful three-pointers each of the last five years... Bulls made him 31st pick in 1982 draft... Born Jan. 31, 1960, in Monroe, La.... Made $500,000 in 1990-91.

Year	Team	G	FG	FG Pct.	FT	FT Pct.	Reb.	Ast.	TP	Avg.
1982-83	Chicago	82	313	.448	209	.792	366	175	848	10.3
1983-84	Chicago	78	193	.447	113	.724	206	116	500	6.4
1984-85	Chicago	68	119	.441	60	.667	147	73	308	4.5
1985-86	Sea.-S.A.-N.J.-Chi	30	39	.368	19	.704	51	24	98	3.3
1986-87	Golden State	73	214	.519	200	.833	237	96	631	8.6
1987-88	Golden State	68	381	.526	273	.848	293	188	1054	15.5
1988-89	Golden State	81	301	.476	188	.821	376	160	856	10.6
1989-90	Golden State	82	304	.481	234	.821	422	129	909	11.1
1990-91	Golden State	82	259	.463	185	.819	354	113	776	9.5
	Totals	644	2123	.475	1481	.805	2452	1074	5980	9.3

MITCH RICHMOND 26 6-5 215   Guard

Second on team in scoring and 10th in NBA ...Went into funk after not making All-Star team, but mostly took it out on the opposition ...Had 40 points and career-high seven steals against Clippers in first game after snub... Grabbed 12 rebounds, tying personal-best, five nights later against Spurs...Post-up specialist because he's so strong...Became the first player to win Rookie of the Year and then improve scoring average each of next two seasons since Phil Ford in late 70s-early 80s... League's fourth-best rebounding guard...Scored 5,000th career point March 25 in 220th NBA game...Wilt Chamberlain (131 games) and Rick Barry (167) are only Warriors to reach milestone faster...Attended Kansas State and was fifth pick in 1988 draft ...Born June 30, 1965, in Fort Lauderdale, Fla....Made $850,000 in 1990-91.

Year	Team	G	FG	FG Pct.	FT	FT Pct.	Reb.	Ast.	TP	Avg.
1988-89	Golden State	79	649	.468	410	.810	468	334	1741	22.0
1989-90	Golden State	78	640	.497	406	.866	360	223	1720	22.1
1990-91	Golden State	77	703	.494	394	.847	452	238	1840	23.9
	Totals	234	1992	.486	1210	.840	1280	795	5301	22.7

SARUNAS MARCIULIONIS 27 6-5 200   Guard

Scoring average dipped in second season of basketball in the United States, but he left a good last impression with play in postseason ...Trade talk swirls, but salary presents heavy baggage...Still needs work on outside shot—when he takes it...Drives more than most Los Angeles motorists...That drives Don Nelson crazy...The upshot: averaged one free throw every four minutes to rank among the league leaders for second consecutive season...But didn't take enough advantage of it, converting just 72.4 percent of attempts...Leading scorer for Soviet Union in 1988 Olympics...Signed as free agent in 1989 ...Born June 13, 1964, in Kaunas, Lithuania...Made $1,270,000 in 1990-91.

Year	Team	G	FG	FG Pct.	FT	FT Pct.	Reb.	Ast.	TP	Avg.
1989-90	Golden State	75	289	.519	317	.787	221	121	905	12.1
1990-91	Golden State	50	183	.501	178	.724	118	85	545	10.9
	Totals	125	472	.512	495	.763	339	206	1450	11.6

TIM HARDAWAY 25 6-0 175   Guard

People make so much noise about all the general managers who passed on Karl Malone in 1985? Let's do some IQ tests on those who let Hardaway fall to 14th pick in '89 coming out of Texas-El Paso . . . Sacramento's Jerry Reynolds said if the draft was held again today, Hardaway would go No. 1 . . . Originally taken to combat the speed of Kevin Johnson, he's turned into a star . . . Doesn't get pushed around despite lack of size . . . Has a knuckleball jump shot with no rotation . . . Magic Johnson: "He's the king of the crossover [dribble] now. It's 'bang, bang, you're dead.' I love it." . . . Only Oscar Robertson racked up more points and assists by the end of his second season . . . The youngest player in the 1990 All-Star Game . . . Born Sept. 12, 1966, in Chicago . . . Made $850,000 in 1990-91.

Year	Team	G	FG	FG Pct.	FT	FT Pct.	Reb.	Ast.	TP	Avg.
1989-90	Golden State	79	464	.471	211	.764	310	689	1162	14.7
1990-91	Golden State	82	739	.476	306	.803	332	793	1881	22.9
	Totals	161	1203	.474	517	.787	642	1103	3043	18.9

MARIO ELIE 27 6-5 210   Guard

One night he had 19 points, eight assists and six rebounds to help Albany beat Pensacola in a CBA game . . . The next night, he had 14 points on four-of-five shooting, in 27 minutes for Warriors at Denver . . . Stature only increased from there . . . Finished as very pleasant surprise . . . Cut by Lakers in training camp, he came back to cause them problems in second round of playoffs . . . Originally drafted by Don Nelson in Milwaukee in 1985's seventh round . . . Played in Portugal, Argentina and Ireland and Miami of USBL before joining Albany for 1989-90 . . . Had a 10-day contract with 76ers before returning to Patroons . . . Then got call from Warriors . . . Speaks Spanish, Portugese, French and English . . . So what college did he attend? American International . . . Played on junior varsity at New York's Power Memorial High with Chris Mullin . . . Born Nov. 26, 1963, in New York . . . Made $50,000 in 1990-91.

Year	Team	G	FG	FG Pct.	FT	FT Pct.	Reb.	Ast.	TP	Avg.
1990-91	Phil.-G.S.	33	79	.497	75	.843	110	45	237	7.2

TOM TOLBERT 26 6-7 240   Forward

Consummate overachiever has carved a niche as a power forward despite size . . . Playing in Don Nelson's lineup helps, but so does his toughness . . . Nicknamed ''Bobcat'' because of scraggly hair . . . Started 32 games . . . Wonder if Hornets regret giving up on him after 14 games in 1988-89? . . . Born Oct. 16, 1965, in Long Beach, Cal. . . . Attended three colleges: UC-Irvine, Cerritos and Arizona, where he averaged 14.0 ppg from 1986 to 1988 . . . A second-round pick by Charlotte in 1988 . . . Made $405,000 in 1990-91.

Year	Team	G	FG	FG Pct.	FT	FT Pct.	Reb.	Ast.	TP	Avg.
1988-89	Charlotte	14	17	.459	6	.500	21	7	40	2.9
1989-90	Golden State	70	218	.493	175	.726	363	58	616	8.8
1990-91	Golden State	62	183	.423	127	.738	275	76	500	8.1
	Totals	146	418	.458	308	.725	659	141	1156	7.9

ALTON LISTER 33 7-0 240   Center-Forward

Has nine years playoff experience, topped only by Mychal Thompson's 11 and Dave Corzine's 10 among Western Conference centers . . . Came back after ruptured right Achilles tendon forced him to sit out final 79 games of 1989-90 to start in 65 of his 77 appearances and average 20.2 minutes an outing . . . Had missed only 13 of 656 games before that in first eight NBA seasons with Milwaukee and Seattle . . . Has two more guaranteed years on contract . . . Moving to backup role would cut down minutes and make playing at 35 seem reasonable . . . Born Oct. 1, 1958, in Dallas . . . Chosen 21st by Bucks in 1981 . . . Made $1,700,000 in 1990-91.

Year	Team	G	FG	FG Pct.	FT	FT Pct.	Reb.	Ast.	TP	Avg.
1981-82	Milwaukee	80	149	.519	64	.520	387	84	362	4.5
1982-83	Milwaukee	80	272	.529	130	.537	568	111	674	8.4
1983-84	Milwaukee	82	256	.500	114	.626	603	110	626	7.6
1984-85	Milwaukee	81	322	.538	154	.588	647	127	798	9.9
1985-86	Milwaukee	81	318	.551	160	.602	592	101	796	9.8
1986-87	Seattle	75	346	.504	179	.675	705	110	871	11.6
1987-88	Seattle	82	173	.504	114	.606	627	58	461	5.6
1988-89	Seattle	82	271	.499	115	.646	545	54	657	8.0
1989-90	Golden State	3	4	.500	4	.571	8	2	12	4.0
1990-91	Golden State	77	188	.478	115	.569	483	93	491	6.4
	Totals	723	2299	.515	1149	.600	5165	850	5748	8.0

TYRONE HILL 23 6-9 243   Forward

Was supposed to be Don Nelson's answer for Warrior rebounding woes when he was drafted 11th . . . Proves Nelson doesn't have an answer for everything . . . Had six double-figure rebound games, five against playoff teams, but lost job in starting lineup . . . Warriors considered his rookie season a disappointment . . . Did have a 16-rebound game against Derrick Coleman in matchup of first two power forwards selected . . . Offered around as trade bait at season's end, but will be welcomed back if not dealt on theory that most players struggle as rookies . . . Was fourth-leading rebounder in the nation in 1990 as a senior at Xavier . . . Midwestern Collegiate Conference Player of the Year . . . Born March 17, 1968, in Cincinnati . . . Made $1,000,000 in 1990-91.

Year	Team	G	FG	FG Pct.	FT	FT Pct.	Reb.	Ast.	TP	Avg.
1990-91	Golden State	74	147	.492	96	.632	383	19	390	5.3

JIM PETERSEN 29 6-10 235   Forward-Center

Inconsistent season ended with a good showing in the playoffs, most notably against San Antonio . . . Uncertain spot in the rotation didn't help, sometimes going from starter to did-not-play . . . Averaged 13.5 minutes in 62 appearances . . . Played more than 20 minutes only eight times . . . The only Warrior to ever participate in NBA Finals . . . He was with the Rockets in 1986 championship series against Boston . . . Can regularly hit baseline jumper . . . Born Feb. 22, 1962, in Minneapolis . . . Hometown star at Minnesota . . . A third-round pick by Rockets in 1984 . . . Made $1,235,000 in 1990-91.

Year	Team	G	FG	FG Pct.	FT	FT Pct.	Reb.	Ast.	TP	Avg.
1984-85	Houston	60	70	.486	50	.758	147	29	190	3.2
1985-86	Houston	82	196	.477	113	.706	396	85	505	6.2
1986-87	Houston	82	386	.511	152	.727	557	127	924	11.3
1987-88	Houston	69	249	.510	114	.745	436	106	613	8.9
1988-89	Sacramento	66	278	.459	115	.747	413	81	671	10.2
1989-90	Golden State	43	60	.426	52	.712	160	23	172	4.0
1990-91	Golden State	62	114	.483	50	.658	200	27	279	4.5
	Totals	464	1353	.487	646	.725	2309	478	3354	7.2

VINCENT ASKEW 25 6-6 226   Guard

Another CBA claimer... Signed by Golden State March 5 for remainder of 1990-91 and this season... Averaged 4.7 points in seven games... Spot for 1991-92 made easier when Kevin Pritchard was traded to San Antonio for second-round pick... Can defend bigger guards... Originally 39th selection overall by 76ers in 1987 following junior year at Memphis State... Played 14 games for Philadelphia before being waived ... Also played in World Basketball League and Italy... First player twice named CBA Most Valuable Player... Set league's single-season scoring record in 1989-90 with 1,484 points... Teammate at Albany with current Warrior Mario Elie... Born Feb. 28, 1966, in Memphis, Tenn.

Year	Team	G	FG	FG Pct.	FT	FT Pct.	Reb.	Ast.	TP	Avg.
1987-88	Philadelphia	14	22	.297	8	.727	22	33	52	3.7
1990-91	Golden State	7	12	.480	9	.818	11	13	33	4.7
	Totals	21	34	.343	17	.773	33	46	85	4.0

LES JEPSEN 24 7-0 237   Center

First and foremost, a project... First pick of 1990 second round after earning third-team All-Big Ten honors at Iowa... Averaged only 5.0 minutes in 21 games as a rookie... Made $505,000 anyway... Wasn't on the playoff roster... Enrolled at Iowa in 1985 with recruiting class that included B.J. Armstrong, Roy Marble, Ed Horton and Kevin Gamble... Sight we'd like to have seen: Jepsen running the relays for track team at Bowbells (N.D.) High... Born June 24, 1967, in Bowbells, a farm community of about 800 people 15 miles south of Canadian border and 100 miles east of Montana.

Year	Team	G	FG	FG Pct.	FT	FT Pct.	Reb.	Ast.	TP	Avg.
1990-91	Golden State	21	11	.306	6	.667	37	1	28	1.3

THE ROOKIES

CHRIS GATLING 24 6-10 220   Forward

Averaged 21.3 points in three seasons at Old Dominion after

transferring from Pitt . . . Also touted for defensive and shot-blocking abilities . . . Two-time Sun Belt Player of the Year . . . Career shooting percentage of 60.6 is highest in conference history . . . No. 16 pick . . . Played for U.S. national team in world championships in Argentina before senior year . . . Born Sept. 3, 1967, in Elizabeth City, N.C.

VICTOR ALEXANDER 22 6-9 265   **Forward-Center**
When Don Nelson beefs up the front line, he beefs up the front line . . . Chris Gatling at 16 and then Alexander, who should have "wide load" sign attached, at 17 . . . Bulk may allow him to play some center in the J.R. Reid, Michael Cage mold . . . Led Big 8 in scoring and ranked second in blocked shots and shooting percentage as a senior . . . Iowa State's third all-time leading scorer, behind Jeff Grayer and Barry Stevens . . . Born Aug. 31, 1969, in Detroit.

COACH DON NELSON: His reputation runneth over . . . Warriors upsetting Spurs in last season's playoff and then giving Lakers a run before falling only adds to the resume . . . Moved into 10th spot all-time for playoff coaching victories and is fifth among active coaches . . . Led a team into postseason for 11th time in 14-year career . . . Only Red Auerbach (19 times), Jack Ramsay (16), Dick Motta (14) and Doug Moe (12) have more . . . Has 664-466 lifetime mark in regular season . . . Only Auerbach has more wins and a higher winning percentage . . . Disappointment came with not being selected coach of 1992 U.S. Olympic team . . . Told people he would love to have the job and was so interested he paid his own way to Argentina to watch 1988 world championships . . . People perceived that as politicking for the spot, and he was passed over in favor of Chuck Daly . . . Now fighting sentiment that he should not try to continue as both coach and general manager because of time constraints . . . Born May 15, 1949, in Muskegon, Mich. . . . Starred at Iowa before playing 14 seasons in NBA, mostly for Boston.

GREATEST TEAM

Why you can go against a team that won the NBA title and get away with it: the 1974-75 Warriors had Keith (later Jamaal)

Chris Mullin's double-figures are only a part of his game.

Wilkes win Rookie of the Year, Rick Barry average 30.6 points a game, and they won the championship, but they also went 48-34. The next season they were 59-23.

Feel free to argue, but don't overlook what the 1975-76 team did just because they didn't win it all. There was balanced scoring with Barry at 21.0, Phil Smith at 20.0 and Wilkes at 17.8, and more than a few team memories. They reached Game 7 of the Western Conference finals before losing to Phoenix and had one midseason stretch of 18 victories in 21 games. They also closed by winning 11 of 14.

In case of a tie between the above, feel free to consider 1966-67 as the compromise candidate. Known as the San Francisco Warriors, they finished only 44-37, but stayed alive until losing to Philadelphia in six games in the Finals, and Barry led the league in scoring at 35.6 points per game and was named MVP of the All-Star Game.

ALL-TIME WARRIOR LEADERS

SEASON

Points: Wilt Chamberlain, 4,029, 1961-62
Assists: Eric Floyd, 848, 1986-87
Rebounds: Wilt Chamberlain, 2,149, 1960-61

GAME

Points: Wilt Chamberlain, 100 vs. New York, 3/2/62
Assists: Guy Rodgers, 28 vs. St. Louis, 3/14/63
Rebounds: Wilt Chamberlain, 55 vs. Boston, 11/24/60

CAREER

Points: Wilt Chamberlain, 17,783, 1959-65
Assists: Guy Rodgers, 4,845, 1958-70
Rebounds: Nate Thurmond, 12,771, 1963-74

HOUSTON ROCKETS

TEAM DIRECTORY: Chairman: Charlie Thomas; Pres.: Edward Schmidt; GM: Steve Patterson; Dir. Media Inf.: Jay Goldberg; Coach: Don Chaney; Asst. Coaches: Carroll Dawson, Rudy Tomjanovich, Calvin Murphy, John Killilea. Arena: The Summit (16,279). Colors: Red and gold.

Hakeem Olajuwon took blocked-shots crown despite injury.

SCOUTING REPORT

SHOOTING: For the first time since 1972-73, four Rockets averaged at least 17 points a game: Hakeem Olajuwon (21.2), Kenny Smith (17.7), Otis Thorpe (17.5) and Vernon Maxwell (17.0). So although they were only 10th in the league in scoring at 106.7, they spread it around. Consider that in the final 42 games, during which Houston went 32-10, six different players led in scoring at least six times.

Only Denver took more three-point shots, and the difference was but 70 attempts, less than one a game. Houston converted 316 of their 989 tries, the fourth-best total in league history. Both stand as personal monuments to Maxwell.

But this is still not a real good shooting team. Only Thorpe (.556, seventh-best in the NBA), Smith (.520) and Olajuwon (.508) broke 50 percent.

PLAYMAKING: Smith, the former No. 6 pick overall by Sacramento, seemed to have a breakthrough season, but his assist-to-turnover ratio of 554-237 is nothing special. That is an area that needs work, since only four teams averaged more than the Rockets' 17.1 turnovers. Smith finished 17th in assists.

That Houston has depth here, though, is a definite plus. Sleepy Floyd was sixth in the league in assists just two seasons ago and played all 82 games in 1990-91, but started just four.

DEFENSE: This may be a better defensive team than the numbers show, and that's saying something. The Rockets held opponents to less than 100 points a franchise-record 40 times, the fifth-highest mark in the league, and to 103.2 points per game, the second-best showing in franchise history. And they did it without their No. 1 defender, Olajuwon, for 26 games, which means there's still room to improve.

REBOUNDING: For the first time since 1985-86, two Rockets finished in double figures in the category, Olajuwon at 13.8 and Thorpe at 10.3, the latter ninth-best in the league. Olajuwon's eye injury kept him from reaching the qualifying minimum, but that number would have surpassed David Robinson (13.0) for the crown.

But as a team, even with Larry Smith at 8.8 in just 23.7 minutes an outing, Houston was only 12th-best. So they went for bulk in the draft by picking John Turner.

ROCKET ROSTER

No.	Veterans	Pos.	Ht.	Wt.	Age	Yrs. Pro	College
50	Matt Bullard	F	6-10	225	24	1	Iowa
21	Eric Floyd	G	6-3	183	31	9	Georgetown
32	Dave Jamerson	G	6-5	192	24	1	Ohio State
1	Buck Johnson	F	6-7	206	27	5	Alabama
11	Vernon Maxwell	G	6-4	190	26	3	Florida
34	Hakeem Olajuwon	C	7-0	258	28	7	Houston
30	Kenny Smith	G	6-3	170	26	4	North Carolina
13	Larry Smith	F-C	6-8	251	33	11	Alcorn State
33	Otis Thorpe	F	6-10	246	29	7	Providence
20	Kennard Winchester	G	6-5	212	25	1	Averett
10	David Wood	F	6-9	228	26	2	Nevada-Reno

Rd.	Rookies	Sel. No.	Pos.	Ht.	Wt.	College
1	John Turner	20	F	6-7	245	Phillips

OUTLOOK: For a time last season, Coach of the Year Don Chaney's Rockets were the best the NBA offered, but it will take another good showing to prove they weren't just playing over their collective heads. The same showing combined with 82 games from Olajuwon should do it.

If the backcourt shoots well—note that Floyd finished at .411 and Maxwell at .404—the odds suddenly get a lot better. But at least they have the three-guard rotation many still desire, and a frontline in a similar position with Larry Smith.

ROCKET PROFILES

HAKEEM OLAJUWON 28 7-0 258   Center

Went from Akeem to Hakeem . . . Had his most star-crossed season as a pro . . . Won second straight blocked-shots title and came within 30 rebounds and 14 games played of third straight rebounding championship . . . Missed 25 games after inadvertent elbow from Bill Cartwright caused a fracture around the right eye . . . Rockets went 15-10 in that stretch . . . Some silly people suggested that made a trade logical, getting plenty for him and keeping the rest of the successful group intact . . . A reserve the first six games after coming back, the first time he hadn't started as a pro . . . Born Jan. 21, 1963, in Lagos, Nigeria . . . Starred at University of Houston, where he led Cougars to Final Four three straight years . . . No. 1 overall pick by Houston in 1984 draft and was NBA Rookie of the Year in 1984-85 . . . Injury last season meant that for the first time in his seven-year career he didn't play in the All-Star Game . . . But he made third-team All-NBA . . . Was paid $3,175,000.

Year	Team	G	FG	FG Pct.	FT	FT Pct.	Reb.	Ast.	TP	Avg.
1984-85	Houston	82	677	.538	338	.613	974	111	1692	20.6
1985-86	Houston	68	625	.526	347	.645	781	137	1597	23.5
1986-87	Houston	75	677	.508	400	.702	858	220	1755	23.4
1987-88	Houston	79	712	.514	381	.695	959	163	1805	22.8
1988-89	Houston	82	790	.508	454	.696	1105	149	2034	24.8
1989-90	Houston	82	806	.501	382	.713	1149	234	1995	24.3
1990-91	Houston	56	487	.508	213	.769	770	131	1187	21.2
	Totals	524	4774	.514	2515	.685	6596	1145	12065	23.0

ERIC (SLEEPY) FLOYD 31 6-3 183　　　　Guard

Has scored 1,000 points or more for eight straight seasons (1,005 in 1990-91) . . . Only Magic Johnson and Rolando Blackman have longer streaks among active guards . . . Started just four games . . . Scored 20 points or more 18 times, most by a Rocket reserve since Calvin Murphy in 1980-81 . . . Forty points off the bench Feb. 26 at Denver was first time in franchise history a Rocket scored 40 points in less than 30 minutes . . . Born March 6, 1960, in Gastonia, N.C. . . . Area rival there of Laker James Worthy . . . Former Georgetown star has years left because he can score off the bench . . . Was 13th pick by Nets in 1982 draft . . . Made $1,400,000.

Year	Team	G	FG	FG Pct.	FT	FT Pct.	Reb.	Ast.	TP	Avg.
1982-83	N.J.-G.S.	76	226	.429	150	.833	137	138	612	8.1
1983-84	Golden State	77	484	.463	315	.816	271	269	1291	16.8
1984-85	Golden State	82	610	.445	336	.810	202	406	1598	19.5
1985-86	Golden State	82	510	.506	351	.796	297	746	1410	17.2
1986-87	Golden State	82	503	.488	462	.860	268	848	1541	18.8
1987-88	G.S.-Hou.	77	420	.433	301	.850	296	544	1155	15.0
1988-89	Houston	82	396	.443	261	.845	306	709	1162	14.2
1989-90	Houston	82	362	.451	187	.806	198	600	1000	12.2
1990-91	Houston	82	386	.411	185	.752	159	317	1005	12.3
	Totals	722	3897	.454	2548	.822	2134	4577	10774	14.9

BUCK JOHNSON 27 6-7 206 Forward

Had string of 118 consecutive appearances (93 starts) snapped when sprained left arch forced him to miss first nine games of 1990-91 . . . Scored career-high 32 points March 31 at Miami . . . Scoring dropped for the first time after three consecutive seasons of increase . . . Was fourth-leading scorer in history at Alabama, where he played big role in Crimson Tide's four straight NCAA appearances . . . Houston took him with 20th pick in 1986 draft . . . Best season was 1989-90, when his 104 steals were second on team to Hakeem Olajuwon . . . Born Alfonso Johnson Jr., Jan. 3, 1964, in Birmingham, Ala. . . . Made $675,000.

Year	Team	G	FG	FG Pct.	FT	FT Pct.	Reb.	Ast.	TP	Avg.
1986-87	Houston	60	94	.468	40	.690	88	40	228	3.8
1987-88	Houston	70	155	.520	67	.736	168	49	378	5.4
1988-89	Houston	67	270	.524	101	.754	286	126	642	9.6
1989-90	Houston	82	504	.495	205	.759	381	252	1215	14.8
1990-91	Houston	73	416	.477	157	.727	330	142	991	13.6
	Totals	352	1439	.495	570	.741	1253	609	3454	9.8

VERNON MAXWELL 26 6-4 190 Guard

Mad Max: the adventure continues . . . Made 172 three-pointers for NBA single-season record . . . With good reason, though: Had 510 attempts, one of only two players to launch at least 500 . . . Led Rockets in scoring (19.2) during April playoff charge . . . Finished No. 4 on the team in that department . . . Oh, yeah: the shooting guard shot 40.4 percent . . . Played 2,870 minutes, most by a Rocket guard since Calvin Murphy in 1978-79 . . . Born Sept. 12, 1965, in Gainesville, Fla. . . . Grew up four miles from University of Florida, the school he later attended . . . Drafted 47th in 1988 by Denver, which traded his rights to San Antonio for a 1989 second-rounder . . . Lasted year-and-a-half with the Spurs before Houston bought him for cash Feb. 21, 1990 . . . Made $250,000.

Year	Team	G	FG	FG Pct.	FT	FT Pct.	Reb.	Ast.	TP	Avg.
1988-89	San Antonio	79	357	.432	181	.745	202	301	927	11.7
1989-90	S.A.-Hou.	79	275	.439	136	.645	228	296	714	9.0
1990-91	Houston	82	504	.404	217	.733	238	303	1397	17.0
	Totals	240	1136	.421	534	.712	668	900	3038	12.7

OTIS THORPE 29 6-10 246   Forward

Played all 82 games . . . Ho-hum . . . It's the sixth time in his seven-year career that has happened . . . Only NBA player to start every game last five seasons . . . That makes his streak of 460 consecutive games the longest in the league . . . Got some much-deserved attention when Hakeem Olajuwon was out . . . Averaged 21.1 points, 11.7 rebounds, 3.6 assists and shot 57 percent in those 25 games . . . Nice quickness for a power forward . . . NBA Player of the Week Jan. 28-Feb. 3 . . . Finished season with a career-best 10.3 rebounds, ninth-best in the league, and shot a franchise-record 55.6 percent, seventh-best . . . Born Aug. 5, 1962, in Boynton Beach, Fla. . . . Former Providence star should be a high choice on somebody's all-underrated team . . . Chosen ninth by Kansas City Kings in 1984 draft . . . Made $1,760,000.

Year	Team	G	FG	FG Pct.	FT	FT Pct.	Reb.	Ast.	TP	Avg.
1984-85	Kansas City	82	411	.600	230	.620	556	111	1052	12.8
1985-86	Sacramento	75	289	.587	164	.661	420	84	742	9.9
1986-87	Sacramento	82	567	.540	413	.761	819	201	1547	18.9
1987-88	Sacramento	82	622	.507	460	.755	837	266	1704	20.8
1988-89	Houston	82	521	.542	328	.729	787	202	1370	16.7
1989-90	Houston	82	547	.548	307	.688	734	261	1401	17.1
1990-91	Houston	82	549	.556	334	.696	846	197	1435	17.5
	Totals	567	3506	.548	2236	.711	4999	1322	9251	16.3

DAVE JAMERSON 24 6-5 192   Guard

No. 15 pick in 1990 draft by Heat . . . Rights traded on Draft Day along with Carl Herrera for rights to Alec Kessler (12th pick) . . . Big disappointment as rookie . . . Did not play 45 times . . . Finished with best games at end of season, scoring 20 points in 26 minutes of final three outings . . . Was third-leading NCAA Division I scorer and Mid-American Conference Player of Year as senior at Ohio University . . . Scored a MAC-record 60 points against Charleston . . . Father, John, was MVP of 1968 NAIA Tournament and a year later was a draft pick of ABA's Indiana Pacers . . . Born Aug. 13, 1967, in Stow, Ohio . . . Made $650,000.

Year	Team	G	FG	FG Pct.	FT	FT Pct.	Reb.	Ast.	TP	Avg.
1990-91	Houston	37	43	.381	22	.815	30	27	113	3.1

DAVID WOOD 26 6-9 228   Forward

Wound up in the NBA later than most, after two years in Europe . . . Rockets liked what they saw in 1990 mini-camp and summer league, signed him and he played all 82 games, starting the first 12 . . . Good outside touch for big man . . . Born Nov. 30, 1964, in Spokane, Wash. . . . Starting center for two years (1985-86, 1986-87) at Nevada-Reno, he was signed as a free agent by Bulls in September 1988 and waived two months later . . . Played briefly in CBA, then off to Europe, where his teams (Enichem Livorno and Barcelona) reached the European Cup championships in consecutive seasons . . . Made $300,000 in 1990-91.

Year	Team	G	FG	FG Pct.	FT	FT Pct.	Reb.	Ast.	TP	Avg.
1988-89	Chicago	2	0	.000	0	.000	0	0	0	0.0
1990-91	Houston	82	148	.424	108	.812	246	94	432	5.3
	Totals	84	148	.424	108	.812	246	94	432	5.1

KENNY SMITH 26 6-3 170   Guard

Writes own material for weekly segment on ABC-TV affiliate in Houston . . . Couldn't have scripted his 1990-91 much better . . . Acquired from Atlanta before training camp along with Roy Marble for John Lucas, who retired soon after, and Tim McCormick . . . From there, he finished second on team in scoring and field-goal percentage and third in steals . . . Fourth-best shooter among all NBA guards (52 percent) and tops in Western Conference . . . Only John Paxson (54.8), Michael Jordan (53.9) and Vern Fleming (53.1) were better . . . While playing for third team in two seasons, his career got stability and a transfusion . . . Was No. 6 pick by Sacramento in 1987 after fine career at North Carolina . . . Born March 8, 1965, in Queens, N.Y. . . . Made $700,000.

Year	Team	G	FG	FG Pct.	FT	FT Pct.	Reb.	Ast.	TP	Avg.
1987-88	Sacramento	61	331	.477	167	.819	138	434	841	13.8
1988-89	Sacramento	81	547	.462	263	.737	226	621	1403	17.3
1989-90	Sac.-Atl.	79	378	.466	161	.821	157	445	943	11.9
1990-91	Houston	78	522	.520	287	.844	163	554	1380	17.7
	Totals	299	1778	.482	878	.800	684	2054	4567	15.3

LARRY SMITH 33 6-8 251   Forward-Center

Mr. Mean had a pleasant 11th pro season . . . Too old? . . . Try again . . . At No. 18, only non-starter to finish in top 20 of league in rebounding . . . Got votes for NBA's Sixth Man Award . . . Started 28 games when Hakeem Olajuwon was out and averaged 14.4 rebounds . . . That made him a 6-8 center who in February had five 20-plus rebound games, the most in a month since Michael Cage in April 1988 . . . Also held 11 of 12 counterparts below their scoring averages and had 73 offensive rebounds to opponents' 29 . . . The trademark lives on . . . Golden State has been desperate for rebounding, but Warriors let him go as an unrestricted free agent . . . Shot 24 percent on free throws . . . That's not a misprint . . . The good news: He only went to the line 50 times . . . Former Alcorn State standout was born Jan. 18, 1958, in Rolling Fork, Miss. . . . Picked in second round by Warriors in 1980 . . . Made $800,000 in 1990-91.

Year	Team	G	FG	FG Pct.	FT	FT Pct.	Reb.	Ast.	TP	Avg.
1980-81	Golden State	82	304	.512	177	.588	994	93	785	9.6
1981-82	Golden State	74	220	.534	88	.553	813	83	528	7.1
1982-83	Golden State	49	180	.588	53	.535	485	46	413	8.4
1983-84	Golden State	75	244	.560	94	.560	672	72	582	7.8
1984-85	Golden State	80	366	.530	155	.605	869	96	887	11.1
1985-86	Golden State	77	314	.536	112	.493	856	95	740	9.6
1986-87	Golden State	80	297	.546	113	.574	917	95	707	8.8
1987-88	Golden State	20	58	.472	11	.407	182	25	127	6.4
1988-89	Golden State	80	219	.552	18	.310	652	118	456	5.7
1989-90	Houston	74	101	.474	20	.364	452	69	222	3.0
1990-91	Houston	81	128	.487	12	.240	709	88	268	3.3
	Totals	772	2431	.533	853	.534	7601	880	5715	7.4

MATT BULLARD 24 6-10 225   Forward

Played in 18 games as a rookie, with two stints on the injured list because of tendinitis in his left knee . . . Best game: six points, three rebounds in nine minutes April 16 at Portland . . . If uniform No. 50 is any indication, he'll be around for a long time . . . Joe Meriweather, who played 10 seasons, and current veterans Robert Reid and Ralph Sampson also wore the half-century uniform . . . Born June 5, 1967, in West Des Moines,

Iowa . . . Played two years at Colorado, where he led the team in scoring in his second season, and transferred to Iowa . . . Undrafted, he proved himself to Rockets in summer league in 1990 and signed for the year at $120,000.

Year	Team	G	FG	FG Pct.	FT	FT Pct.	Reb.	Ast.	TP	Avg.
1990-91	Houston	18	14	.452	11	.647	14	2	39	2.2

THE ROOKIE

JOHN TURNER 23 6-7 245   Forward
The 20th selection, out of Phillips University, where he was an NAIA All-American and Sooner Athletic Conference Player of the Year . . . Started career at Alleghany (Md.) CC and had a year at Georgetown before transferring to Phillips . . . Draft value enhanced when he was named MVP at Portsmouth Invitation and made all-tournament at Orlando All-Star Classic, both pre-draft showcases . . . Has skills to play small forward and strength to play power forward . . . Born Nov. 30, 1967, in Greenbelt, Md.

COACH DON CHANEY: Nice guys do finish first . . . Named 1990-91 Coach of the Year for guiding Rockets to third-place finish in the Midwest Division with great second half . . . Did it all with issue of contract running out at end of season . . . Renewed during offseason . . . What a bold move! . . . Has 138-108 record in three seasons with Houston, a franchise-best percentage of 56.1 . . . Got his 100th Rockets' victory in 189th game, quickest in franchise history. Bill Fitch needed 199 . . . Played 11 years in the NBA (with Boston except for a season-plus with the Lakers) and one year in the ABA (Spirits of St. Louis) . . . Only player in Celtic history to have been teammates with Bill Russell and Larry Bird . . . Former head coach with Clippers and assistant with Atlanta, Detroit and the Clippers . . . Overall pro record: 191-240 . . . Born March 22, 1946, in Baton Rouge, La. . . . Was teammate of Elvin Hayes when both were first black basketball players at University of Houston.

Kenny Smith soared in new life as a Rocket.

GREATEST TEAM

The Twin Towers were the most dramatic piece of NBA architecture in years, and the Rockets nearly reached the summit in 1985-86 before losing to Boston in the Finals. Still, that was their only season in the championship series. They won a franchise-record 20 in a row at home and the Midwest Division title.

The rotation went nine deep. Hakeem Olajuwon averaged 23.5 points and 11.5 rebounds and Ralph Sampson got 19 points and 11 rebounds. No Sampson basket will ever be remembered more than his off-balance toss at the Forum that gave the Rockets the Western Conference title.

The challenger was last season's team, when, with the possibility of a sale looming, the Rockets finished third in the division but won a franchise-record 52 games, set or tied 63 team marks and had Don Chaney named Coach of the Year.

ALL-TIME ROCKET LEADERS

SEASON

Points: Moses Malone, 2,520, 1980-81
Assists: John Lucas, 768, 1977-78
Rebounds: Moses Malone, 1,444, 1978-79

GAME

Points: Calvin Murphy, 57 vs. New Jersey, 3/18/78
Assists: Art Williams, 22 vs. San Francisco, 2/14/70
        Art Williams, 22 vs. Phoenix, 12/28/68
Rebounds: Moses Malone, 37 vs. New Orleans, 2/9/79

CAREER

Points: Calvin Murphy, 17,949, 1970-83
Assists: Calvin Murphy, 4,402, 1970-83
Rebounds: Elvin Hayes, 6,974, 1968-72, 1981-84

LOS ANGELES CLIPPERS

TEAM DIRECTORY: Owner: Donald Sterling; Exec. VP-GM: Elgin Baylor; Exec. VP-Business Oper.: Andy Roeser; VP-Pub. Rel.: Mike Williams; Exec. VP: Harley Frankel; Coach: Mike Schuler; Asst. Coaches: Alvin Gentry, John Hammond. Arena: Los Angeles Sports Arena (16,150). Colors: Red, white and blue.

Versatile Charles Smith arm-wrestles with David Robinson.

SCOUTING REPORT

SHOOTING: Mike Schuler has no shortage of shooters here; smart shooters is another matter. Ron Harper has decided he wants to add an outside game to his driving and slashing, so, in the closing seconds of one contest, he tried a baseline jumper over Mark Eaton and got it blocked instead of using an obvious speed advantage to go around him.

It's enough to drive a coach crazy. Or get him fired. Fact is, though, only Danny Manning, Ken Norman and Olden Polynice among regulars shot better than 50 percent. Charles Smith was .469. Among guards, Gary Grant led at .451. The three shooting guards in the rotation, Harper, Bo Kimble and now-gone Jeff Martin, went .391, .380 and .422, respectively. From the start to the end of the season, Kimble went from starter to being so far down the bench he might as well have been in another area code.

Obviously, improvement is needed here, as the Clippers continue their long search for an outside shooter to provide some distraction for defenses against collapsing on the forwards.

The trade that brought James Edwards from the Pistons (for Martin) adds a low-post scorer, assuming that Edwards doesn't figure a way to play in Italy.

PLAYMAKING: He comes riding in from the East as the Clippers' knight in white, the answer to their troubles at point guard and in the clubhouse. They hope. The investment to get Doc Rivers from Atlanta was relatively minor—draft picks, which they had plenty of and little desire to use—but at the same time, hefty. They can hardly afford another setback and delay in getting the starting lineup finalized.

After eight years, Rivers has nothing to prove to the league. But in the organization and among Clipper fans, everyone will be watching, hoping. Grant, the ousted starter, moves to No. 2 on the depth chart.

DEFENSE: It is a contradiction to a team that is billed for its offensive explosiveness, but almost all sightings of Clipper good fortune is highlighted by defense. When they play team defense and rotate and force turnovers and get into the transition game they desire, the fourth-quarter rallies come.

So they went 31-51 last season, and only nine teams surrendered more than the Clippers' 107 points per game. When the defense comes with greater consistency, so will the wins.

CLIPPER ROSTER

No.	Veterans	Pos.	Ht.	Wt.	Age	Yrs. Pro	College
1	Gary Grant	G	6-3	196	26	3	Michigan
53	James Edwards	C	7-1	252	35	14	Washington
4	Ron Harper	G	6-6	198	27	5	Miami (Ohio)
30	Bo Kimble	G	6-4	190	25	1	Loyola Marymount
5	Danny Manning	F	6-10	230	25	3	Kansas
15	Jeff Martin	G	6-5	195	24	2	Murray State
3	Ken Norman	F	6-9	219	27	4	Illinois
0	Olden Polynice	C	7-0	245	26	4	Virginia
25	Doc Rivers	G	6-4	185	30	8	Marquette
54	Charles Smith	F	6-10	238	26	3	Pittsburgh
35	Loy Vaught	F	6-9	230	24	1	Michigan

Rd.	Rookies	Sel. No.	Pos.	Ht.	Wt.	College
1	LeRon Ellis	22	F-C	6-9	250	Syracuse
2	Elliot Perry	37	G	6-0	155	Memphis State

REBOUNDING: Only five teams had a better rebounding percentage than the Clippers, and all made the playoffs. So this isn't the problem area. Polynice, given a chance to be a full-time starter for the first time, averaged 9.1 rebounds in his 31 games as a Clipper. Smith, knocked for his continued insistence on fallaway jumpers instead of aggressive moves to the basket, deserved credit for improving his work on the boards from 6.7 in his second season to 8.2 in 1990-91.

OUTLOOK: Fools rush in where wise men fear to go. Ricky Nelson? That, or anyone who jumps on the Clipper bandwagon and expects to ride into the playoffs this season. It may happen, but how about they back up all the hype before buying all the swampland?

It should say something that the players agree with that notion themselves, that they are sick of the talk and realize the only real statements come on the court. The excitement is for those who sell season tickets. The reality is that this is a team with much to prove and a history of disappointing.

Will the chemistry again be like a cancer, as one player described it last season? Will second-year player Loy Vaught, who has played as though he deserves more time, and rookie LeRon Ellis, who will need to prove he can play a power game, cancel each other out and make this another failed draft class? Will the insurance company pull coverage of Clipper injuries before being forced into bankruptcy from having to pay up so often?

Tune in. At least it's never boring.

CLIPPER PROFILES

CHARLES SMITH 26 6-10 238   Forward

The player all the other teams want... They won't get him... Versatile offensive game is his strength... Can shoot from the outside because of agility and dribbling ability most 6-10 men would love to have... Tied Bob McAdoo's 15-year-old franchise record with 52 points Dec. 1 at Denver... That also tied for second-highest outing of season in the league ... Finished 22nd in NBA in scoring and first on team... Clippers were 1-7 for the eight games he didn't play... Made strides in improving his defense during second half of season, at one stage reaching top 10 in blocked shots... Showed versatility again, doing good work on small forwards Lionel Simmons and Dennis Scott back-to-back in April... Entering final year of contract, so Clippers went into summer hoping to give him new long-term deal ... Played center at Pitt, but more comfortable in set-up that allows him flexibility to roam perimeter... Played 394 more minutes than any other Clipper... Born July 16, 1965, in Bridgeport, Conn.... Drafted No. 3 by Philadelphia in 1988, then had rights traded to Clippers for rights to Hersey Hawkins and 1989 first-round choice... Made $1,000,000.

Year	Team	G	FG	FG Pct.	FT	FT Pct.	Reb.	Ast.	TP	Avg.
1988-89	L.A. Clippers	71	435	.495	285	.725	465	103	1155	16.3
1989-90	L.A. Clippers	78	595	.520	454	.794	524	114	1645	21.1
1990-91	L.A. Clippers	74	548	.469	384	.793	608	134	1480	20.0
	Totals	223	1578	.495	1123	.775	1597	351	4280	19.2

GLENN (DOC) RIVERS 30 6-4 185   Guard

Came to Clippers from Hawks with two future second-round draft picks for first-round pick in '91... Outside shot is decent, but not first-rate off-guard caliber... Has spent his career setting others up and is a touch light in the aggressive scoring department... Still has real good, sound first step... Smart player, solid defender who'll use his body against anybody.

Won't back down . . . Stayed healthy for the first time in three years . . . Career-best scoring at 15.2, 16th in NBA for steals at 1.9 . . . Hawks' all-time leader in assists and steals . . . Led Hawks' regulars in playoff shooting (.469) . . . All-Interview team . . . A warm, friendly guy . . . Born Oct. 13, 1961, in Chicago . . . Second-round pick out of Marquette by Hawks in '83 . . . Made $895,000.

Year	Team	G	FG	FG Pct.	FT	FT Pct.	Reb.	Ast.	TP	Avg.
1983-84	Atlanta	81	250	.462	255	.785	220	314	757	9.3
1984-85	Atlanta	69	334	.476	291	.770	214	410	974	14.1
1985-86	Atlanta	53	220	.474	172	.608	162	443	612	11.5
1986-87	Atlanta	82	342	.451	365	.828	299	823	1053	12.8
1987-88	Atlanta	80	403	.453	319	.758	366	747	1134	14.2
1988-89	Atlanta	76	371	.455	247	.861	286	525	1032	13.6
1989-90	Atlanta	48	218	.454	138	.812	200	264	598	12.5
1990-91	Atlanta	79	444	.435	221	.844	253	340	1197	15.2
	Totals	568	2582	.455	2008	.782	2000	3866	7357	13.0

RON HARPER 27 6-6 198   Guard

Had successful return from reconstructive surgery on his right knee after missing 54 weeks with torn cartilage and ligament . . . But struggled with his shot, hitting just 39.1 percent . . . Some of problem was simply finishing relatively easy attempts . . . Clippers write that off as a matter of him getting his timing back . . . What should be of concern is that he altered his game a bit . . . He took more outside shots, even in favor of driving and slashing through the lane . . . Harper says the jumpers will make his game more complete and open things up in the long run . . . Clippers were 16-18 when he started . . . Got big new contract while rehabilitating, a gamble by organization . . . Made $1,365,000 . . . Born Jan. 20, 1964, in Dayton, Ohio, and stayed local to attend Miami of Ohio . . . Eighth draft pick by Cavs in 1986.

Year	Team	G	FG	FG Pct.	FT	FT Pct.	Reb.	Ast.	TP	Avg.
1986-87	Cleveland	82	734	.455	386	.684	392	394	1874	22.9
1987-88	Cleveland	57	340	.464	196	.705	223	281	879	15.4
1988-89	Cleveland	82	587	.511	323	.751	409	434	1526	18.6
1989-90	Clev.-LAC.	35	301	.473	182	.788	206	182	798	22.8
1990-91	L.A. Clippers	39	285	.391	145	.668	188	209	763	19.6
	Totals	295	2247	.462	1232	.716	1418	1500	5840	19.8

DANNY MANNING 25 6-10 230   Forward

Showed during second half of season that any thought of trading him would have been a mistake . . . Wasn't exactly broken-hearted over prospect of leaving the organization . . . Moved past Ken Norman to take over starting small-forward job . . . Played every position except shooting guard last season . . . Brought the ball upcourt even when a point guard was in . . . Former No. 1 pick from Kansas who may never make an All-Star team, but who could be the difference between a good team and a very good one . . . Offense is jump hooks, quick jumpers and other assorted junk . . . Has quick hands, but don't expect him to match up well with power forwards . . . Father, Ed, is former pro player and current assistant at San Antonio . . . Born May 17, 1966, in Hattiesburg, Miss. . . . Made $2,200,000.

Year	Team	G	FG	FG Pct.	FT	FT Pct.	Reb.	Ast.	TP	Avg.
1988-89	L.A. Clippers	26	177	.494	79	.767	171	81	434	16.7
1989-90	L.A. Clippers	71	440	.533	274	.741	422	187	1154	16.3
1990-91	L.A. Clippers	73	470	.519	219	.716	426	196	1159	15.9
	Totals	170	1087	.520	572	.734	1019	464	2747	16.2

KEN NORMAN 27 6-9 219   Forward

Went into offseason knowing there was a good chance he'd be traded after becoming sixth man . . . If he returns, it remains to be seen how well he'll handle being full-time reserve . . . Originally the last of Clippers' three first-round picks in 1987, he has clearly become the best . . . Used that as motivation . . . Strong-willed player who has criticized team officials for putting him on injured list, later admitting it was for best . . . Team leader in near-fights before arrival of Olden Polynice . . . Bothered for a couple of years by nagging bumps and bruises, but it's impossible to show up at start of a season in better shape than Norman . . . Tied a career high with 20 rebounds at Philadelphia . . . Born Sept. 5, 1964, in Chicago . . . Attended Illinois . . . Made $1,050,000.

Year	Team	G	FG	FG Pct.	FT	FT Pct.	Reb.	Ast.	TP	Avg.
1987-88	L.A. Clippers	66	241	.482	87	.512	263	78	569	8.6
1988-89	L.A. Clippers	80	638	.502	170	.630	667	277	1450	18.1
1989-90	L.A. Clippers	70	484	.510	153	.632	470	160	1128	16.1
1990-91	L.A. Clippers	70	520	.501	173	.629	497	159	1219	17.4
	Totals	286	1883	.501	583	.609	1897	674	4366	15.3

OLDEN POLYNICE 26 7-0 245 Center

It wasn't like this in the Olden days . . . With Seattle, strictly a backup . . . Acquired by Clippers Feb. 20 in Benoit Benjamin deal, he became a starter almost immediately and never surrendered the spot . . . Scrappy player who tangled with Danny Ferry (enough to become an all-time L.A. favorite on the spot), got into shouting match with teammate Gary Grant after Polynice perceived him as laughing after a loss, and chastised Ron Harper for helping an opponent up during a stoppage in play . . . The Clippers needed this type of fire-and-brimstone play, especially after Benjamin . . . Doesn't have nearly the physical tools of Big Ben, but there's no contest in spirit and approach . . . Averaged 12.3 points, 9.1 rebounds and 36.5 minutes in 31 games after trade . . . Terrible hands . . . Born Nov. 21, 1964, in Port-Au-Prince, Haiti . . . Attended Virginia . . . Drafted by Bulls as Virginia undergraduate in 1987 . . . Made $600,000.

Year	Team	G	FG	FG Pct.	FT	FT Pct.	Reb.	Ast.	TP	Avg.
1987-88	Seattle	82	118	.465	101	.639	330	33	337	4.1
1988-89	Seattle	80	91	.506	51	.593	206	21	233	2.9
1989-90	Seattle	79	156	.540	47	.475	300	15	360	4.6
1990-91	Sea.-LAC	79	316	.560	146	.579	553	42	778	9.8
	Totals	320	681	.529	345	.580	1389	111	1708	5.3

LOY VAUGHT 24 6-9 230 Forward

For once, a Clipper draft choice (No. 13) as good as advertised . . . Much-needed role player who doesn't want headlines, just rebounds . . . Considers "blue collar" label a compliment because his father, a former carpenter, is his hero . . . Good enough shot from around 12 feet to keep defenses honest . . . When Clippers held trade talks during summer, several teams asked that he be included . . . Logjam at forward cost him more playing time than the 16.1 minutes he got . . . First name a combination of three relatives: L for Uncle Louis, O for Uncle Oliver and Y for Aunt Yvonne . . . Member of 1989 NCAA championship team at Michigan . . . Born Feb. 27, 1967, in Grand Rapids, Mich. . . . Made $825,000.

Year	Team	G	FG	FG Pct.	FT	FT Pct.	Reb.	Ast.	TP	Avg.
1990-91	L.A. Clippers	73	175	.487	49	.662	349	40	399	5.5

GARY GRANT 26 6-3 196   Guard

Started first 61 games of season at point guard, then went downhill . . . Free fall is more like it . . . Missed three games with bruised thigh, then eight more with sore knee . . . Clippers started winning, and Mike Schuler scrubbed rule that says a starter can't lose his job to an injury . . . Low point came near end, when he was held out of three games . . . Finished eighth in league in assists . . . Trade value is almost nil, so prospect of having to cut him and eat the remainder of his contract is a possibility . . . Organization frustrated that he never matured—on the court, where he had too many turnovers and made bad decisions, and off . . . If Clippers don't want him, he has enough natural ability to hook on somewhere . . . Once drafted as an outfielder by Kansas City Royals . . . Born April 21, 1965, in Parson, Kan. . . . Chosen 15th by Seattle in 1988 . . . Made $530,000.

Year	Team	G	FG	FG Pct.	FT	FT Pct.	Reb.	Ast.	TP	Avg.
1988-89	L.A. Clippers	71	361	.435	119	.735	238	506	846	11.9
1989-90	L.A. Clippers	44	241	.466	88	.779	195	442	575	13.1
1990-91	L.A. Clippers	68	265	.451	51	.689	209	587	590	8.7
	Totals	183	867	.448	258	.739	642	1535	2011	11.0

GREG (BO) KIMBLE 25 6-4 190   Guard

Tough rookie season on many fronts . . . Shot just 38 percent overall and 29.2 on three-pointers . . . Lost his starting job . . . Lost his confidence . . . Lost his shine after memorable senior season at Loyola Marymount when accusations were leveled that he took money to play for Lions and that he was benefiting from death of friend Hank Gathers . . . Most popular Clipper at majority of road arenas . . . Still a favorite in Los Angeles despite struggles . . . Realizes importance of putting forth positive image to fans . . . Among other things, he tries to wear suit and tie for TV interviews away from arena and appearances . . . Coaches want him to improve defense and ball-handling . . . Clippers were 9-13 when he started . . . Born April 9, 1966, in Philadelphia . . . Second-round pick in 1989 . . . Made $950,000.

Year	Team	G	FG	FG Pct.	FT	FT Pct.	Reb.	Ast.	TP	Avg.
1990-91	L.A. Clippers	62	159	.380	92	.773	119	76	429	6.9

JAMES EDWARDS 35 7-1 252   Center

"Buddha" did not enjoy peace, contentment and inner tranquility last season with Pistons . . . Clamored for contract extension that never came. What did come in August was a trade for Jeff Martin and 1995 second-round draft pick . . . Solid low-post scorer, he was one of the pieces Pistons needed to get over championship hump in '89 . . . Averaged 13.6 points, 13th time in 14 seasons in double figures . . . Not a good defender, but he takes up space. Just 30 blocks—and don't forget he's 7-1 . . . Bad rebounder, especially on the defensive side . . . Bad playoff series against the Bulls: shot .400, averaged less than half (6.3) of seasonal output . . . A real steal from Suns Feb. 24, 1988 . . . Detroit gave up Ron Moore and a second-rounder . . . Lakers tabbed him on third round in '77 out of Washington . . . Born Nov. 22, 1955, in Seattle . . . Angered over $935,000 salary.

Year	Team	G	FG	FG Pct.	FT	FT Pct.	Reb.	Ast.	TP	Avg.
1977-78	L.A.-Ind.	83	495	.453	272	.646	615	85	1252	15.2
1978-79	Indiana	82	534	.501	298	.676	693	92	1366	16.7
1979-80	Indiana	82	528	.512	231	.681	578	127	1287	15.7
1980-81	Indiana	81	511	.509	244	.703	571	212	1266	15.6
1981-82	Cleveland	77	528	.511	232	.684	581	123	1288	16.7
1982-83	Clev.-Phoe	31	128	.487	69	.639	155	40	325	10.5
1983-84	Phoenix	72	438	.536	183	.720	348	184	1059	14.7
1984-85	Phoenix	70	384	.501	276	.746	387	153	1044	14.9
1985-86	Phoenix	52	318	.542	212	.702	301	74	848	16.3
1986-87	Phoenix	14	57	.518	54	.771	60	19	168	12.0
1987-88	Phoe.-Det.	69	302	.470	210	.654	412	78	814	11.8
1988-89	Detroit	76	211	.500	133	.686	231	49	555	7.3
1989-90	Detroit	82	462	.498	265	.749	345	63	1189	14.5
1990-91	Detroit	72	383	.484	215	.729	277	65	982	13.6
	Totals	943	5279	.500	2894	.697	5554	1364	13453	14.3

THE ROOKIES

LeRON ELLIS 22 6-9 250   Forward-Center

Unless Clippers get another center between the draft and the regular season, he'll be the backup . . . So what if his preference is to be a forward? . . . Clippers say he can play both and like his versatility . . . His selection at No. 22 was booed when announced at the Sports Arena . . . Maybe they knew of his reputation as a soft player at Syracuse . . . Needs weight program . . . His father,

LeRoy, played 14 seasons in NBA with Lakers, Bullets, Trail Blazers and 76ers... Born April 28, 1969, in Tustin, Cal.

ELLIOT PERRY 22 6-0 155   **Guard**
Those goggles... That quickness... That dunking ability... Never has been one for subtlety... In a backcourt that already has Ron Harper, he could add even more excitement if he sticks ... Get ready to count number of times phrase "like a waterbug" is used in reference to Memphis State product... Only 10th player in NCAA history to accumulate more than 300 career steals... No. 37 pick who could restore depth to Clipper backcourt after Winston Garland was traded and Tom Garrick was not re-signed ... Born March 28, 1969, in Memphis, Tenn.

COACH MIKE SCHULER: At least he didn't fall out of chair when named coach May 25, 1990... He did that when he became Portland coach... The real fall came soon enough... Had 127-84 record (.602) as NBA coach at beginning of 1990-91, winning 53 and 49 games in two full seasons at Portland... Then went 31-51 with Clippers... Reputation as taskmaster with intensity levels that break the needle dogged him since being fired by Trail Blazers... Clipper players can understand why... But they appreciate his organization, knowledge of game and desire to win... NBA Coach of the Year at Portland in 1986-87... Gained experience as an assistant under Bobby Knight at Army, Terry Holland at Virginia, Larry Brown with the Nets and Don Nelson with the Bucks and Warriors... Nelson lobbied for his friend to get Clipper job... Also interviewed for vacant spot year before that eventually went to Don Casey... Born Sept. 23, 1940, in Portsmouth, Ohio... Attended Ohio U.

GREATEST TEAM

In the seven years since they moved north from San Diego, no Clipper team has won more than 32 games. So we'll go with that 1985-86 group, which set the standard.

In truth, there were more than one or two things to like. There was the pre-knee-injury Derek Smith, a rising star. Marques Johnson averaged 20.3 points. Norm Nixon had his last healthy season as a pro.

And consider this as an indicator of the talent: Smith, Benoit Benjamin, Michael Cage and Darnell Valentine are still in the league. Likewise, head coach Don Chaney is still coaching, and the assistants, Don Casey and Brad Greenberg, respectively, are Celtic assistant and the player personnel director at Portland.

ALL-TIME CLIPPER LEADERS

SEASON

Points: Bob McAdoo, 2,831, 1974-75
Assists: Norm Nixon, 914, 1983-84
Rebounds: Swen Nater, 1,216, 1979-80

GAME

Points: Bob McAdoo, 52 vs. Seattle, 3/17/76
       Bob McAdoo, 52 vs. Boston, 2/22/74
       Charles Smith, 52 vs. Denver, 12/1/90
Assists: Ernie DiGregorio, 25 vs. Portland, 1/1/74
Rebounds: Swen Nater, 32 vs. Denver, 12/14/79

CAREER

Points: Randy Smith, 12,735, 1971-79, 1982-83
Assists: Randy Smith, 3,498, 1971-79, 1982-83
Rebounds: Bob McAdoo, 4,229, 1972-76

LOS ANGELES LAKERS

TEAM DIRECTORY: Owner: Jerry Buss; GM: Jerry West; Dir. Pub. Rel.: John Black; Coach: Mike Dunleavy; Asst. Coaches: Bill Bertka, Randy Pfund, Jim Eyen. Arena: The Great Western Forum (17,505). Colors: Royal purple and gold.

SCOUTING REPORT

SHOOTING: Trade rumors have covered his last two offseasons, but Byron Scott—not Magic Johnson or James Worthy or Sam Perkins—is the key now that "Showtime" makes only cameo appearances.

As defenses collapsed inside on the Lakers' slowdown and post-up game, especially in the playoffs, Scott got countless open shots. In the opening rounds, he made the opposition pay, but when it got to the Finals, he disappeared, and, soon enough, so did the rest of the team. This is not to put the championship-series skid marks on Scott's lap, but to illustrate how crucial his continued presence is in an offense in which he averaged just 14.5 points, the lowest since his rookie season.

The other key is diversity. In Johnson, Worthy, Perkins and Vlade Divac, the Lakers are able to post four players at any time, and the dump-it-in approach is the new norm. But Worthy and Perkins can also hit from outside, and Magis is dangerous anytime he has the ball.

PLAYMAKING: It would normally qualify as heresy to suggest that a team with Magic at the point needs help, but he's not the problem. Finding a backup was the No. 1 concern heading into the summer, a move that wasn't aided by having only the 52nd pick in the draft. They don't need much behind Magic, but there is no question they need something. Tony Smith remains the backup until then.

DEFENSE: They were one of only two teams to end the season sub-100 on defense, a testament magnified in that it was a drop of approximately four points from 1989-90. Mike Dunleavy the player would be proud of Mike Dunleavy the coach. There is no reason this should not continue as an area of strength, because good team defense comes from hard work, and no Laker dogs it.

Magic's prodding has helped in emergence of Vlade Divac.

LAKER ROSTER

No.	Veterans	Pos.	Ht.	Wt.	Age	Yrs. Pro	College
41	Elden Campbell	F-C	6-11	215	23	1	Clemson
12	Vlade Divac	C	7-1	248	23	2	Yugoslavia
10	Larry Drew	G	6-2	190	33	10	Missouri
45	A.C. Green	F	6-9	224	28	6	Oregon State
32	Earvin Johnson	G	6-9	220	32	12	Michigan State
14	Sam Perkins	F-C	6-9	257	30	7	North Carolina
4	Byron Scott	G	6-4	193	30	8	Arizona State
34	Tony Smith	G	6-4	195	23	1	Marquette
20	Terry Teagle	F-G	6-5	195	31	9	Baylor
30	Irving Thomas	F	6-8	225	25	1	Florida State
43	Mychal Thompson	C-F	6-10	235	36	13	Minnesota
42	James Worthy	F	6-9	225	30	9	North Carolina

Rd.	Rookies	Sel. No.	Pos.	Ht.	Wt.	College
2	Anthony Jones	52	F	6-7	200	Oral Roberts

REBOUNDING: What day of the week are we talking? Check the mood rings and then decide their fortunes for the evening. Sometimes, the Lakers hit the boards and get every free ball. Other times, the boards hit back. Sequence that will be engrained: David Robinson missing a 20 footer—and then rushing in to get his own rebound. Returning to Wall Street probably looked good to Dunleavy right about then.

OUTLOOK: Reports of their death were greatly exaggerated. Those experts around the country who predicted before last season the Laker demise and the Clipper rise at the same time were a bit off the mark.

A quick rule of thumb: Don't go against any team with Magic and Worthy and a general manager like Jerry West until they prove negative worth. The stock may be in decline, but this isn't a crash. Fans in Los Angeles, who after the Lakers got much farther than most expected and still talked in the postseason autopsy of dismantling the core, should keep that in mind, too. The stale act is still the hippest.

LAKER PROFILES

EARVIN (MAGIC) JOHNSON 32 6-9 220   Guard

Another year, another piece of property on Mt. Olympus... Became NBA's all-time assists leader April 15, passing Oscar Robertson... Current total at 9,921... With far less fanfare, also established franchise single-season record with 989... Finished second in MVP balloting ... Thirteen triple-doubles led league... Had double-digit assists in 64 of 79 games... Business portfolio expanding faster than his trophy case... Will he be inducted into Hall of Fame or reach the Fortune 500 first?... A personality and a class act against which all others are measured against in L.A. sports... Born Aug. 14, 1959, in Lansing, Mich.... Lakers made him No. 1 overall pick in 1979 draft... Made $2,400,000 in 1990-91.

Year	Team	G	FG	FG Pct.	FT	FT Pct.	Reb.	Ast.	TP	Avg.
1979-80	Los Angeles	77	503	.530	374	.810	596	563	1387	18.0
1980-81	Los Angeles	37	312	.532	171	.760	320	317	798	21.6
1981-82	Los Angeles	78	556	.537	329	.760	751	743	1447	18.6
1982-83	Los Angeles	79	511	.548	304	.800	683	829	1326	16.8
1983-84	Los Angeles	67	441	.565	290	.810	491	875	1178	17.6
1984-85	L.A. Lakers	77	504	.561	391	.843	476	968	1406	18.3
1985-86	L.A. Lakers	72	483	.526	378	.871	426	907	1354	18.8
1986-87	L.A. Lakers	80	683	.522	535	.848	504	977	1909	23.9
1987-88	L.A. Lakers	72	490	.492	417	.853	449	858	1408	19.6
1988-89	L.A. Lakers	77	579	.509	513	.911	607	988	1730	22.5
1989-90	L.A. Lakers	79	546	.480	567	.890	522	907	1765	22.3
1990-91	L.A. Lakers	79	466	.477	519	.906	551	989	1531	19.4
	Totals	874	6074	.521	4788	.848	6376	9921	17239	19.7

VLADE DIVAC 23 7-1 248   Center

Quickness most 7-footers could only hope for ... Moved well despite having Magic Johnson riding him half the time... Had 27 double-doubles in 1990-91, 18 more than the season before... Led team in field-goal percentage at 56.5, fifth-best in league... Only Laker to shoot better than 50 percent... Intensity in games and practices improved since start of previous season... Still doesn't play smart every game... Played Hakeem Olajuwon tough in the first round of the playoffs, a key to the L.A. sweep... Bothered Laker brass by coming to 1990 training camp in bad shape... Born Feb. 2, 1968, in Prijepolje, Yugoslavia... Lakers took him with their only pick (No. 26) in 1989 draft... Made $770,000.

Year	Team	G	FG	FG Pct.	FT	FT Pct.	Reb.	Ast.	TP	Avg.
1989-90	L.A. Lakers	82	274	.499	153	.708	512	75	701	8.5
1990-91	L.A. Lakers	82	360	.565	196	.703	666	92	921	11.2
	Totals	164	634	.535	349	.705	1178	167	1622	9.9

SAM PERKINS 30 6-9 257   Forward-Center

Shored up soft middle for Lakers, especially on defense... Continued to improve on low-post moves developed year before in Dallas... Spent six years with Mavericks before signing six-year contract worth $19.2 million with Lakers... Finished second on the team in rebounding (7.4) and blocked shots (78) and was fourth in scoring (13.5)... Hit winning three-point shot in Game 1 of NBA Finals at Chicago... Had a good series, except for a 1-for-15 in Game 4... Compared to some teammates, that was average... Born June 14, 1961, in New York City... Co-captain of 1984 Olympic team that won the gold medal... Played at North Carolina... Made $1,970,000.

Year	Team	G	FG	FG Pct.	FT	FT Pct.	Reb.	Ast.	TP	Avg.
1984-85	Dallas	82	347	.471	200	.820	605	135	903	11.0
1985-86	Dallas	80	458	.503	307	.814	685	153	1234	15.4
1986-87	Dallas	80	461	.482	245	.828	616	146	1186	14.8
1987-88	Dallas	75	394	.450	273	.822	601	118	1066	14.2
1988-89	Dallas	78	445	.464	274	.833	688	127	1171	15.0
1989-90	Dallas	76	435	.493	330	.778	572	175	1206	15.9
1990-91	L.A. Lakers	73	368	.495	229	.821	538	108	983	13.5
	Totals	544	2908	.479	1858	.815	4305	962	7749	14.2

JAMES WORTHY 30 6-9 225   Forward

Led team in scoring for first time in nine-year career... The 21.4 average was also 18th-best in league... Improved scoring average fourth year in a row... But the 49.2 percent from the field was lowest of his career and far below NBA average of 54.6... Sprained left ankle in Game 5 of Western Conference finals at Portland limited production rest of playoffs... Difficult season off court, with arrest in Houston on misdemeanor counts of solicitation and later contract squabbles . . . Scored 20 points or more 50 times . . . Great combination of speed in the open court and moves in the low post . . . Drafted by Lakers (first pick) as a North Carolina undergraduate in 1982 . . . Born Feb. 27, 1961, in Gastonia, N.C. . . . Made $1,600,000.

Year	Team	G	FG	FG Pct.	FT	FT Pct.	Reb.	Ast.	TP	Avg.
1982-83	Los Angeles	77	447	.579	138	.624	399	132	1033	13.4
1983-84	Los Angeles	82	495	.556	195	.759	515	207	1185	14.5
1984-85	L.A. Lakers	80	610	.572	190	.776	511	201	1410	17.6
1985-86	L.A. Lakers	75	629	.579	242	.771	387	201	1500	20.0
1986-87	L.A. Lakers	82	651	.539	292	.751	466	226	1594	19.4
1987-88	L.A. Lakers	75	617	.531	242	.796	374	289	1478	19.7
1988-89	L.A. Lakers	81	702	.548	251	.782	489	288	1657	20.5
1989-90	L.A. Lakers	80	711	.548	248	.782	478	288	1685	21.1
1990-91	L.A. Lakers	78	716	.492	212	.797	356	275	1670	21.4
	Totals	710	5578	.546	2010	.763	3975	2107	13212	18.6

BYRON SCOTT 30 6-4 193   Guard

Hit a ton of key shots in the playoffs before disappearing in the Finals . . . Wrongly, the downside is what he'll be remembered for from 1990-91 . . . Otherwise, one of most upbeat seasons in years . . . Scoring average was his lowest since rookie season, but accomplished preseason goal by playing in all 82 games for first time since 1986-87 . . . Should give Kevin Johnson the number of the man who worked on his hamstrings . . . Healthy in playoffs for first time since 1989 Finals against Detroit until bruised shoulder forced him out of Game 5 of Chicago series . . . Five three-point baskets away from Michael Cooper's Laker career record . . . Drafted by San Diego as an undergraduate out of Arizona State (fourth pick) in 1983 . . . Born March 28, 1961, in Ogden, Utah . . . Made $1,110,000.

Year	Team	G	FG	FG Pct.	FT	FT Pct.	Reb.	Ast.	TP	Avg.
1983-84	Los Angeles	74	334	.484	112	.806	164	177	788	10.6
1984-85	L.A. Lakers	81	541	.539	187	.820	210	244	1295	16.0
1985-86	L.A. Lakers	76	507	.513	138	.784	189	164	1174	15.4
1986-87	L.A. Lakers	82	554	.489	224	.892	286	281	1397	17.0
1987-88	L.A. Lakers	81	710	.527	272	.858	333	335	1754	21.7
1988-89	L.A. Lakers	74	588	.491	195	.863	302	231	1448	19.6
1989-90	L.A. Lakers	77	472	.470	160	.766	242	274	1197	15.5
1990-91	L.A. Lakers	82	501	.477	118	.797	246	177	1191	14.5
	Totals	627	4207	.500	1406	.830	1972	1883	10244	16.3

A.C. GREEN 28 6-9 224   Forward

Only reliable Laker reserve in postseason... Played all 82 games for fourth consecutive season... The difference: He was a reserve for most of it, behind newcomer Sam Perkins... Numbers were down, but not because he wasn't working as hard as ever... Has second-longest streak (403) for consecutive games played among active players, behind Houston's Otis Thorpe... Last missed a game, regular season or playoff, on Nov. 18, 1986... Started 21 times in 1990-91... Born Oct. 4, 1963, in Portland, Ore.... Played key role in beating hometown Trail Blazers in Western Conference finals... Oregon State product was 23rd pick in 1985 draft... Made $1,750,000.

Year	Team	G	FG	FG Pct.	FT	FT Pct.	Reb.	Ast.	TP	Avg.
1985-86	L.A. Lakers	82	209	.539	102	.611	381	54	521	6.4
1986-87	L.A. Lakers	79	316	.538	220	.780	615	84	852	10.8
1987-88	L.A. Lakers	82	322	.503	293	.773	710	93	937	11.4
1988-89	L.A. Lakers	82	401	.529	282	.786	739	103	1088	13.3
1989-90	L.A. Lakers	82	385	.478	278	.751	712	90	1061	12.9
1990-91	L.A. Lakers	82	258	.476	223	.738	516	71	750	9.1
	Totals	489	1891	.508	1398	.752	3673	495	5209	10.7

TONY SMITH 23 6-4 195   Guard

Backup to Magic Johnson most of season before being replaced by Larry Drew... Moment of glory came Feb. 3, when he filled in for injured Johnson and outscored Michael Jordan in fourth quarter, 6-4... NBC named him Player of the Game... Played 10 minutes in the playoffs... Background as off-guard, but Lakers fashion him at point... Shot 44.1 percent as a rookie and missed all seven three-point attempts... Born June 14, 1968, in East Wauwatosa, Wis.... Starred nearby at Marquette... Chosen No. 51 in 1990 draft... Made $120,000.

Year	Team	G	FG	FG Pct.	FT	FT Pct.	Reb.	Ast.	TP	Avg.
1990-91	L.A. Lakers	64	97	.441	40	.702	71	135	234	3.7

TERRY TEAGLE 31 6-5 195   Forward-Guard

The 44.3 percent from field was his lowest mark since rookie season of 1982-83 . . . But he provided scoring off the bench, exactly what he was acquired for . . . Typical streak shooter . . . Struggled much of season, but closed with 17.2 points and 49 percent shooting in last 11 games of the regular season . . . Finished at 9.9 points overall in 18.3 minutes, a ratio only Magic Johnson and James Worthy could match on Lakers . . . A disaster in the playoffs . . . Lakers gave up 1991 first-round draft choice to get him from Golden State . . . Born April 10, 1960, in Broaddus, Tex., and attended Baylor . . . Broaddus is a community of about 200 people, some of whom put up satellite dishes to watch Teagle . . . Was 16th pick (Houston) in 1982 draft . . . Made $550,000.

Year	Team	G	FG	FG Pct.	FT	FT Pct.	Reb.	Ast.	TP	Avg.
1982-83	Houston........	73	332	.428	87	.696	194	150	761	10.4
1983-84	Houston........	68	148	.470	37	.841	78	63	340	5.0
1984-85	Det.-G.S........	21	74	.540	25	.714	43	14	175	8.3
1985-86	Golden State.....	82	475	.496	211	.796	235	115	1165	14.2
1986-87	Golden State.....	82	370	.458	182	.778	175	105	922	11.2
1987-88	Golden State.....	47	248	.454	97	.802	81	61	594	12.6
1988-89	Golden State.....	66	409	.476	182	.809	263	96	1002	15.2
1989-90	Golden State.....	82	538	.480	244	.830	367	155	1323	16.1
1990-91	L.A. Lakers......	82	335	.443	145	.819	181	82	815	9.9
	Totals	603	2929	.467	1210	.796	1617	841	7097	11.8

ELDEN CAMPBELL 23 6-11 215   Forward-Center

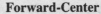

Agility as a leaper, especially for his size . . . Good shot-blocker, too . . . Not much of an offensive game yet . . . Played in 52 games . . . Athletic ability makes him a worthwhile investment . . . Attended Morningside High School in Inglewood, the same city as the Forum . . . Lakers' first-round pick (No. 27) last year after finishing college career as leading scorer in Clemson history . . . Survived several cuts in 1988 Olympic trials, making the final 27 . . . Born July 23, 1968, in Inglewood, Cal. . . . Made $575,000.

Year	Team	G	FG	FG Pct.	FT	FT Pct.	Reb.	Ast.	TP	Avg.
1990-91	L.A. Lakers......	52	56	.455	32	.653	96	10	144	2.8

LARRY DREW 33 6-2 190   Guard

Third-string point guard in regular season behind Magic Johnson and rookie Tony Smith . . . Elevated to backup in the playoffs because of his experience . . . It didn't help . . . Never complained about his role, even when third on the depth chart . . . Hard worker . . . Started two games for injured Johnson in January . . . Had 14 assists against Golden State . . . Expects to return to Europe, but most teams can always use a backup point guard . . . Born April 2, 1958, in Kansas City, Kan., and went to Missouri . . . Drafted No. 17 by Detroit in 1980 . . . Made $550,000.

Year	Team	G	FG	FG Pct.	FT	FT Pct.	Reb.	Ast.	TP	Avg.
1980-81	Detroit	76	197	.407	106	.797	120	249	504	6.6
1981-82	Kansas City	81	358	.473	150	.794	149	419	874	10.8
1982-83	Kansas City	75	599	.492	310	.820	207	610	1510	20.1
1983-84	Kansas City	73	474	.462	243	.776	146	558	1194	16.4
1984-85	Kansas City	72	457	.501	154	.794	164	484	1075	14.9
1985-86	Sacramento	75	376	.485	128	.795	125	338	890	11.9
1986-87	L.A. Clippers	60	295	.432	139	.837	103	326	741	12.4
1987-88	L.A. Clippers	74	328	.456	83	.769	119	383	765	10.3
1989-90	L.A. Lakers	80	170	.444	46	.767	98	217	418	5.2
1990-91	L.A. Lakers	48	54	.432	17	.773	34	118	139	2.9
	Totals	714	3308	.467	1376	.798	1265	3702	8110	11.4

IRVING THOMAS 25 6-8 225   Forward

Rookie free agent got to play in only 26 games in regular season and five minutes total in three playoff games . . . Center at Florida State, where he left as No. 2 on school's all-time scoring list . . . Transferred from Kentucky . . . Needs to make transition to small forward . . . Non-drafted in 1990, he impressed Lakers in summer league, but landed in Greece for less than a month before signing with L.A. . . . Born Jan. 2, 1966, in Brooklyn, N.Y., and grew up in Miami, where he was an All-American at Carol City H.S. . . . Made $120,000.

Year	Team	G	FG	FG Pct.	FT	FT Pct.	Reb.	Ast.	TP	Avg.
1990-91	L.A. Lakers	26	17	.340	12	.571	31	10	46	1.8

MYCHAL THOMPSON 36 6-10 235   Center-Forward

Still Mychal after all these years . . . Personality and witty comments made him a media favorite during the Finals, even though he barely played . . . Says he wants to play two more years . . . That may be fine with Lakers, as long as it's somewhere else . . . Would be happy to finish career with Miami or Orlando, close to his roots in the Bahamas and Florida . . . Appeared in 72 games, averaging 15 minutes per . . . Born Jan. 30, 1955, in Nassau, Bahamas, and played collegiately at Minnesota . . . First player selected in 1978 draft, by Portland . . . Made $615,000.

Year	Team	G	FG	FG Pct.	FT	FT Pct.	Reb.	Ast.	TP	Avg.
1978-79	Portland	73	460	.490	154	.572	604	176	1074	14.7
1979-80	Portland					Injured				
1980-81	Portland	79	569	.494	207	.641	686	284	1345	17.0
1981-82	Portland	79	681	.523	280	.628	921	319	1642	20.8
1982-83	Portland	80	505	.489	249	.621	753	380	1259	15.7
1983-84	Portland	79	487	.524	266	.667	688	308	1240	15.7
1984-85	Portland	79	572	.515	307	.684	618	205	1451	18.4
1985-86	Portland	82	503	.498	198	.641	608	176	1204	14.7
1986-87	S.A.-LAL	82	359	.450	219	.737	412	115	938	11.4
1987-88	L.A. Lakers	80	370	.512	185	.634	489	66	925	11.6
1988-89	L.A. Lakers	80	291	.559	156	.678	467	48	738	9.2
1989-90	L.A. Lakers	70	281	.500	144	.706	477	43	706	10.1
1990-91	L.A. Lakers	72	113	.496	62	.705	228	21	288	4.0
	Totals	935	5191	.504	2427	.655	6951	2141	12810	13.7

THE ROOKIE

ANTHONY JONES 24 6-7 200   Forward

Next stop will be fourth in five years . . . Spent freshman and sophomore years at Connors (Okla.) State Junior College, the next at Union (Ky.) College and the last at Oral Roberts . . . Honorable mention NAIA All-American . . . Chances of making Lakers are slim, but not impossible . . . Last year, they kept three rookies, including undrafted Irving Thomas . . . High-school teammate of Chicago's Stacey King . . . Born March 21, 1967, in Lawton, Okla.

Magic erased Oscar Robertson's all-time assists mark.

COACH MIKE DUNLEAVY: First-time head coach was given the keys to a Rolls-Royce . . . He didn't crash, though 2-5 start caused a few worries . . . By the end of the season, no one was asking if turning over Magic Johnson, James Worthy, et al, to rookie coach was a mistake . . . Former sixth-round draft choice by Philadelphia out of the University of South Carolina . . . Later played for Houston and San Antonio, then left  to work for Merrill Lynch on Wall Street . . . Returned to basketball when injury-depleted Bucks called . . . Supposedly retired as a player 19 games into 1984-85 when airplane suddenly jerked while taxiing, causing back injury . . . Became assistant coach with Bucks, but played on 10-day contracts when injuries came again each of his last two seasons there, making 10 appearances in 1989-90 . . . Born March 21, 1954, in Brooklyn, N.Y.

GREATEST TEAM

This is a little like picking the best Mike Tyson punch. You prefer Magic Johnson and Kareem Abdul-Jabbar, or Wilt Chamberlain and Jerry West? Thirty-three consecutive wins, or back-to-back titles?

For several, somewhat emotional, reasons, we gave 1986-87 the nod over 1971-72, the latter of which was highlighted by 33 victories in a row and 69 overall, both NBA records. But '87 was the first of Magic Johnson's MVP seasons and the season the Lakers went 65-17 to answer many doubters after losing to Houston the year before. They capped the season with their fourth title of the decade to break a tie with Boston.

And they beat the Celtics in six games in the Finals to seal the accomplishment. Their one victory at Boston Garden came on Johnson's memorable baby hook with two seconds remaining, and the three at the Forum were all convincing, as convincing as the notion that the Lakers had re-established themselves.

ALL-TIME LAKER LEADERS

SEASON

Points: Elgin Baylor, 2,719, 1962-63
Assists: Earvin (Magic) Johnson, 989, 1990-91
Rebounds: Wilt Chamberlain, 1,712, 1968-69

GAME

Points: Elgin Baylor, 71 vs. New York, 11/15/60
Assists: Jerry West, 23 vs. Philadelphia, 2/1/67
       Earvin (Magic) Johnson, 23 vs. Seattle, 2/21/84
Rebounds: Wilt Chamberlain, 42 vs. Boston, 3/7/69

CAREER

Points: Jerry West, 25,192, 1960-74
Assists: Earvin (Magic) Johnson, 9,921, 1980-91
Rebounds: Elgin Baylor, 11,463, 1958-72

MINNESOTA TIMBERWOLVES

TEAM DIRECTORY: Owners: Harvey Ratner, Marv Wolfenson; Pres.: Bob Stein; VP-Marketing: Len Komoroski; VP-Sales: Chris Wright: Dir. Player Personnel: Jim Brewer; Dir. Media Rel.: Bill Robertson; Coach: Jimmy Rodgers; Asst. Coaches: Jim Brewer, Sidney Lowe. Arena: Target Center (19,006). Colors: Blue, green and silver.

SCOUTING REPORT

SHOOTING: Events of the past should be forgotten, if not purged. Any team that drafts Pooh Richardson and Gerald Glass and an agile center like Felton Spencer and then runs a slowdown game doesn't deserve the kind of fan support the Timberwolves have gotten their first two years. But that wasn't the only problem. Spencer was the only player to hit better than 50 percent, and he took only 4.7 shots a game. Tony Campbell, whose 1,502 attempts was 152 more than second-place Richardson despite getting 261 fewer minutes, finished at .434.

What imagination comes to this offense with the arrival of Jimmy Rodgers as new coach remains to be seen. At least it can't get worse. Myron Brown, the rookie shooting guard and leader from Slippery Rock, may help.

PLAYMAKING: Among the many things to like about Richardson is that he doesn't beat his own team a lot, something you can't say about a lot of young players given the keys to an offense. Last season, he finished seventh in the league in assists, but more important had only 2.1 turnovers to 9.0 assists. This is a carryover from his rookie season, when his final 41 games resulted in just 87 turnovers.

The Timberwolves' continuous two-man game obviously helps cut down mistakes. But even if Richardson's turnovers go up when someone adds an accelerator to the offense, so will his enjoyment of showing up. That can only help.

DEFENSE: Only three teams allowed higher shooting percentages, and only one, Denver, came from the Western Conference. But the Wolves had the ability to give people trouble because defense comes from hard work and concentration (compared to execution for offense) and Bill Musselman had plenty of hungry rescued CBAers.

Pooh Richardson welcomes new era under Jimmy Rodgers.

That aspect will be sorted out as the roster develops properly. What should improve in the meantime is the shot-blocking abilities of a team with Spencer, Randy Breuer and rookie Luc Longley. The Timberwolves of 1990-91 finished 10th in the league in blocks.

REBOUNDING: Twelve teams had better percentages last season. Only by having a couple good rebounding forwards, 6-6 Tyrone Corbin (7.2 boards a game) and 6-7 Sam Mitchell (6.3), did they get that high. So when the Timberwolves went into the draft needing a power forward, they took a center, Longley. What that gets them beyond potentially great scrimmages is anyone's guess.

TIMBERWOLF ROSTER

No.	Veterans	Pos.	Ht.	Wt.	Age	Yrs. Pro	College
45	Randy Breuer	C	7-3	258	31	8	Minnesota
1	Scott Brooks	G	5-11	165	26	3	Cal-Irvine
19	Tony Campbell	G-F	6-7	215	29	7	Ohio State
23	Tyrone Corbin	F	6-6	222	28	6	DePaul
22	Gerald Glass	G-F	6-6	221	22	1	Mississippi
52	Dan Godfread	F-C	6-10	250	24	1	Evansville
42	Sam Mitchell	F	6-7	210	28	2	Mercer
4	Tod Murphy	F	6-10	220	27	3	Cal-Irvine
24	Jerome Richardson	G	6-1	180	25	2	UCLA
50	Felton Spencer	C	7-0	265	23	1	Louisville
5	Doug West	G	6-6	200	24	2	Villanova

Rd.	Rookies	Sel. No.	Pos.	Ht.	Wt.	College
1	Luc Longley	7	C	7-2	265	New Mexico
2	Myron Brown	34	G	6-3	180	Slippery Rock

OUTLOOK: They're the only team in the Western Conference with a new coach and, therefore, are something of an uncertainty, especially when a change of philosophy is in the air. For one thing, the firing of Musselman was a vote for long-term gains over immediate wins and showed the desire of the front office to let the young players learn, which is good. On the other hand, the Timberwolves didn't help themselves much in the summer, which is bad. Denver did and Dallas will, simply by staying healthy, all of which makes last place a possibility.

TIMBERWOLF PROFILES

JEROME (POOH) RICHARDSON 25 6-1 180   Guard

The only player in the league who can play all 164 games his first two seasons, starting the last 124, and claim no one saw him . . . On the court, no one will benefit more from Bill Musselman's firing . . . Slowdown offense did nothing to showcase his talents . . . Flashy player who was sometimes victimized by passes going off hands of teammates . . . Nine assists per game was seventh-best average in NBA . . . Also third in league in assist-to-turnover ratio behind Muggsy Bogues and John Paxson, though here's where Minnesota's style of play obviously helped . . . A player with this much ability absolutely, positively has to shoot better than 58.9 percent (rookie) and 53.9 percent (last season) from the line . . . Former UCLA star gets clobbered when forced to play one-on-one defense against penetrating guards, too . . . Tenth pick in 1989 draft . . . Born May 4, 1966, in Philadelphia . . . Made $615,000.

Year	Team	G	FG	FG Pct.	FT	FT Pct.	Reb.	Ast.	TP	Avg.
1989-90	Minnesota	82	426	.461	63	.589	217	554	938	11.4
1990-91	Minnesota	82	635	.470	89	.539	286	734	1401	17.1
	Totals	164	1061	.466	152	.559	503	1288	2339	14.3

TONY CAMPBELL 29 6-7 215   Guard-Forward

Again led Timberwolves in scoring, finishing 15th in the league, but actually had two seasons in one in 1990-91 . . . The beginning and the end were Campbell of old, posting up smaller guards in the Bill Musselman dump-it-in offense . . . The middle was a time of unhappiness and frustration with the coach . . . Took 157 more shots than any other Timberwolf even though he played five fewer games than runnerup Pooh Richardson . . . There was talk they tried to trade him before February deadline, when his complaints may have gotten old, but strong finish and Musselman's departure should be worth new life . . . Minnesota was 12-12 when he shot 50 percent or better . . . First-round pick out of Ohio State in 1984 by Pistons . . . Born May 7, 1962, in Teaneck, N.J. . . . Made $1,200,000.

Year	Team	G	FG	FG Pct.	FT	FT Pct.	Reb.	Ast.	TP	Avg.
1984-85	Detroit	56	130	.496	56	.800	89	24	316	5.6
1985-86	Detroit	82	294	.484	58	.795	236	45	648	7.9
1986-87	Detroit	40	57	.393	24	.615	58	19	138	3.5
1987-88	L.A. Lakers	13	57	.564	28	.718	27	15	143	11.0
1988-89	L.A. Lakers	63	158	.458	70	.843	130	47	388	6.2
1989-90	Minnesota	82	723	.457	448	.787	451	213	1903	23.2
1990-91	Minnesota	77	652	.434	358	.803	346	214	1678	21.8
	Totals	413	2071	.456	1042	.790	1337	577	5214	12.6

TYRONE CORBIN 28 6-6 222   Forward

Established career highs in scoring, assists and blocked shots in 1990-91 . . . Only Larry Bird and Scottie Pippen had more assists among NBA forwards . . . Only Pippen and Chris Mullin averaged more steals . . . Posted first triple-double in franchise history, Jan. 2 vs. Dallas . . . Scored 20 points or more 34 times . . . Ranked fourth in NBA in minutes played . . . Only Timberwolf left from expansion draft . . . A hard worker and a leader, but more by example than voice . . . Nothing flashy about him . . . Good medium-range shooter . . . Spent two seasons in a row with same team for first time in six-year pro career . . . Drafted by Spurs in second round of 1985 draft after fine career at DePaul . . . Born Dec. 31, 1962, in Columbia, S.C. . . . Made $830,000.

Year	Team	G	FG	FG Pct.	FT	FT Pct.	Reb.	Ast.	TP	Avg.
1985-86	San Antonio	16	27	.422	10	.714	25	11	64	4.0
1986-87	S.A.-Clev.	63	156	.409	91	.734	215	97	404	6.4
1987-88	Clev.-Phoe.	84	257	.490	110	.797	350	115	625	7.4
1988-89	Phoenix	77	245	.540	141	.788	398	118	631	8.2
1989-90	Minnesota	82	521	.481	161	.770	604	216	1203	14.7
1990-91	Minnesota	82	587	.448	296	.798	589	347	1472	18.0
	Totals	404	1793	.470	809	.782	2181	904	4399	10.9

FELTON SPENCER 23 7-0 265   Center

Along with Derrick Coleman and Lionel Simmons, the only rookie to get 500 points and 500 rebounds . . . Proved to be very agile for a big man and a hard worker . . . Needs to develop more offensive capabilities . . . Most of baskets came off junk inside and offensive rebounds . . . Wolves' president Bob Stein has said he would take Spencer over Coleman with the No. 1, given the choice between the two after a year in the pros . . . Minnesota writer responded by asking Stein if the NBA was considering drug-testing team executives . . . Give Spencer time and and he'll only get better . . . Sixth pick in 1990 draft out of Louisville . . . No. 7 offensive rebounder in league (272) and No. 20 in blocked shots . . . Born Jan. 5, 1968, in Louisville . . . Made $1,070,000.

Year	Team	G	FG	FG Pct.	FT	FT Pct.	Reb.	Ast.	TP	Avg.
1990-91	Minnesota	81	195	.512	182	.722	641	25	572	7.1

TOD MURPHY 27 6-10 220 — Forward

Encouraging first season with Minnesota was followed by disappointing, injury-plagued 1990-91 . . . Biggest problem was recurring back spasms that put him out for 26 games in a row from the end of November to the end of January . . . Shot 50 percent before back problems, 35.4 after . . . Minutes disappeared, and so did his confidence . . . Started 19 times . . . Drafted 53rd by Seattle out of Cal-Irvine in 1986 . . . Cut by Sonics, played briefly in Italy before suffering knee injury in exhibition game . . . Had one game in 1987-88 with Clippers before the CBA experience in which he was MVP of the league's 1988 Championship Series under Bill Musselman . . . Played in Spain following season and became a Timberwolf in 1989 . . . Born Dec. 24, 1963, in Lakewood, Cal. . . . Made $590,000.

Year	Team	G	FG	FG Pct.	FT	FT Pct.	Reb.	Ast.	TP	Avg.
1987-88	L.A. Clippers	1	1	1.000	3	.750	2	2	5	5.0
1989-90	Minnesota	82	260	.471	144	.709	564	106	680	8.3
1990-91	Minnesota	52	90	.396	70	.667	255	60	251	4.8
	Totals	135	351	.450	217	.696	821	168	936	6.9

SCOTT BROOKS 26 5-11 165 — Guard

Plays like he's generating electricity for entire Twin Cities . . . Fans behind bench yell for him to take tranquilizers when he looks out of control . . . Played very well last six weeks of season . . . Team at times responded better with him than with Pooh Richardson . . . Signed five-year contract, four of which are guaranteed, two days after season ended . . . Not bad for a guy who was not drafted out of Cal-Irvine and came to Timberwolves for a second-round draft choice . . . Led team in three-point attempts . . . Born July 31, 1965, in Lathrop, Cal. . . . Made $295,000.

Year	Team	G	FG	FG Pct.	FT	FT Pct.	Reb.	Ast.	TP	Avg.
1988-89	Philadelphia	82	156	.420	61	.884	94	306	428	5.2
1989-90	Philadelphia	72	119	.431	50	.877	64	207	319	4.4
1990-91	Minnesota	80	159	.430	61	.847	72	204	424	5.3
	Totals	234	434	.427	172	.869	230	717	1171	5.0

RANDY BREUER 31 7-3 258   Center

Teams could do worse in their second year of existence than having him for a backup center ... It's just that no one pegged him as defensive specialist against point guards ... But there he was, playing Magic Johnson in December in a Bill Musselman special ... Started some at power forward with Felton Spencer at center ... Hurt by inconsistent rotation, but that didn't make him any different than most teammates ... Can score a little with hook shot ... Had only nine double-digit rebound games in 73 appearances, 44 of which were starts ... Born Oct. 11, 1960, in Lake City, Minn., and stayed at home to star at Minnesota ... Drafted 18th by Milwaukee in 1983 ... Made $1,150,000.

Year	Team	G	FG	FG Pct.	FT	FT Pct.	Reb.	Ast.	TP	Avg.
1983-84	Milwaukee	57	68	.384	32	.696	109	17	168	2.9
1984-85	Milwaukee	78	162	.511	89	.701	256	40	413	5.3
1985-86	Milwaukee	82	272	.477	141	.712	458	114	685	8.4
1986-87	Milwaukee	76	241	.485	118	.584	350	47	600	7.9
1987-88	Milwaukee	81	390	.495	188	.657	551	103	968	12.0
1988-89	Milwaukee	48	86	.480	28	.549	135	22	200	4.2
1989-90	Mil.-Minn.	81	298	.428	126	.653	417	97	722	8.9
1990-91	Minnesota	73	197	.453	35	.443	345	73	429	5.9
	Totals	576	1714	.468	757	.640	2621	513	4185	7.3

GERALD GLASS 22 6-6 221   Guard-Forward

As expected coming out of college, he had trouble finding his right position ... Not quick enough to handle guards and not strong enough for some forwards ... Athleticism makes up for some deficiencies. No one on Wolves averaged more points per 48 minutes than his 27.9 ... Had a three-game stretch on a December road swing when he hit Phoenix, Golden State and the Lakers for 27, 24 and 32 ... Next game, Dennis Rodman shut him down and he quickly became a memory ... Disappeared from rotation when Bill Musselman got down on him ... Got 20 minutes in final 22 games ... Was probably delighted to see Musselman leave ... Former Mississippi standout shows signs of a positive future ... Was 20th pick in 1990 draft ... Born Nov. 12, 1968, in Greenwood, Miss. ... Made $575,000.

Year	Team	G	FG	FG Pct.	FT	FT Pct.	Reb.	Ast.	TP	Avg.
1990-91	Minnesota	51	149	.438	52	.684	102	42	352	6.9

DAN GODFREAD 24 6-10 250   Forward-Center

Does he have anything going for him besides being 6-10? Who knows? . . . Played a total of 20 minutes in his 10 games . . . In practice, at least, he showed a bit of a shooting touch from the outside for a big man . . . Originally got 10-day contract in December . . . Signed for rest of season Jan. 18 and the next night made his first NBA basket on a resounding dunk against Golden State . . . Averaged 17.8 points and 8.8 rebounds before that for Rockford of the CBA . . . Played at Evansville, where he set school record for blocked shots . . . Born July 14, 1967, in Fort Wayne, Ind.

Year	Team	G	FG	FG Pct.	FT	FT Pct.	Reb.	Ast.	TP	Avg.
1990-91	Minnesota.	10	5	.417	3	.750	2	0	13	1.3

SAM MITCHELL 28 6-7 210   Forward

Continues to prove himself as a legitimate player after bouncing around from NBA camps to Europe to CBA . . . Started 60 games, but is realistically seventh or eighth man . . . Versatile as he was persistent to get here . . . Played a lot of power forward because Minnesota needed him there, though he's better suited for small forward . . . Defended everyone from Kevin Johnson to Magic Johnson to David Robinson . . . Solid baseline shooter from around 15 feet . . . Born Sept. 9, 1963, in Columbus, Ga., and went on to star at Mercer College . . . Drafted 54th by Houston in 1985 . . . Made $500,000.

Year	Team	G	FG	FG Pct.	FT	FT Pct.	Reb.	Ast.	TP	Avg.
1989-90	Minnesota.	80	372	.446	268	.768	462	89	1012	12.7
1990-91	Minnesota.	82	445	.441	307	.775	520	133	1197	14.6
	Totals	162	817	.443	575	.772	982	222	2209	13.6

DOUG WEST 24 6-6 200   Guard

Improved a lot during second pro season . . . A year ago, he was close to being cut as some within the organization thought he was lazy . . . A crowd favorite with soaring slams off the break . . . Great athlete with questionable outside shooting . . . Swingman who played primarily small forward in 1990-91 . . . Timberwolves were 11-12 when he played at least

15 minutes . . . There's a stat to use to bargain for time . . . Born May 27, 1967, in Altoona, Pa., and was four-year starter at Villanova after being highly recruited as MVP in Pittsburgh's Dapper Dan Classic . . . Taken in second round (No. 38) by Minnesota in 1989 . . . Made $230,000.

Year	Team	G	FG	FG Pct.	FT	FT Pct.	Reb.	Ast.	TP	Avg.
1989-90	Minnesota.	52	53	.393	26	.813	70	18	135	2.6
1990-91	Minnesota.	75	118	.480	58	.690	136	48	294	3.9
	Totals	127	171	.449	84	.724	206	66	429	3.4

Tony Campbell never saw a shot he didn't like.

THE ROOKIES

LUC LONGLEY 22 7-2 265   **Center**
Good mobility and passing skills for a player his size, but how
much time will he get to move around on a team that already is
developing Felton Spencer?... When so many teams desperate
for a center wanted him, it would be a shame to have him as
second-string or platooning... Picked seventh... First New
Mexico player since Michael Cooper in late '70s named first-team
All-Western Athletic Conference in consecutive seasons... Born
Jan. 19, 1969, in Perth, Australia.

MYRON BROWN 22 6-3 180   **Guard**
You won't recognize the name or the competition, but the Division
II All-American from Slippery Rock was good enough to get first-
round mention and was ultimately picked at 34... NBA director
of scouting Marty Blake said, ''Myron Brown can play. My job
is to find prospects, and he is one.''... Missed only one of 117
games during career in which he averaged 22.6 ppg and finished
as all-time leading scorer in Pennsylvania State Athletic Conference... Born Nov. 3, 1969, in Pittsburgh.

COACH JIMMY RODGERS: Named to replace Bill Musselman June 19... Fired by Celtics May 8,
1990, after first-round playoff loss to Knicks
... Went 42-40 and 52-30 in two seasons at
Boston, where he'd previously been an assistant
for eight years... Superb basketball mind and
fine judge of talent... Began coaching career
as assistant to Bill Fitch at North Dakota...
Elevated to No. 1 spot when Fitch left... Spent
one season as Arkansas assistant, then reunited with Fitch as chief
scout and assistant for newly formed Cleveland Cavaliers...
Named team's director of player personnel for 1979-80... Was
three-year starter at guard at Iowa... Born March 12, 1943, in
Franklin Park, Ill.

GREATEST TEAM

This won't do much for the now-departed Bill Musselman, but
the Timberwolves improved by seven wins from their first season

to the second, going 29-53 in 1990-91. That was good for fifth place in the seven-team Midwest Division, just two games out of fourth and ahead of established franchises Dallas and Denver.

It may have been a season of internal unrest, but the Wolves went 21-20 at the Target Center, their permanent home after spending the first season at the cavernous Metrodome. Pooh Richardson averaged nine assists a game despite running a sloooowdown offense, and Tony Campbell averaged 21.8 points.

This was three yards and a cloud of dust brought to the NBA. The Timberwolves may have been boring, but that also helped make sure they didn't beat themselves—their 13 turnovers a game were fewer than anyone.

ALL-TIME TIMBERWOLF LEADERS

SEASON

Points: Tony Campbell, 1,903, 1989-90
Assists: Jerome Richardson, 554, 1989-90
Rebounds: Felton Spencer, 641, 1990-91

GAME

Points: Tony Campbell, 44 vs. Boston, 2/2/90
Assists: Sidney Lowe, 17 vs. Golden State, 3/20/90
Rebounds: Todd Murphy, 20 vs. L.A. Clippers, 1/2/90

CAREER

Points: Tony Campbell, 3,581, 1989-91
Assists: Jerome Richardson, 1,288, 1989-91
Rebounds: Tyrone Corbin, 2,181, 1989-91

PHOENIX SUNS

TEAM DIRECTORY: Pres./CEO: Jerry Colangelo; VP-Dir. Pub. Rel.: Tom Ambrose; Dir. Media Rel.: Barry Ringel; Dir. Player Personnel/Coach: Cotton Fitzsimmons; Asst. Coaches: Paul Westphal, Lionel Hollins. Arena: Veterans Memorial Coliseum (14,471). Colors: Purple, orange and copper.

Suns will shine if Dan Majerle recovers from back surgery.

SCOUTING REPORT

SHOOTING: This never has been much of a problem area. Six players who appeared in at least half the games (counting Xavier McDaniel's Suns totals) shot 50 percent or better—three regular starters and both centers, Mark West and Andrew Lang, and reserve forward Tim Perry. None finished among the top 10 in the league, but the team still finished No. 3 at 49.6 percent.

The noticeable absentee from the plus-.500 group, of course, is Tom Chambers, coming off a career-low .437. The return to health (his back) and his game will tell a lot about the Suns' pulse.

PLAYMAKING: The Suns are probably in better shape than any other NBA team. Kevin Johnson isn't the best point guard in the West, but he is very good, and Negele Knight and Jeff Hornacek are behind him. That's a security blanket to cover the Grand Canyon. Knight is the true backup, Hornacek merely the solid shooting guard who used to be the No. 1 ball-handler.

DEFENSE: The comeback of Dan Majerle from offseason back surgery is imperative because the Suns aren't a great defensive team to begin with. Having their main stopper hobbled would only make things worse. Phoenix allowed 107.5 points an outing last season, tied for 20th. West dropping out of the starting lineup, taking his shot-blocking abilities along, didn't help, but Johnson finished ninth in steals.

REBOUNDING: They try to improve through the draft again. A year ago, Phoenix used its No. 1 pick on Jayson Williams for power forward, but he had contract problems and was traded to Philadelphia. This time, the Suns went with more bulk, choosing Creighton's Chad Gallagher early in the second round.

Help is needed. No Sun had more than the 6.9 boards a game of McDaniel and West. The Suns finished the season tied for 10th in the league and tied for fourth in the Pacific Division.

OUTLOOK: Last season's third-place finish in the Pacific may have been a disappointment, but it wasn't a surprise. The Trail Blazers and Lakers both made more significant moves to improve.

It looks like the same fate faces Cotton Fitzsimmons' team this season. The talent, as in the past, is undeniable, but there are too many unresolved issues to not make at least a small bit of difference in the game's most competitive division. Will they find the right complement for Chambers at the other forward? Will Chambers

SUN ROSTER

No.	Veterans	Pos.	Ht.	Wt.	Age	Yrs. Pro	College
2	Joe Barry Carroll	C	7-1	255	33	10	Purdue
23	Cedric Ceballos	F	6-6	210	22	1	Cal-Fullerton
24	Tom Chambers	F	6-10	230	32	10	Utah
14	Jeff Hornacek	G	6-4	190	28	5	Iowa State
7	Kevin Johnson	G	6-1	190	25	4	California
32	Negele Knight	G	6-1	182	24	1	Dayton
28	Andrew Lang	C	6-11	250	25	3	Arkansas
51	Ian Lockhart	F-C	6-8	240	24	1	Tennessee
9	Dan Majerle	G-F	6-6	220	26	3	Central Michigan
35	Xavier McDaniel	F	6-8	205	28	6	Wichita State
45	Ed Nealy	F	6-7	240	31	8	Kansas State
34	Tim Perry	F	6-9	220	26	3	Temple
31	Kurt Rambis	F	6-8	213	33	10	Santa Clara
41	Mark West	C	6-10	246	30	8	Old Dominion

Rd.	Rookies	Sel. No.	Pos.	Ht.	Wt.	College
2	Chad Gallagher	32	F	6-9	245	Creighton
2	Richard Dumas	46	F	6-6	200	Oklahoma State
2	Joey Wright	50	G	6-3	185	Texas

and Majerle be 100 percent? And, most important, will the Suns finally reach their potential?

In other words, replace the question marks with an exclamation point.

SUN PROFILES

DAN MAJERLE 26 6-6 220   Guard-Forward

Maybe the MVP on the team . . . Defends power players like Charles Barkley and guards with detonation-like quickness like Michael Jordan and Ron Harper with success . . . When everyone was still learning how to pronounce his name (MAR-lee), Cotton Fitzsimmons said Central Michigan product would be like this . . . Until end of the regular season, the ultimate bargain-basement guy . . . Will still get in neighborhood of $500,000 each of next two years, but extension signed near end of last season puts him at approximately $11 million over the three years after that . . . Had offseason surgery to remove benign cyst from lower back . . . Caused numbness and pain in legs by pressing against a nerve . . . In the playoffs, he faced Jazz when right leg had no reflexes . . . Born Sept. 9, 1965, in Traverse City, Mich. . . . Fourth pick in 1988.

Year	Team	G	FG	FG Pct.	FT	FT Pct.	Reb.	Ast.	TP	Avg.
1988-89	Phoenix	54	181	.419	78	.614	209	130	467	8.6
1989-90	Phoenix	73	296	.424	198	.762	430	188	809	11.1
1990-91	Phoenix	77	397	.484	227	.762	418	216	1051	13.6
	Totals	204	874	.448	503	.734	1057	534	2327	11.4

JEFF HORNACEK 28 6-4 190   Guard

Had most consistent season as a pro . . . Steady and versatile . . . Finished third in the league in three-point shooting and eighth in free throws with career-best 89.7 percent . . . Team's top outside shooter . . . Occasionally went back to point guard, his original position with Suns, when Cotton Fitzsimmons used a big lineup with Dan Majerle in the backcourt . . . No. 1 among guards in field-goal percentage in 1989-90 . . . Born April 3, 1963, in Elmhurst, Ill. . . . Suns' fourth pick of 1986 draft . . . Attended Iowa State . . . Made $1.1 million.

Year	Team	G	FG	FG Pct.	FT	FT Pct.	Reb.	Ast.	TP	Avg.
1986-87	Phoenix	80	159	.454	94	.777	184	361	424	5.3
1987-88	Phoenix	82	306	.506	152	.822	262	540	781	9.5
1988-89	Phoenix	78	440	.495	147	.826	266	465	1054	13.5
1989-90	Phoenix	67	483	.536	173	.856	313	337	1179	17.6
1990-91	Phoenix	80	544	.518	201	.897	321	409	1350	16.9
	Totals	387	1932	.509	767	.843	1346	2112	4788	12.4

TOM CHAMBERS 32 6-10 230   Forward

Found the bottom of the Valley of the Sun in 1990-91 . . . Frustration was such that in post-season evaluation with management he volunteered to come off bench this fall . . . Had career-low shooting mark . . . Also lowest scoring average since 1985-86 . . . Muscle problem in back added to problems . . . Went through first special offseason conditioning program of his career . . . Off to a bad start before back problems kicked in . . . All of the above hit him like a flash flood . . . Wasn't it only a year earlier he was celebrating his best season? . . . Mobility is a key because his game is running the court and outside shooting . . . All-Star Game MVP in 1987 while with Seattle . . . Born June

21, 1959, in Ogden, Utah, and drafted eighth out of Utah by Clippers in 1981 . . . Made $2.06 million.

Year	Team	G	FG	FG Pct.	FT	FT Pct.	Reb.	Ast.	TP	Avg.
1981-82	San Diego	81	554	.525	284	.620	561	146	1392	17.2
1982-83	San Diego	79	519	.472	353	.723	519	192	1391	17.6
1983-84	Seattle	82	554	.499	375	.800	532	133	1483	18.1
1984-85	Seattle	81	629	.483	475	.832	579	209	1739	21.5
1985-86	Seattle	66	432	.466	346	.836	431	132	1223	18.5
1986-87	Seattle	82	660	.456	535	.849	545	245	1909	23.3
1987-88	Seattle	82	611	.448	419	.807	490	212	1674	20.4
1988-89	Phoenix	81	774	.471	509	.851	684	231	2085	25.7
1989-90	Phoenix	81	810	.501	557	.861	571	190	2201	27.2
1990-91	Phoenix	76	556	.437	379	.826	490	194	1511	19.9
	Totals	791	6099	.475	4232	.806	5402	1884	16608	21.0

CEDRIC CEBALLOS 22 6-6 210   Forward

One year in the league and he's already developed a reputation . . . Throws up wild shots from weird angles while charging toward the basket and gets many of them to go in . . . First time or two, it looked like luck . . . From there, it became a knack . . . Should have been teaching himself some defense along the way . . . A player whose offense can change the tempo of a game . . . Like on April 14 against Denver: 34 points in 32 minutes . . . Played one season of varsity ball at Dominguez High School in Compton, Cal., before advancing to Ventura (Calif.) JC and Cal State-Fullerton . . . Was 48th pick in 1990 . . . Born Aug. 2, 1969, in Maui, Hawaii . . . Made $175,000.

Year	Team	G	FG	FG Pct.	FT	FT Pct.	Reb.	Ast.	TP	Avg.
1990-91	Phoenix	63	204	.487	110	.663	150	35	519	8.2

KEVIN JOHNSON 25 6-1 190   Guard

Walk-on-water status evaporated last season . . . When an injured KJ watched a late-season game at Golden State but skipped another road game two nights later against the Lakers to attend a fund-raiser for a favorite charity in hometown Sacramento, some players and management wondered about his commitment to the team . . . Grumbles also developed when he opted for pull-up jumpers more than passing off . . . Remains one of game's best point guards, but he's not a floor leader in the vein of Magic Johnson and John Stockton . . . Led team in scoring, assists and steals, but barely reached double figures in assists . . . His 10.1 assists was fourth-best in the league . . . Named winner of J. Walter Kennedy Citizenship Award . . . Born March 4, 1966, in Sacramento . . . Played at California being being first-round draft choice (No. 7) by Cleveland . . . Made $1.75 million.

Year	Team	G	FG	FG Pct.	FT	FT Pct.	Reb.	Ast.	TP	Avg.
1987-88	Clev.-Phoe.	80	275	.461	177	.839	191	437	732	9.2
1988-89	Phoenix	81	570	.505	508	.882	340	991	1650	20.4
1989-90	Phoenix	74	578	.499	501	.838	270	846	1665	22.5
1990-91	Phoenix	77	591	.516	519	.843	271	781	1710	22.2
	Totals	312	2014	.500	1705	.852	1072	3055	5757	18.5

MARK WEST 30 6-10 246   Center

The starter of the future may become the starter of the past much sooner than most would have expected after 1989-90 . . . Led NBA in field-goal percentage that season and played key role in ousting Lakers in playoffs . . . After that, he crumbled . . . Did not seem to play with same intensity . . . A reserve for most of team's successful March run . . . Moved back into starting lineup when Negele Knight stepped in for injured Kevin Johnson and Cotton Fitzsimmons wanted additional experience . . . Played every game for fourth consecutive season . . . Did not get enough attempts to qualify for second field-goal percentage title . . . Actually was in 83 games in 1987-88, when he was traded in February from Cleveland to Phoenix . . . Has 255 consecutive appearances . . . Attended Petersburg High School in Virginia, which produced Moses Malone . . . Then went to Old Dominion . . . A second-rounder drafted by Mavericks in 1983 . . . Born Nov. 5, 1960, in Fort Campbell, Ky. . . . Made $875,000.

Year	Team	G	FG	FG Pct.	FT	FT Pct.	Reb.	Ast.	TP	Avg.
1983-84	Dallas	34	15	.357	7	.318	46	13	37	1.1
1984-85	Mil.-Clev.	66	106	.546	43	.494	251	15	255	3.9
1985-86	Cleveland	67	113	.541	54	.524	322	20	280	4.2
1986-87	Cleveland	78	209	.543	89	.514	339	41	507	6.5
1987-88	Clev.-Phoe.	83	316	.551	170	.596	523	74	802	9.7
1988-89	Phoenix	82	243	.653	108	.535	551	39	594	7.2
1989-90	Phoenix	82	331	.625	199	.691	728	45	861	10.5
1990-91	Phoenix	82	247	.647	135	.655	564	37	629	7.7
	Totals	574	1580	.588	805	.589	3324	284	3965	6.9

JOE BARRY CARROLL 33 7-1 255   Center

Stands a good chance to make team despite presence of several other centers . . . His $1 million guarantee—tough to trade or eat—says so . . . Signed as free agent in late January after having not been re-signed by Denver . . . Put on suspended list to get in shape . . . Played 10 games before injuring his hamstring March 15 and going on injured list . . . Returned to action for season finale . . . Still is threat as low-post scorer . . . Can pass and rebound . . . No. 1 pick overall in 1980 by Golden State after playing at Purdue . . . Has played with Golden State, Houston, New Jersey, Denver and Phoenix in last four seasons . . . Made $350,000 . . . Born July 24, 1958, in Pine Bluff, Ark.

Year	Team	G	FG	FG Pct.	FT	FT Pct.	Reb.	Ast.	TP	Avg.
1980-81	Golden State	82	616	.491	315	.716	759	117	1547	18.9
1981-82	Golden State	76	527	.519	235	.728	633	64	1289	17.0
1982-83	Golden State	79	785	.513	337	.719	688	169	1907	24.1
1983-84	Golden State	80	663	.477	313	.723	636	198	1639	20.5
1985-86	Golden State	79	650	.463	377	.752	670	176	1677	21.2
1986-87	Golden State	81	690	.472	340	.787	589	214	1720	21.2
1987-88	G.S.-Hou.	77	402	.435	172	.764	489	113	976	12.7
1988-89	New Jersey	64	363	.448	176	.800	473	105	902	14.1
1989-90	N.J.-Denver	76	312	.411	137	.774	443	97	761	10.0
1990-91	Phoenix	11	13	.361	11	.917	24	11	37	3.4
	Totals	705	5021	.474	2413	.747	5404	1264	12455	17.7

NEGELE KNIGHT 24 6-1 182   Guard

A lot of teams are kicking themselves for passing him all the way down to 31st in 1990 draft . . . Solid backup to Kevin Johnson as a rookie out of Dayton who could become much more . . . Had especially good showings at end of the season, but really opened eyes because they came against teams like Warriors, Lakers and Spurs . . . Not tall, but muscular . . . A tough-nosed player who, unlike many rookies, was not eaten alive on defense . . . All-time assist leader at Dayton . . . Born March 6, 1967, in Dayton . . . Made $468,000.

Year	Team	G	FG	FG Pct.	FT	FT Pct.	Reb.	Ast.	TP	Avg.
1990-91	Phoenix	64	131	.425	71	.602	71	191	339	5.3

XAVIER McDANIEL 28 6-8 205 Forward

Was more like the ex-X for Suns... Not the rebounder and intimidator they wanted after sending Eddie Johnson and a couple of No. 1s to Seattle... The shaved head remained, not the style... Suns' president Jerry Colangelo: "I told him I wanted the old X."... Suns tried trading him during offseason... Led team in rebounding at 7.2... If that was disappointing, somebody should remind them McDaniel averaged 7.0 in his career heading into 1990-91... Set Veterans Memorial Coliseum record by making 20 consecutive field goals over two games... An All-Star in 1988 who shouldn't be counted out yet... Born June 4, 1963, in Columbia, S.C.... Led NCAA in scoring and rebounding in 1984-85 at Wichita State... Seattle made him fourth pick in 1985... Made $1.4 million.

Year	Team	G	FG	FG Pct.	FT	FT Pct.	Reb.	Ast.	TP	Avg.
1985-86	Seattle	82	576	.490	250	.687	655	193	1404	17.1
1986-87	Seattle	82	806	.509	275	.696	705	207	1890	23.0
1987-88	Seattle	78	687	.488	281	.715	518	263	1669	21.4
1988-89	Seattle	82	677	.489	312	.732	433	134	1677	20.5
1989-90	Seattle	69	611	.496	244	.733	447	171	1471	21.3
1990-91	Sea.-Phoe.	81	590	.497	193	.723	557	187	1373	17.0
	Totals	474	3947	.495	1555	.714	3315	1155	9484	20.0

ANDREW LANG 25 6-11 250 Center

Suffered stress fracture in his leg in August 1990, and didn't get back to 100 percent until February... Still wrested starting job away from Mark West... Offensive rebounding improved... Set team and Veterans Memorial Coliseum record with seven blocks in first half vs. Orlando Feb. 27... Led Suns in blocks per minute and ranked among best in NBA in that department... Coaches wanted him to work on offensive game in summer league... Free-throw percentage has improved each of first three years as a pro... Arkansas product a second-round pick (No. 28) by Suns in 1988... Born June 28, 1966, in Pine Bluff, Ark.... Made $600,000.

Year	Team	G	FG	FG Pct.	FT	FT Pct.	Reb.	Ast.	TP	Avg.
1988-89	Phoenix	62	60	.513	39	.650	147	9	159	2.6
1989-90	Phoenix	74	97	.557	64	.653	271	21	258	3.5
1990-91	Phoenix	63	109	.577	93	.715	303	27	311	4.9
	Totals	199	266	.554	196	.681	721	57	728	3.7

KURT RAMBIS 33 6-8 213   Forward

When Xavier McDaniel came in, Rambis went out . . . Had fewest appearances since 1983-84 . . . Postponed surgery to remove bone spurs from both ankles in summer of '90 . . . Came back in 1990-91, only to have pain return . . . Still a positive influence behind the scenes . . . But he is going to be 34 . . . As popular in Phoenix as he was in Los Angeles and Charlotte, which is saying something . . . Has anyone ever seen him not hustle or not hit the floor chasing a loose ball? . . . Born Feb. 25, 1958, in Cupertino, Cal., and attended Santa Clara . . . Drafted on third round by Knicks in 1980, but ended up in Greece . . . Joined Lakers and left with four championship rings . . . Made $900,000.

Year	Team	G	FG	FG Pct.	FT	FT Pct.	Reb.	Ast.	TP	Avg.
1981-82	Los Angeles	64	118	.518	59	.504	348	56	295	4.6
1982-83	Los Angeles	78	235	.569	114	.687	531	90	584	7.5
1983-84	Los Angeles	47	63	.558	42	.636	266	34	168	3.6
1984-85	L.A. Lakers	82	181	.554	68	.660	528	69	430	5.2
1985-86	L.A. Lakers	74	160	.595	88	.721	517	69	408	5.5
1986-87	L.A. Lakers	78	163	.521	120	.764	453	63	446	5.7
1987-88	L.A. Lakers	70	102	.548	73	.785	268	54	277	4.0
1988-89	Charlotte	75	325	.518	182	.734	703	159	832	11.1
1989-90	Char.-Phoe.	74	190	.509	82	.646	525	135	462	6.2
1990-91	Phoenix	62	83	.497	60	.706	266	64	226	3.6
	Totals	704	1620	.537	888	.692	4405	793	4128	5.9

TIM PERRY 26 6-9 220   Forward

Once a No. 7 pick overall . . . Gulp . . . Runs and jumps well, but still looks like he's trying to make the transition to pro game . . . Or maybe he's just catching up, period . . . Didn't play competitively until junior year in high school . . . At least his defense is improving . . . Played 46 games last season, fewest since coming out of Temple . . . Competed in 1989 Slam Dunk competition at All-Star Weekend . . . Atlantic 10 Conference Player of the Year as a senior for the Owls . . . Born June 4, 1965, in Freehold, N.J. . . . Made $675,000.

Year	Team	G	FG	FG Pct.	FT	FT Pct.	Reb.	Ast.	TP	Avg.
1988-89	Phoenix	62	108	.537	40	.615	132	18	257	4.1
1989-90	Phoenix	60	100	.513	53	.589	152	17	254	4.2
1990-91	Phoenix	46	75	.521	43	.614	126	27	193	4.2
	Totals	168	283	.524	136	.604	410	62	704	4.2

ED NEALY 31 6-7 240   Forward

Somebody woke him up from the dream life
. . . Made an impact for Chicago in 1990 playoffs . . . Left as free agent and got first multi-
year guaranteed contract of his career . . . Averaged just 10.4 minutes for Suns, then watched
former team win the title . . . Strictly blue-collar
player who sets a mean pick . . . Second stint
with Phoenix . . . First time, he lasted just 30
games after being traded from Chicago, then went back to Bulls
. . . Originally an eighth-round pick by Kansas City Kings after
playing at Kansas State . . . Born Feb. 19, 1960, in Pittsburg, Kan.
. . . Made $550,000.

Year	Team	G	FG	FG Pct.	FT	FT Pct.	Reb.	Ast.	TP	Avg.
1982-83	Kansas City	82	147	.595	70	.614	485	62	364	4.4
1983-84	Kansas City	71	63	.500	48	.800	222	50	174	2.5
1984-85	Kansas City	22	26	.591	10	.526	44	18	62	2.8
1986-87	San Antonio	60	84	.438	51	.739	284	83	223	3.7
1987-88	San Antonio	68	50	.459	41	.651	222	49	142	2.1
1988-89	Chi.-Phoe.	43	13	.361	4	.444	78	14	30	0.7
1989-90	Chicago	46	37	.529	30	.732	138	28	104	2.3
1990-91	Phoenix	55	45	.464	28	.737	151	36	123	2.2
	Totals	447	465	.505	282	.683	1624	340	1222	2.7

IAN LOCKHART 24 6-8 240   Forward-Center

The only one of the 14 players on the roster at
the end of 1990-91 without a guaranteed contract . . . That doesn't bode well for second-year
player from Tennessee . . . Invited back to
rookie/free-agent camp during offseason . . .
Also played in Puerto Rico . . . A good rebounder . . . Averaged 10.9 boards as a senior for
Vols . . . Fifth player in school history to grab
at least 300 rebounds in a season . . . Signed as a free agent by
Suns after going undrafted . . . Born June 25, 1967, in Nassau,
Bahamas . . . Made $130,000.

Year	Team	G	FG	FG Pct.	FT	FT Pct.	Reb.	Ast.	TP	Avg.
1990-91	Phoenix	1	1	1.000	2	1.000	0	0	4	4.0

THE ROOKIES

CHAD GALLAGHER 22 6-9 245   Center
Mentioned as possible first-round pick, but went 32nd . . . Missouri

Valley Conference Player of the Year as a senior at Creighton . . .
Two-time all-conference selection on defense . . . Never shot below 54.9 percent final three years and finished career at .551,
third-best ever for the Bluejays . . . Born May 30, 1969, in Rockford, Ill.

JOEY WRIGHT 22 6-1 185   Guard
Third-leading scorer in Texas history behind Travis Mays and Ron
Baxter . . . But scored more points in three years than any other
Longhorn . . . Spent freshman season at Drake . . . Averaged 18.8
ppg in Texas career highlighted in 1989-90 when he led Longhorns
to NCAA final eight . . . Had career-high 46 points against Stetson
in junior year and a 6-for-6 three-point performance against DePaul
as a senior . . . Suns, seemingly set in the backcourt, made him
50th choice . . . Born Sept. 4, 1969, in Hammond, Ind.

RICHARD DUMAS 22 6-6 200   Forward
Had big freshman year at Oklahoma State in 1987-88 . . . Averaged
17.4 points and 6.4 rebounds . . . Set school record for steals in a
season (69) and a game (7) . . . Named second-team All-Big 8 and
freshman All-American . . . Led Cowboys in scoring the next season . . . Left college after two years for personal reasons . . . Played
last season in Israel . . . Born May 19, 1969, in Tulsa, Okla.

COACH COTTON FITZSIMMONS: Stop staring . . . He'll
leave when he's good and ready . . . Seemed to
be ready when, following team's horrendous
showing at Houston last season, he volunteered
to resign . . . President Jerry Colangelo assured
him there was no need for that . . . Fitzsimmons, despite additional title as director of
player personnel, is a coach . . . Why else
would he have gotten back into it in
1989? . . . Has three consecutive 50-win seasons, the only ones
of an NBA career that includes two stints in Phoenix (first in
1970-71), Atlanta, Buffalo, KC and San Antonio . . . The 55 wins
in 1988-89 was most in Phoenix history and earned him Coach
of the Year honors, something he previously achieved with the
KC Kings in 1978-79 . . . Born Oct. 7, 1931, in Hannibal, Mo.,
he's in Missouri Basketball Hall of Fame and National Junior
College Hall of Fame . . . Played at Midwestern State (Wichita

Falls, Tex.) and was head coach at Kansas State before his initial swing with the Suns.

GREATEST TEAM

The most memorable team in franchise history was 1975-76, when the Suns reached the NBA Finals and played one of the greatest championship-round games ever, a triple-overtime marathon with Boston. But that team also went 42-40 during the regular season and during one stretch lost 18 of 22.

The best team in franchise history comes down to 1980-81—when the Suns went 57-25, were out of first place in the Pacific Division for only two games all season, and never lost more than two in a row—and 1989-90. We give it to the latter, which won 54 games and reached the Western Conference finals.

Those Suns led the league in point-differential and during one stretch won 19 in a row at home. This was a team of speed and athleticism with Kevin Johnson, Tom Chambers and Dan Majerle, combined with the invaluable midseason acquisition of Kurt Rambis. Mark West had his best season as a pro and finished No. 1 in field-goal percentage.

ALL-TIME SUN LEADERS

SEASON

Points: Tom Chambers, 2,201, 1989-90
Assists: Kevin Johnson, 991, 1988-89
Rebounds: Paul Silas, 1,015, 1970-71

GAME

Points: Tom Chambers, 60 vs. Seattle, 3/24/90
Assists: Gail Goodrich, 19 vs. Philadelphia, 10/22/69
Rebounds: Paul Silas, 27 vs. Cincinnati, 1/18/71

CAREER

Points: Walter Davis, 15,666, 1977-88
Assists: Alvan Adams, 4,012, 1975-88
Rebounds: Alvan Adams, 6,937, 1975-88

PORTLAND TRAIL BLAZERS

TEAM DIRECTORY: Chairman: Paul Allen; Pres.: Harry Glickman; Dir. Media Services: John Lashway; Coach: Rick Adelman; Asst. Coaches: Jack Schalow, John Wetzel. Arena: Memorial Coliseum (12,884). Colors: Red, black and white.

Clyde the Glide aims at title that eluded Blazers in '91.

SCOUTING REPORT

SHOOTING: Welcome to the paradox. Buck Williams' 60.2 percent led the league, but didn't make much of a difference. This category for the Trail Blazers is about the guards, with Clyde Drexler, Terry Porter and Danny Ainge having taken 41 percent of last season's shots. Ainge played 872 less minutes than Williams and still had 119 more attempts.

So they will advance with guarded optimism, pun intended. The upshot is that acquiring Ainge and putting him in the unit gave Portland the best three-point shooting team in the league. As long as that is mixed in with the lethal transition game, the Trail Blazers are in good shape.

They finished, after all, third-best in the league at 114.7 points an outing. There were signs last season of the wealth being spread, the Blazers being the only team in the league to have eight players average double figures. But don't be fooled. Among those is Walter Davis, whose numbers were just 6.1 as a Blazer after being traded by Denver. Rookie Lamont Strothers brings impressive double-figure stats from Division III Christopher Newport.

PLAYMAKING: Porter is enough to make most other teams envious, especially since he's only 28 and getting better all the time. But, again, trading for Ainge while having to give up little— Byron Irvin was the only player, the 27th spot in the 1991 draft the highest pick—makes a big difference. He couldn't start for any Pacific Division team at full strength, but who wouldn't want him as a third guard with experience as a ball-handler? That's a secure feeling for Rick Adelman.

DEFENSE: Seeing as this is a team built on athleticism, the Trail Blazers are often able to make up for their failed gambles in the open court. But an even more important factor is their now-established familiarity, a factor overlooked. The five on the floor know where teammates will be for help, and opponents' scoring should continue to drop. The 106 points allowed per game in 1990-91 is nothing to earn a trademark, but it was the best for the franchise since 1982-83.

REBOUNDING: Utah swept aside any notion of invincibility during the second round of last season's playoffs, but rebounding is definitely a Blazer strength. Without having any one player in double figures, they ranked first or second in total boards and defensive rebounding all 1990-91, finishing No. 2 to Detroit in

TRAIL BLAZER ROSTER

No.	Veterans	Pos.	Ht.	Wt.	Age	Yrs. Pro	College
31	Alaa Abdelnaby	F	6-10	240	23	1	Duke
9	Danny Ainge	G	6-5	185	32	10	Brigham Young
2	Mark Bryant	F	6-9	245	26	3	Seton Hall
42	Wayne Cooper	C	6-10	220	34	13	New Orleans
6	Walter Davis	G-F	6-7	207	37	14	North Carolina
22	Clyde Drexler	G	6-7	222	29	8	Houston
00	Kevin Duckworth	C	7-0	270	27	5	Eastern Illinois
25	Jerome Kersey	F	6-7	225	29	7	Longwood
30	Terry Porter	G	6-3	195	28	6	Wis.-Stevens Pt.
3	Cliff Robinson	F	6-10	225	24	2	Connecticut
52	Buck Williams	F	6-8	225	31	10	Maryland
21	Danny Young	G	6-4	175	29	7	Wake Forest

Rd.	Rookies	Sel. No.	Pos.	Ht.	Wt.	College
2	Lamont Strothers	43	G	6-4	192	Chris. Newport

both. Since Adelman took over in February 1989, Portland has 15 consecutive months of positive rebounding margins.

OUTLOOK: The strange thing is that there was more panic in Los Angeles after the Lakers lost in the NBA Finals than in Portland following the Trail Blazers' defeat in the Western Conference championship series. Maybe that's because everyone realizes, disappointing finish aside, this is still the team to beat in the West, barring any preseason deals. We're still waiting to see the day when a Blazer has to pay for a meal around town.

TRAIL BLAZER PROFILES

CLYDE DREXLER 29 6-7 222   Guard

Has led Trail Blazers in scoring four straight seasons . . . Career 20-point scorer despite only 7.7 as rookie out of Houston . . . Still takes bad shots . . . Competed in three-point shootout at 1991 All-Star Weekend but is still first and foremost Clyde the Glide . . . Finished only 21.2 percent on threes . . . His game remains pyrotechnics: slam dunks, the transition game and great offensive rebounding... Worked hard to improve defense last season... Holds club record for games played, minutes, scoring, field-goals made and attempted, free-throws made and attempted, offensive rebounds and steals... Played in five All-Star Games... Born June 22, 1962, in New Orleans... Made $1.18 million, fourth-highest on team... Drafted as Houston undergraduate in 1983.

Year	Team	G	FG	FG Pct.	FT	FT Pct.	Reb.	Ast.	TP	Avg.
1983-84	Portland	82	252	.451	123	.728	235	153	628	7.7
1984-85	Portland	80	573	.494	223	.759	476	441	1377	17.2
1985-86	Portland	75	542	.475	293	.769	421	600	1389	18.5
1986-87	Portland	82	707	.502	357	.760	518	566	1782	21.7
1987-88	Portland	81	849	.506	476	.811	533	467	2185	27.0
1988-89	Portland	78	829	.496	438	.799	615	450	2123	27.2
1989-90	Portland	73	670	.494	333	.774	507	432	1703	23.3
1990-91	Portland	82	645	.482	416	.794	546	493	1767	21.5
	Totals	633	5067	.491	2659	.781	3851	3602	12954	20.5

TERRY PORTER 28 6-3 195   Guard

Keep reminding yourself while watching him turn into one of top point guards: he was a small forward in college, he was a small forward in college... At an NAIA school, at an NAIA school... No. 4 in NBA in three-point shooting at 41.5 percent... Had 10 double-doubles in first 19 games... Placed 12th in NBA assists, 14th in steals... Has never sat out more than three games in a season, and has missed only nine in six-year career... Five of those games came in first two seasons after being first-round selection from Wisconsin-Stevens Point... Born April 8, 1963, in Milwaukee... Made $2 million.

Year	Team	G	FG	FG Pct.	FT	FT Pct.	Reb.	Ast.	TP	Avg.
1985-86	Portland	79	212	.474	125	.806	117	198	562	7.1
1986-87	Portland	80	376	.488	280	.838	337	715	1045	13.1
1987-88	Portland	82	462	.519	274	.846	378	831	1222	14.9
1988-89	Portland	81	540	.471	272	.840	367	770	1431	17.7
1989-90	Portland	80	448	.462	421	.892	272	726	1406	17.6
1990-91	Portland	81	486	.515	279	.823	282	649	1381	17.0
	Totals	483	2524	.489	1651	.848	1753	3889	7047	14.6

KEVIN DUCKWORTH 27 7-0 270   Center

Fake nose and glasses won't let him go out in Portland without being noticed . . . That's unfortunate for him . . . He's catching the most heat for team's disappointing showing in the playoffs . . . Has been in All-Star Game two of last three seasons, including 1991 . . . Continues to add range to his jumper . . . Now hits consistently from around 17 feet and may be best medium-range shooter on the team . . . Bad passer and not a shot-blocker . . . Not much of a rebounder for 7-footer, but his assignment is to keep opposing center off the boards and let other Blazers crash the lane . . . NBA's Most Improved Player in 1987-88 . . . Portland considered drafting him, took Walter Berry instead, and then saved long-term mistake by trading Berry to Spurs for Duckworth after a season . . . Born April 1, 1964, in Dalton, Ill. . . . Another of Trail Blazers' small-college guys, he played at Eastern Illinois . . . Was 33rd pick in 1986 draft . . . Made $1.71 million.

Year	Team	G	FG	FG Pct.	FT	FT Pct.	Reb.	Ast.	TP	Avg.
1986-87	S.A.-Port.	65	130	.476	92	.687	223	29	352	5.4
1987-88	Portland	78	450	.496	331	.770	576	66	1231	15.8
1988-89	Portland	79	554	.477	324	.757	635	60	1432	18.1
1989-90	Portland	82	548	.478	231	.740	509	91	1327	16.2
1990-91	Portland	81	521	.481	240	.772	531	89	1282	15.8
	Totals	385	2203	.482	1218	.754	2474	335	5624	14.6

BUCK WILLIAMS 31 6-8 225   Forward

Simply, every team should have a player like this . . . Better, a guy like this in the clubhouse . . . Named to All-Defensive team for second season in a row . . . Doesn't have big numbers on blocked shots or steals, but very tough on power forwards on the low block . . . Did as nice a job on Karl Malone in the second round of the playoffs as anyone could . . . NBA field-goal champion last season at 60.2 percent . . . The first Blazer ever to finish atop that category and the fifth Portland player to rank first in any department . . . Only Dave Twardzik, at 61.2 percent in 1976-77, has better single-season mark in franchise history . . . But at least Williams' beard is neatly trimmed . . . Twenty-one rebounds April 5 at Orlando was most by a Blazer since Kenny Carr in December 1986 . . . Born March 8, 1960, in Rocky Mount,

N.C. . . . Drafted No. 3 by Nets as Maryland undergraduate in 1981 . . . Made $1.55 million.

Year	Team	G	FG	FG Pct.	FT	FT Pct.	Reb.	Ast.	TP	Avg.
1981-82	New Jersey	82	513	.582	242	.624	1005	107	1268	15.5
1982-83	New Jersey	82	536	.588	324	.620	1027	125	1396	17.0
1983-84	New Jersey	81	495	.535	284	.570	1000	130	1274	15.7
1984-85	New Jersey	82	577	.530	336	.625	1005	167	1491	18.2
1985-86	New Jersey	82	500	.523	301	.676	986	131	1301	15.9
1986-87	New Jersey	82	521	.557	430	.731	1023	129	1472	18.0
1987-88	New Jersey	70	466	.560	346	.668	834	109	1279	18.3
1988-89	New Jersey	74	373	.531	213	.666	696	78	959	13.0
1989-90	Portland	82	413	.548	288	.706	800	116	1114	13.6
1990-91	Portland	80	358	.602	217	.705	751	97	933	11.7
	Totals	797	4752	.554	2981	.657	9127	1189	12487	15.7

WALTER DAVIS 37 6-6 207   Guard-Forward

Averaged 6.1 points and 13.7 minutes in 32 games after going from Denver to Portland Jan. 23 in three-way trade that also included New Jersey . . . Trail Blazers got him two-thirds for own use and one-third to keep him away from other suitors Chicago and San Antonio, possible playoff opponents . . . Some feared Portland chemistry would be hurt by having someone adjust from being in regular rotation to moving down the bench, but it didn't happen . . . Ranks 20th on all-time scoring list and sixth among active players . . . Needs 936 points to reach 20,000 . . . Had 924 last season, 728 of which came with Nuggets . . . Born Sept. 9, 1954, in Pineville, N.C. . . . Played for North Carolina and 1976 Olympic team . . . Drafted fifth by Phoenix in 1977 . . . Made $900,000.

Year	Team	G	FG	FG Pct.	FT	FT Pct.	Reb.	Ast.	TP	Avg.
1977-78	Phoenix	81	786	.526	387	.830	484	273	1959	24.2
1978-79	Phoenix	79	764	.561	340	.831	373	339	1868	23.6
1979-80	Phoenix	75	657	.563	299	.819	272	337	1613	21.5
1980-81	Phoenix	78	593	.539	209	.836	200	302	1402	18.0
1981-82	Phoenix	55	350	.523	91	.820	103	162	794	14.4
1982-83	Phoenix	80	665	.516	184	.818	197	397	1521	19.0
1983-84	Phoenix	78	652	.512	233	.863	202	429	1557	20.0
1984-85	Phoenix	23	139	.450	64	.877	35	98	345	15.0
1985-86	Phoenix	70	624	.485	257	.843	203	361	1523	21.8
1986-87	Phoenix	79	779	.514	288	.862	244	364	1867	23.6
1987-88	Phoenix	68	488	.473	205	.887	159	278	1217	17.9
1988-89	Denver	81	536	.498	175	.879	151	190	1267	15.6
1989-90	Denver	69	497	.481	207	.912	179	155	1207	17.5
1990-91	Den.-Port.	71	403	.468	107	.915	181	125	924	13.0
	Totals	987	7933	.513	3046	.850	2983	3810	19064	19.3

JEROME KERSEY 29 6-7 225   Forward

Becomes more of a daredevil going for loose balls every year . . . Plays with reckless abandon . . . That's great to see, but it may start taking its toll if the body won't hold up . . . Example A of Trail Blazer plan to go after great athletes even if they're raw . . . And he was very raw . . . Ten-foot jumpers were an adventure for him at Longwood College in Virginia . . . Got so few scholarship offers that he jokes about choosing the Division II school because of its ratio of men to women . . . Chosen 46th in 1984 . . . Runnerup to Michael Jordan in 1987 slam-dunk competition at All-Star Weekend . . . Born June 26, 1962, in Clarksville, Va. . . . Drafted 46th in 1984 . . . Made $550,000.

Year	Team	G	FG	FG Pct.	FT	FT Pct.	Reb.	Ast.	TP	Avg.
1984-85	Portland	77	178	.478	117	.646	206	63	473	6.1
1985-86	Portland	79	258	.549	156	.681	293	83	672	8.5
1986-87	Portland	82	373	.509	262	.720	496	194	1009	12.3
1987-88	Portland	79	611	.499	291	.735	657	243	1516	19.2
1988-89	Portland	76	533	.469	258	.694	629	243	1330	17.5
1989-90	Portland	82	519	.478	269	.690	690	188	1310	16.0
1990-91	Portland	73	424	.478	232	.709	481	227	1084	14.8
	Totals	548	2896	.490	1585	.702	3452	1241	7394	13.5

CLIFF ROBINSON 24 6-10 225   Forward

The emergence continues . . . Former second-round selection was knocked for being soft at Connecticut, but he's shown ability to defend all three frontcourt positions . . . Portland's leading scorer off the bench . . . Along with Clyde Drexler, only Blazer to play all 82 games . . . Has quick feet and shot-blocking talent . . . Has a scorer's mentality to go with it, but only made improvement after making better shot selection . . . Jump in field-goal percentage will attest to that . . . Has played all 164 games since coming into league, first Blazer ever to do that, and has longest current streak on the team . . . Born Dec. 16, 1966, in Buffalo . . . Made $250,000.

Year	Team	G	FG	FG Pct.	FT	FT Pct.	Reb.	Ast.	TP	Avg.
1989-90	Portland	82	298	.397	138	.550	308	72	746	9.1
1990-91	Portland	82	373	.463	205	.653	349	151	957	11.7
	Totals	164	671	.431	343	.607	657	223	1703	10.4

DANNY AINGE 32 6-5 185   Guard

Despite inconsistent playoffs, when they counted on him most, he was still a great acquisition from Sacramento... Cost the Blazers Byron Irvin, a first-round choice in the poor draft of 1991, Chicago's 1992 second-round pick and cash... High-school star in nearby Eugene who came home, or close enough... Attended Brigham Young... Had good regular season as first guard off the bench... Finished sixth in league in three-point shooting (40.6 percent)... Second to Dale Ellis among active players in career three-pointers... Valuable because he can play both backcourt positions... Seldom used in three-guard attack with Clyde Drexler and Terry Porter... Born March 17, 1959, in Eugene, Ore.... Second-round pick by Celtics in 1981 ... Made $725,000.

Year	Team	G	FG	FG Pct.	FT	FT Pct.	Reb.	Ast.	TP	Avg.
1981-82	Boston	53	79	.357	56	.862	56	87	219	4.1
1982-83	Boston	80	357	.496	72	.742	214	251	791	9.9
1983-84	Boston	71	166	.460	46	.821	116	162	384	5.4
1984-85	Boston	75	419	.529	118	.868	268	399	971	12.9
1985-86	Boston	80	353	.504	123	.904	235	405	855	10.7
1986-87	Boston	71	410	.486	148	.897	242	400	1053	14.8
1987-88	Boston	81	482	.491	158	.878	249	503	1270	15.7
1988-89	Bos.-Sac.	73	480	.457	205	.854	255	402	1281	17.5
1989-90	Sacramento	75	506	.438	222	.831	326	453	1342	17.9
1990-91	Portland	80	337	.472	114	.826	205	285	890	11.1
	Totals	739	3589	.476	1262	.853	2166	3347	9056	12.3

MARK BRYANT 26 6-9 245   Forward

Finally showed signs of an offensive game last season... Missed 27 games after fracturing right foot Feb. 17 against the Lakers... Backup center... All-Big East selection at Seton Hall before becoming 21st player picked in 1988 draft... Averaged 20.5 points and 9.1 rebounds to earn Haggerty Award as top player in New York City area in 1988... Member of U.S. team that competed in 1987 World University Games in Yugoslavia... Born April 25, 1965, in Glen Ridge, N.J.

. . . Made $405,000.

Year	Team	G	FG	FG Pct.	FT	FT Pct.	Reb.	Ast.	TP	Avg.
1988-89	Portland	56	120	.486	40	.580	179	33	280	5.0
1989-90	Portland	58	70	.458	28	.560	146	13	168	2.9
1990-91	Portland	53	99	.488	74	.733	190	27	272	5.1
	Totals	167	289	.479	142	.645	515	73	720	4.3

DANNY YOUNG 29 6-4 175   Guard

Nice role player as fourth guard . . . Steady and a pretty good defender . . . Coming off career-low season from the floor . . . Played for current Blazer assistant Jack Schalow with Wyoming of CBA . . . Former Wake Forest star was waived twice during four-year stint with Seattle, which drafted him 39th in 1984 . . . Was involved in 85 victories during college career, more than any player in school history, and is third on Deacons' assist list . . . Born July 26, 1962, in Raleigh, N.C. . . . Made $450,000.

Year	Team	G	FG	FG Pct.	FT	FT Pct.	Reb.	Ast.	TP	Avg.
1984-85	Seattle	3	2	.200	0	.000	3	2	4	1.3
1985-86	Seattle	82	227	.506	90	.849	120	303	568	6.9
1986-87	Seattle	73	132	.458	59	.831	113	353	352	4.8
1987-88	Seattle	77	89	.408	43	.811	75	218	243	3.2
1988-89	Portland	48	115	.460	50	.781	74	123	297	6.2
1989-90	Portland	82	138	.421	91	.813	122	231	383	4.7
1990-91	Portland	75	103	.380	41	.911	75	141	283	3.8
	Totals	440	806	.444	374	.829	582	1371	2130	4.8

ALAA ABDELNABY 23 6-10 240   Forward

Made only 43 appearances as rookie, but had expanded role after Mark Bryant's foot injury . . . Shot 52.9 percent in those 27 games . . . Quick jumper who could be good offensive rebounder . . . Coaches are counting on successful summer program for improvement . . . No. 25 selection in draft after playing in three Final Fours with Duke . . . Named All-ACC as a senior when he finished career with .599 shooting, a Blue Devil record . . . Born June 24, 1968, in Alexandria, Egypt . . . Moved with parents to United States in 1971 . . . All-everything at Bloomfield High in New Jersey, where he also played first base for baseball team and goalie for the soccer team . . . Made $395,000.

Year	Team	G	FG	FG Pct.	FT	FT Pct.	Reb.	Ast.	TP	Avg.
1990-91	Portland	43	55	.474	25	.568	89	12	135	3.1

WAYNE COOPER 34 6-10 220   Center

Coming into the final year of his contract, when playing time should decrease even more in favor of developing Mark Bryant and Alaa Abdelnaby . . . But he's great dealing with young players and a good tutor who should earn his money being a mentor . . . Played 11.1 minutes in his 67 games, with one start . . . Played at least 20 minutes only five times . . . Slowed final two weeks of regular season with strained tendon . . . Has spent 13 seasons with six teams (Portland twice), but has yet to leave Western Conference . . . Born Nov. 16, 1956, in Milan, Ga. . . . Attended New Orleans . . . Was second-round pick by Golden State in 1978 . . . Made $1.1 million.

Year	Team	G	FG	FG Pct.	FT	FT Pct.	Reb.	Ast.	TP	Avg.
1978-79	Golden State	65	128	.437	41	.672	280	21	297	4.6
1979-80	Golden State	79	367	.489	136	.751	507	42	871	11.0
1980-81	Utah	71	213	.452	62	.689	440	52	489	6.9
1981-82	Dallas	76	281	.420	119	.744	550	115	682	9.0
1982-83	Portland	80	320	.443	135	.685	611	116	775	9.7
1983-84	Portland	81	304	.459	185	.804	476	76	793	9.8
1984-85	Denver	80	404	.472	161	.685	631	86	969	12.1
1985-86	Denver	78	422	.466	174	.795	610	81	1021	13.1
1986-87	Denver	69	235	.448	79	.725	473	68	549	8.0
1987-88	Denver	45	118	.437	50	.746	270	30	286	6.4
1988-89	Denver	79	220	.495	79	.745	619	78	520	6.6
1989-90	Portland	79	138	.454	25	.641	339	44	301	3.8
1990-91	Portland	67	57	.393	33	.786	188	22	147	2.2
	Totals	949	3207	.457	1279	.737	5996	831	7700	8.1

THE ROOKIE

LAMONT STROTHERS 23 6-4 192   Guard

Drafted by Warriors and traded to Blazers on Draft Day . . . Only Division III player drafted . . . Christopher Newport product went 43rd . . . Set all-time NCAA record for any division with 116 consecutive games scoring in double figures, every game of career

. . . Third all-time leading scorer (2,709) in Division III . . . Never averaged fewer than 21.5 points any season . . . Born May 10, 1968, in Suffolk, Va.

COACH RICK ADELMAN: Bill Walton's favorite coach . . .  Had the Blazers met expectations and won the title, Portland, one writer suggested, would have become Rick City . . . As it was, he coached them to franchise-record 61 victories . . . Has 136-63 (.683) record . . . Win No. 128 passed predecessor Mike Schuler for second place on Blazers' all-time coaching list . . . Jack Ramsay holds franchise record with 453 victories . . . First Blazer captain and an original member of franchise . . . Played seven NBA seasons with five teams . . . Seventh coach in Portland history . . . Born June 16, 1946, in Downey, Cal . . . Was record-setting scorer at Loyola (now Loyola Marymount) . . . After retiring as NBA player, he earned master's degree in history at Loyola . . . Coached six years at Oregon's Chemeketa Community College before joining Ramsay as an assistant in 1983.

GREATEST TEAM

It was announcer Bill Schonely and Rip City. It was Blazermania. It was Bill Walton playing 65 games, his most during five seasons in Portland. It was 1976-1977.

More than the only championship in franchise history, it was what every Blazer team since has strived to be. The Blazers of 1989-90 were very good, reaching the NBA Finals, but that stirred nostalgia as much as excitement.

Many of the names now hang from the rafters of Memorial Coliseum, their uniforms retired: Walton, Maurice Lucas, Bob Gross, Lionel Hollins and Dave Twardzik. That was the starting lineup. They may have won only 49 regular-season games, but they got the four that mattered most, getting a grand slam after losing the first two games in the Finals against Philadelphia.

What will never be known is whether the next season's team

could have been better. The Trail Blazers of 1977-78 opened 50-10 before Walton, the eventual MVP, got hurt, the start of the downfall that culminated in a 58-22 record and a loss in the conference semifinals.

ALL-TIME TRAIL BLAZER LEADERS

SEASON

Points: Clyde Drexler, 2,185, 1987-88
Assists: Terry Porter, 831, 1987-88
Rebounds: Lloyd Neal, 967, 1972-73

GAME

Points: Geoff Petrie, 51 vs. Houston, 1/20/73
        Geoff Petrie, 51 vs. Houston, 3/16/73
Assists: Terry Porter, 19 vs. Utah, 4/14/88
Rebounds: Sidney Wicks, 27 vs. Los Angeles, 2/26/75

CAREER

Points: Clyde Drexler, 12,954, 1984-91
Assists: Clyde Drexler, 3,602, 1984-91
Rebounds: Mychal Thompson, 4,878, 1978-86

SACRAMENTO KINGS

TEAM DIRECTORY: Managing General Partner: Gregg Lukenbill; Pres.: Rick Benner; Dir. Player Personnel: Jerry Reynolds; Dir. Pub. Rel.: Julie Fie; Coach: Dick Motta; Asst. Coach: Rex Hughes. Arena: ARCO Arena (17,014); Colors: Red, white and blue.

SCOUTING REPORT

SHOOTING: Only three teams shot worse than the .453 by the Kings, whose Antoine Carr led at .511. This is surprising since so much of their game is to get the ball to the forwards at the post.

Billy Owens, the boy from Syracuse, was No. 3 in draft.

What's not surprising is that a team with no decent point guard to direct the flow would be erratic. The injury to Wayman Tisdale and an abundance of rookies learning as they go didn't help, either. Spud Webb, acquired from Atlanta just after the draft, should be an improvement because he is a ball-handler and experienced.

PLAYMAKING: Again, they look to Webb, standing 5-7 but much taller on that pedestal waiting for his arrival. Maybe it's worth keeping in mind that he averaged just 5.6 assists in 75 games, 64 of which were starts, last season for Atlanta, a team that scored 109.8 points an outing.

The Kings averaged a league-low 96.7. How many more baskets will Webb be worth, especially in an offense that focuses on getting the ball inside to post players? Spud's specialty is sprinting up and down the court.

DEFENSE: The signs are encouraging. The points-against was a respectable 103.5 last season, but, even better, an improvement of 3.3 points from 1989-90. How much Webb becomes a defensive liability because of his size could be a factor, but the healthy return of Bobby Hansen to provide a big body in the backcourt would be a help.

The impact of rookie Duane Causwell was apparent, too. He led the way as the Kings finished No. 5 in the league in blocked shots.

REBOUNDING: Anthony Bonner, drafted for his rebounding, played only 34 games. Tisdale showed improvement in the area, but he had only 33 appearances. So, the team's leading rebounder turned out to be—a small forward. That probably says more about Sacramento's thin board work than the versatility of Lionel Simmons.

The power players who remained at the end were Causwell and Carr, and neither is known as a rebounder. Even with the return of Bonner and Tisdale, Pete Chilcutt, the first-round pick from North Carolina, can make an impact if he can rebound.

OUTLOOK: The turnovers continue on and off the court. Last season, 11 of the 14 players who were in at least one-fourth of the games were newcomers. Now, there are chances for five more: Webb, and rookies Chilcutt, Billy Owens, Randy Brown and Steve Hood.

The only threat Dick Motta's team will pose, though, is exhaustion to the people who sew the names on the back of uniforms.

KING ROSTER

No.	Veterans	Pos.	Ht.	Wt.	Age	Yrs. Pro	College
24	Anthony Bonner	F	6-8	225	23	1	St. Louis
35	Antoine Carr	F	6-9	265	30	7	Wichita State
31	Duane Causwell	C	7-0	240	23	1	Temple
20	Bobby Hansen	G	6-6	200	30	8	Iowa
33	Jim Les	G	5-11	165	28	3	Bradley
50	Ralph Sampson	C	7-4	250	31	8	Virginia
22	Lionel Simmons	F	6-7	210	22	1	La Salle
23	Wayman Tisdale	F	6-9	260	27	6	Oklahoma
4	Spud Webb	G	5-7	135	28	6	North Carolina State

Rd.	Rookies	Sel. No.	Pos.	Ht.	Wt.	College
1	Billy Owens	3	F	6-9	225	Syracuse
1	Pete Chilcutt	27	F-C	6-10	232	North Carolina
2	Randy Brown	31	G	6-3	190	New Mexico State
2	Steve Hood	42	G	6-7	185	James Madison

It won't help that, given the chance to improve with the third pick in the draft, Sacramento went with Owens, which would have been a great addition if not for the fact that it already has Simmons at small forward. So maybe Owens plays out of position. Or maybe gets traded. Or maybe the Kings will make everyone else look foolish this season. OK, next guess.

KING PROFILES

ANTOINE CARR 30 6-9 265   Forward

Led team in scoring at 20.1 points in 32.8 minutes, both career-bests... Averaged 23.5 points after All-Star break and 26.1 the final month... Four of top five single-game point totals came in 1990-91... Was sixth man with Wayman Tisdale healthy, a starter otherwise ... Occasionally part of offense-minded lineup with Tisdale and Lionel Simmons... Deadly shot from top of the key... Can create better than most players his size... Knock is lack of rebounding and defense... Detroit tabbed former Wichita State star No. 8 in 1983 draft... Came to Sacramento on Feb. 13, 1990, with Sedric Toney and a 1991 second-round pick for Kenny Smith and Mike Williams . . . Born July 23, 1961, in Oklahoma City, Okla. . . . Made $610,000.

Year	Team	G	FG	FG Pct.	FT	FT Pct.	Reb.	Ast.	TP	Avg.
1984-85	Atlanta	62	198	.528	101	.789	232	80	499	8.0
1985-86	Atlanta	17	49	.527	18	.667	52	14	116	6.8
1986-87	Atlanta	65	134	.506	73	.709	156	34	342	5.3
1987-88	Atlanta	80	281	.544	142	.780	289	103	705	8.8
1988-89	Atlanta	78	226	.480	130	.855	274	91	582	7.5
1989-90	Atl.-Sac.	77	356	.494	237	.795	322	119	949	12.3
1990-91	Sacramento	77	628	.511	295	.758	420	191	1551	20.1
	Totals	456	1872	.510	996	.779	1745	632	4744	10.4

LIONEL SIMMONS 22 6-7 210   Forward

Look for him in an All-Star Game near you someday . . . Nuggets should be kicking themselves for not drafting him four picks earlier . . . Finished second in balloting for Rookie of the Year . . . Scoring average (18.0) and minutes (37.7) most ever for rookie in 19-year history of Kings . . . Stats were impressive, but here's what doesn't show up: He loves to take big shot in close games . . . Scoring got most attention, but he's a good rebounder . . . Shortcoming—for now—is inability to consistently hit jumpers in 17-to-20-foot range that a wing needs to convert . . . Played some off-guard, but is better at small forward . . . Born Nov. 14, 1968, in Philadelphia . . . Played at hometown LaSalle, where he averaged 24.6 points in four-year career . . . Seventh pick in 1990 draft . . . Made $930,000.

Year	Team	G	FG	FG Pct.	FT	FT Pct.	Reb.	Ast.	TP	Avg.
1990-91	Sacramento	79	549	.422	320	.736	697	315	1421	18.0

WAYMAN TISDALE 27 6-9 260   Forward

Among most difficult low-post scorers in the league to stop . . . His play demands double-teaming . . . Perfect for Dick Motta's forward-oriented offense . . . Has made himself into effective rebounder . . . Played in just 33 games, fewest as a pro, because of ruptured tendon in right foot in early January . . . Last appearance came March 12 . . . It was first time he missed more than three games in a season . . . Was leading team in points (21.2) and rebounds (8.2) prior to injury . . . Three-time All-American at Oklahoma . . . Indiana made him No. 2 pick in 1985 draft behind Patrick Ewing . . . Born June 9, 1964, in Tulsa, Okla. . . . Made $2,330,000.

Year	Team	G	FG	FG Pct.	FT	FT Pct.	Reb.	Ast.	TP	Avg.
1985-86	Indiana.	81	516	.515	160	.684	584	79	1192	14.7
1986-87	Indiana.	81	458	.513	258	.709	475	117	1174	14.5
1987-88	Indiana.	79	511	.512	246	.783	491	103	1268	16.1
1988-89	Ind.-Sac.	79	532	.514	317	.773	609	128	1381	17.5
1989-90	Sacramento.	79	726	.525	306	.783	595	108	1758	22.3
1990-91	Sacramento.	33	262	.483	136	.800	253	66	660	20.0
	Totals	432	3005	.513	1423	.756	3007	601	7433	17.2

DUANE CAUSWELL 23 7-0 240   Center

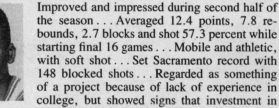

Improved and impressed during second half of the season . . . Averaged 12.4 points, 7.8 rebounds, 2.7 blocks and shot 57.3 percent while starting final 16 games . . . Mobile and athletic, with soft shot . . . Set Sacramento record with 148 blocked shots . . . Regarded as something of a project because of lack of experience in college, but showed signs that investment in No. 18 pick could pay off . . . Not real physical, so he needs work on rebounding . . . Born May 31, 1968, in Queens, N.Y. . . . Was the nation's No. 2 shot-blocker as junior at Temple . . . Kings took him as 18th pick in draft . . . Made $650,000.

Year	Team	G	FG	FG Pct.	FT	FT Pct.	Reb.	Ast.	TP	Avg.
1990-91	Sacramento.	76	210	.508	105	.636	391	69	525	6.9

ANTHONY (SPUD) WEBB 28 5-7 135   Guard

Kings acquired him from Hawks in offseason trade for Travis Mays . . . Lifted weights before 1990-91 season at insistence of pal Ron Harper . . . Result was a marvel of a season . . . Range on his shot increased by twice his size. Staggering stat: in first five NBA seasons, Webb made seven three-point shots. Last season, 54 . . . Got off to a bad 11-game start as a sub and shot .306. Given starting point job in late November and shot 48 percent rest of the way . . . Career-high points and steals . . . Typically disruptive defensive season . . . Gambled a lot and won with 118 steals . . . Yeah, he can still leap like he did in '86 when he won Slam Dunk title . . . Made $510,000 . . . Born July 13, 1963, in Dallas . . . Drafted out of North Carolina State on fourth round in '85 by Pistons. Cut and signed as free agent by Hawks, Sept. 26, 1985.

Year	Team	G	FG	FG Pct.	FT	FT Pct.	Reb.	Ast.	TP	Avg.
1985-86	Atlanta	79	199	.483	216	.785	123	337	616	7.8
1986-87	Atlanta	33	71	.438	80	.762	60	167	223	6.8
1987-88	Atlanta	82	191	.475	107	.817	146	337	490	6.0
1988-89	Atlanta	81	133	.459	52	.867	123	284	319	3.9
1989-90	Atlanta	82	294	.477	162	.871	201	477	751	9.2
1990-91	Atlanta	75	359	.447	231	.868	174	417	1003	13.4
	Totals	432	1247	.464	848	.829	827	2019	3402	7.9

RALPH SAMPSON 31 7-4 250   Center

Improved his game after years of decline by accepting role as dirty-work player . . . Decided that was pretty much all he had left . . . Certainly doesn't have any knees left . . . Arthritis in the joints and three surgeries mean he can only squeeze out about 15 minutes a game twice a week . . . Can still alter shots inside and rebound . . . Career lows in every statistic except rebounding in 1990-91 . . . Would have been gone long ago except that Kings still owe him $5 million over next two seasons; that makes it almost impossible to trade him . . . Of all Don Nelson's moves at Golden State, one of his best was unloading the contract and the player for Jim Petersen in 1989 . . . Born July 7, 1960, in Harrisonburg, Va, and played at Virginia . . . First pick in 1983 draft, by Houston . . . Made $2,250,000.

Year	Team	G	FG	FG Pct.	FT	FT Pct.	Reb.	Ast.	TP	Avg.
1983-84	Houston	82	716	.523	287	.661	913	163	1720	21.0
1984-85	Houston	82	753	.502	303	.676	853	224	1809	22.1
1985-86	Houston	79	624	.488	241	.641	879	283	1491	18.9
1986-87	Houston	43	277	.489	118	.624	372	120	672	15.6
1987-88	Hou.-G.S.	48	299	.438	149	.760	462	122	749	15.6
1988-89	Golden State	61	164	.449	62	.653	307	77	393	6.4
1989-90	Sacramento	26	48	.372	12	.522	84	28	109	4.2
1990-91	Sacramento	25	34	.366	5	.263	111	17	74	3.0
	Totals	446	2915	.487	1177	.661	3981	1034	7017	15.7

Ex-Hawk Spud Webb will bring his kind of magic to the Kings.

BOBBY HANSEN 30 6-6 200   Guard

Somebody remind him this isn't a "Twilight Zone" episode . . . After appearing in seven consecutive playoffs with Utah, he was traded to Sacramento before last season . . . Kings won 25 games. They would've needed two seasons like that to equal what Hansen was used to . . . Had two surgeries in 1990-91, on shoulder and knee . . . The shoulder surgery ended his season April 3 . . . Reports on rehabilitation are good, but he's also going to be 31 in January . . . Thirty-six appearances was career-low . . . Hasn't shot better than 56 percent from free-throw line in three seasons . . . Former Iowa star was born Jan. 18, 1961, in Des Moines . . . Helped raise more than $100,000 in late 1980s to aid struggling Iowa farmers and their families . . . Was 54th pick, by Utah, in 1983 draft . . . Made $550,000.

Year	Team	G	FG	FG Pct.	FT	FT Pct.	Reb.	Ast.	TP	Avg.
1983-84	Utah	55	65	.448	18	.643	48	44	148	2.7
1984-85	Utah	54	110	.489	40	.556	70	75	261	4.8
1985-86	Utah	82	299	.476	95	.720	244	193	710	8.7
1986-87	Utah	72	272	.453	136	.760	203	102	696	9.7
1987-88	Utah	81	316	.517	113	.743	187	175	777	9.6
1988-89	Utah	46	140	.467	42	.560	128	50	341	7.4
1989-90	Utah	81	265	.467	33	.516	229	149	617	7.6
1990-91	Sacramento	36	96	.375	18	.500	96	90	229	6.4
	Totals	507	1563	.469	495	.671	1205	878	3779	7.5

ANTHONY BONNER 23 6-8 225   Forward

Drafted for rebounding and athletic ability . . . The next sign of a regular offensive game will be the first . . . Missed first 17 games of 1990-91 with stress fracture in his foot and played the next 27 before a fracture was found . . . Appeared in 34 games . . . Led St. Louis University to NIT championship game twice in a row . . . NCAA's No. 1 rebounder as a senior . . . Finished career as school's all-time leader in points, rebounds, steals and games played . . . Born June 8, 1968, in St. Louis.

Year	Team	G	FG	FG Pct.	FT	FT Pct.	Reb.	Ast.	TP	Avg.
1990-91	Sacramento	34	103	.448	44	.579	161	49	250	7.4

Antoine Carr uncorked his highest-scoring season ever.

JIM LES 28 5-11 165   Guard

Cup-of-coffee guy who earned a permanent job by winning NBA three-point title . . . Decided long-range shooting was his best bet after being cut by Clippers . . . Needs time to square up, but makes teams pay for double-teaming Wayman Tisdale or Antoine Carr . . . Shot 46.1 percent on threes, 44.4 overall . . . Capped college career at Bradley in 1986 by winning Francis Pomeroy-Naismith Basketball Hall of Fame award as best player in the country under six feet . . . Played in same Bradley backcourt as 76ers' Hersey Hawkins . . . Born Aug. 13, 1963, in Niles, Ill. . . . Played at Cleveland State and Bradley . . . Drafted by Atlanta as 70th pick in 1986.

Year	Team	G	FG	FG Pct.	FT	FT Pct.	Reb.	Ast.	TP	Avg.
1988-89	Utah	82	40	.301	57	.781	87	215	138	1.7
1989-90	Utah-LAC	7	5	.357	13	.765	7	21	23	3.3
1990-91	Sacramento	55	119	.444	86	.835	111	299	395	7.2
	Totals	144	164	.395	156	.808	205	535	556	3.9

THE ROOKIES

BILLY OWENS 22 6-9 225   Forward
Best all-around player in the draft . . . But why Sacramento, an apparent conflict at small forward with Lionel Simmons? . . . Landed at No. 3 after being passed over by New Jersey . . . Early-entry candidate after junior season at Syracuse . . . Big East Player of the Year in 1991 after leading Orangemen to regular-season conference title . . . Joined Derrick Coleman as only players in school history to top 1,800 points and 900 rebounds . . . Born May 1, 1969, in Carlisle, Pa.

PETE CHILCUTT 23 6-10 232   Forward-Center
The Kings passed on Dikembe Mutombo at No. 3, so Chilcutt has become Duane Causwell's competition for the starting center job . . . Final pick of first round . . . Played in all 140 possible games at North Carolina to set a school record with two senior classmates . . . Didn't average double-figure scoring until last season and finished Tar Heel career at 8.2 . . . Ranks seventh on all-time North Carolina list for blocked shots . . . Born Sept. 14, 1968, in Eutaw, Ala.

RANDY BROWN 23 6-0 190   Guard
Broke the Rebel barrier in Big West last season . . . Only non-UNLV player selected first-team all-conference . . . It was his second straight year so honored . . . Led New Mexico State to 23-6 record and set school record for assists in a season and steals in a career . . . Played freshman and sophomore years at Houston . . . Attended, but did not play at, Howard County (Tex.) Junior College between stints at Houston and New Mexico State . . . Went 31st . . . Born May 22, 1968, in Chicago.

STEVE HOOD 23 6-7 185   Guard
Colonial Conference Player of the Year at James Madison last two years . . . But what should be at the top of his resume: he scored 32 points against UNLV, the most by any Runnin' Rebel opponent in 1990-91 . . . Spent first two years at Maryland before transferring to James Madison . . . Another Morgan Wootten product from DeMatha High School in Hyattsville, Md., where he was born April 4, 1968.

COACH DICK MOTTA: How much longer will he stick with  Kings? . . . Talked about quitting in a moment of frustration last season . . . Third-winningest coach of all time, behind Red Auerbach and Jack Ramsay . . . Needs 15 more wins to pass Ramsay with 865 . . . Auerbach seems untouchable at 938 . . . Current coaches Rick Adelman, Matt Goukas, Jerry Sloan, Wes Unseld and Bob Weiss all played for him . . . Prototype "old school" coach . . . He came back in 1990-91 after "retiring" at Dallas in 1987 after 19 NBA seasons that began with Chicago in 1968-69 when he inherited a 29-game winner . . . Two years later, his Bulls won 51 games and he was Coach of the Year . . . Led Washington to successive Finals and won the championship in 1977-78 . . . So he's had it all . . . The son of a farmer, he was born Sept. 3, 1931, in Medvale, Utah, and is a graduate of Utah State . . . He and his wife, Janice, own the BlueBird Chocolate Factory in Logan, Utah . . . The scene ain't so sweet in Sacramento.

GREATEST TEAM

To find the greatest team in Kings' history, go East—to the beginnings. They were known as the Royals—first in Rochester, then in Cincinnati. The Rochester Royals, champions of the old National Basketball League in 1945-46 with such stars as Bob Davies, Al Cervi and Red Holzman, joined the Basketball Association of America in 1948-49. The BAA was the forerunner of the NBA.

In the BAA, Rochester, which had added Bobby Wanzer, was one of the dominant teams. And they would have been more than a match for the best of the Royals' teams that landed in Cincinnati, beginning in 1957-58.

It was Oscar Robertson's Cincinnati Royals of 1963-64 who stand out as the greatest in the franchise over the last 30 years. They never won an NBA championship, or even a division title, but Robertson, Rookie of the Year Jerry Lucas, Jack Twyman, Wayne Embry, Tom Hawkins and Adrian Smith teamed for 55 victories that year (the Celtics had 59) and made it to the Eastern Division finals before losing in five to Boston.

The Royals became the Kansas City-Omaha Kings in 1972-73,

deleted the Omaha in 1975-76 and then got to be the Sacramento Kings in 1985-86. So for whatever solace, Sacramento can point to a franchise with a gloried history.

ALL-TIME KING LEADERS

SEASON

Points: Nate Archibald, 2,719, 1972-73
Assists: Nate Archibald, 910, 1972-73
Rebounds: Jerry Lucas, 1,688, 1965-66

GAME

Points: Jack Twyman, 59 vs. Minneapolis, 1/15/60
Assists: Phil Ford, 22 vs. Milwaukee, 2/21/79
    Oscar Robertson, 22 vs. New York, 3/5/66
    Oscar Robertson, 22 vs. Syracuse, 10/29/61
Rebounds: Jerry Lucas, 40 vs. Philadelphia, 2/29/64

CAREER

Points: Oscar Robertson, 22,009, 1960-70
Assists: Oscar Robertson, 7,721, 1960-70
Rebounds: Jerry Lucas, 8,831, 1963-69

SAN ANTONIO SPURS

TEAM DIRECTORY: Chairman: Red McCombs; Pres.: Gary Woods; VP-Basketball Oper.: Bob Bass; Exec. VP: Russ Bookbinder; Media Services Dir.: Matt Sperisen; Media Services Mgr.: Tom James; Coach: Larry Brown; Asst. Coaches: Gregg Popovich, R.C. Buford, Ed Manning. Arena: HemisFair Arena (16,057). Colors: Metallic silver and black.

David Robinson shot 25.6 ppg and won NBA rebound title.

SCOUTING REPORT

SHOOTING: San Antonio shot 48.8 percent last season. But take away David Robinson and his 55.2, they drop to 47.2. And since Robinson's offensive game around the post is still developing, much of the team-high 25.6 points a game coming from offensive rebounds and straight athleticism, the Spurs as a whole have to develop, too.

The four other starters—Terry Cummings, Sean Elliott, Willie Anderson and Rod Strickland—are all legitimate scoring threats, something not many teams can boast. But there is no three-point shooting—Elliott's 64 attempts led—and a lack of outside firepower gives opponents too many opportunities to collapse on Robinson and Cummings inside. But having a group that runs the court so well means the Spurs don't always give defenses a chance to get set.

PLAYMAKING: Strickland has the flash and the ability, but he is a powderkeg in more ways than one. For the good of the Spurs, his offseason regimen better have included learning how to be more responsible. Avery Johnson and Kevin Pritchard, acquired from Golden State, are his backups.

DEFENSE: The 44.8 percentage against was No. 1 last season and the 102.6 points allowed was No. 5, and no wonder. Robinson's quickness was the key to him and the team finishing second in blocked shots. Cummings provided more muscle inside and several other athletic types who could cover a lot of ground took care of the rest.

Strickland would have finished 12th in steals at 2.02 per game had he qualified, and Robinson was at 1.55. But San Antonio committed nearly two more turnovers a game than it forced.

REBOUNDING: David is Goliath, No. 1 in the league in 1990-91 after finishing second to Hakeem Olajuwon as a rookie. Collectively, the Spurs aren't far behind: No. 3 behind Detroit and Portland in both defensive boards and overall rebounding.

Robinson is enough to pull an entire team along, but he has help with the heavy lifting. Cummings, though his numbers are dropping, is still a factor at 7.8 a game.

OUTLOOK: Teams don't win championships without stability, which means the Spurs have far more to prove than discovering an outside shooter. Some organizations say it's a distraction when

SPUR ROSTER

No.	Veterans	Pos.	Ht.	Wt.	Age	Yrs. Pro	College
40	Willie Anderson	G-F	6-8	185	24	3	Georgia
34	Terry Cummings	F	6-9	235	30	9	DePaul
32	Sean Elliott	F	6-8	205	23	2	Arizona
21	Sidney Green	F	6-9	230	30	8	Nevada-Las Vegas
3	Sean Higgins	F	6-9	195	22	1	Michigan
15	Avery Johnson	G	5-11	175	26	3	Southern
45	Tony Massenburg	F	6-9	230	24	1	Maryland
8	Paul Pressey	G-F	6-5	203	32	9	Tulsa
14	Kevin Pritchard	G	6-3	180	24	1	Kansas
50	David Robinson	C	7-1	235	26	2	Navy
24	Dwayne Schintzius	C	7-2	260	23	1	Florida
1	Rod Strickland	G	6-3	175	25	3	DePaul

Rd.	Rookies	Sel. No.	Pos.	Ht.	Wt.	College
2	Greg Sutton	49	G	6-2	170	Oral Roberts

little things like a move to Memphis or Cincinnati is mentioned. But their players stay out until ridiculous hours the morning before a day playoff game and their coach, Larry Brown, seems to constantly figure that better opportunities are elsewhere.

At some point, that may catch up to them. The Spurs have won back-to-back Midwest Division titles, but they can thank Utah for that. Two seasons ago, the Jazz dropped four of their last six and finished a game back. In 1990-91, they were upset by Golden State on the final day and again San Antonio won by a game.

SPUR PROFILES

DAVID ROBINSON 26 7-1 235   **Center**

His only disappointment in 1990-91 was tailing off in the second half . . . Even with that, his greatness prevailed . . . All-NBA first team for the first time . . . Finished first in rebounding, second in blocked shots, and ninth in scoring and field-goal percentage . . . Had three triple-doubles . . . MVP-type first half of season . . . Flash-powder quickness . . . Sight of him coming from other side of the lane to block a shot is as breathtaking as any slam . . . Not even close to reaching his full potential . . . Wait until he develops some sort of post game . . . All-American at Naval Academy who was No. 1 pick by Spurs in 1987 . . . Fulfilled two-year military obligation and played in 1988 Olympics before joining Spurs in 1989 . . . Born Aug. 6, 1965, in Key West, Fla. . . . Made $2.265 million.

Year	Team	G	FG	FG Pct.	FT	FT Pct.	Reb.	Ast.	TP	Avg.
1989-90	San Antonio	82	690	.531	613	.732	983	164	1993	24.3
1990-91	San Antonio	82	754	.552	592	.762	1063	208	2101	25.6
	Totals	164	1444	.542	1205	.747	2046	372	4094	25.0

SEAN ELLIOTT 23 6-8 205   Forward

That's more like it . . . Showed tremendous improvement over rookie season . . . Stats went up almost as much as confidence . . . Either bought ear plugs or realized that Larry Brown's constant yelling was just his way of encouraging improvement . . . A year earlier and just out of Arizona as third pick in draft, Brown's riding distracted Elliott and got under his skin . . . Last season, he shot a lot better and drove stronger and more often . . . Needs to get better on rebounding . . . Played a little off-guard . . . Born Feb. 2, 1968, in Tucson, Ariz. . . . Gym at Tucson's Cholla High is named for him . . . Made $1.8 million.

Year	Team	G	FG	FG Pct.	FT	FT Pct.	Reb.	Ast.	TP	Avg.
1989-90	San Antonio	81	311	.481	187	.866	297	154	810	10.0
1990-91	San Antonio	82	478	.490	325	.808	456	238	1301	15.9
	Totals	163	789	.486	512	.828	753	392	2111	13.0

WILLIE ANDERSON 24 6-8 185   Guard-Forward

Faced most difficult season as a pro, following offseason trade rumors . . . Year before, he focused on weathering sophomore jinx and succeeded . . . Came 1990-91, he seemed to be thinking about every move on the court instead of relying on natural reaction . . . Quick, lanky player who can make athletic moves better than many his size . . . Game reminds Spurs' fans of George Gervin . . . Doesn't take enough advantage of putting ball on the floor or driving . . . Missed first seven games last season because of stress fracture in his leg . . . Affected lateral mobility on defense . . . Born Jan. 8, 1967, in Greenville, S.C. . . . Tenth pick in 1988, out of Georgia . . . Made $725,000.

Year	Team	G	FG	FG Pct.	FT	FT Pct.	Reb.	Ast.	TP	Avg.
1988-89	San Antonio	81	640	.498	224	.775	417	372	1508	18.6
1989-90	San Antonio	82	532	.492	217	.748	372	364	1288	15.7
1990-91	San Antonio	75	453	.457	170	.798	351	358	1083	14.4
	Totals	238	1625	.484	611	.771	1140	1094	3879	16.3

ROD STRICKLAND 25 6-3 175   Guard

May turn into one of great what-could-have-beens . . . Showed flashes of brilliance in first full season in San Antonio . . . Problem was, he showed as much stupidity . . . Stayed out until 4 A.M. before noon playoff game in first-round series against Golden State . . . Also went into summer facing indecent-exposure charges filed in Seattle . . . Was often late to practice and games . . . Spurs worried about his true commitment . . . Restricted free agent, but a good bet to be re-signed or have any reasonable offer sheet matched because Spurs need him . . . Great quickness . . . With only three years experience since coming out of DePaul, he looks like a veteran when slicing down the lane and dishing off or scoring . . . Knicks drafted him 19th in 1988 . . . Made some errors with bad passes, but is getting better . . . Born July 11, 1966, in Bronx, N.Y. . . . Made $400,000.

Year	Team	G	FG	FG Pct.	FT	FT Pct.	Reb.	Ast.	TP	Avg.
1988-89	New York	81	265	.467	172	.745	160	319	721	8.9
1989-90	N.Y.-S.A.	82	343	.454	174	.626	259	468	868	10.6
1990-91	San Antonio	58	314	.482	161	.763	219	463	800	13.8
	Totals	221	922	.467	507	.704	638	1250	2389	10.8

TERRY CUMMINGS 30 6-9 235   Forward

Enters 10th NBA season in unusual position of having something to prove . . . Came into 1990 training camp at 257 pounds, about 22 more than normal playing weight . . . Said he wanted to get stronger, but admitted later it was a mistake and that it slowed him down . . . No longer the first option in offense because of development of David Robinson . . . Concentration shifts more to defense and rebounding . . . Posted career low in scoring and dropped below 20-point mark for only second time in the NBA . . . Ordained Pentecostal minister/evangelist . . . Also an accomplished musician who has produced two songs, he carries portable keyboard on the road to compose and once sung national anthem before game in Milwaukee . . . Born March 15, 1961, in Chicago . . . Drafted 59th by Bucks as DePaul undergraduate in 1978 . . . Made $1.86 million.

Year	Team	G	FG	FG Pct.	FT	FT Pct.	Reb.	Ast.	TP	Avg.
1982-83	San Diego	70	684	.523	292	.709	744	177	1660	23.7
1983-84	San Diego	81	737	.494	380	.720	777	139	1854	22.9
1984-85	Milwaukee	79	759	.495	343	.741	716	228	1861	23.6
1985-86	Milwaukee	82	681	.474	265	.656	694	193	1627	19.8
1986-87	Milwaukee	82	729	.511	249	.662	700	229	1707	20.8
1987-88	Milwaukee	76	675	.485	270	.665	553	181	1621	21.3
1988-89	Milwaukee	80	730	.467	362	.787	650	198	1829	22.9
1989-90	San Antonio	81	728	.475	343	.780	677	219	1818	22.4
1990-91	San Antonio	67	503	.484	164	.683	521	157	1177	17.6
	Totals	698	6226	.489	2668	.715	6032	1721	15154	21.7

SIDNEY GREEN 30 6-9 230   Forward

Spurs gave No. 1 pick to Orlando for him before last season . . . By end of season, there were reports Spurs were ready to dump him . . . Green maintained no one was seeing the real Green . . . Spurs still waiting . . . He vowed to have a great playoffs, but got very little time because of matchups against Golden State . . . San Antonio expected enforcer/rebounder type, but didn't get anything close to that . . . Was more offense-minded than team wanted, especially at beginning of season . . . His 313 rebounds were fewest in a season when he's played more than 48 games . . . Bone spurs on his ankle didn't help him get into rhythm . . . Born Jan. 4, 1961, in Brooklyn, N.Y. . . . No. 5 pick in 1983 from Nevada-Las Vegas by Chicago . . . Made $837,000.

Year	Team	G	FG	FG Pct.	FT	FT Pct.	Reb.	Ast.	TP	Avg.
1983-84	Chicago	49	100	.439	55	.714	174	25	255	5.2
1984-85	Chicago	48	108	.432	79	.806	246	29	295	6.1
1985-86	Chicago	80	407	.465	262	.782	658	139	1076	13.5
1986-87	Detroit	80	256	.472	119	.672	653	62	631	7.9
1987-88	New York	82	258	.441	126	.663	642	93	642	7.8
1988-89	New York	82	194	.460	129	.759	394	76	517	6.3
1989-90	Orlando	73	312	.468	136	.651	588	99	761	10.4
1990-91	San Antonio	66	177	.461	89	.848	313	52	443	6.7
	Totals	560	1812	.458	995	.731	3668	575	4620	8.3

PAUL PRESSEY 32 6-5 203   Guard-Forward

Will be in seat beside Sidney Green on next train out ... On-again, off-again first season with Spurs after being acquired from Bucks for Frank Brickowski Aug. 1, 1990 ... Showed no scoring punch ... Larry Brown noted occasional good showings on defense, but Pressey didn't provide consistent stopping hoped for ... Twice named to All-Defensive first team during eight years at Milwaukee, and was twice second team ... Bucks picked him 20th in 1982 draft out of Tulsa ... Born Dec. 24, 1958, in Richmond, Va. ... Made $900,000.

Year	Team	G	FG	FG Pct.	FT	FT Pct.	Reb.	Ast.	TP	Avg.
1982-83	Milwaukee	79	213	.457	105	.597	281	207	532	6.7
1983-84	Milwaukee	81	276	.523	120	.600	282	252	674	8.3
1984-85	Milwaukee	80	480	.517	317	.758	429	543	1284	16.1
1985-86	Milwaukee	80	411	.488	316	.806	399	623	1146	14.3
1986-87	Milwaukee	61	294	.477	242	.738	296	441	846	13.9
1987-88	Milwaukee	75	345	.491	285	.798	375	523	983	13.1
1988-89	Milwaukee	67	307	.474	187	.776	262	439	813	12.1
1989-90	Milwaukee	57	239	.472	144	.758	172	244	628	11.0
1990-91	San Antonio	70	201	.472	110	.827	176	271	528	7.5
	Totals	650	2766	.488	1826	.750	2672	3543	7434	11.4

AVERY JOHNSON 26 5-11 175   Guard

Became team sparkplug after being signed as a free agent Jan. 17 ... Started 10 games with Spurs, but was mostly backup point guard ... Also made Seattle as free agent two years in a row after originally going undrafted from Southern University ... David Robinson said, "I couldn't imagine anybody else coming in in that situation and lifting the team like he did." ... Hard work gets it done ... Good at entering in closing seconds of a quarter and quickly pushing up ball for a score ... Had career high in shooting last season, though it wouldn't have taken much ... Good-natured ... Born March 25, 1965, in New Orleans.

Year	Team	G	FG	FG Pct.	FT	FT Pct.	Reb.	Ast.	TP	Avg.
1988-89	Seattle	43	29	.349	9	.563	24	73	68	1.6
1989-90	Seattle	53	55	.387	29	.725	43	162	140	2.6
1990-91	Den.-S.A.	68	130	.469	59	.678	77	230	320	4.7
	Totals	164	214	.426	97	.678	144	465	528	3.2

SEAN HIGGINS 22 6-9 195   Forward

Considering last season would have been his senior year at Michigan, Spurs regarded rookie season as an investment . . . A player they want to try and develop . . . Obviously could have used another year of college ball . . . Also, it's a good bet he would have gone higher than 54th in draft . . . Averaged just 9.3 minutes . . . Probably best shooter on the team . . . Born Dec. 30, 1968, in Los Angeles . . . Hit game-winning basket for Michigan in 1989 Final Four semifinal win over Illinois . . . His father, Earle, played at Eastern Michigan and one year with Indiana Pacers . . . Made $150,000.

Year	Team	G	FG	FG Pct.	FT	FT Pct.	Reb.	Ast.	TP	Avg.
1990-91	San Antonio	50	97	.458	28	.848	63	35	225	4.5

TONY MASSENBURG 24 6-9 230   Forward

A leaper and all-around athlete . . . Was 43rd pick overall in 1990 draft after making second-team All-ACC at Maryland . . . One of only two players in ACC to finish season averaging double figures in points (18) and rebounds (10) . . . Got most of points with Spurs converting offensive rebounds . . . Any talk of other offensive game is based purely on potential . . . Has yet to start an NBA game after being in opening lineup two years in a row at Maryland . . . Born July 31, 1967, in Sussex, Va. . . . Made $150,000.

Year	Team	G	FG	FG Pct.	FT	FT Pct.	Reb.	Ast.	TP	Avg.
1990-91	San Antonio	35	27	.450	28	.622	58	4	82	2.3

DWAYNE SCHINTZIUS 23 7-2 260   Center

The most perplexing case of 1990 draft . . . Florida product may have been most talented player coming out but he dropped to 24th pick because of what was viewed as discipline problems and poor work habits . . . So he showed up at summer league at 300 pounds . . . Stayed around desired 260 most of season, but had trouble getting in basketball shape . . . Common sight was his heaving and gasping for air after practice . . . Nice

guy with easy-going attitude who isn't afraid to poke fun at himself
. . . Good passer for a center, he has a nice touch and good hands
. . . Needs to become more aggressive . . . Too passive going back
up with offensive rebounds and gets pushed off the blocks inside
. . . Physique doesn't say finesse player, but style does . . . Spurs
insist it may be two more years before investment shows a return
. . . Not on playoff roster because of back injury . . . Early indi-
cations on rehabilitation were positive . . . Born Oct. 14, 1968, in
Brandon, Fla. . . . Made $520,000.

Year	Team	G	FG	FG Pct.	FT	FT Pct.	Reb.	Ast.	TP	Avg.
1990-91	San Antonio	42	68	.439	22	.550	121	17	158	3.8

KEVIN PRITCHARD 24 6-3 180   Guard

Traded to Spurs by Golden State for second-
round draft pick in 1991 . . . Reunited with
Larry Brown, his coach at Kansas . . . Figures
to contend with Avery Johnson for backup point
guard spot . . . Had poor assist-to-turnover ratio
of 81-59 as rookie with Warriors . . . All-Big
Eight selection as a senior at Kansas . . . Twice
made all-conference defensive team . . . Played
on Jayhawks' 1988 NCAA championship team . . . College teammates with several current NBAers, including Danny Manning,
Tyrone Hill and Rick Calloway . . . High-jumped 6-8 in high
school in Tulsa, Okla. . . . Born July 18, 1967, in Bloomington,
Ind. . . . Warriors selected him 34th in 1990 . . . Made $185,000.

Year	Team	G	FG	FG Pct.	FT	FT Pct.	Reb.	Ast.	TP	Avg.
1990-91	Golden State	62	88	.384	62	.805	65	81	243	3.9

THE ROOKIE

GREG SUTTON 23 6-2 170   Guard

NBA scouting director Marty Blake called him ''a great talent . . .
one of the greatest shooters I have seen in years.'' . . . So why did
he last until No. 49? . . . NAIA Player of the Year as a senior at
Oral Roberts . . . Scoring average of 34.3 was second-highest in
the division . . . Set school records for career scoring average, assists and free-throws made . . . Scored 68 points against Oklahoma
City during 1990-91 . . . Born Dec. 3, 1967, in Oklahoma City,
Okla.

Sean Elliott got spurs that jingled in second season.

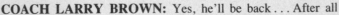

COACH LARRY BROWN: Yes, he'll be back ... After all

that "will-he-or-won't-he?" go to South Carolina, he launches third season with Spurs ... It will be one more than he had with Carolina (ABA), and two less than with Denver (ABA-NBA), one more than with the Nets, two less than with Kansas ... In 19 seasons as a pro and college coach, he's had only one losing year (21-61 with Spurs in 1988-89) and has led 17 teams to the playoffs ... Combined college and pro record of

753-444 (.629)... ABA-NBA: 576-383 (.601)... Owns one title: NCAA, Kansas, 1988... Born Sept. 14, 1940, in Brooklyn, N.Y.... Played at North Carolina, in AAU ball, in the Olympics, five years in ABA (5-9 guard was MVP of the first ABA All-Star Game in 1968).

GREATEST TEAM

There were rookie mistakes, all right—mistakes by those who doubted the rookie.

But by the time 1989-90 was over, David Robinson had won over everyone, just as the Spurs had won the Midwest Division title with a 56-26 record, three more victories than any other Spur club. His 24.3 per-game average was supported by Terry Cumming's 22.4 and the continued emergence of another young player, Willie Anderson.

It ended with a playoff loss to Portland, but the Spurs, who won just 21 games the previous season, had already set an NBA record for the biggest single-season turnaround.

ALL-TIME SPUR LEADERS

SEASON

Points: George Gervin, 2,585, 1979-80
Assists: Johnny Moore, 816, 1984-85
Rebounds: Swen Nater, 1,279, 1974-75 (ABA)

GAME

Points: George Gervin, 63 vs. New Orleans, 4/9/78
Assists: John Lucas, 24 vs. Denver, 4/15/84
Rebounds: Manny Leaks, 35 vs. Kentucky, 11/27/70 (ABA)

CAREER

Points: George Gervin, 23,602, 1974-85
Assists: Johnny Moore, 3,663, 1980-87
Rebounds: George Gervin, 4,841, 1974-85

SEATTLE SUPERSONICS

TEAM DIRECTORY: Chairman: Barry Ackerley; Pres.: Bob Whitsitt; Dir. Pub. Rel.: Jim Rupp; Coach: K.C. Jones; Asst. Coaches: Bob Kloppenburg, Kip Motta. Arena: Seattle Center Coliseum (14,132). Colors: Green and yellow.

SCOUTING REPORT

SHOOTING: They finished tied for fifth in the league in 1990-91 and can improve off that even more with an entire season together. Three important ingredients—Eddie Johnson, Benoit Benjamin and Ricky Pierce—all joined after December.

In Pierce and Johnson, K.C. Jones has great shooters to work with, E.J. having regained much of what he lost at Phoenix. Derrick McKey averaged 15.3 points and shot 51.7 percent and still seems to have untapped potential. Benjamin and Shawn Kemp as the bookends on the blocks provide versatility.

PLAYMAKING: People wouldn't be so loud in their criticism of Gary Payton had he not painted the target on himself with brash talk before playing a single NBA game. In truth, he was a rookie who struggled like most rookies. Nate McMillan, who figured to move to small forward, was asked to stick around in the backcourt for stability.

Payton should be ready to solo this season. His improved finish to 1990-91 gave the Sonics plenty of upbeat feelings heading into the summer.

DEFENSE: The notion of finishing 12th in shooting percentage against and 19th in blocked shots, as the Sonics did last season, will go out the window if Benjamin plays to potential. Not the potential of what he might be, a pressure that has always shadowed him, but the potential of what he has been at times in the past. He finished ninth in blocks, but got 2.33 a game with the Clippers and 1.74 in 31 outings with Seattle.

Elsewhere, Kemp will only get better, McKey gets good marks for his defense, and Sedale Threatt and Payton in the backcourt and McMillan as the swingman give reason to believe the Sonics will cut down on the 105.4 points they allowed last season.

REBOUNDING: Benjamin again can make a huge difference. Seattle finished fifth in rebounding percentage as it was, and

Shawn Kemp got to start and came of age as NBA sophomore.

No. 1 in work on the offensive boards. Michael Cage may have
fallen down on the depth chart, but there's proof that he still has
influence. For additional help, the SuperSonics used their first-
round pick on 7-2 center Rich King.

SONIC ROSTER

No.	Veterans	Pos.	Ht.	Wt.	Age	Yrs. Pro	College
11	Dana Barros	G	5-11	163	24	2	Boston College
00	Benoit Benjamin	C	7-0	260	26	6	Creighton
44	Michael Cage	F-C	6-9	245	29	7	San Diego State
20	Quintin Dailey	G	6-2	207	30	9	San Francisco
22	Eddie Johnson	F	6-7	215	32	10	Illinois
40	Shawn Kemp	F	6-10	240	21	2	Trinity JC
31	Derrick McKey	F	6-9	210	25	4	Alabama
10	Nate McMillan	F-G	6-5	197	27	5	North Carolina State
8	Scott Meents	F	6-10	235	27	2	Illinois
2	Gary Payton	G	6-4	190	23	1	Oregon State
21	Ricky Pierce	G	6-4	210	32	9	Rice
4	Sedale Threatt	G	6-2	177	30	8	W. Virginia Tech

Rd.	Rookies	Sel. No.	Pos.	Ht.	Wt.	College
1	Rich King	14	C	7-2	260	Nebraska

OUTLOOK: Wait and watch with the rest of the Western Conference because no team may be viewed with more curiosity than the SuperSonics, who made some noise in their short time as a unit last season. They have size, strength, scoring and veterans; now all they have to do is prove they can come together. The good thing is that the final two months of 1990-91 may have been the breaking-in stage; that's better than having to do it early this season.

SUPERSONIC PROFILES

EDDIE JOHNSON 32 6-7 215   **Forward**

When Seattle traded Xavier McDaniel to Phoenix for E.J. and a couple of future first-round picks, the payoff for the SuperSonics wasn't supposed to come until later. Johnson proved that theory wrong . . . Regained shooting touch and confidence he once had, but had lost, at Phoenix . . . Sonics consider him a good clubhouse leader . . . Replaced Derrick McKey in opening lineup at small forward toward end of season . . . Seattle was 18-9 when he started . . . Made 98 of 104 free-throw attempts (94.2 percent) with Seattle and finished ninth in the league overall at 89.1 . . . Won NBA's Sixth Man Award in 1988-89 . . . Born May 1, 1959, in Chicago, and attended Illinois . . . Was 29th pick (KC Kings) in 1981 . . . Made $1,000,000.

Year	Team	G	FG	FG Pct.	FT	FT Pct.	Reb.	Ast.	TP	Avg.
1981-82	Kansas City	74	295	.459	99	.664	322	109	690	9.3
1982-83	Kansas City	82	677	.494	247	.779	501	216	1621	19.8
1983-84	Kansas City	82	753	.485	268	.810	455	296	1794	21.9
1984-85	Kansas City	82	769	.491	325	.871	407	273	1876	22.9
1985-86	Sacramento	82	623	.475	280	.816	419	214	1530	18.7
1986-87	Sacramento	81	606	.463	267	.829	353	251	1516	18.7
1987-88	Phoenix	73	533	.480	204	.850	318	180	1294	17.7
1988-89	Phoenix	70	608	.497	217	.868	306	162	1504	21.5
1989-90	Phoenix	64	411	.453	188	.917	246	107	1080	16.9
1990-91	Phoe.-Sea.	81	543	.484	229	.891	271	111	1354	16.7
	Totals	771	5818	.480	2324	.834	3598	1919	14259	18.5

SHAWN KEMP 21 6-10 240   Forward

Words "man child" seem to come up a lot for some reason when people describe him . . . Showed great improvement on the offensive end during 1990-91, but was erratic overall from late February on . . . Became permanent starter at power forward after Xavier McDaniel deal opened spot for Derrick McKey at small forward . . . Had franchise-record 10 blocked shots Jan. 18 against Lakers . . . Must learn when to put the ball on the floor . . . Youngest player in the league last season, his second after leaving Trinity Valley (Tex.) JC . . . SuperSonics took a flier on him with No. 17 pick in 1989 and, considering his physical talents and potential, there are no regrets . . . Born Nov. 26, 1969, in Elkhart, Ind. . . . Made $350,000.

Year	Team	G	FG	FG Pct.	FT	FT Pct.	Reb.	Ast.	TP	Avg.
1989-90	Seattle	81	203	.479	117	.736	346	26	525	6.5
1990-91	Seattle	81	462	.508	288	.661	679	144	1214	15.0
	Totals	162	665	.499	405	.681	1025	170	1739	10.7

BENOIT BENJAMIN 26 7-0 260   Center

No doubt he has physical ability to be in second echelon of centers behind Robinson/Ewing/Olajuwon... No doubt he has wasted much of it... Traded from Clippers to Seattle in February for package that included Olden Polynice... Blamed Los Angeles media for treating him too harshly... Should play in New York or Philadelphia and miss a practice with bruised buttocks or skip through running drills and then see what harsh is ... A nice guy who wouldn't hurt a fly... Clipper organization got a good chuckle when Sonics signed him to a contract worth a guaranteed $17.7 million... Finished eighth in the league in rebounding and ninth in blocked shots... Had dominating stretch for the Clippers Jan. 5-26, when he averaged 19.2 points, 17.6 rebounds and 3.1 blocks... Born Nov. 22, 1964, in Monroe, La.... Starred at Creighton... Clippers chose him No. 3 in 1985 draft... Made $1,750,000.

Year	Team	G	FG	FG Pct.	FT	FT Pct.	Reb.	Ast.	TP	Avg.
1985-86	L.A. Clippers	79	324	.490	229	.746	600	79	878	11.1
1986-87	L.A. Clippers	72	320	.449	188	.715	586	135	828	11.5
1987-88	L.A. Clippers	66	340	.491	180	.706	530	172	860	13.0
1988-89	L.A. Clippers	79	491	.541	317	.744	696	157	1299	16.4
1989-90	L.A. Clippers	71	362	.526	235	.732	657	159	959	13.5
1990-91	LAC-Sea.	70	386	.496	210	.712	723	119	982	14.0
	Totals	437	2223	.501	1359	.728	3792	821	5806	13.3

DERRICK McKEY 25 6-9 210   Forward

Sonics liken him to James Worthy because of potent low-post skills and also speed in the open court... Most unselfish player on the team, maybe even too much... Needs to be more aggressive... Has been told to shoot more, but he'll still pass up open 15-footers... A top defensive player... Opened season at power forward, but moved to small forward, a more natural position, after Xavier McDaniel was traded to Phoenix... Replaced in starting lineup late by Eddie Johnson and came off the bench in season's final 16 games... Shot 59.1 percent (78-of-132) in that stretch... Finished with career-best 51.7 per-

cent . . . Born Oct. 10, 1966, in Meridian, Miss. . . . Drafted ninth
as Alabama undergraduate in 1987 . . . Made $962,000.

Year	Team	G	FG	FG Pct.	FT	FT Pct.	Reb.	Ast.	TP	Avg.
1987-88	Seattle	82	255	.491	173	.772	328	107	694	8.5
1988-89	Seattle	82	487	.502	301	.803	464	219	1305	15.9
1989-90	Seattle	80	468	.493	315	.782	489	187	1254	15.7
1990-91	Seattle	73	438	.517	235	.845	423	169	1115	15.3
	Totals	317	1648	.502	1024	.800	1704	682	4368	13.8

NATE McMILLAN 27 6-5 197   Forward-Guard

Last season was supposed to be one of movement, from point guard to small forward . . .
But he still ended up as point when rookie Gary
Payton was slow in developing . . . Showed versatility in playing both . . . Team captain who
accepts any role . . . Some see him as a coach
of the future . . . People person . . . Has shown
he is capable of defending big and small opponents, so Sonics foresee him as a Michael Cooper-type . . .
Came off the bench all 78 games in 1990-91, but still led team
in assists 27 times . . . Needs just 211 more assists to pass Fred
Brown and become all-time Seattle leader . . . A second-round
Sonic pick out of North Carolina State in 1986 . . . Born Aug. 3,
1964, in Raleigh, N.C. . . . Made $658,000.

Year	Team	G	FG	FG Pct.	FT	FT Pct.	Reb.	Ast.	TP	Avg.
1986-87	Seattle	71	143	.475	87	.617	331	583	373	5.3
1987-88	Seattle	82	235	.474	145	.707	338	702	624	7.6
1988-89	Seattle	75	199	.410	119	.630	388	696	532	7.1
1989-90	Seattle	82	207	.473	98	.641	403	598	523	6.4
1990-91	Seattle	78	132	.433	57	.613	251	371	338	4.3
	Totals	388	916	.452	506	.648	1711	2950	2390	6.2

GARY PAYTON 23 6-4 190   Guard

About that comment that guards like him and
Magic Johnson come along once every 10 years
. . . Would you believe 11? . . . The No. 2 pick
from Oregon State, Payton was a major disappointment early . . . No player at his position
had been drafted as high as second since Isiah
Thomas . . . Started all 82 games . . . Never
showed any consistent jump shot and struggled
with floor leadership until late in season . . . Nice showing in play-

offs against Portland gave Sonics some encouragement . . . Proved to be tenacious defender on big and small guards . . . Great passing instincts . . . Finished 12th in the league in steals and 20th in assists . . . Led all rookies in both departments . . . Born July 23, 1968, in Oakland . . . Made $1,685,000.

Year	Team	G	FG	FG Pct.	FT	FT Pct.	Reb.	Ast.	TP	Avg.
1990-91	Seattle	82	259	.450	69	.711	243	528	588	7.2

DANA BARROS 24 5-11 163   Guard

Odd-man-out of backcourt rotation . . . Got 600 fewer minutes in 1990-91 than as a rookie, even though he averaged 19.6 minutes final seven games of the season . . . Got 10.4 minutes before that, with 15 did-not-plays . . . Sonics still haven't decided if he's an off-guard or point . . . A defensive liability because of size at the former, but he dribbles too much and hasn't yet developed skills for the latter . . . Improved ability to penetrate and quickness allows him to break traps . . . Nice shooting range . . . Shot 91.8 percent from the line . . . Born April 13, 1967, in Boston and starred at Boston College . . . Sonics made him 16th pick in 1989 . . . Made $500,000.

Year	Team	G	FG	FG Pct.	FT	FT Pct.	Reb.	Ast.	TP	Avg.
1989-90	Seattle	81	299	.405	89	.809	132	205	782	9.7
1990-91	Seattle	66	154	.495	78	.918	71	111	418	6.3
	Totals	147	453	.432	167	.856	203	316	1200	8.2

RICKY PIERCE 32 6-4 210   Guard

Acquired from Milwaukee in exchange for Dale Ellis in February . . . Only guard ever to win NBA's Sixth Man Award . . . Has won it twice, 1987 and '90 . . . One-on-one scorer who slumped at the wrong time . . . Finished regular season with 14-of-39 slump (35.9 percent) and then had horrible playoffs . . . One-dimensional . . . Finished No. 3 in NBA in free-throw percentage at 91.3, the best mark of his career . . . Had streak of 46 shots without a miss at the line, four shy of all-time Seattle record . . . But finished with lowest field-goal percentage since 1983-84 . . . SuperSonics were 16-16 with him in the lineup . . . Born Aug.

19, 1959, in Dallas . . . Pistons drafted him No. 18 out of Rice in 1982 . . . Made $1,110,000.

Year	Team	G	FG	FG Pct.	FT	FT Pct.	Reb.	Ast.	TP	Avg.
1982-83	Detroit	39	33	.375	18	.563	35	14	85	2.2
1983-84	San Diego.	69	268	.470	149	.861	135	60	685	9.9
1984-85	Milwaukee	44	165	.537	102	.823	117	94	433	9.8
1985-86	Milwaukee	81	429	.538	266	.858	231	177	1127	13.9
1986-87	Milwaukee	79	575	.534	387	.880	266	144	1540	19.5
1987-88	Milwaukee	37	248	.510	107	.877	83	73	606	16.4
1988-89	Milwaukee	75	527	.518	255	.859	197	156	1317	17.6
1989-90	Milwaukee	59	503	.510	307	.839	167	133	1359	23.0
1990-91	Mil.-Sea.	78	561	.485	430	.913	191	168	1598	20.5
	Totals	561	3309	.510	2021	.866	1422	1019	8750	15.6

MICHAEL CAGE 29 6-9 245   Forward-Center

Started first 51 games, then lost job after acquisition of Benoit Benjamin . . . Finished out of top 10 in rebounding for first time since 1985-86 . . . Great offensive rebounder . . . Solid low-post defender, but there's nothing there on offense . . . By the end of 1990-91, he still didn't know all the offensive and defensive sets . . . Has played at least 80 games four of the last five seasons and has missed only two contests last three combined . . . Born Jan. 28, 1962, in West Memphis, Ark. . . . All-time scoring and rebounding leader when he left San Diego State . . . Clippers selected him 14th in 1984 draft . . . Made $910,000.

Year	Team	G	FG	FG Pct.	FT	FT Pct.	Reb.	Ast.	TP	Avg.
1984-85	L.A. Clippers.	75	216	.543	101	.737	392	51	533	7.1
1985-86	L.A. Clippers.	78	204	.479	113	.649	417	81	521	6.7
1986-87	L.A. Clippers.	80	457	.521	341	.730	922	131	1255	15.7
1987-88	L.A. Clippers.	72	360	.470	326	.688	938	110	1046	14.5
1988-89	Seattle	80	314	.498	197	.743	765	126	825	10.3
1989-90	Seattle	82	325	.504	148	.698	821	70	798	9.7
1990-91	Seattle	82	226	.508	70	.625	558	89	522	6.4
	Totals	549	2102	.502	1296	.704	4813	658	5500	10.0

QUINTIN DAILEY 30 6-2 207   Guard

Nickname is "Q," but it should be The Cat, because he always lands on his feet . . . Proud of his self-described role as a survivor after offcourt problems in college and pros . . . Says he should be a referee after retiring because he's so used to being booed in most arenas . . . Just hanging on? He has been for years . . . Ran into an old problem during 1990-91, gaining weight in midseason . . . Had role as a scorer off the bench early, but got little time at the end . . . Talks openly about his time at the Adult Substance Abuse Program in Southern California in hopes that it will help others . . . Born Jan. 22, 1961, in Baltimore . . . Drafted No. 7 by Bulls as undergraduate at San Francisco in 1982 . . . Made $425,000.

Year	Team	G	FG	FG Pct.	FT	FT Pct.	Reb.	Ast.	TP	Avg.
1982-83	Chicago	76	470	.466	206	.730	260	280	1151	15.1
1983-84	Chicago	82	583	.474	321	.811	235	254	1491	18.2
1984-85	Chicago	79	525	.473	205	.817	208	191	1262	16.0
1985-86	Chicago	35	203	.432	163	.823	68	67	569	16.3
1986-87	L.A. Clippers	49	200	.407	119	.768	83	79	520	10.6
1987-88	L.A. Clippers	67	328	.434	243	.776	154	109	901	13.4
1988-89	L.A. Clippers	69	448	.465	217	.759	204	154	1114	16.1
1989-90	Seattle	30	97	.404	52	.788	51	34	247	8.2
1990-91	Seattle	30	73	.471	38	.613	32	16	184	6.1
	Totals	517	2927	.456	1564	.778	1295	1184	7439	14.4

SEDALE THREATT 30 6-2 177   Guard

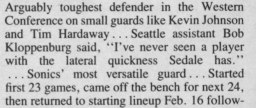

Arguably toughest defender in the Western Conference on small guards like Kevin Johnson and Tim Hardaway . . . Seattle assistant Bob Kloppenburg said, ''I've never seen a player with the lateral quickness Sedale has.'' . . . Sonics' most versatile guard . . . Started first 23 games, came off the bench for next 24, then returned to starting lineup Feb. 16 following Dale Ellis trade . . . Good perimeter shooter . . . Persistent contract squabbles created problems with front office . . . Sixth-round pick by Philadelphia in 1983 after career at West Virginia Institute of Technology . . . Lowest selection still active in NBA . . . Born Oct. 10, 1961, in Atlanta . . . Made $650,000.

Year	Team	G	FG	FG Pct.	FT	FT Pct.	Reb.	Ast.	TP	Avg.
1983-84	Philadelphia	45	62	.419	23	.821	40	41	148	3.3
1984-85	Philadelphia	82	188	.452	66	.733	99	175	446	5.4
1985-86	Philadelphia	70	310	.453	75	.833	121	193	696	9.9
1986-87	Phil.-Chi.	68	239	.448	95	.798	108	259	580	8.5
1987-88	Chi.-Sea.	71	216	.508	57	.803	88	160	492	6.9
1988-89	Seattle	63	235	.494	63	.818	117	238	544	8.6
1989-90	Seattle	65	303	.506	130	.828	115	216	744	11.4
1990-91	Seattle	80	433	.519	137	.792	99	273	1013	12.7
	Totals	544	1986	.482	646	.802	787	1555	4663	8.6

SCOTT MEENTS 27 6-10 235   **Forward**

The biggest move he made from first season with Seattle to next? He switched from jersey No. 50 to No. 8 . . . Wore the latter in Europe during 1988-89 . . . Missed 41 games in 1990-91 with strained right arch . . . Fifty-three minutes played was fewest on team . . . Didn't get to play in the NBA until Sonics signed him at beginning of 1989-90 season . . . Injuries were a factor in his playing only 148 minutes in 26 games . . . Was fourth-round pick by the Bulls out of Illinois in 1986 . . . Born Jan. 4, 1964, in Kankakee, Ill. . . . Made $300,000.

Year	Team	G	FG	FG Pct.	FT	FT Pct.	Reb.	Ast.	TP	Avg.
1989-90	Seattle	26	19	.432	17	.739	30	7	55	2.1
1990-91	Seattle	13	7	.250	2	.500	10	8	17	1.3
	Totals	39	26	.361	19	.704	40	15	72	1.8

THE ROOKIE

RICH KING 22 7-2 260   **Center**

Developing, and in a good spot to do it because of presence of Benoit Benjamin . . . Shouldn't be any pressure to produce immediately . . . No. 14 selection, the third center taken and the first from America . . . Stock helped by all-tournament showing at Orlando All-Star Classic . . . Cornhusker to the cob who is from Omaha and played at Nebraska . . . His 57.4 percent from the field as a senior set school record and led the Big 8 . . . Born April 4, 1969.

COACH K.C. JONES: Has been a head coach at collegiate or

pro level in four decades . . . Got 500th career NBA victory with April 8 win over Denver . . . Any roundtable discussion of great teams has to include him . . . A guard on Bill Russell-led 1955-56 NCAA champions at the University of San Francisco . . . Played on 1956 Olympic team that won the gold medal in Melbourne, Australia . . . Second-round pick of Boston in 1956 and then won eight championship rings in nine seasons as an active player with Celtics . . . Assistant coach to Bill Sharman on Lakers' squad that had record 33-game winning streak in 1971-72 and also won the championship . . . Coached his own title team in Boston in 1983-84 . . . Joined SuperSonics in August 1989 as assistant to friend Bernie Bickerstaff . . . Took over as head coach before last season . . . Inducted into Hall of Fame May 9, 1989 . . . Born May 25, 1932, in San Francisco.

Eddie Johnson shone as he once did under the Sun.

GREATEST TEAM

Fifty-two wins is four short of the franchise record, set the following season, but 1978-79 is about a couple of ones: the Sonics' only Pacific Division title and only NBA championship.

Came the playoffs, they pushed aside the Lakers and Bullets in five games and were threatened only by a seven-game series with the Suns. And when they beat the Bullets in the Finals, it was by winning four in a row after dropping the opener.

Gus Williams, Dennis Johnson, Jack Sikma, Fred "Downtown" Brown, Lonnie Shelton: names of history in a town that hasn't enjoyed much sports success.

ALL-TIME SUPERSONIC LEADERS

SEASON

Points: Spencer Haywood, 2,251, 1972-73
Assists: Lenny Wilkens, 766, 1971-72
Rebounds: Jack Sikma, 1,038, 1981-82

GAME

Points: Fred Brown, 58 vs. Golden State, 3/23/74
Assists: Nate McMillan, 25 vs. LA Clippers, 2/23/87
Rebounds: Jim Fox, 30 vs. Los Angeles, 12/26/73

CAREER

Points: Fred Brown, 14,018, 1971-84
Assists: Fred Brown, 3,160, 1971-84
Rebounds: Jack Sikma, 7,729, 1977-86

UTAH JAZZ

TEAM DIRECTORY: Owner: Larry Miller; Pres.: Frank Layden; GM: R. Tim Howells; Dir. Player Personnel: Scott Layden; VP-Pub. Rel.: David Allred; Dir. Media Services: Kim Turner; Coach: Jerry Sloan; Asst. Coaches: Phil Johnson, David Fredman, Gordon Chiesa. Arena: New Salt Lake Arena (20,000). Colors: Purple, gold and green.

SCOUTING REPORT

SHOOTING: Beyond being tied for No. 5 in the league last season at 49.2 percent, the Jazz succeed because everyone knows his range and plays within it. Five regulars finished at better than 50 percent: Mark Eaton (.579), Karl Malone (.527), Blue Edwards (.526), Jeff Malone (.508) and John Stockton (.507).

The acquisition of Jeff Malone from Washington worked as planned, with his outside shooting keeping defenses from hounding Karl Malone inside, Karl, meanwhile, improved his jumper, anyway. Stockton, once someone team officials wondered out loud if he could or would shoot, has upped the number of three-point attempts by 102 in two seasons.

Eric Murdock, the team's first-round pick out of Providence, has impressive credentials—No. 1 in scoring and steals in the Big East—but he walked out of the Jazz rookie free-agent camp.

PLAYMAKING: Consistent doesn't begin to describe Stockton, who has between 1,118 and 1,164 assists each of the last four seasons and scoring averages of 17.2, 17.2 and 17.1 the last three. Durability comes into play and so do smarts.

Even with records coming quicker than at Motown—the label, not the town—Stockton probably doesn't get his due. He certainly will never make the All-NBA first team until Magic Johnson or Michael Jordan retires, get hurt or Johnson moves to forward.

DEFENSE: Opponents shot just .459 against Utah last season, sixth-best in the NBA. They got just 100.7 points, third-best.

There's not a lot of quickness (Eaton) or size (Edwards) around Karl Malone on the frontline, but they make do. Even as Eaton's blocked shots decline, his mere presence is still a factor.

REBOUNDING: Twenty-one teams had a better rebounding percentage, and the Jazz, surprisingly, were dead last in offensive

John Stockton broke his own NBA season-assists record.

boards, even with Karl Malone finishing fourth in the league.

Retaining Mike Brown, a free agent during the offseason, could be key to holding at 21. That, or a big showing from second-round draft choice Isaac Austin from Arizona State.

OUTLOOK: Getting upset by Golden State on the final day of the regular season, which cost Utah the Midwest Division title, is only the most recent late disappointment for Jerry Sloan's Jazz. There have been others, and that is the real red flag here.

JAZZ ROSTER

No.	Veterans	Pos.	Ht.	Wt.	Age	Yrs. Pro	College
41	Thurl Bailey	F	6-5	200	26	8	North Carolina State
54	Alan Bannister	C	7-5	300	24	0	Arkansas State
40	Mike Brown	F	6-9	260	28	5	George Washington
53	Mark Eaton	C	7-4	290	34	9	UCLA
30	Theodore Edwards	F	6-5	200	26	2	East Carolina
35	Darrell Griffith	G	6-4	195	33	11	Louisville
24	Jeff Malone	G	6-4	205	30	8	Mississippi State
32	Karl Malone	F	6-9	256	28	6	Louisiana Tech
33	Walter Palmer	C	7-1	215	22	1	Dartmouth
11	Delaney Rudd	G	6-2	195	29	2	Wake Forest
12	John Stockton	G	6-1	175	29	7	Gonzaga

Rd.	Rookies	Sel. No.	Pos.	Ht.	Wt.	College
1	Eric Murdock	21	G	6-2	189	Providence
2	Isaac Austin	48	C	6-10	255	Arizona State

Except that this time, after the loss to the Warriors forced a first-round matchup with tougher Phoenix, the Jazz proved their real worth under gut-check conditions. They first beat the Suns and then, while being eliminated by Portland, never gave up and had several big second-half comebacks to turn blowouts into white-knuckle rides for the Trail Blazers.

They remain a puzzling group, though, capable of greatness or heartbreak. Any team with a pair of superstars, as the Jazz have in Stockton and Karl Malone, will contend, but it's been proven two can carry them only so far.

JAZZ PROFILES

KARL MALONE 28 6-9 256   Forward

As if the status quo isn't terrifying enough for opponents, he continues to improve all-around game . . . Had career highs in assists and blocked shots last season . . . More than a very good rebounder, he's a very good rebounder on a poor rebounding team . . . Opposition should be able to concentrate on keeping him off the boards, but it doesn't work . . . Finished

second in league in scoring and fourth in rebounding . . . Outside
shot has gotten better, but it will always be the ugly sister next
to his dominating post game . . . Temper will sometimes get best
of him . . . Great personality who handles all the attention well . . .
Born July 24, 1963, in Summerfield, La. . . . Jazz picked him 13th
as Louisiana Tech undergraduate in 1985 . . . Made $2.26 million.

Year	Team	G	FG	FG Pct.	FT	FT Pct.	Reb.	Ast.	TP	Avg.
1985-86	Utah	81	504	.496	195	.481	718	236	1203	14.9
1986-87	Utah	82	728	.512	323	.598	855	158	1779	21.7
1987-88	Utah	82	858	.520	552	.700	986	199	2268	27.7
1988-89	Utah	80	809	.519	703	.766	853	219	2326	29.1
1989-90	Utah	82	914	.562	696	.762	911	226	2540	31.0
1990-91	Utah	82	847	.527	684	.770	967	270	2382	29.0
	Totals	489	4660	.525	3153	.708	5290	1308	12498	25.6

JOHN STOCKTON 29 6-1 175   Guard

All he does is set records and then hide from the publicity they bring . . . Again established NBA's single-season assist mark . . . Only player ever to have four 1,000-assist seasons . . . Had four games of 20 assists or more, with a season high of 28 against San Antonio Jan. 28 . . . Also second in league in steals . . . But will he ever make first team All-NBA?
. . . What doesn't show up on stat sheet is toughness despite size
. . . Constantly getting knocked down and pressured but has played
all 82 games six of seven seasons . . . Always seems under control
with the ball, making it look like extension of his arm . . . Gen-
uinely disdains the spotlight, so can be hard for media to deal
with . . . Instead of shy, he's more like curt . . . Born March 26,
1962, in Spokane, Wash., grew up competing against Mark Ry-
pien and Ryne Sandberg and stayed local to attend Gonzaga . . .
Was 16th pick in 1984 draft . . . Made $2 million.

Year	Team	G	FG	FG Pct.	FT	FT Pct.	Reb.	Ast.	TP	Avg.
1984-85	Utah	82	157	.471	142	.736	105	415	458	5.6
1985-86	Utah	82	228	.489	172	.839	179	610	630	7.7
1986-87	Utah	82	231	.499	179	.782	151	670	648	7.9
1987-88	Utah	82	454	.574	272	.840	237	1128	1204	14.7
1988-89	Utah	82	497	.538	390	.863	248	1118	1400	17.1
1989-90	Utah	78	472	.514	354	.819	206	1134	1345	17.2
1990-91	Utah	82	496	.507	363	.836	237	1164	1413	17.2
	Totals	570	2535	.520	1872	.825	1363	6239	7098	12.5

MARK EATON 34 7-4 290   Center

The song remains the same: alter shots inside and grab seven or eight rebounds a game . . . Number of attempts has dropped way off—541 in 1987-88 to 407 to 300 to 292 last season—but his shooting has never been better . . . Hit 52.7 percent in 1989-90, then a career-high 57.9 last season to lead team . . . Took advantage of double-teaming on Karl Malone to get open for dunks . . . Failed to get at least 200 blocked shots for first time in career, finishing at 188 . . . Streak of 291 consecutive-games played, sixth-best in league, was snapped when missed two games in December with the flu . . . Born Jan. 24, 1957, in Westminster, Cal. . . . Attended, but played little, at UCLA . . . Was fourth-round choice in 1982 . . . Made $2 million.

Year	Team	G	FG	FG Pct.	FT	FT Pct.	Reb.	Ast.	TP	Avg.
1982-83	Utah	81	146	.414	59	.656	462	112	351	4.3
1983-84	Utah	82	194	.466	73	.593	595	113	461	5.6
1984-85	Utah	82	302	.449	190	.712	927	124	794	9.7
1985-86	Utah	80	277	.470	122	.604	675	101	676	8.5
1986-87	Utah	79	234	.400	140	.657	697	105	608	7.7
1987-88	Utah	82	226	.418	119	.623	717	55	571	7.0
1988-89	Utah	82	188	.462	132	.660	843	83	508	6.2
1989-90	Utah	82	158	.527	79	.669	601	39	395	4.8
1990-91	Utah	80	169	.579	71	.634	667	51	409	5.1
	Totals	730	1894	.456	985	.650	6184	783	4773	6.5

JEFF MALONE 30 6-4 205   Guard

Provided Jazz new weapon with outside shooting . . . Beyond his own scoring, he helps spread defenses to allow more room for Karl Malone and John Stockton to operate . . . Finished second on team in scoring . . . Had career-high shooting percentage . . . Also made 91.7 percent from the line, No. 2 in the league just behind the 91.8 by Indiana's Reggie Miller . . . Restricted free agent heading into the summer . . . A better defender than people realize . . . Other subtle talent is his ability to occasionally bring the ball upcourt to provide brief relief for Stockton . . . Streak shooter . . . Born June 28, 1961, in Mobile, Ala. . . . Attended Mississippi State . . . Drafted 10th by Bullets in

1983 . . . Made $815,000.

Year	Team	G	FG	FG Pct.	FT	FT Pct.	Reb.	Ast.	TP	Avg.
1983-84	Washington	81	408	.444	142	.826	155	151	982	12.1
1984-85	Washington	76	605	.499	211	.844	206	184	1436	18.9
1985-86	Washington	80	735	.483	322	.868	288	191	1795	22.4
1986-87	Washington	80	689	.457	376	.885	218	298	1758	22.0
1987-88	Washington	80	648	.476	335	.882	206	237	1641	20.5
1988-89	Washington	76	677	.480	296	.871	179	219	1651	21.7
1989-90	Washington	75	781	.491	257	.877	206	243	1820	24.3
1990-91	Utah	69	525	.508	231	.917	206	143	1282	18.6
	Totals	617	5068	.480	2170	.874	1664	1666	12365	20.0

THEODORE (BLUE) EDWARDS 26 6-5 200   Forward

Natural position is probably off-guard, but Jeff Malone is there . . . Started 56 games last season, mostly at small forward . . . Can still drive and penetrate as well as anybody on team . . . Also improved his outside shot . . . Had injury-plagued season that caused him to miss 20 games with broken nose and severely sprained ankle . . . New nickname should be "Black and Blue" . . . Got original monicker from an older sister who found year-old Theodore choking on a baby bottle in a crib . . . Career 51.6 percent from the field as a pro after hitting 55.5 percent at East Carolina . . . Lakers made him a third-rounder in 1977 . . . Born Oct. 31, 1965, in Washington, D.C. . . . Made $360,000.

Year	Team	G	FG	FG Pct.	FT	FT Pct.	Reb.	Ast.	TP	Avg.
1989-90	Utah	82	286	.507	146	.719	251	145	727	8.9
1990-91	Utah	62	244	.526	82	.701	201	108	576	9.3
	Totals	144	530	.516	228	.713	452	253	1303	9.0

THURL BAILEY 30 6-11 232   Forward

Durable as always after playing 348 consecutive games, but stats have dipped two seasons in a row . . . Part of that due to arrival of Jeff Malone, which thrust Bailey into more of a role of rebounder and defender . . . But he's not much of a rebounder for his size . . . Primarily a sixth man who started 22 times, six to open season and 16 more for injured Blue Edwards . . . No. 3 on all-time Jazz list for games played and minutes, and fourth in scoring . . . Born April 7, 1961, in Washington, D.C.

... Won NCAA championship with North Carolina State in 1983
... Utah got him as No. 7 pick in 1983 draft ... Made $1 million.

Year	Team	G	FG	FG Pct.	FT	FT Pct.	Reb.	Ast.	TP	Avg.
1983-84	Utah	81	302	.512	88	.752	464	129	692	8.5
1984-85	Utah	80	507	.490	197	.842	525	138	1212	15.2
1985-86	Utah	82	483	.448	230	.830	493	153	1196	14.6
1986-87	Utah	81	463	.447	190	.805	432	102	1116	13.8
1987-88	Utah	82	633	.492	337	.826	531	158	1604	19.6
1988-89	Utah	82	615	.483	363	.825	447	138	1595	19.5
1989-90	Utah	82	470	.481	222	.779	410	137	1162	14.2
1990-91	Utah	82	399	.458	219	.808	407	124	1017	12.4
	Totals	652	3872	.475	1846	.814	3709	1079	9594	14.7

DELANEY RUDD 29 6-2 195   Guard

After going three full seasons between being drafted out of Wake Forest and getting a minute in the regular season, he's turned into role player who's played 159 of a possible 164 games last two seasons ... Shooting guard in college, he's a point guard in pros ... Hears criticism that everything falls apart when John Stockton is out ... Doesn't get a lot of minutes behind Stockton, but coaches are happy with his work ... Has good attitude about time constraints ... Not a lot of quickness to match up with new breed of jet-like point guards ... Born Nov. 8, 1962, in Hollister, N.C. ... A fourth-round draft pick in 1985 ... Made $215,000.

Year	Team	G	FG	FG Pct.	FT	FT Pct.	Reb.	Ast.	TP	Avg.
1989-90	Utah	77	111	.429	35	.660	55	177	273	3.5
1990-91	Utah	82	124	.435	59	.831	66	216	324	4.0
	Totals	159	235	.432	94	.758	121	393	597	3.8

MIKE BROWN 28 6-9 260   Forward

Had so-so 1990-91 before good showing in playoffs ... Hurt Portland on the boards and practically split time with Mark Eaton ... So guess who's suddenly a hot commodity as an unrestricted free agent? ... Even before the draft, he had a $5-million, three-year offer on the table from Il Messaggero of Italian League ... Has played in Italy before; he speaks the language and his wife is from the country ... Has thug look about him because he's so big and burly, but in truth he's a nice guy who deserves credit as hard worker... Graduated from George Washington University in 3½ years... Drafted by Bulls on third round in 1985... Born July 9, 1963, in Newark, N.J.... Made $650,000.

Year	Team	G	FG	FG Pct.	FT	FT Pct.	Reb.	Ast.	TP	Avg.
1986-87	Chicago	62	106	.527	46	.639	214	24	258	4.2
1987-88	Chicago	46	78	.448	41	.577	159	28	197	4.3
1988-89	Utah	66	104	.419	92	.708	258	41	300	4.5
1989-90	Utah	82	177	.515	157	.789	373	47	512	6.2
1990-91	Utah	82	129	.454	132	.742	337	49	390	4.8
	Totals	338	594	.475	468	.720	1341	189	1657	4.9

DARRELL GRIFFITH 33 6-4 195   Guard

Dr. Dunkenstein may be through operating in Salt Lake City... At draft time, it was questionable whether he'd be back... Has one guaranteed year left on contract... Played very little down the stretch and in the playoffs... Had first career did-not-plays/coach's decision in 1990-91, missing seven games in March and April... Averaged career-low 5.7 points... Still a pleasure to watch his pretty three-point shot, even during warmups... Shot below 40 percent for first time in his career, but had second-best season ever at the line... All-time Jazz leader in games played, field-goals made and attempted and three-pointers... Born June 16, 1958, in Louisville, Ky., and led hometown Cardinals to NCAA crown in 1980, when he was also NCAA Player of the Year... Second pick in 1980 draft... Made $850,000.

Year	Team	G	FG	FG Pct.	FT	FT Pct.	Reb.	Ast.	TP	Avg.
1980-81	Utah	81	716	.464	229	.716	288	194	1671	20.6
1981-82	Utah	80	689	.482	189	.697	305	187	1582	19.8
1982-83	Utah	77	752	.484	167	.679	304	270	1709	22.2
1983-84	Utah	82	697	.490	151	.696	338	283	1636	20.0
1984-85	Utah	78	728	.457	216	.725	344	243	1764	22.6
1985-86	Utah					Injured				
1986-87	Utah	76	463	.446	149	.703	227	129	1142	15.0
1987-88	Utah	52	251	.429	59	.641	127	91	589	11.3
1988-89	Utah	82	466	.446	142	.780	330	130	1135	13.8
1989-90	Utah	82	301	.464	51	.654	166	63	733	8.9
1990-91	Utah	75	174	.391	34	.756	90	37	430	5.7
	Totals	765	5237	.463	1387	.707	2519	1627	12391	16.2

WALTER PALMER 22 7-1 215   Center

Utah's only 1990 draft pick, 33rd overall . . . Averaged just 3.0 minutes in 28 appearances . . . Good outside shooter for center . . . May end up as Laimbeer/Sikma type of player . . . Still needs to get stronger and add bulk . . . Would be better at 230-240 . . . Played four years at Dartmouth . . . As a senior he was 10th in nation in shot-blocking average and made All-Ivy . . . Set Ivy League mark with 12 blocked shots against Harvard . . . His dad and Rudy LaRusso were Dartmouth teammates . . . Born Oct. 23, 1968, in Lexington, Mass. . . . Made $225,000.

Year	Team	G	FG	FG Pct.	FT	FT Pct.	Reb.	Ast.	TP	Avg.
1990-91	Utah	28	15	.333	10	.667	21	6	40	1.4

ALAN BANNISTER 24 7-5 300   Center

From the team that brought you Mark Eaton . . . This gets even better . . . Raised in England, where he was a high-school star and also lettered in swimming, cricket and rugby . . . Reportedly had 80 scholarship offers, including Big East and ACC teams, before deciding on Oklahoma State . . . Transferred to Arkansas State . . . Undrafted, Jazz signed him as free agent and thought so much of his potential that they kept him on the payroll despite knee surgery in training camp that sidelined him all of 1990-91 . . . An investment . . . Or maybe owner Larry Miller was starting a world-class snooker team to rival his prized softball outfit . . . Born June 12, 1967, in Horwich, England . . . Made $50,000.

THE ROOKIES

ERIC MURDOCK 23 6-2 189   Guard

NCAA's all-time leader in steals may turn out to be the same at No. 21 . . . Kentucky coach Rick Pitino says he had the quickest hands in college basketball . . . Probably second-best defender among guards coming out, behind Mark Macon . . . Second-team All-American as a senior at Providence, former home of current Jazz assistant Gordon Chiesa . . . Led Big East in scoring in 1991 and set conference record with 435 points . . . Born June 14, 1968, in Bridgewater, N.J.

ISAAC AUSTIN 22 6-10 255 **Center**

Isn't starting his rookie season on the right foot, thanks to knee surgery early in the summer that was expected to sideline him for two months . . . No. 48 pick . . . Arizona State product averaged 16.3 points and 8.7 rebounds while leading Sun Devils to second round of 1991 NCAA tournament . . . Played two seasons at Kings River Junior College in native Reedley, Cal., where he was born Aug. 18, 1969.

COACH JERRY SLOAN: Reputation got a break when Jazz finally got past first round of playoffs . . . That was only part of it . . . Jazz, hindered by opening season with two games at Tokyo, opened 2-5, prompting talk that Sloan was in trouble . . . But they closed regular season 52-23 despite not having regular starting lineup intact for about a month . . . Lifetime NBA coaching record in six seasons with Utah and Chicago is 243-201 . . . He's 149-80 with Jazz . . . Personality has evolved as much as career . . . Very intense player with Bulls who used to arrive at Chicago Stadium an hour before coach Dick Motta . . . As Jazz coach, he's far more mellow than most would expect . . . Dramatic change came after crash of plane carrying Evansville University basketball team in 1977 . . . Sloan was supposed to coach that team, and would have been on that plane, but he'd resigned as the coach months earlier . . . Crash made him realize that life is too short to revolve around basketball . . . Lasting impression he leaves now: genuine good guy . . . Still a small-town guy at heart who returns to McLeansboro, Ill., every summer . . . Born March 14, 1946, in Louisville, Ky.

Karl Malone made All-NBA first team for third straight year.

GREATEST TEAM

From a distance, there is questionable evidence to support the 1988-89 team that won four fewer games than the next season and then got swept in the first round by Golden State in one of the NBA's greatest playoff upsets ever.

On the other hand . . .

Jerry Sloan's first year as Jazz coach in 1988-89 resulted in winning the Midwest Division title by six games. John Stockton, Mark Eaton and Karl Malone made the All-Star team and Malone was named MVP of the game. The team had a 37-19 finish and 20 wins by 15 points or more. The 1989-90 team, 55-game winners, finished 2-4 to lose the division and won only 11 games by 15 points or more.

ALL-TIME JAZZ LEADERS

SEASON

Points: Karl Malone, 2,540, 1989-90
Assists: John Stockton, 1,164, 1990-91
Rebounds: Len Robinson, 1,288, 1977-78

GAME

Points: Pete Maravich, 68 vs. New York, 2/25/77
Assists: John Stockton, 26 vs. Portland, 4/14/88
Rebounds: Len Robinson, 27 vs. Los Angeles, 11/11/77

CAREER

Points: Adrian Dantley, 13,545, 1979-86
Assists: John Stockton, 6,239, 1984-91
Rebounds: Mark Eaton, 6,184, 1982-91

1991 NBA COLLEGE DRAFT

Sel. No.	Team	Name	College	Ht.
	FIRST ROUND			
1.	Charlotte	Larry Johnson	UNLV	6-5
2.	New Jersey	Kenny Anderson	Georgia Tech	6-0
3.	Sacramento	Billy Owens	Syracuse	6-9
4.	Denver	Dikembe Mutombo	Georgetown	7-1
5.	Miami	Steve Smith	Michigan State	6-6
6.	Dallas	Doug Smith	Missouri	6-10
7.	Minnesota	Luc Longley	New Mexico	7-2
8.	Denver (from Washington)	Mark Macon	Temple	6-3
9.	Atlanta (from L.A. Clippers)	Stacey Augmon	UNLV	6-6

Missouri's Doug Smith was drafted sixth by the Mavericks.

T-Wolves made New Mexico's Luc Longley seventh pick.

Sel. No.	Team	Name	College	Ht.
10.	Orlando	Brian Williams	Arizona	6-9
11.	Cleveland	Terrell Brandon	Oregon	5-11
12.	New York	Greg Anthony	UNLV	6-0
13.	Indiana	Dale Davis	Clemson	6-9
14.	Seattle	Rich King	Nebraska	7-2
15.	a- Atlanta	Anthony Avent	Seton Hall	6-8
16.	Golden State (from Philadelphia)	Chris Gatling	Old Dominion	6-10
17.	Golden State	Victor Alexander	Iowa State	6-9
18.	b- Milwaukee	Kevin Brooks	SW Louisiana	6-6
19.	Washington (from Detroit, via Dallas and Denver)	LaBradford Smith	Louisville	6-3
20.	Houston	John Turner	Phillips	6-7
21.	Utah	Eric Murdock	Providence	6-2
22.	L.A. Clippers (from Phoenix via Seattle)	LeRon Ellis	Syracuse	6-9
23.	Orlando (from San Antonio)	Stanley Roberts	LSU	6-11
24.	Boston	Rick Fox	North Carolina	6-6
25.	Golden State (from L.A. Lakers)	Shaun Vandiver	Colorado	6-10
26.	Chicago	Mark Randall	Kansas	6-7
27.	Sacramento (from Portland)	Pete Chilcutt	North Carolina	6-10

a-Traded to Denver, then to Milwaukee
b-Traded to Denver

Nuggets took Temple's Mark Macon with eighth selection.

Sel. No.	Team	Name	College	Ht.
	SECOND ROUND			
28.	Charlotte (from Denver)	Kevin Lynch	Minnesota	6-5
29.	Miami	George Ackles	UNLV	6-8
30.	Atlanta (from Sacramento)	Rodney Monroe	North Carolina State	6-2
31.	Sacramento (from New Jersey)	Randy Brown	New Mexico State	6-0
32.	Phoenix (from Charlotte)	Chad Gallagher	Creighton	6-9
33.	Dallas	Donald Hodge	Temple	7-0
34.	Minnesota	Myron Brown	Slippery Rock	6-3
35.	Dallas (from Washington via Sacramento)	Mike Iuzzolino	St. Francis (Pa.)	5-10
36.	Orlando	Chris Corchiani	North Carolina State	5-11
37.	L.A. Clippers	Elliot Perry	Memphis State	6-0
38.	c- L.A. Clippers (from Cleveland)	Joe Wylie	Miami (Fla.)	6-9
39.	Cleveland (from New York via Charlotte)	Jimmy Oliver	Purdue	6-5
40.	Detroit (from Seattle)	Doug Overton	La Salle	6-1
41.	Indiana	Sean Green	Iona	6-5
42.	Sacramento (from Atlanta)	Steve Hood	James Madison	6-7

UNLV's Stacey Augmon got draft call (No. 9) from Hawks.

Sel. No.	Team	Name	College	Ht.
43.	d- Golden State	Lamont Strothers	Christopher Newport	6-4
44.	Philadelphia	Alvaro Teheran	Houston	7-1
45.	Milwaukee	Bobby Phills	Southern	6-4
46.	Phoenix (from Detroit)	Richard Dumas	Oklahoma State	6-6
47.	e- Houston	Keith Hughes	Rutgers	6-6
48.	Utah	Isaac Austin	Arizona State	6-10
49.	San Antonio	Greg Sutton	Oral Roberts	6-2
50.	Phoenix	Joey Wright	Texas	6-1
51.	Houston (from Boston, via New Jersey and Cleveland)	Zan Tabak	POP 84 Split	6-11
52.	L.A. Lakers	Anthony Jones	Oral Roberts	6-7
53.	New Jersey (from Chicago)	Von McDade	Wisconsin-Milwaukee	6-2
54.	Portland	Marcus Kennedy	Eastern Michigan	6-6

c-Traded to New York
d-Traded to Portland
e-Traded to Cleveland

1990–91
NATIONAL BASKETBALL ASSOCIATION

FINAL STANDINGS

EASTERN CONFERENCE

Atlantic Division	Won	Lost	Pct.
Boston	56	26	.683
Philadelphia	44	38	.537
New York	39	43	.476
Washington	30	52	.366
New Jersey	26	56	.317
Miami	24	58	.293

Central Division	Won	Lost	Pct.
Chicago	61	21	.744
Detroit	50	32	.610
Milwaukee	48	34	.585
Atlanta	43	39	.524
Indiana	41	41	.500
Cleveland	33	49	.402
Charlotte	26	56	.317

WESTERN CONFERENCE

Midwest Division	Won	Lost	Pct.
San Antonio	55	27	.671
Utah	54	28	.659
Houston	52	30	.634
Orlando	31	51	.378
Minnesota	29	53	.354
Dallas	28	54	.341
Denver	20	62	.244

Pacific Division	Won	Lost	Pct.
Portland	63	19	.768
L.A. Lakers	58	24	.707
Phoenix	55	27	.671
Golden State	44	38	.537
Seattle	41	41	.500
L.A. Clippers	31	51	.378
Sacramento	25	57	.305

PLAYOFFS

EASTERN CONFERENCE
First Round
Chicago defeated New York (3-0)
Philadelphia defeated Milwaukee (3-0)
Boston defeated Indiana (3-2)
Detroit defeated Atlanta (4-2)
Semifinals
Chicago defeated Philadelphia (4-1)
Detroit defeated Boston (4-2)
Finals
Chicago defeated Detroit (4-0)

WESTERN CONFERENCE
First Round
Portland defeated Seattle (3-2)
Utah defeated Phoenix (3-1)
Gold. St. defeated San Antonio (3-1)
L.A. Lakers defeated Houston (3-0)
Semifinals
Portland defeated Utah (4-1)
L.A. Lakers defeated Gold. St. (4-1)
Finals
L.A. Lakers defeated Portland (4-2)

CHAMPIONSHIP
Chicago defeated L.A. Lakers (4-1)

1990-91 INDIVIDUAL HIGHS

Most Minutes Played, Season: 3,315, Mullin, Golden State
Most Minutes Played, Game: 58, Mitchell, Minnesota vs. Philadelphia, 2/3 (2 OT)
48, 41 times, most recently by Skiles, Orlando vs. New Jersey, 4/21; Corbin, Minnesota vs. Washington, 4/21
Most Points, Game: 54, Adams, Denver vs. Milwaukee, 3/23 (OT)
52, Smith, L.A. Clippers vs. Denver, 12/1; King, Washington vs. Denver, 12/29
Most Field Goals Made, Game: 22, Ewing, New York vs. Charlotte, 12/1
Most Field Goal Attempts, Game: 38, King Washington vs. New York, 2/26 (2 OT)
35, Three times, most recently by King, Washington vs. New Jersey, 2/7
Most 3-Pt. Field Goals Made, Game: 9, Adams, Denver vs. L.A. Clippers, 4/12
Most 3-Pt. Field Goals Attempted, Game: 20, Adams, Denver vs. L.A. Clippers, 4/12
Most Free Throws Made, Game: 22, Floyd, Houston, vs. Golden State, 2/3 (2 OT)
19, Maxwell, Houston vs. Cleveland, 1/26
Most Free Throw Attempts, Game: 27, Floyd, Houston vs. Golden State, 2/3 (2 OT)
26, Seikaly, Miami vs. Dallas, 11/14
Most Rebounds, Game: 25, Three times, most recently by Lane, Denver vs. Houston, 4/21
Most Offensive Rebounds, Game: 15, L. Smith, Houston vs. Phoenix, 2/16
Most Defensive Rebounds, Game: 20, Daugherty, Cleveland vs. Sacramento, 3/8
Most Offensive Rebounds, Season: 361, Rodman, Detroit
Most Defensive Rebounds, Season: 731, K. Malone, Utah
Most Assists, Game: 30, Skiles, Orlando, vs. Denver, 12/30
Most Blocked Shots, Game: 11, Three times, most recently by Robinson, San Antonio vs. Utah, 1/12
Most Steals, Game: 10, Robertson, Milwaukee vs. Utah, 11/19
Most Personal Fouls, Season: 338, Mitchell, Minnesota
Most Games Disqualified, Season: 15, Rasmussen, Denver

INDIVIDUAL SCORING LEADERS
Minimum 70 games or 1,400 points

	G	FG	FT	Pts.	Avg.
Jordan, Chicago	82	990	571	2580	31.5
K. Malone, Utah	82	847	684	2382	29.0
King, Washington	64	713	383	1817	28.4
Barkley, Philadelphia	67	665	475	1849	27.6
Ewing, New York	81	845	464	2154	26.6
Adams, Denver	66	560	465	1752	26.5
Wilkins, Atlanta	81	770	476	2101	25.9
Mullin, Golden State	82	777	513	2107	25.7
Robinson, San Antonio	82	754	592	2101	25.6
Richmond, Golden State	77	703	394	1840	23.9
Hardaway, Golden State	82	739	306	1881	22.9
Miller, Indiana	82	596	551	1855	22.6
K. Johnson, Phoenix	77	591	519	1710	22.2
Hawkins, Philadelphia	80	590	479	1767	22.1
Campbell, Minnesota	77	652	358	1678	21.8
Daugherty, Cleveland	76	605	435	1645	21.6
Drexler, Portland	82	645	416	1767	21.5
Worthy, L.A. Lakers	78	716	212	1670	21.4
Pierce, Milw.-Sea.	78	561	430	1598	20.5
Dumars, Detroit	80	622	371	1629	20.4

REBOUND LEADERS
Minimum 70 games or 800 rebounds

	G	Off.	Def.	Tot.	Avg.
Robinson, San Antonio	82	335	728	1063	13.0
Rodman, Detroit	82	361	665	1026	12.5
Oakley, New York	76	305	615	920	12.1
K. Malone, Utah	82	236	731	967	11.8
Ewing, New York	81	194	711	905	11.2
Daugherty, Cleveland	76	177	353	830	10.9
Parish, Boston	81	271	585	856	10.6
Benjamin, LAC-Sea.	70	157	566	723	10.3
Thorpe, Houston	82	287	559	846	10.3
Coleman, New Jersey	74	269	490	759	10.3
Rasmussen, Denver	70	170	508	678	9.7
Williams, Portland	80	227	524	751	9.4
Wilkins, Atlanta	81	261	471	732	9.0
Laimbeer, Detroit	82	173	564	737	9.0
Donaldson, Dallas	82	201	526	727	8.9
Simmons, Sacramento	79	193	504	697	8.8
Willis, Atlanta	80	259	445	704	8.8
L. Smith, Houston	81	302	407	709	8.8
Nance, Cleveland	80	201	485	686	8.6
Grant, Chicago	78	266	393	659	8.4

FIELD-GOAL LEADERS
Minimum 300 FG Made

	FG	FGA	Pct.
Williams, Portland	358	595	.602
Parish, Boston	485	811	.598
Gamble, Boston	548	933	.587
Barkley, Philadelphia	665	1167	.570
Divac, L.A. Clippers	360	637	.565
Polynice, Sea.-LAC	316	564	.560
Thorpe, Houston	549	988	.556
McHale, Boston	504	912	.553
Robinson, San Antonio	754	1366	.552
Paxson, Chicago	317	578	.548
Grant, Chicago	401	733	.547
Jordan, Chicago	990	1837	.539
Mullin, Golden State	777	1449	.536
Roberts, Milwaukee	357	670	.533

3-POINT FIELD-GOAL LEADERS
Minimum 50 Made

	FG	FGA	Pct.
Les, Sacramento	71	154	.461
Tucker, New York	64	153	.418
Hornacek, Phoenix	61	146	.418
Porter, Portland	130	313	.415
Skiles, Orlando	93	228	.408
Ainge, Portland	102	251	.406
Hawkins, Philadelphia	108	270	.400
Bird, Boston	77	198	.389
Rice, Miami	71	184	.386
Hardaway, Golden State	97	252	.385
Scott, Orlando	125	334	.374
Humphries, Milwaukee	60	161	.373
Mays, Sacramento	72	197	.365
Ellis, Milwaukee	57	!57	.363

FREE-THROW LEADERS
Minimum 125 FT Made

	FT	FTA	Pct.
Miller, Indiana	551	600	.918
J. Malone, Utah	231	252	.917
Pierce, Milw.-Sea.	430	471	.913
Tripucka, Charlotte	152	167	.910
Johnson, L.A. Lakers	519	573	.906
Skiles, Orlando	340	377	.902
Vandeweghe, New York	259	288	.899
Hornacek, Phoenix	201	224	.897
Johnson, Seattle	229	257	.891
Bird, Boston	163	183	.891

ASSISTS LEADERS
Minimum 70 games or 400 assists

	G	A	Avg.
Stockton, Utah	82	1164	14.2
Johnson, L.A. Lakers	79	989	12.5
Adams, Denver	66	693	10.5
K. Johnson, Phoenix	77	781	10.1
Hardaway, Golden State	82	793	9.7
Thomas, Detroit	48	446	9.3
Richardson, Minnesota	82	734	9.0
Grant, L.A. Clippers	68	587	8.6
Douglas, Miami	73	624	8.5
Skiles, Orlando	79	660	8.4

STEALS LEADERS
Minimum 70 games or 125 steals

	G	St.	Avg.
Robertson, Milwaukee	81	246	3.04
Stockton, Utah	82	234	2.85
Jordan, Chicago	82	223	2.72
Hardaway, Golden State	82	214	2.61
Pippen, Chicago	82	193	2.35
Blaylock, New Jersey	72	169	2.35
Adams, Denver	66	147	2.23
Hawkins, Philadelphia	80	178	2.23
K. Johnson, Phoenix	77	163	2.12
Mullin, Golden State	82	173	2.11
M. Williams, Indiana	73	150	2.05
Payton, Seattle	82	165	2.01

BLOCKED-SHOTS LEADERS
Minimum 70 games or 100 blocked shots

	G	Blk.	Avg.
Olajuwon, Houston	56	221	3.95
Robinson, San Antonio	82	320	3.90
Ewing, New York	81	258	3.19
Bol, Philadelphia	82	247	3.01
Dudley, New Jersey	61	153	2.51
Nance, Cleveland	80	200	2.50
Eaton, Utah	80	188	2.35
McHale, Boston	68	146	2.15
Benjamin, LAC-Sea.	70	145	2.07
Ellison, Washington	76	157	2.07
Lang, Phoenix	63	127	2.02
Jones, Washington	62	124	2.00

1990-91 ALL-NBA TEAM

FIRST		SECOND	
Pos.	Player, Team	Pos.	Player, Team
G	Michael Jordan, Bulls	G	Kevin Johnson, Suns
G	Magic Johnson, Lakers	G	Clyde Drexler, Blazers
C	David Robinson, Spurs	C	Patrick Ewing, Knicks
F	Karl Malone, Jazz	F	Dominique Wilkins, Hawks
F	Charles Barkley, 76ers	F	Chris Mullin, Warriors

THIRD	
Pos.	Player, Team
G	John Stockton, Jazz
G	Joe Dumars, Pistons
C	Hakeem Olajuwon, Rockets
F	James Worthy, Lakers
F	Bernard King, Bullets

*1990-91 NBA ALL-ROOKIE TEAM

FIRST	SECOND
Kendall Gill, Hornets	Chris Jackson, Nuggets
Dennis Scott, Magic	Gary Payton, Sonics
Dee Brown, Celtics	Felton Spencer, Timberwolves
Lionel Simmons, Kings	Travis Mays, Kings
Derrick Coleman, Nets	Willie Burton, Heat

*Chosen without regard for position

1990-91 NBA ALL-DEFENSIVE TEAM

FIRST		SECOND	
Pos.	Player, Team	Pos.	Player, Team
G	Michael Jordan, Bulls	G	Joe Dumars, Pistons
G	Alvin Robertson, Bucks	G	John Stockton, Jazz
C	David Robinson, Spurs	C	Hakeem Olajuwon, Rockets
F	Dennis Rodman, Pistons	F	Scottie Pippen, Bulls
F	Buck Williams, Blazers	F	Dan Majerle, Suns

MOST VALUABLE PLAYER

1955-56	Bob Pettit, St. Louis	1973-74	Kareem Abdul-Jabbar, Milwaukee
1956-57	Bob Cousy, Boston	1974-75	Bob McAdoo, Buffalo
1957-58	Bill Russell, Boston	1975-76	Kareem Abdul-Jabbar, L.A.
1958-59	Bob Pettit, St. Louis	1976-77	Kareem Abdul-Jabbar, L.A.
1959-60	Wilt Chamberlain, Philadelphia	1977-78	Bill Walton, Portland
1960-61	Bill Russell, Boston	1978-79	Moses Malone, Houston
1961-62	Bill Russell, Boston	1979-80	Kareem Abdul-Jabbar, L.A.
1962-63	Bill Russell, Boston	1980-81	Julius Erving, Philadelphia
1963-64	Oscar Robertson, Cincinnati	1981-82	Moses Malone, Houston
1964-65	Bill Russell, Boston	1982-83	Moses Malone, Philadelphia
1965-66	Wilt Chamberlain, Philadelphia	1983-84	Larry Bird, Boston
1966-67	Wilt Chamberlain, Philadelphia	1984-85	Larry Bird, Boston
1967-68	Wilt Chamberlain, Philadelphia	1985-86	Larry Bird, Boston
1968-69	Wes Unseld, Baltimore	1986-87	Magic Johnson, L.A. Lakers
1969-70	Willis Reed, New York	1987-88	Michael Jordan, Chicago
1970-71	Lew Alcindor, Milwaukee	1988-89	Magic Johnson, L.A. Lakers
1971-72	Kareem Adbul-Jabbar, Milwaukee	1989-90	Magic Johnson, L.A. Lakers
1972-73	Dave Cowens, Boston	1990-91	Michael Jordan, Chicago

FINALS MVP AWARD

1969	Jerry West, Los Angeles	1981	Cedric Maxwell, Boston
1970	Willis Reed, New York	1982	Magic Johnson, Los Angeles
1971	Kareem Abdul-Jabbar, Milwaukee	1983	Moses Malone, Philadelphia
1972	Wilt Chamberlain, Los Angeles	1984	Larry Bird, Boston
1973	Willis Reed, New York	1985	K. Abdul-Jabbar, L.A. Lakers
1974	John Havlicek, Boston	1986	Larry Bird, Boston
1975	Rick Barry, Golden State	1987	Magic Johnson, L.A. Lakers
1976	Jo Jo White, Boston	1988	James Worthy, L.A.
1977	Bill Walton, Portland	1989	Joe Dumars, Detroit
1978	Wes Unseld, Washington	1990	Isiah Thomas, Detroit
1979	Dennis Johnson, Seattle	1991	Michael Jordan, Chicago
1980	Magic Johnson, Los Angeles		

ROOKIE OF THE YEAR

1952-53	Don Meincke, Fort Wayne	1971-72	Sidney Wicks, Portland
1953-54	Ray Felix, Baltimore	1972-73	Bob McAdoo, Buffalo
1954-55	Bob Pettit, Milwaukee	1973-74	Ernie DiGregorio, Buffalo
1955-56	Maurice Stokes, Rochester	1974-75	Keith Wilkes, Golden State
1956-57	Tom Heinsohn, Boston	1975-76	Alvan Adams, Phoenix
1957-58	Woody Sauldsberry, Philadelphia	1976-77	Adrian Dantley, Buffalo
1958-59	Elgin Baylor, Minneapolis	1978-79	Phil Ford, Kansas City
1959-60	Wilt Chamberlain, Philadelphia	1977-78	Walter Davis, Phoenix
1960-61	Oscar Robertson, Cincinnati	1979-80	Larry Bird, Boston
1961-62	Walt Bellamy, Chicago	1980-81	Darrell Griffith, Utah
1962-63	Terry Dischinger, Chicago	1981-82	Buck Williams, New Jersey
1963-64	Jerry Lucas, Cincinnati	1982-83	Terry Cummings, San Diego
1964-65	Willis Reed, New York	1983-84	Ralph Sampson, Houston
1965-66	Rick Barry, San Francisco	1984-85	Michael Jordan, Chicago
1966-67	Dave Bing, Detroit	1985-86	Patrick Ewing, New York
1967-68	Earl Monroe, Baltimore	1986-87	Chuck Person, Indiana
1968-69	Wes Unseld, Baltimore	1987-88	Mark Jackson, New York
1969-70	Lew Alcindor, Milwaukee	1988-89	Mitch Richmond, Golden State
1970-71	Dave Cowens, Boston	1989-90	David Robinson, San Antonio
	Geoff Petrie, Portland	1990-91	Derrick Coleman, New Jersey

DEFENSIVE PLAYER OF THE YEAR

1982-83	Sidney Moncrief, Milwaukee	1987-88	Michael Jordan, Chicago
1983-84	Sidney Moncrief, Milwaukee	1988-89	Mark Eaton, Utah
1984-85	Mark Eaton, Utah	1989-90	Dennis Rodman, Detroit
1985-86	Alvin Robertson, San Antonio	1990-91	Dennis Rodman, Detroit
1986-87	Michael Cooper, L.A. Lakers		

SIXTH MAN AWARD

1982-83	Bobby Jones, Philadelphia	1987-88	Roy Tarpley, Dallas
1983-84	Kevin McHale, Boston	1988-89	Eddie Johnson, Phoenix
1984-85	Kevin McHale, Boston	1989-90	Ricky Pierce, Milwaukee
1985-86	Bill Walton, Boston	1990-91	Detlef Schrempf, Indiana
1986-87	Ricky Pierce, Milwaukee		

MOST IMPROVED PLAYER

1985-86 Alvin Robertson, San Antonio	1988-89 Kevin Johnson, Phoenix
1986-87 Dale Ellis, Seattle	1989-90 Rony Seikaly, Miami
1987-88 Kevin Duckworth, Portland	1990-91 Scott Skiles, Orlando

SCHICK AWARD
Determined by Computer Formula

1983-84 Magic Johnson, Los Angeles	1987-88 Charles Barkley, Philadelphia
1984-85 Michael Jordan, Chicago	1988-89 Michael Jordan, Chicago
1985-86 Charles Barkley, Philadelphia	1989-90 David Robinson, San Antonio
1986-87 Charles Barkley, Philadelphia	1990-91 David Robinson, San Antonio

COACH OF THE YEAR

1962-63 Harry Gallatin, St. Louis	1977-78 Hubie Brown, Atlanta
1963-64 Alex Hannum, San Francisco	1978-79 Cotton Fitzsimmons, Kansas City
1964-65 Red Auerbach, Boston	1979-80 Bill Fitch, Boston
1965-66 Dolph Schayes, Philadelphia	1980-81 Jack McKinney, Indiana
1966-67 Johnny Kerr, Chicago	1981-82 Gene Shue, Washington
1967-68 Richie Guerin, St. Louis	1982-83 Don Nelson, Milwaukee
1968-69 Gene Shue, Baltimore	1983-84 Frank Layden, Utah
1969-70 Red Holzman, New York	1984-85 Don Nelson, Milwaukee
1970-71 Dick Motta, Chicago	1985-86 Mike Fratello, Atlanta
1971-72 Bill Sharman, Los Angeles	1986-87 Mike Schuler, Portland
1972-73 Tom Heinsohn, Boston	1987-88 Doug Moe, Denver
1973-74 Ray Scott, Detroit	1988-89 Cotton Fitzsimmons, Phoenix
1974-75 Phil Johnson, Kansas City-Omaha	1989-90 Pat Riley, L.A. Lakers
1975-76 Bill Fitch, Cleveland	1990-91 Don Chaney, Houston
1976-77 Tom Nissalke, Houston	

J. WALTER KENNEDY CITIZENSHIP AWARD

1974-75 Wes Unseld, Washington	1983-84 Frank Layden, Utah
1975-76 Slick Watts, Seattle	1984-85 Dan Issel, Denver
1976-77 Dave Bing, Washington	1985-86 Michael Cooper, L.A. Lakers
1977-78 Bob Lanier, Detroit	Rory Sparrow, New York
1978-79 Calvin Murphy, Houston	1986-87 Isiah Thomas, Detroit
1979-80 Austin Carr, Cleveland	1987-88 Alex English, Denver
1980-81 Mike Glenn, New York	1988-89 Thurl Bailey, Utah
1981-82 Kent Benson, Detroit	1989-90 Glenn Rivers, Atlanta
1982-83 Julius Erving, Philadelphia	1990-91 Kevin Johnson, Phoenix

NBA SCORING CHAMPIONS

Season	Pts./Avg.	Top Scorer	Team
1946-47	1389	Joe Fulks	Philadelphia
1947-48	1007	Max Zaslofsky	Chicago
1948-49	1698	George Mikan	Minneapolis
1949-50	1865	George Mikan	Minneapolis
1950-51	1932	George Mikan	Minneapolis
1951-52	1674	Paul Arizin	Philadelphia
1952-53	1564	Neil Johnston	Philadelphia
1953-54	1759	Neil Johnston	Philadelphia
1954-55	1631	Neil Johnston	Philadelphia
1955-56	1849	Bob Pettit	St. Louis
1956-57	1817	Paul Arizin	Philadelphia
1957-58	2001	George Yardley	Detroit
1958-59	2105	Bob Pettit	St. Louis
1959-60	2707	Wilt Chamberlain	Philadelphia
1960-61	3033	Wilt Chamberlain	Philadelphia
1961-62	4029	Wilt Chamberlain	Philadelphia
1962-63	3586	Wilt Chamberlain	San Francisco
1963-64	2948	Wilt Chamberlain	San Francisco
1964-65	2534	Wilt Chamberlain	San Fran.-Phila.
1965-66	2649	Wilt Chamberlain	Philadelphia
1966-67	2775	Rick Barry	San Francisco
1967-68	2142	Dave Bing	Detroit
1968-69	2327	Elvin Hayes	San Diego
1969-70	*31.2	Jerry West	Los Angeles
1970-71	*31.7	Lew Alcindor	Milwaukee
1971-72	*34.8	K. Abdul-Jabbar	Milwaukee
1972-73	*34.0	Nate Archibald	K.C.-Omaha
1973-74	*30.6	Bob McAdoo	Buffalo
1974-75	*34.5	Bob McAdoo	Buffalo
1975-76	*31.1	Bob McAdoo	Buffalo
1976-77	*31.1	Pete Maravich	New Orleans
1977-78	*27.2	George Gervin	San Antonio
1978-79	*29.6	George Gervin	San Antonio
1979-80	*33.1	George Gervin	San Antonio
1980-81	*30.7	Adrian Dantley	Utah
1981-82	*32.3	George Gervin	San Antonio
1982-83	*28.4	Alex English	Denver
1983-84	*30.6	Adrian Dantley	Utah
1984-85	*32.9	Bernard King	New York
1985-86	*30.3	Dominique Wilkins	Atlanta

Season	Pts./Avg.	Top Scorer	Team
1986-87	*37.1	Michael Jordan	Chicago
1987-88	*35.0	Michael Jordan	Chicago
1988-89	*32.5	Michael Jordan	Chicago
1989-90	*33.6	Michael Jordan	Chicago
1990-91	*31.2	Michael Jordan	Chicago

*Scoring title based on best average with at least 70 games played

NBA CHAMPIONS

Season	Champion	Eastern Division W.	L.		Western Division W.	L.	
1946-47	Philadelphia	49	11	Washington	39	22	Chicago
1947-48	Baltimore	27	21	Philadelphia	29	19	St. Louis
1948-49	Minneapolis	38	22	Washington	45	15	Rochester
1949-50	Minneapolis	51	13	Syracuse	39	25	Indianap.*
1950-51	Rochester	40	26	Philadelphia	44	24	Minneapolis
1951-52	Minneapolis	40	26	Syracuse	41	25	Rochester
1952-53	Minneapolis	47	23	New York	48	22	Minneapolis
1953-54	Minneapolis	44	28	New York	46	26	Minneapolis
1954-55	Syracuse	43	29	Syracuse	43	29	Ft. Wayne
1955-56	Philadelphia	45	27	Philadelphia	37	35	Ft. Wayne
1956-57	Boston	44	28	Boston	34	38	StL-Mpl-FtW
1957-58	St. Louis	49	23	Boston	41	31	St. Louis
1958-59	Boston	52	20	Boston	49	23	St. Louis
1959-60	Boston	59	16	Boston	46	29	St. Louis
1960-61	Boston	57	22	Boston	51	28	St. Louis
1961-62	Boston	60	20	Boston	54	26	Los Angeles
1962-63	Boston	58	22	Boston	53	27	Los Angeles
1963-64	Boston	59	21	Boston	48	32	San Fran.
1964-65	Boston	62	18	Boston	49	31	Los Angeles
1965-66	Boston	54	26	Boston	45	35	Los Angeles
1966-67	Philadelphia	68	13	Philadelphia	44	37	San Fran.
1967-68	Boston	54	28	Boston	52	30	Los Angeles
1968-69	Boston	48	34	Boston	55	27	Los Angeles
1969-70	New York	60	22	New York	46	36	Los Angeles
1970-71	Milwaukee	42	40	Baltimore	66	16	Milwaukee
1971-72	Los Angeles	48	34	New York	69	13	Los Angeles
1972-73	New York	57	25	New York	60	22	Los Angeles
1973-74	Boston	56	26	Boston	59	23	Milwaukee
1974-75	Golden State	60	22	Washington	48	34	Golden State
1975-76	Boston	54	28	Boston	42	40	Phoenix
1976-77	Portland	50	32	Philadelphia	49	33	Portland

Season	Champion	Eastern Division			Western Division		
		W.	L.		W.	L.	
1977-78	Washington	44	38	Washington	47	35	Seattle
1978-79	Seattle	54	28	Washington	52	30	Seattle
1979-80	Los Angeles	59	23	Philadelphia	60	22	Los Angeles
1980-81	Boston	62	20	Boston	40	42	Houston
1981-82	Los Angeles	58	24	Philadelphia	57	25	Los Angeles
1982-83	Philadelphia	65	17	Philadelphia	58	24	Los Angeles
1983-84	Boston	62	20	Boston	54	28	Los Angeles
1984-85	L.A. Lakers	63	19	Boston	62	20	L.A. Lakers
1985-86	Boston	67	15	Boston	51	31	Houston
1986-87	L.A. Lakers	59	23	Boston	65	17	L.A. Lakers
1987-88	L.A. Lakers	54	28	Detroit	62	20	L.A. Lakers
1988-89	Detroit	63	19	Detroit	57	25	L.A. Lakers
1989-90	Detroit	59	23	Detroit	59	23	Portland
1990-91	Chicago	61	21	Chicago	58	24	L.A. Lakers

*1949-50 Central Division Champion: Minneapolis and Rochester tied 51-17.

ALL-TIME NBA RECORDS

INDIVIDUAL

Single Game

Most Points: 100, Wilt Chamberlain, Philadelphia vs New York, at Hershey, Pa., Mar. 2, 1962

Most FG Attempted: 63, Wilt Chamberlain, Philadelphia vs New York, at Hershey, Pa., Mar. 2, 1962

Most FG Made: 36, Wilt Chamberlain, Philadelphia vs New York, at Hershey, Pa., Mar. 2, 1962

Most Consecutive FG Made: 18, Wilt Chamberlain, San Francisco vs New York, at Boston, Nov. 27, 1963; Wilt Chamberlain, Philadelphia vs Baltimore, at Pittsburgh, Feb. 24, 1967

Most 3-Pt. FG Attempted: 15, Michael Adams, Denver vs Utah, at Denver, March 14, 1988

Most 3-Pt. FG Made: 9, Dale Ellis, Seattle vs L.A. Clippers, at Seattle, April 20, 1990; Michael Adams, Denver vs Utah, at Utah, April 13, 1991

Most FT Attempted: 34, Wilt Chamberlain, Philadelphia vs St. Louis, at Philadelphia, Feb. 22, 1962

Most FT Made: 28, Wilt Chamberlain, Philadelphia vs New York, at Hershey, Pa., Mar. 2, 1962; Adrian Dantley, Utah vs Houston at Las Vegas, Nev., Jan. 4, 1984

Most Consecutive FT Made: 19, Bob Pettit, St. Louis vs Boston, at Boston, Nov. 22, 1961; Bill Cartwright, New York vs Kansas City, at N.Y., Nov. 17, 1981; Adrian Dantley, Detroit vs Chicago, at Chicago, Dec. 15, 1987 (OT)

Most FT Missed: 22, Wilt Chamberlain, Philadelphia vs Seattle, at Boston, Dec. 1, 1967

Most Assists: 30, Scott Skiles, Orlando vs Denver, at Orlando, Dec. 30, 1990

Most Personal Fouls: 8, Don Otten, Tri-Cities at Sheboygan, Nov. 24, 1949

Season

Most Points: 4,029, Wilt Chamberlain, Philadelphia, 1961-62

Highest Average: 50.4, Wilt Chamberlain, Philadelphia, 1961-62

Most FG Attempted: 3,159, Wilt Chamberlain, Philadelphia, 1961-62

Most FG Made: 1,597, Wilt Chamberlain, Philadelphia, 1961-62

Highest FG Percentage: .727, Wilt Chamberlain, Los Angeles, 1972-73

Most 3-Pt. FG Attempted: 529, Michael Adams, Denver, 1990-91

Most 3-Pt. FG Made: 167, Michael Adams, Denver, 1990-91

Most FT Attempted: 1,363, Wilt Chamberlain, Philadelphia, 1961-62

Most FT Made: 840, Jerry West, Los Angeles, 1965-66

Highest FT Percentage: .958, Calvin Murphy, Houston, 1980-81

Most Rebounds: 2,149, Wilt Chamberlain, Philadelphia, 1960-61

Most Assists: 1,164, John Stockton, Utah, 1990-91

Most Personal Fouls: 386, Darryl Dawkins, New Jersey, 1983-84

Most Disqualifications: 26, Don Meineke, Fort Wayne, 1952-53

Career

Most Points Scored: 38,387, Kareem Abdul-Jabbar, Milwaukee and Los Angeles Lakers, 1970-89

Highest Scoring Average: 32.6, Michael Jordan, Chicago, 1984-91

Most FG Attempted: 28,307, Kareem Abdul-Jabbar, Milwaukee and Los Angeles Lakers, 1970-89

Most FG Made: 15,837, Kareem Abdul-Jabbar, 1970-89

Highest FG Percentage: .599, Artis Gilmore, Chicago, San Antonio, Chicago, Boston, l976-88

Most 3-Pt. FG Attempted: 1,571, Michael Adams, Sacramento, Washington, Denver, 1985-91

Most 3-Pt. FG Made: 658, Michael Adams, Sacramento, Washington, Denver, 1985-91

Most FT Attempted: 11,862, Wilt Chamberlain, 1960-73

Most FT Made: 7,999, Moses Malone, Buffalo, Houston, Philadelphia, Washington, Atlanta, 1976-91

1961-74 Highest FT Percentage: .900, Rick Barry, San Francisco/ Golden State Warriors, Houston, 1965-67, 1972-80

Most Rebounds: 23,924, Wilt Chamberlain, 1960-73

Most Assists: 9,921, Magic Johnson, Los Angeles, 1979-91

Most Minutes: 57,446, Kareem Abdul-Jabbar, Milwaukee and Los Angeles Lakers, 1970-89

Most Games: 1,560, Kareem Abdul-Jabbar, Milwaukee and Los Angeles Lakers, 1970-89

Most Personal Fouls: 4,657, Kareem Abdul-Jabbar, Milwaukee and Los Angeles Lakers, 1970-89

Most Times Disqualified: 127, Vern Mikkelsen, Minneapolis, 1950-59

TEAM RECORDS
Single Game

Most Points, One Team: 173, Boston, vs Minneapolis at Boston, Feb. 27, 1959; Phoenix, vs Denver at Phoenix, Nov. 10, 1990; 186, Detroit, vs Denver at Denver, Dec. 13, 1983 (3 overtimes)

Most Points, Two Teams: 320, Golden State 162 vs Denver 158 at Denver, Nov. 2, 1990; 370, Detroit 186 vs Denver 184 at Denver, Dec. 13, 1983 (3 overtimes)

Most FG Attempted, One Team: 153, Philadelphia, vs Los Angeles at Philadelphia (3 overtimes), Dec. 8, 1961

Most FG Attempted, Two Teams: 291, Philadelphia 153 vs Los Angeles 138 at Philadelphia (3 overtimes), Dec. 8, 1961

Most FG Made, One Team: 72, Boston, vs Minneapolis at Boston, Feb. 27, 1959; 74, Denver, vs Detroit at Denver, Dec. 13, 1983 (3 overtimes)

Most FG Made, Two Teams: 142, Detroit 74 vs Denver 68 at Denver, Dec. 13, 1983 (3 overtimes)

Most FT Attempted, One Team: 86, Syracuse, vs Anderson at Syracuse (5 overtimes), Nov. 24, 1949

Most FT Attempted, Two Teams: 160, Syracuse 86 vs Anderson 74 at Syracuse (5 overtimes), Nov. 24, 1949

Most FT Made, One Team: 61, Phoenix, vs Utah, April 4, 1990 (1 overtime)

Most FT Made, Two Teams: 116, Syracuse 59 vs Anderson 57 at Syracuse (5 overtimes), Nov. 24, 1949

Most Rebounds, One Team: 109, Boston, vs Detroit at Boston, Dec. 24, 1960

Most Rebounds, Two Teams: 188, Philadelphia 98 vs Los Angeles 90 at Philadelphia, Dec. 8, 1961 (3 overtimes)

Most Assists, One Team: 53, Milwaukee, vs Detroit at Detroit, Dec. 26, 1978

Most Assists, Two Teams: 88, Phoenix 47 vs San Diego 41 at Tucson, Ariz., Mar. 15, 1969; San Antonio 50 vs Denver 38 at San Antonio, April 15, 1984

Most Assists, Two Teams, OT: 93, Detroit 47 vs Denver 46 at Denver, Dec. 13, 1983 (3 overtimes)

Most Personal Fouls, One Team: 66, Anderson, at Syracuse (5 overtimes), Nov. 24, 1949

Most Personal Fouls, Two Teams: 122, Anderson 66 vs Syracuse 56 at Syracuse (5 overtimes), Nov. 24, 1949

Most Disqualifications, One Team: 8, Syracuse, vs Baltimore at Syracuse (1 overtime), Nov. 15, 1952

Most Disqualifications, Two Teams: 13, Syracuse 8 vs Baltimore 5 at Syracuse (1 overtime), Nov. 15 1952

Most Points in a Losing Game: 184, Denver, vs Detroit at Denver Dec. 13, 1983 (3 overtimes)

Widest Point Spread: 63, Los Angeles 162 vs Golden State 99 at Los Angeles, Mar. 19, 1972

Most Consecutive Points in a Game: 24, Philadelphia, vs Baltimore at Baltimore, Mar. 20, 1966

Season

Most Games Won: 69, Los Angeles, 1971-72

Most Games Lost: 73, Philadelphia, 1972-73

Longest Winning Streak: 33, Los Angeles, Nov. 5, 1971 to Jan. 7, 1972

Longest Losing Streak: 20, Philadelphia, Jan. 9, 1973 to Feb. 11, 1973

Most Points Scored: 10,731, Denver, 1981-82

Most Points Allowed 10,328, Denver, 1981-82

Highest Scoring Average: 126.5, Denver, 1981-82

Highest Average, Points Allowed: 130.8, Denver, 1990-91

Most FG Attempted: 9,295, Boston, 1960-61

Most FG Made: 3,980, Denver, 1981-82

Highest FG Percentage: .545, Los Angeles, 1984-85

Most FT Attempted: 3,411, Philadelphia, 1966-67

Most FT Made: 2,313, Golden State, 1989-90

Highest FT Percentage: .832, Boston, 1989-90

Official 1991–92 NBA Schedule

*Afternoon Game

Fri Nov 1
Char at Bos
NY at Orl
Mil at Det
Wash at Ind
Phil at Chi
Utah at Minn
LAL at Hou
Dal at SA
GS at Den
LAC at Sac
Cle at Port
Phoe at Sea

Sat Nov 2
Orl at Phil
Bos at Wash
NY at Mia
NJ at Char
Det at Atl
Utah at Ind
Chi at Mil
LAL at Dal
Hou at Den
Cle at LAC
Sac at GS
Phoe at Port

Sun Nov 3
SA at Sea

Tue Nov 5
Mil at NY
Phil at Wash
Bos at Mia
Utah at Atl
Char at Det
GS at Chi
Cle at Dal
Port at Hou
SA at Den
Ind at Phoe
LAC at LAL
Sac at Sea

Wed Nov 6
Chi at Bos

NJ at Phil
Wash at Orl
Atl at Char
GS at Mil
Dal at Minn
Port at SA
Phoe at LAC
Ind at Sac

Thu Nov 7
Orl at NY
Mia at NJ
Minn at Den
Sea at Utah

Fri Nov 8
Atl at Bos
GS at Phil
Mil at Char
Dal at Chi
Cle at SA
LAL at Phoe
Den at LAC
Ind at Port

Sat Nov 9
Char at NY
Det at NJ
GS at Wash
Mia at Atl
Orl at Chi
Dal at Mil
Phoe at Hou
LAC at Utah
Minn at Sac
Ind at Sea

Sun Nov 10
Wash at Det
Minn at LAL
*Bos at Port

Mon Nov 11
Mil at Phil
Sac at Utah
Ind at LAC

Tue Nov 12
NJ at NY
Orl at Wash
Char at Atl
Mil at Cle
Det at Chi
Hou at Dal
Phoe at GS
Bos at Sac
Den at Port

Wed Nov 13
Utah at NJ
Phil at Orl
Det at Mia
Chi at Char
NY at Ind
Wash at Minn
LAC at SA
Bos at Phoe

Thu Nov 14
Sea at Cle
LAC at Dal
LAL at GS
Atl at Sac

Fri Nov 15
Phil at Bos
Wash at NJ
Char at Mia
Utah at Det
Sea at Ind
Mil at Chi
Port at Minn
Atl at Phoe
Hou at LAL

Sat Nov 16
Utah at Wash
NJ at Orl
Bos at Char
Ind at Cle
Phil at Det
Mia at Mil
Phoe at Dal
NY at SA

Port at Den
GS at LAC
Hou at Sac

Sun Nov 17
Sea at Minn
Atl at LAL

Mon Nov 18
Det at Ind

Tue Nov 19
Sac at NJ
Sea at Wash
Utah at Mia
Char at Mil
NY at Hou
Dal at Den
Phoe at LAL
LAC at Port

Wed Nov 20
Ind at Bos
Mia at Phil
Utah at Orl
Cle at Char
Sac at Atl
Sea at Det
NY at Dal
Minn at SA
Den at Phoe
Chi at GS

Thu Nov 21
NJ at Cle
Wash at Mil
Minn at Hou
Port at LAC

Fri Nov 22
Atl at Phil
Sac at Mia
Ind at Char
NY at Det
Den at Utah
LAC at Phoe
SA at LAL

GS at Port
Chi at Sea

Sat Nov 23
Phil at NY
Bos at NJ
Atl at Wash
Sac at Orl
Det at Cle
Mia at Ind
Hou at Minn
Utah at Dal
Chi at Den
Mil at GS

Sun Nov 24
Sea at LAC
Mil at LAL
*SA at Port

Mon Nov 25
Wash vs Bos
at Hart

Tue Nov 26
Mia at NY
Cle at Phil
LAL at Orl
Det at Atl
NJ at Hou
Char at Den
Chi at LAC
Phoe at Sac
Mil at Port
GS at Sea

Wed Nov 27
Orl at Bos
LAL at Mia
Phil at Cle
Atl at Det
Den at Minn
Ind at Dal
NJ at SA
Char at Utah
Sac at Phoe

Fri Nov 29
LAL at Bos
Phil at Mia
SA at Atl
Orl at Cle
Hou at Ind
NJ at Dal
Sea at Den
GS at Utah
Char at Phoe
Wash at LAC
Chi at Port

Sat Nov 30
*Det at NY
LAL at Phil
Mia at Orl
Bos at Atl
Ind at Mil
Minn at Dal
Sea at SA
NJ at Den
Utah at Phoe
Char at LAC
Chi at Sac

Sun Dec 1
*Hou at Det
*Wash at Port

Mon Dec 2
NY at Char

Tue Dec 3
Phil at NJ
Port at Mia
Ind at Det
LAL at Mil
Phoe at Minn
Atl at Dal
Den at Hou
Utah at GS
SA at Sac
Wash at Sea

Wed Dec 4
Mia at Bos
Port at Orl
LAL at Char
Phoe at Ind
Cle at Chi
Wash at Utah
SA at LAC

Thu Dec 5
Cle at Det

NJ at Mil
Atl at Hou
Dal at GS

Fri Dec 6
NY at Bos
LAL at NJ
Port at Phil
Det at Wash
Phoe at Orl
Mil at Ind
Char at Chi
Utah at SA
LAC at Den
Minn at Sea

Sat Dec 7
Chi at Phil
Char at Orl
Phoe at Mia
NY at Atl
Wash at Cle
Port at Ind
Utah at Hou
Minn at LAC
Sac at GS
Dal at Sea

Sun Dec 8
SA at Mil
Dal at LAL

Mon Dec 9
Den at Bos

Tue Dec 10
NY at NJ
Mil at Atl
SA at Ind
Sea at Chi
Mia at Dal
Orl at Utah
Det at Phoe
LAC at GS
LAL at Sac
Hou at Port

Wed Dec 11
Sea at NY
Den at Phil
Cle at Mia
Dal at Char
SA at Minn
Det at LAC
Utah at LAL

Thu Dec 12
Den at NJ
Mil at Wash
Atl at Cle
Hou at GS
Orl at Sac

Fri Dec 13
Sea at Bos
Mia at Char
Dal at Ind
NY at Chi
Phil at Minn
Phoe at SA
Utah at LAC
Det at Port

Sat Dec 14
Bos at NY
Char at NJ
Sea at Phil
Chi at Wash
Atl at Mia
Dal at Cle
Den at Ind
Minn at Mil
SA at Hou
Det at Utah
Orl at GS
Sac at Port

Sun Dec 15
Orl at LAC
Sac at LAL

Mon Dec 16
Den at Det
Minn at Port

Tue Dec 17
NJ at NY
Bos at Orl
Utah at Char
Ind at Atl
Mia at Cle
LAL at Chi
SA at Dal
Wash at Hou
Minn at GS
LAC at Sea

Wed Dec 18
Mil at Bos
Cle at NJ
Utah at Phil

Ind at Mia
Char at Det
Wash at SA
Phoe at Den
GS at LAC

Thu Dec 19
Mil at Orl
LAL at Minn
Sac at Hou
Den at Sea

Fri Dec 20
Utah at Bos
Chi at NJ
Mia at Phil
Hou at Char
Cle at Atl
LAL at Det
Wash at Dal
SA at Phoe
Port at GS

Sat Dec 21
Utah at NY
Bos at Mia
Char at Cle
NJ at Ind
Atl at Chi
Phil at Mil
LAC at Minn
Sac at Dal
Wash at Den
GS at Sea

Sun Dec 22
Hou at Orl
Phoe at LAL
Sea at Port

Mon Dec 23
Atl at NJ
Char at Phil
Orl at Mia
Utah at Cle
NY at Minn
Dal at Hou
Sac at SA

Wed Dec 25
*LAL at LAC
Bos at Chi

Thu Dec 26
SA at NY

Hou at NJ
Det at Orl
Chi at Atl
Phil at Ind
Cle at Mil
GS at Den
LAC at Utah
Mia at Phoe
Sea at Sac
Dal at Port

Fri Dec 27
Hou at Wash
NJ at Char
SA at Cle
Orl at Det
GS at Minn
Bos at Sea

Sat Dec 28
Ind at NY
Char vs. Wash
  at Balt
Minn at Atl
Sac at Chi
Bos at Den
*Mia at Utah
Dal at Phoe
Phil at LAC
Port at LAL

Sun Dec 29
SA at Orl
Hou at Mil
Mia at Port

Mon Dec 30
Orl at NJ
SA at Wash
Hou at Cle
Phoe at Det
Chi at Ind
Sac at Minn
Phil at Den
Bos at LAC
GS at LAL

Thu Jan 2
Cle at NY
LAC at Char
Phoe at Atl
Mil at Minn
Det at Hou
Port at Utah

Den at GS
Phil at Sac
Mia at Sea

Fri Jan 3
Cle at Bos
Wash at NJ
Chi at Mil
Det at Dal
Ind at LAL

Sat Jan 4
NY at Wash
Phoe at Char
LAC at Atl
NJ at Chi
Bos at Minn
Hou at SA
Orl at Den
Dal at Utah
Ind at GS
Mia at Sac
Phil at Sea

Sun Jan 5
Phoe at NY
Mia at LAL
Phil at Port

Mon Jan 6
Sac at Bos
LAC at NJ
Hou at Atl
Det at SA
Ind at Utah

Tue Jan 7
Atl at NY
Wash at Chi
Cle at Minn
LAL at Dal
Sea at Den
Orl at Port

Wed Jan 8
NY at Bos
Minn at NJ
Hou at Phil
Chi at Mia
Sac at Det
LAC at Ind
Utah at Mil
LAL at SA
Den at Phoe
Orl at Sea

Thu Jan 9
Cle at Wash
Sac at Char
Dal at Atl

Fri Jan 10
Minn at Bos
Mil at NJ
LAC at Phil
Hou at Mia
Port at Det
Utah at Chi
Sea at Dal
Orl at Phoe
Den at LAL
SA at GS

Sat Jan 11
Bos at NY
LAC at Wash
Port at Char
Phil at Cle
NJ at Det
Atl at Ind
Mia at Chi
Sac at Mil
Utah at Minn
Sea at Hou
SA at Den
GS at Phoe

Sun Jan 12
Orl at LAL

Mon Jan 13
Dal at Det
Sac at Den
Minn at Phoe
Sea at LAC

Tue Jan 14
Dal at NJ
Ind at Wash
NY at Orl
Mil at Atl
Port at Cle
Phil at Chi
Den at Hou
GS at SA
Minn at Utah
Char at Sea

Wed Jan 15
NJ at Bos
Port at NY

Mil at Mia
Det at Ind
Char at LAL
Phoe at Sac

Thu Jan 16
Mia at Wash
Chi at Cle
SA at Minn
Den at Dal
GS at Hou
Atl at Utah
LAC at Sea

Fri Jan 17
Phil at Bos
Orl at Ind
SA at Chi
NY at Mil
Sac at Phoe
Atl at LAC
Char at Port

Sat Jan 18
Phil vs. Wash
    at Balt
NY at Cle
Mia at Ind
NJ at Minn
GS at Dal
Hou at Utah
Char at Sac
LAL at Sea

Sun Jan 19
*SA at Bos
*Chi at Det
*Orl at Mil
*Atl at Den
*Port at Phoe

Mon Jan 20
*Ind at NY
Wash at Phil
Minn at Mia
*Bos at Cle
*Sea at LAL
*Char at GS

Tue Jan 21
Minn at Orl
Phoe at Chi
Mil at Hou
LAC at SA
Den at Sac

*LAL at Port
Atl at Sea

Wed Jan 22
Orl at Bos
Phoe at NJ
NY at Phil
Wash at Mia
Chi at Char
Ind at Cle
Mil at Dal
SA at Utah
Atl at GS

Thu Jan 23
Det at Minn
LAC at Hou
Utah at Den
LAL at Sac
Port at Sea

Fri Jan 24
Phoe at Bos
Mia at NJ
Minn at Phil
Dal at Orl
Cle at Ind
Det at Chi
Mil at SA
Sac at LAL
NY at GS
Atl at Port

Sat Jan 25
NJ at Phil
Phoe at Wash
Cle at Orl
Dal at Mia
Ind at Char
Hou at Chi
Mil at Den
NY at LAC
Utah at Sea

Sun Jan 26
*Det at Bos

Mon Jan 27
NY at Utah

Tue Jan 28
Bos at Wash
Sea at Orl
Det at Char
Phil at Atl

Minn at Hou
Chi at SA
Port at GS
NJ at Sac

Wed Jan 29
Wash at NY
Ind at Phil
Sea at Mia
Cle at Det
Atl at Mil
SA at Dal
Sac at Utah
NJ at Phoe
GS at LAL

Thu Jan 30
Orl at Cle
Chi at Hou
LAL at Den

Fri Jan 31
Orl at Phil
NY at Wash
Sea at Char
Mia at Det
Atl at Ind
Bos at Mil
Chi at Dal
Minn at SA
Phoe at Utah
Den at GS
LAC at Sac
NJ at Port

Sat Feb 1
Bos at Phil
Det at Atl
Utah at Dal
Hou at Phoe
NJ at LAC

Sun Feb 2
*GS at NY
*Orl at Wash
*Char at Mia
*Minn at Cle
*Sea at Mil
*Ind at Den
*Chi at LAL
*Sac at Port

Mon Feb 3
GS at Orl
Sea at Atl

Den at Minn
Ind at Hou
Chi at Utah
LAL at Phoe
Dal at Sac

Tue Feb 4
Mia at NY
Wash at Char
Port at SA
Dal at LAC

Wed Feb 5
Hou at Bos
Sea at NJ
Cle at Phil
GS at Mia
Mil at Det
Orl at Minn
Chi at Phoe
LAC at LAL
Utah at Sac

Thu Feb 6
Hou at NY
NJ at Wash
GS at Char
Orl at Atl
Det at Cle
Den at Mil
Port at Dal
Ind at SA

Sun Feb 9
*All-Star Game
at Orl

Tue Feb 11
Ind at Orl
Phil at Mia
Char at Atl
NJ at Chi
Det at Mil
LAL at Minn
Bos at SA
Cle at Utah
Wash at GS
Den at Port
Hou at Sea

Wed Feb 12
NJ at Phil
NY at Ind
Bos at Dal
Cle at Den

Port at Phoe
Hou at LAC
Wash at Sac

Thu Feb 13
Chi at NY
Atl at Mia
Minn at Det
Char at Mil
LAL at Utah
SA at GS

Fri Feb 14
Phil at NJ
Atl at Orl
Mil at Ind
Bos at Hou
Dal at Den
Phoe at LAC
Wash at LAL
Port at Sac
SA at Sea

Sat Feb 15
NJ at Cle
NY at Chi
Ind at Minn
Hou at Dal
Den at Utah
Wash at Phoe
Sea at GS

Sun Feb 16
*Det at Phil
*Mil at Orl
*Mia at Char
*Bos at LAL
SA at Sac
LAC at Port

Mon Feb 17
*Atl vs. Wash
at Balt
NY at Mia
Char at Ind
Cle at Chi
Minn at Hou
Bos at Utah
SA at LAC
LAL at GS
Phoe at Sea

Tue Feb 18
Sac at NY
Orl at Det

Cle at Mil
Phil at Dal
Phoe at Port

Wed Feb 19
Det at NJ
Chi at Orl
Den at Char
Wash at Atl
Sac at Ind
Minn at SA
Dal at Utah
LAL at LAC
*Bos at GS

Thu Feb 20
Cle at NY
Mia at Mil
Phil at Hou
LAL at Sea

Fri Feb 21
Char vs. Bos
at Hart
Ind at NJ
Den at Wash
Det at Orl
Chi at Atl
Sac at Cle
Minn at Dal
Phil at SA
Hou at Utah
Port at LAC
Phoe at GS

Sat Feb 22
Den at NY
Det at Mia
Orl at Char
NJ at Atl
Minn at Chi
LAC at Phoe
GS at LAL
Port at Sea

Sun Feb 23
*Sac at Wash
*Mil at Cle
*Bos at Ind
*SA at Hou

Mon Feb 24
Sac at Phil
Den at Atl
Sea at Minn

GS at Dal
NY at Phoe
Utah at Port

Tue Feb 25
Bos at NJ
Mil at Char
Chi at Det
Mia at SA
Utah at LAC

Wed Feb 26
Ind at Bos
Phil at Orl
Wash at Chi
Dal at Minn
GS at Hou
Mia at Den
Cle at Phoe
NY at LAL

Thu Feb 27
Port at NJ
Phil at Char
Mil at Det
GS at SA
Sea at Utah
NY at Sac

Fri Feb 28
Port at Wash
Bos at Atl
Orl at Ind
Chi at Mil
Phoe at Dal
Hou at Den
Mia at LAC
Cle at LAL

Sat Feb 29
*Minn at NY
Phil at Wash
Ind at Char
NJ at Det
Den at SA
Mia at GS
Sea at Sac

Sun Mar 1
Dal at Bos
NY at NJ
*LAC at Orl
*Port at Chi
*Atl at Mil
*Utah at Phoe

Hou at LAL
Cle at Sea

Mon Mar 2
Wash at Det
GS at Sac

Tue Mar 3
Dal at NY
Wash at Orl
LAC at Mia
Ind at Chi
SA at Minn
Hou at Phoe
Utah at GS
LAL at Port
Den at Sea

Wed Mar 4
Orl at Bos
Atl at Phil
Ind at Det
Char at Mil
Port at Den
SA at Utah
NJ at LAL
Cle at Sac

Thu Mar 5
LAC at NY
Dal at Wash
Chi at Minn
Mia at Hou
Sea at Phoe
Cle at GS

Fri Mar 6
LAC at Bos
Dal at Phil
Ind at Atl
Mia at Chi
Orl at Mil
Det at Den
NJ at Utah
Sac at Port

Sat Mar 7
Char at NY
Mil vs. Wash
at Balt
Cle at Atl
Minn at Ind
Phoe at SA
Hou at GS
NJ at Sea

Sun Mar 8
*Chi at Phil
Bos at Orl
Wash at Mia
SA at Dal
Utah at Den
GS at LAC
*Det at LAL
Hou at Sac
Sea at Port

Mon Mar 9
NY at Phil

Tue Mar 10
LAL at NY
Den at Orl
Bos at Mia
Minn at Char
Phoe at Cle
Wash at Ind
Port at Mil
Dal at Hou
Atl at SA
NJ at GS
LAC at Sac
Det at Sea

Wed Mar 11
Ind at Phil
LAL at Atl
Bos at Chi
Port at Minn
Char at Dal
Sea at LAC

Thu Mar 12
Phoe at Mil
Hou at SA
Det at GS
Utah at Sac

Fri Mar 13
NJ vs. Bos
at Hart
Phoe at Phil
Minn at Wash
Ind at Orl
Den at Mia
Port at Atl
LAL at Cle
Char at Hou
Dal at LAC

Sat Mar 14
NJ at NY
LAL at Wash
Chi at Orl
Mia at Atl
Phil at Mil
Utah at SA
Det at Sac

Sun Mar 15
*Port at Bos
*Den at Cle
*Phoe at Minn
Utah at Hou
Sac at LAC
Dal at Sea

Mon Mar 16
Cle at Wash
Chi at Mia
Atl at Det
LAL at Ind
Char at SA

Tue Mar 17
Chi at NJ
NY at Orl
Bos at Mil
LAC at Hou
Sac at Den
Dal at Phoe
Minn at Port
GS at Sea

Wed Mar 18
Cle at Bos
Ind at Mia
Orl at Atl
Phil at Det
LAC at Dal
Sac at SA
Port at LAL
Minn at GS

Thu Mar 19
Mil at NY
Char at Phil
Chi at Wash
Sea at Hou
Den at Utah

Fri Mar 20
Wash at NJ
Atl at Char
GS at Cle

Bos at Det
Mil at Ind
Sac at Dal
LAC at Phoe
Minn at LAL

Sat Mar 21
Mia at NY
Orl at Chi
Sac at Hou
Sea at SA
LAC at Den
Port at Utah
Minn at Phoe

Sun Mar 22
*GS at Bos
NJ at Mia
*Det at Char
*Atl at Cle
*Phil at Ind
*Wash at Mil
Sea at Dal

Mon Mar 23
Char at NJ
SA at Phil
GS at Atl
Den at Minn

Tue Mar 24
Orl at NY
Ind at Cle
Den at Chi
Mil at Sac
Dal at Port
Hou at Sea

Wed Mar 25
Bos at NJ
Ind at Wash
Cle at Orl
SA at Char
GS at Det
Mia at Minn
Phil at Utah
Mil at Phoe

Thu Mar 26
Wash at Atl
NY at Den
Hou at LAC
Dal at LAL
Port at Sac

Fri Mar 27
Det at Bos
SA at Mia
Cle at Char
GS at Ind
Atl at Minn
LAL at Utah
Phil at Phoe
Mil at Sea

Sat Mar 28
GS at NJ
Char at Wash
Mia at Orl
Cle at Chi
Phoe at Den
Mil at LAC
Hou at Port
NY at Sea

Sun Mar 29
Atl at Bos
*SA at Det
*Sac at Minn
Den at Dal
Phil at LAL
NY at Port

Mon Mar 30
SA at NJ
Orl at Char
Mil at Utah
Phil at GS

Tue Mar 31
Chi at NY
Mia at Cle
LAC at Det
LAL at Hou
Minn at Den
Port at Phoe
GS at Sac
Utah at Seattle

Wed Apr 1
Wash at Bos
Mia at Phil
Atl at Ind
Char at Chi
NJ at Mil
Orl at Dal
LAL at SA

Thu Apr 2
NY at Char

LAC at Cle
Den at Hou
GS at Phoe
Sea at Sac
Utah at Port

Fri Apr 3
Atl at NY
Mil at NJ
Det at Wash
Cle at Mia
Bos at Ind
LAC at Chi
Minn at Dal
Orl at SA
Phoe at Utah
Sea at LAL
Sac at GS

Sat Apr 4
Wash at Char
Phil at Atl
Orl at Hou

Sun Apr 5
*Chi at Bos
*NY at Cle
Mia at Det
*NJ at Ind
*LAC at Mil
*Utah at Minn
*SA at Den
Phoe at LAL
Port at GS
Dal at Sac

Tue Apr 7
Det at NY
Atl at NJ
Char at Orl
Wash at Mia
Bos at Cle
Mil at Chi
LAC at Minn
Hou at SA
Utah at Den
Sac at Phoe
GS at Port
LAL at Sea

Wed Apr 8
NY at Bos
Det at Phil
NJ at Wash

Lethal Kevin Willis was Hawk leader in FG pct.

Ind at Mil	**Sat Apr 11**	GS at Utah	Port at Dal	**Sat Apr 18**
Dal at GS	Orl at Mia	Den at LAL	LAL at Den	Orl at NJ
	NJ at Atl		Hou at Utah	Wash at Phil
Thu Apr 9	Ind at Chi	**Tue Apr 14**		NY at Mil
Atl at Orl	Dal at Hou	Wash at NY	**Thu Apr 16**	*LAL at Port
Char at Cle	Den at LAC	Bos at Phil	Ind at NJ	
Hou at Minn	*Utah at LAL	NJ at Mia	Orl at Wash	**Sun Apr 19**
Dal at Utah	Phoe at GS	Chi at Cle	Mil at Mia	*Mia at Bos
Port at LAC	Minn at Sac	Char at Ind	SA at Phoe	Atl at Cle
*SA at LAL		Det at Mil	Minn at LAC	*Det at Chi
Den at Sac	**Sun Apr 12**	GS at Minn	LAL at Sac	*Char at Minn
Phoe at Sea	*Mil at Phil	Port at Hou		*Phoe at Hou
	Bos at Char	Dal at SA	**Fri Apr 17**	*Dal at Den
Fri Apr 10	*Wash at Cle	Sea at Phoe	Phil at Char	LAC at LAL
Mil at Bos	*NY at Det	Sac at LAC	Chi at Atl	*Sea at GS
Phil at NY	*SA at Port		Cle at Ind	
Cle at NJ	Minn at Sea	**Wed Apr 15**	Hou at Dal	
Mia at Wash		Phil at Orl	Den at SA	
Char at Det	**Mon Apr 13**	Cle at Char	Minn at Utah	
Chi at Ind	NJ at Orl	NY at Atl	LAC at GS	
Sea at Port	Atl at Chi	Bos at Det	Sac at Sea	

1991–92 NBA ON NBC SCHEDULE

(starting times Eastern)

Day	Date	Game	Time
Sat	Oct 19	McDonald's Open Final (Paris) Featuring LAL	3:30
Wed	Dec 25	LAL at LAC	3:30
		Bos at Chi	9:00
Sun	Jan 19	Chi at Det	12:00
		Port at Phoe	2:30
Sun	Jan 26	Det at Bos	12:30
Sun	Feb 2	GS at NY	1:00
		Chi at LAL	3:30
Sun	Feb 9	42nd ALL-STAR GAME (Orlando Arena)	3:30
Sun	Feb 16	Det at Phil	1:00
		Bos at LAL	3:30
Sun	Feb 23	Bos at Ind or SA at Hou	1:00
Sun	Mar 1	Port at Chi	1:00
		Utah at Phoe	3:30
Sun	Mar 8	Chi at Phil	1:00
		Det at LAL	3:30
Sun	Mar 15	Port at Bos	12:00
Sun	Mar 22	Phil at Ind or Atl at Cle	12:00
Sun	Mar 29	SA at Det	12:00
Sun	Apr 5	Chi at Bos	12:00
Sat	Apr 11	Utah at LAL	3:30
Sun	Apr 12	NY at Det or Milw at Phil	1:00
		SA at Port	3:30
Sat	Apr 18	LAL at Port	3:30
Sun	Apr 19	Det at Chi or Utah at SA or Sea at GS or Phoe at Hou	3:30

1991–92 NBA/TNT SCHEDULE

(starting times Eastern)

Day	Date	Game	Time
Fri	Oct 18	McDonald's Open (Paris) Featuring LA Lakers	8:00
Tue	Oct 29	Hall of Fame Game Chi vs. Mia at Springfield, Mass.	8:00
Fri	Nov 1	Phil at Chi	8:00
		Phoe at Sea	10:30
Tue	Nov 5	Bos at Mia	8:00
		SA at Den	10:30
Fri	Nov 8	Mil at Char	8:00
Tue	Nov 12	Det at Chi	8:00
Fri	Nov 15	Port at Minn	8:00
Tue	Nov 19	NY at Hou	8:00
Fri	Nov 22	Atl at Phil	8:00
Tue	Nov 26	LAL at Orl	8:00
Fri	Nov 29	LAL at Bos	8:00
		Chi at Port	10:30
Tue	Dec 3	Ind at Det	8:00
Fri	Dec 6	Utah at SA	8:00
Tue	Dec 10	NY at NJ	8:00
Fri	Dec 13	Phoe at SA	8:00
		Det at Port	10:30
Tue	Dec 17	LAL at Chi	8:00
Fri	Dec 20	LAL at Det	8:00
		Port at GS	10:30
Thu	Dec 26	SA at NY	8:00
Fri	Dec 27	Hou at Wash	8:00
Fri	Jan 3	Det at Dal	8:00
Wed	Jan 8	LAL at SA	8:00
Fri	Jan 10	Port at Det	8:00
Tue	Jan 14	Port at Cle	8:00
Fri	Jan 17	SA at Chi	8:00
Tue	Jan 21	LAL at Port	8:00
Fri	Jan 24	Det at Chi	8:00
Tue	Jan 28	Chi at SA	8:00
Fri	Jan 31	Bos at Mil	8:00
		LAC at Sac	10:30
Wed	Feb 5	Hou at Bos	8:00
Fri	Feb 7	All-Star Weekend at Orl	TBA
Sat	Feb 8	All-Star Weekend at Orl	7:00
Tue	Feb 11	Bos at SA	8:00
Fri	Feb 14	Mil at Ind	8:00
Wed	Feb 19	Bos at GS	8:00
Fri	Feb 21	Phil at SA	8:00
Tue	Feb 25	Chi at Det	8:00
Fri	Feb 28	Bos at Atl	8:00
Tue	Mar 3	Hou at Phoe	8:00
Tue	Mar 10	LAL at NY	8:00
Wed	Mar 11	Bos at Chi	8:00
Wed	Mar 18	Phil at Det	8:00
		Port at LAL	10:30
Wed	Mar 25	Phil at Utah	8:00
Tue	Mar 31	LAL at Hou	8:00
Fri	Apr 3	Bos at Ind	8:00
		Phoe at Utah	10:30
Thu	Apr 9	SA at LAL	8:00
Wed	Apr 15	Bos at Det	8:00
Fri	Apr 17	Chi at Atl	8:00

Newly revised and updated third edition!

THE ILLUSTRATED SPORTS RECORD BOOK
Zander Hollander and David Schulz

Here, in a single book, are more than 400 all-time—and current—sports records with 50 new stories and 125 action photos so vivid, it's like "being there." Featured is an all-star cast that includes Martina Navratilova, Joe DiMaggio, Joe Montana, Michael Jordan, Jack Nicklaus, Mark Spitz, Wayne Gretzky, Nolan Ryan, Muhammad Ali, Greg LeMond, Hank Aaron, Carl Lewis and Magic Johnson. This is *the* authoritative book that sets the record straight and recreates the feats at the time of achievement!
